SECOND EDITION

Numerical Methods for Physics

Alejandro L. Garcia
San Jose State University

Prentice Hall, Upper Saddle River, New Jersey 07458

Library of Congress Cataloging-in-Publication Data

Garcia, Alejandro L.,
    Numerical methods for physics / Alejandro L. Garcia. – 2nd ed.
    p. cm.
  Includes bibliographical references and index.
  ISBN 0-13-906744-2
  1. Mathematical physics. 2. Differential equations,
Partial–Numerical solutions. 3. Physics–Data processing. I.
Title.
  QC20 .G37 2000
  530.15–dc21

                                        99-28552
                                        CIP

Executive Editor: Alison Reeves
Editor-in-Chief: Paul F. Corey
Assistant Vice President of Production and Manufacturing: David W. Riccardi
Executive Managing Editor: Kathleen Schiaparelli
Assistant Managing Editor: Lisa Kinne
Production Editor: Linda DeLorenzo
Marketing Manager: Steven Sartori
Editorial Assistant: Gillian Buonanno
Manufacturing Manager: Trudy Pisciotti
Art Director: Jayne Conte
Cover Designer: Bruce Kenselaar
Cover Art: John Christiana

Printed in the United States of America

10 9 8 7 6 5 4 3 2 1

ISBN 0-13-906744-2

Prentice-Hall International (UK) Limited, *London*
Prentice-Hall of Australia Pty. Limited, *Sydney*
Prentice-Hall Canada Inc., *Toronto*
Prentice-Hall Hispanoamericana, S.A., *Mexico*
Prentice-Hall of India Private Limited, *New Delhi*
Prentice-Hall of Japan, Inc., *Tokyo*
Prentice-Hall (*Singapore*) Pte Ltd
Editora Prentice-Hall do Brasil, Ltda., *Rio de Janeiro*

Contents

Preface

When I was an undergraduate, computers were just beginning to be introduced into the university curriculum. Physics majors were expected to take a single semester of Pascal taught by the computer science department. We wrote programs to sort lists, process a payroll, and so forth, but were expected to acquire the specialized tools of scientific computing on our own. Most of us wasted many human and computer hours learning them by trial and error.

In recent years, many departments have added a computational physics course, taught by physicists, to their curricula. However, there is still considerable debate as to how this course should be organized. My philosophy is to use the upper division/graduate mathematical physics course as a model. Consider the following parallels between this text and a typical math physics book: A variety of numerical and analytical techniques used in physics are covered. Topics include ordinary and partial differential equations, linear algebra, Fourier transforms, integration, and probability. Because the text is written for physicists, these techniques are applied to solving realistic problems, many of which the students have encountered in other courses.

Numerical Methods for Physics is organized to cover what I believe are the most important, basic computational methods for physicists. The structure of the book differs considerably from the generic numerical analysis text. For example, about a third of the book is devoted to partial differential equations. This emphasis is natural considering the fundamental importance of Maxwell's equations, the Schrödinger equation, the Boltzmann equation, and so forth. Chapters 6 and 7 introduce some methods in computational fluid dynamics, an increasingly important topic in the fields of nonlinear physics, environmental physics, and astrophysics.

Numerical techniques may be classified as basic, advanced, and cutting edge. On the whole, this text covers only fundamental techniques; to work effectively with advanced numerical methods requires that the user first understand the basic algorithms. The discussion in the "Beyond This Chapter" section at the end of each chapter guides the reader to advanced algorithms and indicates when it is appropriate to use them. Unfortunately, the cutting edge moves so quickly that any attempt to summarize the latest algorithms would quickly be out of date.

The material in this text may be arranged in various ways to suit anything from a 10-week, upper-division class to a full-semester, graduate course. Most chapters include optional sections that may be omitted without loss of continuity. Furthermore, entire chapters may be skipped; chapter interdependencies are indicated in the flow chart.

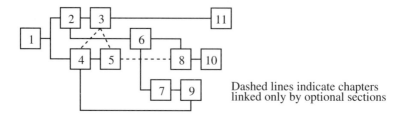

Dashed lines indicate chapters linked only by optional sections

I have tried to present the algorithms in a clear, universal form that would allow the reader to easily implement them in *any* language. The programs are given in outline form in the main text with MATLAB and C++ listings in the appendices. In my classes, the students are allowed to use any language, yet I find that most end up using MATLAB. Its plotting utilities are particularly good—all the graphical results in the book were generated directly from the MATLAB programs. Advanced programmers (and students wishing to improve this skill) prefer using C++. FORTRAN versions of the programs, along with the MATLAB and C++ source code, are available online from Prentice Hall.

The over 250 exercises should be regarded as an essential part of the text. The time needed to do a problem ranges from 30 minutes to 2 days; in my classes, I assign about five exercises per week. Each exercise is labeled as:

[Pencil]   can be solved with pencil and paper.
[Computer]   requires using the computer.
[MATLAB]   best solved using MATLAB.
[C++]   best solved using C++.

While some texts emphasize month-long projects, I find that shorter exercises allow the class to move at a brisker pace, covering a wider variety of topics. Some instructors may wish to give one or two longer assignments, and many of the exercises may be expanded into such projects.

Readers familiar with the first edition will notice the following changes: C++ versions of the programs have been added, along with a new section (1.3) summarizing the language. The MATLAB programs have been updated to version 5. The discussion of derivatives has been moved from Chapter 1 to Chapter 2. A new section (6.3) has been added to Chapter 6. The discussion of hyperbolic partial differential equations has been collected into a new Chapter 7.

I wish to thank the people in my department, especially D. Strandburg, P. Hamill, A. Tucker, and J. Becker, for their strong support; my students and teaching assistants, J. Stroh, S. Moon, and D. Olson, who braved the rough waters of the early drafts; the National Science Foundation for its support of the computational physics program at San Jose State University; my editors at Prentice Hall and the technical staff of The MathWorks Inc. for their assistance; the National Oceanic and Atmospheric Administration Climate Monitoring and Diagnostics Laboratory for the CO_2 data used in Chapter 5. In addition, I appreciate the comments of the following reviewers: David A. Boness, Seattle University; Wolfgang Christian, Davidson College; David M. Cook, Lawrence University; Harvey Gould, Clark University; Cleve Moler, The MathWorks, Inc; Cecile Penland, University of Colorado, Boulder; and Ross L. Spencer, Brigham Young University. Finally, I owe a special debt of gratitude to my entire family for their moral support as I wrote this book.

Alejandro L. Garcia

Dedicated to
Josefina Ovies García
and
Miriam González López

Chapter 1

Preliminaries

This chapter has no physics; to use the computer to do physics, one must first know how to use it to do math. The book presents algorithms in their general form, but when we sit down at the computer we have to give it instructions that it understands. Sections 1.2 and 1.3 present a synopsis of the MATLAB and C++ programming languages, and some simple programs are developed in Section 1.4. The chapter concludes with a discussion of the effect of hardware limitations (e.g., round-off errors) on mathematical calculations.

1.1 PROGRAMMING

General Thoughts

Before we get started, let me warn you that this book does not teach programming. Presumably, you have already learned a programming language (it doesn't really matter which one) and have had some practice in writing programs. This book covers numerical algorithms, specifically those that are most useful in physics. The style of presentation is informal. Instead of rigorously deriving all the details of all possible algorithms, I'll cover only the essential points and stress the practical methods.

If you've had a math course in numerical analysis, you may see some old friends (such as Romberg integration). This book emphasizes the application of such methods to physics problems. You will also learn some specialized techniques generally not presented in a mathematics course. If you have not had numerical analysis, don't worry. The book is organized assuming no prior knowledge of numerical methods.

In your earlier programming course I hope you learned about good programming style. I try to use what I consider good style in the programs, but everyone has personal preferences. The point of good style is to make your life easier by organizing and structuring your program development. Many programs in this book sacrifice efficiency for the sake of clarity. After you understand how a program works, you should make it a regular exercise to improve it. However, always be sure to check your improved version with the original.

Most of the exercises in this book involve programming projects. In the first few chapters, many exercises require only that you modify an existing program. In the later chapters you are asked to write more and more of your own code. The exercises are purposely organized in this fashion to allow you to come up to speed on whatever computer system you choose to use. Unfortunately, computational physics is often like experimental work in the following regard: Debugging and testing is a slow, tedious, but necessary task similar to aligning optics or fixing vacuum leaks.

Programming Languages

In writing this book, one of the most difficult decisions I had to make was choosing a language. The obvious choices were Basic, FORTRAN, MATLAB, C++, and Java. I also considered symbolic manipulators such as Maple and Mathematica. When the first edition of this book appeared, there were significant differences among these choices. Some were more powerful, but difficult to use; others had better graphics, but were not portable across computing platforms, etc. Since that time, advances in software engineering have diminished the deficiencies (and in many ways the distinctiveness) of these languages, making the choice of language for the second edition even more difficult. With my editor's assistance, we put the question to students and instructors using the first edition, and their choices were MATLAB and C++.*

MATLAB is the language that I encourage my students to use in their course work. Although you may not be familiar with MATLAB, it is widely used in both academia and industry. It is especially popular in the engineering community and with applied mathematicians. MATLAB is very portable; it runs on Windows PCs, Macintoshes, and Unix workstations.

MATLAB is an interpreted language with excellent scientific libraries. Because it is an interpreted language, it is easy to use interactively, while the compiled libraries improve its performance. Being an interpreted language also makes MATLAB very clean. Many details (such as dimensioning matrices) are handled automatically. MATLAB has very good graphics facilities, including high-level routines (e.g., contour and surface plots). If you are comfortable using Basic, FORTRAN, or symbolic manipulators, you should have no trouble programming in MATLAB.

C++ is a rich, elegant, and powerful programming language. Most of the applications on your computer were probably written in C++. Arguably, FORTRAN remains the dominant language in the physics community, but C++ is the *lingua franca* of engineering. For these reasons many students are eager to learn this object-oriented language. C++ is difficult to master, but knowing the basics will suffice for programming the algorithms in this book. If you have programming experience with C or Java, you will probably enjoy using C++.

---

*FORTRAN versions of the programs in this book are also available online.

1.2   BASIC ELEMENTS OF MATLAB

This section summarizes the basic elements of MATLAB. Advanced features are introduced in later chapters as we need them. The MATLAB manuals include several tutorial chapters, along with a complete reference to the language. If you don't have a copy of the manual at hand, most of it is available from the built-in help system. For other MATLAB tutorials, see the texts by Etter [44] and by Hanselman and Littlefield [70].

Variables

The fundamental data type in MATLAB is the matrix (MATLAB is an acronym for MATrix LABoratory). A scalar is a 1×1 matrix, a row vector is a $1 \times N$ matrix, and a column vector is an $N \times 1$ matrix. Variables are not declared explicitly; MATLAB just dimensions them as they are used. For example, take the scalars x and y, the vectors $\mathbf{a}$ and $\mathbf{b}$, and the matrices $\mathbf{C}$, $\mathbf{D}$, and $\mathbf{E}$, and give them the values

$$x = 3; \quad y = -2; \quad \mathbf{a} = \begin{bmatrix} 1 \\ 2 \\ 3 \end{bmatrix}; \quad \mathbf{b} = \begin{bmatrix} 0 & 3 & -4 \end{bmatrix};$$

$$\mathbf{C} = \begin{bmatrix} 1 & 0 & 1 \\ 0 & 1 & -1 \\ 1 & 2 & 0 \end{bmatrix}; \quad \mathbf{D} = \begin{bmatrix} 0 & 1 & 1 \\ 2 & 3 & -1 \\ 0 & 0 & 1 \end{bmatrix}; \quad \mathbf{E} = \begin{bmatrix} 1 & \pi \\ 0 & -1 \\ x & \sqrt{-1} \end{bmatrix} \quad (1.1)$$

In MATLAB these variables would be set by the assignment statements

```
x = 3;        % These are some simple assignments
y = -2;
a = [1; 2; 3];    % Column vector a; Row vector b
b = [0 3 -4];
C = [1 0 1; 0 1 -1; 1 2 0];    % Matrices
D = [0 1 1; 2 3 -1; 0 0 1];
E = [1 pi; 0 -1; x sqrt(-1)]; % In MATLAB, pi = 3.14...
```

Variable names in MATLAB, as in most languages, must start with a letter but can be composed of any combination of letters, numbers, and underscores (e.g., `mass`, `mass_of_particle`, `MassOfParticle2`). Anything following a percent sign is considered a comment in MATLAB.

The semicolon at the end of each assignment marks the end of the statement; you can put multiple statements on a line by separating them with semicolons. If this semicolon is omitted, the statement is assumed to end at the end of the line, and the value assigned is displayed on the screen (sometimes useful but more often annoying). Notice that rows in a matrix are separated by semicolons.

Two handy MATLAB functions for creating matrices are `zeros` and `ones`. The statement `A=zeros(M,N)` sets A to be an $M \times N$ matrix, with all elements equal to zero. The `ones` function works in the same fashion, but creates matrices filled with ones.

Mathematics

The basic arithmetic operations are defined in the natural manner. For example, the MATLAB statements

```
z = x - y;      % Some basic operations
t = b * a;
F = C + D;
G = C * E;
```

assign the values

$$z = 5; \quad t = -6; \quad \mathbf{F} = \begin{bmatrix} 1 & 1 & 2 \\ 2 & 4 & -2 \\ 1 & 2 & 1 \end{bmatrix}; \quad \mathbf{G} = \begin{bmatrix} 4 & \pi + i \\ -3 & -1 - i \\ 1 & \pi - 2 \end{bmatrix} \quad (1.2)$$

The power operator is ^, thus 2^3 is $2^3 = 8$. Other mathematical functions are available from MATLAB's large collection of built-in functions (Table 1.1).

MATLAB performs matrix multiplication; thus in the example above, $G_{ij} = \sum_k C_{ik} E_{kj}$. Notice that b*a is just the dot product of these vectors. MATLAB will balk if you try to do a matrix operation when the dimensions don't match (e.g., it will not compute C+E). For matrices, division is implemented by using Gaussian elimination (discussed in Chapter 4).

Sometimes we want to perform operations element by element, so MATLAB defines the operators .* ./ and .^. Here are some examples of these array operations:

```
H = C .* D;     % These operations are performed
J = E .^ x;     % element-by-element
```

In this case $H_{i,j} = C_{i,j} D_{i,j}$ and $J_{i,j} = (E_{i,j})^x$, thus

$$\mathbf{H} = \begin{bmatrix} 0 & 0 & 1 \\ 0 & 3 & 1 \\ 0 & 0 & 0 \end{bmatrix}; \quad \mathbf{J} = \begin{bmatrix} 1 & \pi^3 \\ 0 & -1 \\ 27 & -i \end{bmatrix} \quad (1.3)$$

Individual elements of a matrix may be addressed by using their indices. For example, J(1,2) equals π^3 and J(3,1) equals 27. Similarly, for vectors, b(3) (or b(1,3)) equals -4. Notice that matrix indices start at 1 and not 0.

Matrix $\mathbf{B}$ is the transpose of matrix $\mathbf{A}$ if $A_{ij} = B_{ji}$, that is, the rows and columns are exchanged. The Hermitian conjugate of a matrix is the transpose of its complex conjugate. In MATLAB

```
K = J';      % Hermitian conjugate
L = J.';     % Transpose
```

give the values

$$\mathbf{K} = \begin{bmatrix} 1 & 0 & 27 \\ \pi^3 & -1 & i \end{bmatrix}; \quad \mathbf{L} = \begin{bmatrix} 1 & 0 & 27 \\ \pi^3 & -1 & -i \end{bmatrix} \quad (1.4)$$

The Hermitian conjugate of $\mathbf{J}$ is $\mathbf{K}$, while $\mathbf{L}$ is the transpose of $\mathbf{J}$.

Table 1.1: Selected MATLAB mathematical functions.

`abs(x)`	Absolute value or complex magnitude
`norm(x)`	Magnitude of a vector
`sqrt(x)`	Square root
`sin(x), cos(x)`	Sine and cosine
`tan(x)`	Tangent
`atan2(y,x)`	Arc tangent of y/x in $[0, 2\pi]$
`exp(x)`	Exponential
`log(x), log10(x)`	Natural logarithm and base-10 logarithm
`rem(x,y)`	Remainder (modulo) function (e.g., `rem(10.3,4)=2.3`)
`floor(x)`	Round down to nearest integer (e.g., `floor(3.2)=3`)
`ceil(x)`	Round up to nearest integer (e.g., `ceil(3.2)=4`)
`rand(N)`	Uniformly distributed random numbers from the interval $[0, 1)$. Returns $N \times N$ matrix.
`randn(N)`	Normal (Gaussian) distributed random numbers (zero mean, unit variance). Returns $N \times N$ matrix.

Loops and Conditionals

Repeated operations are performed by using loops. Here is an example of a `for` loop in MATLAB:

```
for i=1:5        % Your basic loop; i goes from 1 to 5
   p(i) = i^2;
end              % This is the end of the loop
```

This loop assigns the value p = [1 4 9 16 25]. The body of the `for` loop (i.e., the set of statements executed in the loop) is terminated by the `end` statement. Notice that p is created as a row vector. If we wanted it to be a column vector, we could build it as

```
for i=1:5        % Your basic loop; i goes from 1 to 5
   p(i,1) = i^2; % p is a column vector
end              % This is the end of the loop
```

or

```
for i=1:5        % Your basic loop; i goes from 1 to 5
   p(i) = i^2;
end              % This is the end of the loop
p = p.';         % Transpose p into a column vector
```

using the transpose operator.

In a `for` loop, the default step is +1, but it is possible to use a different increment. For example, the loop

```
for i=1:2:5      % Loop over odd values of i
  q(i) = i;
  q(i+1) = -i;
end
```

assigns the values q = [1 -1 3 -3 5 -5].

MATLAB also has `while` loops; here is a simple example:

```
while( x > 1 )
  x = x/2;
end
```

A `while` command executes the statements in the body of the loop while the loop condition is true. If $x = 5$ before the loop, then x will equal $\frac{5}{8}$ when the loop completes. The `break` statement can be used to terminate `for` loops or `while` loops.

Here are some examples of how conditionals are implemented; you see that it is quite standard.

```
if( x > 5 )            % A simple conditional
  z = z-1;
  y = MaxHeight;       % Body of this conditional has two statements
end

if( x >= x_min & x <= x_max )   % A more complicated conditional
  status = 1;
else                            % This conditional uses else
  status = 0;
end

if( x == 0 | x == 1)          % Another conditional using elseif
  flag = 1;
elseif( x < 0 & x ~= -1)   % Notice that elseif is ONE WORD
  flag = -1;
else
  flag = 0;
end
```

Notice that equals and not equals are == and ~=, respectively. Logical "and" is & (ampersand), and logical "or" is | (vertical bar). The `end` command terminates both loops and conditionals.

Colon Operator

The colon operator, : , is one of MATLAB's handiest tools.[†] Let's consider a few examples of its use. First, the `for` loop,

---

[†]FORTRAN 90 has a similar colon operator

```
tau = 0.1;
for i=1:100
   time(i) = tau * i;
end
```

could be replaced with

```
tau = 0.1;
i=1:100;
time = tau * i;
```

In the latter, a vector `i=[1 2 ... 100]` is created. We may further abbreviate this to

```
tau = 0.1;
time = tau * (1:100);
```

In all three cases, the vector `time=[0.1 0.2 ... 10.0]` is created.

The colon operator is also useful for looping over rows or columns of a matrix. For example, the loop

```
[M,N] = size(A);   % Find dimensions of A
for i=1:M
   first(i) = A(i,1);
   last(i) = A(i,N);
end
```

copies the first and last columns of matrix `A` into the vectors `first` and `last`. The above can be replaced with

```
[M,N] = size(A);   % Find dimensions of A
first = A(:,1);
last = A(:,N);
```

Not only does using the colon operator abbreviate our code, but it also makes it run faster. The program becomes more efficient because we are explicitly executing a vector operation instead of performing an element-by-element calculation.

Input, Output, and Graphics

MATLAB has various types of input and output facilities. The `input` command prints a prompt to the screen and accepts input from the keyboard. Here is a simple example of its use:

```
x = input('Enter the value of x: ');
```

In this example, you can enter a scalar, a matrix, or any valid MATLAB expression.

The `disp` command may be used to display the value of a variable or to print a string of text:

Table 1.2: Selected MATLAB graphics functions.

`plot(x,y)`	Plot vector y versus vector x
`loglog(x,y)`, `semilogx(x,y)`, `semilogy(x,y)`	Plot vector y versus vector x using log or semilog scales
`polar(theta,rho)`	Polar plot
`contour(z)`	Contour plot of matrix z
`mesh(z)`	3-D wire-mesh plot of matrix z
`title('text')`, `xlabel('text')`, `ylabel('text')`	Write a title on a plot / Write axis labels on a plot
`print`	Print graphics

```
M = [1, 2, 3; 4, 5, 6; 7, 8, 9];
disp('The value of M is ');
disp(M);
```

produces the output

```
The value of M is
      1      2      3
      4      5      6
      7      8      9
```

Formatted output is also available with the `fprintf` command,

```
fprintf('The values of x and y are %g and %g meters \n',x,y)
```

The values of the variables x and y are displayed in place of the %g's. The \n at the end of the text string indicates a carriage return (new line). The MATLAB commands `load` and `save` can be used to read and write data files.

MATLAB has various graphics commands for creating xy plots, contour plots, and three-dimensional wire-mesh plots. Table 1.2 gives a list of a few of the basic graphics commands.

MATLAB Session

When you first enter the MATLAB environment, you are at the command level as indicated by the `>>` prompt (in the regular edition) or the `EDU>>` prompt (in the student edition). From the command line you can enter individual MATLAB commands. To end your MATLAB session, type `quit` or `exit`.

For programming, it is more convenient to enter a set of commands to be executed in a file. In the MATLAB terminology such a script of commands is called an *M-file*. Our programs and functions will all be M-files. You run an M-file by invoking its name (the name of the file) on the command line. Before running a program you need to tell MATLAB where to look for your M-files,

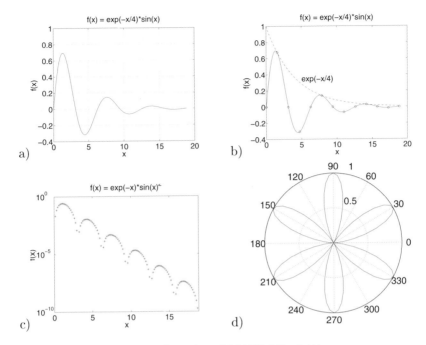

Figure 1.1: Samples of MATLAB plotting.

that is, the directory where your files are located. MATLAB searches for M-files in all locations specified in a list called the "path." Use the `path` command or the "Set path..." menu item to add your directories to MATLAB's path.

After MATLAB executes the commands in the M-file, it returns control to the command line. You can then enter individual commands (for example, to display the values of your variables). The interactive help may be used from the command line. For example,

```
EDU>>  help bessel
```

tells you about MATLAB's Bessel function routines. You can also get help on special characters (e.g., try `help &`).

EXERCISES

(Recommended exercises indicated by boldface numbers)

1. For the matrix `A=[1 2; 3 4]`, use compute MATLAB to find: (a) `A*A`; (b) `A.*A`; (c) `A^2`; (d) `A.^2`; (e) `A/A`; (f) `A./A`. [MATLAB]

2. Given the vectors $\mathbf{x} = [1\ 2\ 3\ldots\ 10]$ and $\mathbf{y} = [1\ 4\ 9\ldots 100]$, plot them in MATLAB using: (a) `plot(x,y)`; (b) `plot(x,y,'+')`; (c) `plot(x,y,'-',x,y,'+')`; (d) `plot(x,y,'-', x(1:2:10), y(1:2:10), '+')`; (e) `semilogy(x,y)`; (f) `loglog(x,y,'+')`. [MATLAB]

3. Reproduce the plots shown in Figure 1.1. Try to be as accurate as possible in your reconstruction. [MATLAB]

4. (a) The MATLAB function `inv(A)` returns the inverse of matrix $\mathbf{A}$. Find the inverse of the matrices

$$\begin{bmatrix} 1 & 2 & 3 \\ 0 & 4 & 5 \\ 0 & 0 & 6 \end{bmatrix}; \quad \begin{bmatrix} 1 & 0 & 0 \\ 0 & 2 & 0 \\ 0 & 0 & 3 \end{bmatrix}; \quad \begin{bmatrix} 1 & 2 & 3 \\ 4 & 5 & 6 \\ 7 & 8 & 9 \end{bmatrix}; \quad \begin{bmatrix} 1 & 1/2 & 1/3 \\ 1/4 & 1/5 & 1/6 \\ 1/7 & 1/8 & 1/9 \end{bmatrix}.$$

Check that a matrix times its inverse equals the identity matrix, whose elements are 1 on the diagonal and 0 elsewhere. (b) The MATLAB function `eig(A)` returns the eigenvalues of matrix $\mathbf{A}$. Find the eigenvalues of each matrix in part (a). [MATLAB]

5. The exponential of a matrix is defined by the expansion

$$e^{\mathbf{A}} = \mathbf{I} + \mathbf{A} + \frac{1}{2!}\mathbf{A}^2 + \frac{1}{3!}\mathbf{A}^3 + \ldots$$

where

$$\mathbf{I} = \begin{bmatrix} 1 & 0 & 0 & \cdots \\ 0 & 1 & 0 & \cdots \\ 0 & 0 & 1 & \cdots \\ \vdots & \vdots & \vdots & \ddots \end{bmatrix}$$

is the identity matrix. For the matrices in the previous exercise, estimate $e^{\mathbf{A}}$ using the first six terms of the expansion. Compare with the exact result given by the MATLAB function `expm(A)`. When does the estimate work, and when does it fail? [MATLAB]

1.3   BASIC ELEMENTS OF C++

This section serves as both a crash course and a pocket reference to C++. For the programs in this book, this synopsis should suffice if you only need reading proficiency in the language. If you are planning to write C++ programs, you'll likely need a supplementary text. There are many tutorial books to choose from ranging from the whimsical, *C++ for Dummies* [38], to the pragmatic, *C++ for FORTRAN Programmers* [103]. The standard reference for the language is Stroustrup [119] and for the libraries is Plauger [101, 102].

Variables

Variables in C++ must be declared before they are used. Our programs use three data types: `int` (integers); `double` (double precision floating-point numbers); and `Matrix` (an object class for matrices). Here are some simple declarations and assignment statements

```
double x;           // Floating-point variable
int i,j;            // Integer variables
i = -7;             // Assignment statements
x = 8.234;
int statusFlag = 0; // Declaration and assignment
```

The `Matrix` class will be introduced in Chapter 4. Notice that each statement is terminated with a semicolon and that // indicates the beginning of a comment. Floating-point values are rounded down when assigned to integers (e.g., `j = x;`). Constants are declared as

```
const double c_light = 2.998e8;  // Speed of light (m/s)
```

The value of a constant cannot be changed after it is declared. User-defined data types, such as structures and classes, are discussed in Chapter 4.

Lists[‡] are declared by giving their type and length. For example,

```
double z[3];     // List with 3 elements
z[0] = 0.5;  z[1] = 1.0;  z[2] = 1.5;
```

Notice that the index of z runs from 0 to 2. Multiple statements can occur on the same line because they are separated by semicolons.

In *Gulliver's Travels*, the kingdoms of Lilliput and Blefuscu are at war over whether an egg should be eaten from the small or large end. A similar debate rages among programmers as to whether array indices should start from zero (as in C++) or one (as in MATLAB and FORTRAN). Like Gulliver, I am loath to take sides, but to maintain a single, consistent notation in the algorithms, indices will run from 1 to N.

For example, in our programs the position vector $\mathbf{r} = [4, -2, 7]$ (i.e., $\mathbf{r}_3 = 7$) is declared and defined as

```
double r[3+1];   // List with 4 elements
r[1] = 4;  r[2] = -2;  r[3] = 7;
```

The declaration `r[3+1]` reminds us that the vector has three components and the list has one extra, unused element, `r[0]`. If the number of elements is variable, the declaration is

```
int nCmp = 3;    // Number of components
double *r;       // Declare r as "pointer to doubles"
r = new double [nCmp+1];  // Allocate memory for 4 elements
```

Functionally, the two ways of declaring `r[]` are equivalent, though the latter is more flexible. Memory allocated by `new` should be released by `delete`; for example,

```
delete [] r;  // Release memory allocated by "new"
```

Make it a habit to check that each `new` has a matching `delete`.

Mathematics

The basic arithmetic operations are defined in the natural manner. For example,

---

[‡]Also called vectors or one-dimensional arrays

Table 1.3: Selected C++ mathematical functions.

`pow(x,y)`	Raising to a power, x^y
`fabs(x)`	Absolute value
`sqrt(x)`	Square root
`sin(x)`, `cos(x)`	Sine and cosine
`tan(x)`	Tangent
`atan2(y,x)`	Arc tangent of y/x in $[0, 2\pi]$
`exp(x)`	Exponential
`log(x)`, `log10(x)`	Natural logarithm and base-10 logarithm
`floor(x)`	Round down to nearest integer (e.g., `floor(3.2)=3`)
`ceil(x)`	Round up to nearest integer (e.g., `ceil(3.2)=4`)
`fmod(x,y)`	Remainder of x/y (e.g., `fmod(7.3,2.0)=1.3`)

```
double x = 4, y = 2.5, z;
z = (3*x - y  + 0.5)/2.0;
```

assigns the value z=5. There is no built-in arithmetic operator to raise a value to a power; use the `pow(x,y)` function (e.g., `pow(2.0,3.0)` is $2^3 = 8$). The modulo operator is %, so 23%4 equals 3 since $\frac{23}{4} = 5\frac{3}{4}$.

C++ provides several shortcuts for common arithmetic operations. The most common is i++ for i=i+1 (similarly, i-- for i=i-1). Other shortcuts are

```
x += 2.5;        // Same as x = x + 2.5;
y -= 3;          // Same as y = y - 3;
z *= x;          // Same as z = z * x;
y /= x + z;      // Same as y = y/(x+z);
```

Commonly used mathematical functions are available in the standard library `<math.h>`. Table 1.3 gives a short list of some of the basic functions.

Loops and Conditionals

Repeated operations are performed by using loops. Here is an example of a `for` loop in C++:

```
int i; double p[5+1];
for( i=1; i<=5; i++ )   // A basic loop; i goes from 1 to 5
   p[i] = i*i;
```

This loop assigns the values 1, 4, ..., 25 to p[1], p[2], ..., p[5]. The body of this `for` loop only contains one statement. Braces, {}, are needed if the body contains multiple statements; for example,

```
int i; double x = 1.0, y = -1.0;
for( i=1; i<=5; i++ ) {
```

```
    x *= i;
    y /= x;
}
```

By convention, the statements within a loop are indented to outline the loop's structure.

C++ also has `while` loops. Here is a simple example:

```
double x = 5;
while( x > 1 )
  x /= 2;
```

The statements in the body of the loop are repeatedly executed while the loop condition is true. In this example x will equal $\frac{5}{8}$ when the loop completes. The `break` statement can be used to terminate `for` loops or `while` loops.

Here are some examples of how conditionals are implemented: First, a simple `if` statement

```
if( x > 5 ) {    // A simple conditional
  z--;
  y = MaxHeight;
}
```

Second, an `if–else` conditional

```
if( x >= x_min && x <= x_max )
  status = 1;
else
  status = 0;
```

Logical "and" is `&&` (two ampersands) and logical "or" is `||` (two vertical bars). This conditional can be written as

```
status = (x >= x_min && x <= x_max) ? 1 : 0;
```

Third, a conditional using `else if`

```
if( x == 0 || x == 1)    // If x equals 0 or 1
  flag = 1;
else if( x < 0 && x != -1)
  flag = -1;
else
  flag = 0;
```

Logical "equals" and "not equals" are `==` and `!=`, respectively.

Input and Output

The introduction of "streams" in C++ is a great improvement over the input and output routines originally available in C. For example, the lines

```
double x = 3.1;
cout << " Value of x is " << x << " meters" << endl;
```

display

```
Value of x is 3.1 meters
```

to standard output (which is normally your screen). The **endl** stream manipulator indicates an end-of-line (i.e., a new line).

Similarly, the input stream **cin** allows us to enter data from the keyboard. The lines

```
double y;
cout << "Enter value of y: ";
cin >> y;
```

display

```
Enter value of y: _
```

to the screen with the cursor (_) waiting for you to enter the value of **y**. Streams can also be used to read and write files.

EXERCISES

6. Find the errors in each set of C++ statements below:

```
// (a) -----------------------------------
const double pi = 3.141592654
double radius, circum = 2*pi*radius;
// (b) -----------------------------------
int i; double x=1;
for( i=1, i<10, i++ )
   x = x+i;    \\ Increment x
// (c) -----------------------------------
int new=1; a=1; b=2;
if( new > 5 )
   a -= new;   new = a;
else
   b += new;   new = b;
// (d) -----------------------------------
double y=1, y_max=50*50;
while( 0 < y <= y_max )
   y *= 2;
```

You can either check these by hand or have the computer help you find the errors. [C++]

7. For each set of C++ statements below, find the value of **x** after the code executes:

```
int i, j; double x, y;
// (a) ------------------------------------
i=3; j=4;
x = (i/j)*(j/i);
// (b) ------------------------------------
x=1;
for( i=1; i<10; i+=2 )
  x /= i;
// (c) ------------------------------------
x=1;
for( i=1; i<=10; i++ )
  if( i > 6 ) x -= i;
  else if( i > 3 ) x = 2*i;
  else x--;
// (d) ------------------------------------
x=-1; y=1;
while( x < y )
  x = ( x*y < 0 ) ? -x : y++;
```

You can either work these out by hand or on the computer. [C++]

8. For each set of C++ statements below, find the value of **x** after the code executes. Warning: Results may not be what you expect.

```
int i,j; double x,y;
// (a) ------------------------------------
x=1;
for( i=1; i<5; i++ )
  x = i+x / 2.0;
// (b) ------------------------------------
x=1;
for( i=1; i<10; i+=2 );
  x /= i;
// (c) ------------------------------------
j=1;
for( i=1; i<=10; i++ )
  if( i > 5 )
    x -= i;
  else
    j = 2*i;
    x = j/2;
// (d) ------------------------------------
x = 1; y = 2;
for( i=1; i<=5; i++ )
  y *= x; x *= y;
```

I recommend that you work these out by hand before checking them on the computer. [C++]

Table 1.4: Outline of program `orthog`, which evaluates the dot product of a pair of three dimensional vectors.

- Initialize the vectors **a** and **b**.

- Evaluate the dot product as $\mathbf{a} \cdot \mathbf{b} = \mathbf{a}_1\mathbf{b}_1 + \mathbf{a}_2\mathbf{b}_2 + \mathbf{a}_3\mathbf{b}_3$.

- Print dot product and state whether vectors are orthogonal.

See pages 31 and 32 for program listings.

1.4   PROGRAMS AND FUNCTIONS

Orthogonality Program in MATLAB

In this section we write some simple programs using MATLAB and C++. Our first example, called `orthog`, tests whether two vectors are orthogonal by computing their dot product. This simple program is outlined in Table 1.4.

We first consider the MATLAB version, listed on page 31. In MATLAB, a program's name is set by the program's file name. In this case, the program is in a file called `orthog.m`. The first few lines of `orthog` are

```
% orthog - Program to test if a pair of vectors
% is orthogonal.  Assumes vectors are in 3D space
clear all;  help orthog;   % Clear the memory and print header
```

The first two lines are comments; if you type `help orthog` from the command line, MATLAB displays these lines. The `clear all` command on the third line clears the memory. The `help` statement on this line serves to display the first two lines each time you run `orthog`.

The next few lines of `orthog` are

```
%* Initialize the vectors a and b
a = input('Enter the first vector: ');
b = input('Enter the second vector: ');
```

The vectors are entered using the `input` command on these lines. The comments that begin with %* are those that have corresponding entries in the program's outline (see Table 1.4).

The next few lines calculate the dot product.

```
%* Evaluate the dot product as sum over products of elements
a_dot_b = 0;
for i=1:3
  a_dot_b = a_dot_b + a(i)*b(i);
end
```

The `for` loop, using index `i`, goes over the components of the vectors. A slicker way to do the same thing would be to use

```
%* Evaluate the dot product as sum over products of elements
a_dot_b = a * b';
```

In this case, we use MATLAB's matrix multiplication to compute the dot product as the vector product of the row vector `a` and column vector `b'` (using the Hermitian conjugate operator `'`).

The last lines of `orthog` are

```
%* Print dot product and state whether vectors are orthogonal
if( a_dot_b == 0 )
  disp('Vectors are orthogonal');
else
  disp('Vectors are NOT orthogonal');
  fprintf('Dot product = %g \n',a_dot_b);
end
```

According to the value of `a_dot_b`, the program displays one of the two possible responses.

Here is the output from a typical run:

```
>>orthog

   orthog - Program to test if a pair of vectors
   is orthogonal.  Assumes vectors are in 3D space

Enter the first vector: [1 1 1]
Enter the second vector: [1 -2 1]
Vectors are orthogonal
```

If, instead, you get the following error message,

```
??? Undefined function or variable 'orthog'.
```

then your MATLAB path probably does not point to the directory containing `orthog.m`.

Orthogonality Program in C++

Now we consider the C++ version of the `orthog` program, which tests if a pair of vectors are orthogonal by computing their dot product. The program is outlined in Table 1.4 and listed on page 32.

The first few lines are

```
// orthog - Program to test if a pair of vectors
// is orthogonal.  Assumes vectors are in 3D space
#include <iostream.h>
```

The first two lines are comments reminding us what the program does. The third line serves to include the `iostream` library, which allows us to use input and output streams. The next line marks the beginning of the main program

```
void main() {
```

with a matching } at the end of the program.

The first lines in the body of the program are

```
//* Initialize the vectors a and b
double a[3+1], b[3+1];
cout << "Enter the first vector" << endl;
int i;
for( i=1; i<=3; i++ ) {
   cout << "   a[" << i << "] = ";
   cin >> a[i];
}
```

Comments marked as `//*` correspond to entries in the program's outline (see Table 1.4). Vectors `a` and `b` are declared as floating-point arrays with four elements, three components plus one unused element (index zero). The output statements (`cout << ...`) display the following prompt to the screen:

```
Enter the first vector
   a[1] = _
```

The input statement (`cin >> a[i];`) reads the value you enter at the keyboard into `a[i]`. The next few lines

```
cout << "Enter the second vector" << endl;
for( i=1; i<=3; i++ ) {
   cout << "   b[" << i << "] = ";
   cin >> b[i];
}
```

read in vector **b** in a similar fashion.

Next, the program evaluates the dot product, using

```
//* Evaluate the dot product as sum over products of elements
double a_dot_b = 0.0;
for( i=1; i<=3; i++ )
   a_dot_b += a[i]*b[i];
```

This `for` loop contains only one statement so braces are not needed. Finally, the lines

```
//* Print dot product and state whether vectors are orthogonal
if( a_dot_b == 0.0 )
   cout << "Vectors are orthogonal" << endl;
else {
```

Table 1.5: Outline of program `interp`, which interpolates and extrapolates data.

- Initialize the data points, (x_1, y_1), (x_2, y_2), and (x_3, y_3) to be fit by a quadratic.

- Establish the range of interpolation (from $x_{\min}$ to $x_{\max}$).

- Find y^* for the desired interpolation values of x^*, using the function `intrpf`.

- Plot the curve given by (x^*, y^*), and mark the orginal data points.

See pages 31 and 33 for program listings.

```
        cout << "Vectors are NOT orthogonal" << endl;
        cout << "Dot product = " << a_dot_b << endl;
    }
```

display the result.

Here is the output from a typical run:

```
Enter the first vector
    a[1] = 1
    a[2] = 1
    a[3] = 1
Enter the second vector
    b[1] = 1
    b[2] = -2
    b[3] = 1
Vectors are orthogonal
```

Although this program may seem excessively simple, it should help you learn to compile, link, and run programs on your system.

Interpolation Program in MATLAB

It is well known that given three (x, y) pairs, one may find a quadratic that fits the desired points. There are various ways to find this polynomial and various ways to write it. The Lagrange form of the polynomial is

$$p(x) = \frac{(x-x_2)(x-x_3)}{(x_1-x_2)(x_1-x_3)}y_1 + \frac{(x-x_1)(x-x_3)}{(x_2-x_1)(x_2-x_3)}y_2 + \frac{(x-x_1)(x-x_2)}{(x_3-x_1)(x_3-x_2)}y_3 \tag{1.5}$$

where (x_1, y_1), (x_2, y_2), (x_3, y_3) are the three data points to be fit. Commonly, such polynomials are used to interpolate between data points.

Table 1.6: Outline of function `intrpf`, which evaluates the Lagrange quadratic (1.5).

- *Inputs*: $\mathbf{x} = [x_1 \; x_2 \; x_3]$, $\mathbf{y} = [y_1 \; y_2 \; y_3]$, and x^*

- *Outputs*: y^*

- Calculate $y^* = p(x^*)$ using the Lagrange polynomial (1.5).

See pages 32 and 34 for program listings.

A simple interpolation program, called `interp`, is outlined in Table 1.5. The MATLAB listing is on page 31; the first few lines are

```
% interp - Program to interpolate data using Lagrange
% polynomial to fit quadratic to three data points
clear all; help interp;  % Clear memory and print header
%* Initialize the data points to be fit by quadratic
disp('Enter data points as x,y pairs (e.g., [1 2])');
for i=1:3
  temp = input('Enter data point: ');
  x(i) = temp(1);
  y(i) = temp(2);
end
%* Establish the range of interpolation (from x_min to x_max)
xr = input('Enter range of x values as [x_min x_max]: ');
```

Here the program reads in the three (x, y) pairs and the range of values for which the data is to be interpolated.

The interpolated value $y^* = p(x^*)$ is computed by the function `intrpf` from $x^* = x_{\min}$ to $x^* = x_{\max}$. These values of y^* (`yi`) are computed in the loop

```
%* Find yi for the desired interpolation values xi using
%  the function intrpf
nplot = 100;     % Number of points for interpolation curve
for i=1:nplot
  xi(i) = xr(1) + (xr(2)-xr(1))*(i-1)/(nplot-1);
  yi(i) = intrpf(xi(i),x,y);  % Use intrpf function to interpolate
end
```

Finally, the results are graphed using MATLAB's plotting routines.

```
%* Plot the curve given by (xi,yi) and mark original data points
plot(x,y,'*',xi,yi,'-');
xlabel('x');
ylabel('y');
```

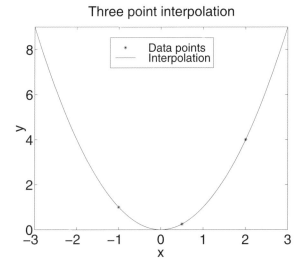

Figure 1.2: Graphical output from the `interp` program. Input data is $(-1, 1)$, $(\frac{1}{2}, \frac{1}{4})$, and $(2, 4)$; interpolation range is from -3 to 3.

```
title('Three point interpolation');
legend('Data points','Interpolation');
```

The interpolation points (x^*, y^*) are plotted as a solid line along with the original data points (x, y) marked by asterisks (see Figure 1.2).

The real work is done by the function `intrpf` (Table 1.6). Functions in MATLAB are implemented as in most languages, except each function must be in a separate file. The file name must match the function name (function `intrpf` is in the file `intrpf.m`). The first lines of `intrpf` are

```
function yi = intrpf(xi,x,y)
% Function to interpolate between data points
% using Lagrange polynomial (quadratic)
% Inputs
%   x     Vector of x coordinates of data points (3 values)
%   y     Vector of y coordinates of data points (3 values)
%   xi    The x value where interpolation is computed
% Output
%   yi    The interpolation polynomial evaluated at xi
```

The `intrpf` function has three input arguments and one output argument. However, a MATLAB function can have a list of output arguments. In Section 3.3 we use an adaptive Runge-Kutta routine that has the calling sequence

```
function [xSmall, t, tau] = rka(x,t,tau,err,derivsRK,param)
```

with six input arguments and three output arguments.

The `intrpf` function is straightforward, since it just evaluates Equation (1.5). The body of the function is

```
%* Calculate yi = p(xi) using Lagrange polynomial
yi = (xi-x(2))*(xi-x(3))/((x(1)-x(2))*(x(1)-x(3)))*y(1) ...
   + (xi-x(1))*(xi-x(3))/((x(2)-x(1))*(x(2)-x(3)))*y(2) ...
   + (xi-x(1))*(xi-x(2))/((x(3)-x(1))*(x(3)-x(2)))*y(3);
return;
```

The ellipsis[§] (...) ending the first two lines signals that they are continued on the next line.

As in most languages, variables in a function are local to that function. For example, if we were to modify the value of `xi` inside the function `intrpf`, the variable `xi` in the main program (`interp`) would be unaffected. Variables in the calling sequence are passed by value (as in C++) and not by reference (as in FORTRAN).

Interpolation Program in C++

The C++ version of `interp`, the Lagrange polynomial interpolation program, is outlined in Table 1.5 (see page 33 for the listing). The first few lines of the program are

```
// interp - Program to interpolate data using Lagrange
// polynomial to fit quadratic to three data points
#include "NumMeth.h"
double intrpf( double xi, double x[], double y[]);
void main() {
```

The include statement refers to the header file `NumMeth.h`, which lists the various libraries that we normally want to include (`<iostream.h>`, `<math.h>`, etc.). The declaration `double intrpf(...` states that the program intends to call the function `intrpf`, which has three inputs (of type `double`) and which returns a value of type `double`.

The next few lines of the program are

```
//* Initialize the data points to be fit by quadratic
double x[3+1], y[3+1];
cout << "Enter data points:" << endl;
int i;
for( i=1; i<=3; i++ ) {
  cout << "x[" << i << "] = ";
  cin >> x[i];
  cout << "y[" << i << "] = ";
  cin >> y[i];
```

[§]An ellipsis (...) is the punctuation mark that indicates an incomplete thought. An ellipse is a geometric object whose name indicates that it is an imperfect circle.

```
  }
  //* Establish the range of interpolation (from x_min to x_max)
  double x_min, x_max;
  cout << "Enter minimum value of x: ";   cin >> x_min;
  cout << "Enter maximum value of x: ";   cin >> x_max;
```

The program prompts you to enter the data points to be fit by the Lagrange polynomial (1.5) and the range of interpolation values.

Next, the arrays xi and yi are declared by

```
  //* Find yi for the desired interpolation values xi using
  //   the function intrpf
  int nplot = 100;       // Number of points for interpolation curve
  double *xi, *yi;
  xi = new double [nplot+1];   // Allocate memory for these
  yi = new double [nplot+1];   // arrays (nplot+1 elements)
```

These lines could be replaced by

```
  const int nplot = 100;   // Number of points for interpolation curve
  double xi[nplot+1], yi[nplot+1];
```

since nplot is a constant in this program, but you should get accustomed to using new for allocating arrays.

The interpolation values of xi and yi are computed by the loop

```
  for( i=1; i<=nplot; i++ ) {
    xi[i] = x_min + (x_max-x_min)*(i-1)/(nplot-1);
    yi[i] = intrpf(xi[i],x,y);  // Use intrpf function to interpolate
  }
```

Note that xi[1]= $x_{\min}$, xi[nplot]= $x_{\max}$, with linearly spaced values in between. The values of yi ($y^* = p(x^*)$) are computed by evaluating Equation (1.5), which is done by the intrpf function.

The program outputs the results, using

```
  //* Print out the plotting variables: x, y, xi, yi
  ofstream xOut("x.txt"), yOut("y.txt"), xiOut("xi.txt"),
           yiOut("yi.txt");
  for( i=1; i<=3; i++ ) {
    xOut << x[i] << endl;
    yOut << y[i] << endl;
  }
  for( i=1; i<=nplot; i++ ) {
    xiOut << xi[i] << endl;
    yiOut << yi[i] << endl;
  }
```

Four data files (x.dat, y.dat, etc.) are created.

Unfortunately, C++ lacks a standard graphics library so we need a separate graphics application to plot this output. The following MATLAB commands

```
load x.txt; load y.txt; load xi.txt; load yi.txt;
plot(x,y,'*',xi,yi,'-');
xlabel('x');  ylabel('y');
title('Three point interpolation');
legend('Data points','Interpolation');
```

load and plot the data (see Figure 1.2).

The last line of the program is

```
delete [] xi, yi;  // Release memory allocated by "new"
```

This line is not absolutely necessary because the program exits right after releasing the memory allocated to xi and yi. However, it is considered good programming style to clean up when you're finished using an array.

The intrpf function, which evaluates the Lagrange polynomial, is listed on page 34, (see outline in Table 1.6). The first few lines of the function are

```
double intrpf( double xi, double x[], double y[]) {
// Function to interpolate between data points
// using Lagrange polynomial (quadratic)
// Inputs
//   xi    The x value where interpolation is computed
//   x     Vector of x coordinates of data points (3 values)
//   y     Vector of y coordinates of data points (3 values)
// Output
//   yi    The interpolation polynomial evaluated at xi
```

The first line gives the function's calling sequence. There are three inputs: xi is a simple variable, and the other two, x and y, are arrays. The function returns a value (yi), which has type double. Functions that do not return a value have type void; such functions are equivalent to FORTRAN subroutines.

The variable xi in intrpf is *local* to the function. That is, the function receives a copy of this variable from the main program; this is called "pass by value." Since the function receives a copy, changing xi within intrpf does not affect its value in interp. If we wanted the function to receive the actual variable, the calling sequence would be

```
double intrpf( double& xi, double x[], double y[]) {
```

The ampersand (double& xi) indicates that xi is "passed by reference." Arrays, on the other hand, are always passed by reference, since what the function receives is not a copy of the array, but rather the memory address where the array begins.

The rest of intrpf is just

```
//* Calculate yi = p(xi) using Lagrange polynomial
double yi = (xi-x[2])*(xi-x[3])/((x[1]-x[2])*(x[1]-x[3]))*y[1]
   + (xi-x[1])*(xi-x[3])/((x[2]-x[1])*(x[2]-x[3]))*y[2]
   + (xi-x[1])*(xi-x[2])/((x[3]-x[1])*(x[3]-x[2]))*y[3];
return (yi);
```

These lines evaluate the Lagrange polynomial, Equation (1.5), and return the resulting value. Notice that this long equation is written across three lines. This is a single statement that ends with the semicolon.

To run the `interp` program with the `intrpf` function, you will need to compile each routine and link them. This procedure varies significantly from system to system (e.g., make files, workspaces), so consult your compiler's documentation or local experts. Resist the temptation to put both routines into a single file, since that solution will be impractical for the programs in the later chapters.

EXERCISES

9. Kernighan and Ritchie, who created the C language, advise that, "The first program to write in any language is the same for all languages: Print the words `hello, world`. This is the basic hurdle; to leap over it you have to be able to create the program text somewhere, compile it successfully, load it, run it, and find out where your output went. With these mechanical details mastered, everything else is comparatively easy." [80] Write, compile and run a `hello` program. [Computer]

10. It is always good to know your limits. For your computer system find: (a) the largest possible floating-point number; (b) the largest integer I such that $(I + 1) - 1$ equals I; (c) the smallest possible positive floating-point number; (d) the smallest positive floating-point number x such that $(1 + x) - 1$ does not equals zero; (e) the largest $N \times N$ matrix allowed by memory; (f) the longest row vector allowed by memory; (g) the maximum number of array dimensions allowed; for example, $a(i, j, k)$ is a three-dimensional array. [Computer]

11. For your computer system, write a program to estimate the number of floating-point operations (e.g., multiplications) that can be performed in one second. In C++, timing routines are available in the `<time.h>` library. In MATLAB, the `tic` and `toc` commands mimic a stopwatch. [Computer]

12. Modify the `orthog` program so that it can handle vectors of any length. Your program should detect and gracefully handle erroneous inputs such as vectors of unequal length. [Computer]

13. Modify the `orthog` program so that it accepts a pair of three- dimensional vectors and outputs a unit vector that is orthogonal to the input vectors. [Computer]

14. Modify `orthog` so that if the second vector is not orthogonal to the first, the program computes a new vector that is orthogonal to the first vector, has the same length as the second vector, and is in the same plane as the two input vectors. This orthogonalization is often used with eigenvectors and is commonly performed using the Gram-Schmidt procedure. [Computer]

15. From tables we find the following values for the zeroth-order Bessel function: $J_0(0) = 1.0$; $J_0(0.5) = 0.9385$; $J_0(1.0) = 0.7652$. Using `intrp`, find the estimated

values of $J_0(x)$ for range $x = 0.3$, 0.9, 1.1, 1.5 and 2.0. Look up the tabulated values and compare. [Computer]

16. Modify `interp` so that it can handle any number of data points by using higher-order polynomials. After testing your program, give it the following values of the Bessel function: $J_0(0) = 1.0$; $J_0(0.2) = 0.9900$; $J_0(0.4) = 0.9604$; $J_0(0.6) = 0.9120$; $J_0(0.8) = 0.8463$; $J_0(1.0) = 0.7652$, and repeat the previous exercise. Do your estimates improve? [Computer]

17. Write a function that is similar to `intrpf` but that returns the estimated derivative at the interpolation point. The function will accept three (x, y) pairs, fit a quadratic to the data, then return the value of the derivative of the quadratic at the desired point. [Computer]

18. A Bézier cubic curve is defined by the parametric equations

$$x(t) = a_x t^3 + b_x t^2 + c_x t + x_1$$
$$y(t) = a_y t^3 + b_y t^2 + c_y t + y_1$$

where $0 \le t \le 1$. The Bézier control points are given by the relations

$$
\begin{array}{ll}
x_2 = x_1 + c_x/3 & y_2 = y_1 + c_y/3 \\
x_3 = x_2 + (c_x + b_x)/3 & y_3 = y_2 + (c_y + b_y)/3 \\
x_4 = x_1 + c_x + b_x + a_x & y_4 = y_1 + c_y + b_y + a_y
\end{array}
$$

The curve goes from $(x(0), y(0)) = (x_1, y_1)$ to $(x(1), y(1)) = (x_4, y_4)$ and is tangent to the lines (x_1, y_1)–(x_2, y_2) and (x_3, y_3)–(x_4, y_4). Write a program to draw a Bézier curve, given the control points (x_1, y_1), ..., (x_4, y_4). Draw the curve with control points (0,0), (2,1), (-1,1), and (1,0). [Computer]

1.5   NUMERICAL ERRORS

Range Error

A computer stores individual floating-point numbers using only a small amount of memory. Typically, single precision (`float` in C++) allocates 4 bytes (32 bits) for the representation of a number, while double precision (`double` in C++; MATLAB's default precision) uses 8 bytes. A floating-point number is represented by its mantissa and exponent (for 1.60×10^{-19}, the decimal mantissa is 1.60 and the exponent is -19). The IEEE format for double precision uses 53 bits to store the mantissa (including one bit for the sign) and the remaining 11 bits for the exponent. Exactly how a computer handles the representation is not as important as knowing the maximum range and the number of significant digits.

The maximum range is the limit on the magnitude of floating-point numbers given the fixed number of bits used for the exponent. For single precision, a typical value is $2^{\pm 127} \approx 10^{\pm 38}$; for double precision it is typically $2^{\pm 1023} \approx 10^{\pm 308}$. Exceeding the single precision range is not difficult. Consider, for example, the evaluation of the Bohr radius in SI units,

$$a_0 = \frac{4\pi\epsilon_0 \hbar^2}{m_e e^2} \approx 5.3 \times 10^{-11} \text{ m} \tag{1.6}$$

While its value lies within the range of a single precision number, the range is exceeded in the calculation of the numerator ($4\pi\epsilon_0\hbar^2 \approx 1.24 \times 10^{-78}$ kg$\cdot$C$^2\cdot$m) and the denominator ($m_e e^2 \approx 2.34 \times 10^{-68}$ kg $\cdot$ C^2). The best solution for dealing with this type of range difficulty is to work in a set of units natural to a problem (e.g., for atomic problems work in units of angstroms, the charge of an electron).

Sometimes range problems arise not from the choice of units but because the numbers in the problem are inherently large. Let's consider an important example, the factorial function. Using the definition

$$n! = n \times (n-1) \times (n-2) \times \ldots 3 \times 2 \times 1 \tag{1.7}$$

it is easy to evaluate $n!$ in C++ as

```
double nFactorial = 1;
int i;
for (i=1; i<=n; i++)
  nFactorial *= i;
```

given that n has been defined.

In MATLAB, using the colon operator this calculation may be performed as

```
nFactorial = prod(1:n);
```

where `prod(x)` is the product of the elements of vector x and `1:n` = [1 2 ... n]. Unfortunately, due to range problems, we cannot compute $n!$ for $n > 170$ using these direct methods of evaluating (1.7).

A common solution to working with very large numbers is to use their logarithm. For the factorial,

$$\log(n!) = \log(n) + \log(n-1) + \ldots + \log(3) + \log(2) + \log(1) \tag{1.8}$$

In MATLAB, this could be evaluated as

```
log_nFactorial = sum( log(1:n) );
```

where `sum(x)` is the sum of the elements of vector x. However, this scheme is computationally expensive if n is large. An even better approach is to combine the use of logarithms with Stirling's formula [2]

$$n! = \sqrt{2n\pi} n^n e^{-n} \left(1 + \frac{1}{12n} + \frac{1}{288n^2} + \ldots \right) \tag{1.9}$$

or

$$\log(n!) = \frac{1}{2}\log(2n\pi) + n\log(n) - n + \log\left(1 + \frac{1}{12n} + \frac{1}{288n^2} + \ldots \right) \tag{1.10}$$

This approximation should be used when n is large ($n > 30$), otherwise the factorial's original definition is preferred.

Finally, if the value of $n!$ needs to be printed, we can as express it as

$$n! = (\text{mantissa}) \times 10^{(\text{exponent})} \tag{1.11}$$

where the exponent is the integer part of $\log_{10}(n!)$, and the mantissa is 10^a where a is the fractional part of $\log_{10}(n!)$. Recall that the conversion between natural and base-10 logarithms is $\log_{10}(x) = \log_{10}(e)\log(x)$.

Round-off Error

Suppose we wanted to numerically compute $f'(x)$, the derivative of a known function $f(x)$. In calculus you learned the following formula for the derivative,

$$f'(x) = \frac{f(x+h) - f(x)}{h} \tag{1.12}$$

with the limit that $h \to 0$. What happens if we evaluate the right-hand side of this expression, setting $h = 0$? Because the computer doesn't understand that the expression is valid only as a limit, the division by zero has several possible outcomes. The computer may assign the value, Inf, which is a special floating-point number reserved for representing infinity. Since the numerator is also zero, the computer may evaluate the quotient to be undefined (Not-a-Number), NaN, another reserved value. Or the calculation might be halted with a scolding diagnostic message.

Clearly, setting $h = 0$ when evaluating (1.12) will not give us anything useful, but what if we set h to a very small value, say $h = 10^{-300}$, using double precision? The answer will still be incorrect due to the second limitation on the representation of floating-point numbers: the finite numer of digits in the mantissa. For single precision, the number of significant digits is typically 6 or 7 decimal digits; for double precision it is about 16 digits. Thus, in double precision, the operation $3 + 10^{-20}$ returns an answer of 3 because of round-off; using $h = 10^{-300}$ in Equation (1.12) will almost certainly return 0 when evaluating the numerator.

Figure 1.3 illustrates the magnitude of the round-off error in a typical calculation of a derivative. Define the absolute error as

$$\Delta(h) = \left| f'(x) - \frac{f(x+h) - f(x)}{h} \right| \tag{1.13}$$

Notice that $\Delta(h)$ decreases as h is made smaller, which is expected given Equation (1.12) is exact as $h \to 0$. Below $h = 10^{-8}$, the error starts increasing due to round-off effects. At the smallest values of h ($\leq 10^{-16}$), the error is so large that the answer is worthless. In the next chapter we'll return to the question of how best to compute derivatives numerically.

To test round-off tolerance, we define ϵ_r as the smallest number that, when added to 1, returns a value different from 1. In MATLAB, the built-in function eps returns ϵ_r; on my computer, eps $\approx 2.22 \times 10^{-16}$. In C++, the <float.h>

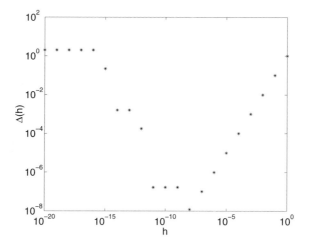

Figure 1.3: Absolute error $\Delta(h)$, Equation (1.13), versus h for $f(x) = x^2$ and $x = 1$.

header defines `DBL_EPSILON` as ϵ_r for double precision. Notice in Figure 1.3 that $\Delta(h)$ plateaus when $h < \epsilon_r$.

Because of round-off errors, most scientific calculations use double precision. The disadvantages of double precision are that it requires more storage and that it is sometimes (but not always) more computationally costly. Modern computer processors are designed to work in double precision, so it can actually be slower to work in single precision. Using double precision sometimes only forestalls the difficulties of round-off. For example, a matrix inverse calculation may work fine in single precision for small matrices of 50×50 elements, but fail because of round-off for larger matrices. Double precision may allow us to work with matrices of 100×100, but if we need to solve even larger systems we will have to use a different algorithm. The best approach is to work with algorithms that are robust against round-off error.

EXERCISES

19. Suppose that we take electron volts as our unit of energy, the mass of the electron as our unit of mass, and set Planck's constant equal to unity. Convert 1 kg, 1 m, and 1 s into these units. [Pencil]

20. Suppose that we take the mean radius of Earth-Sun orbit as the unit of length, the mass of Earth as the unit of mass, and a year as the unit of time. Convert the gravitational constant, G, into these units. What is the force of attraction between Earth and the Moon in these units? Between Earth and the Sun? [Pencil]

21. The probability of flipping N coins and obtaining m "heads" is given by the binomial distribution to be

$$P_N(m) = \frac{N!}{m!(N-m)!} \left(\frac{1}{2}\right)^N$$

What is more probable, flipping 10 coins and getting no heads or flipping 10,000 coins and getting exactly 5000 heads? [Pencil]

22. The double factorial is defined as

$$n!! \equiv n \times (n-2) \times (n-4) \ldots \times \begin{cases} 6 \times 4 \times 2 & n \text{ even} \\ 5 \times 3 \times 1 & n \text{ odd} \end{cases}$$

(a) Write a program that prints out $n!!$ by evaluating its definition using logarithms. Test your program by checking that $1000!! \approx 3.99 \times 10^{1284}$; compute $2001!!$. (b) Obtain an expression for $n!!$ in terms of $n!$. [Pencil] (c) Write a program that prints out $n!!$ by evaluating it using Stirling's approximation when $n > 30$. Compute $10000!!$, $314159!!$ and $(6.02 \times 10^{23})!!$. [Computer]

23. Suppose that you are standing at $40°$ latitude and are 2 m tall. (a) Find the velocity of your feet, v, due to the rotation of Earth. Assume that Earth is a perfect sphere of radius $R = 6378$ km and that a day is exactly 24 h long. (b) Using the result from (a), compute the centripetal acceleration at your feet as $a = v^2/r$. (c) Repeat parts (a) and (b) for your head, and compute the difference between the acceleration at your head and feet. Show how round-off can corrupt your calculation and how to fix the problem. [Pencil]

24.   (a) Write a program to reproduce Figure 1.3. Use $h = 1$, 10^{-1}, $10^{-2}, \ldots$. (b) Modify your program to use $h = 1$, 2^{-1}, $2^{-2}, \ldots$. The results are strikingly different; explain why. [Computer]

25. Write a program to find ϵ_r, the smallest number that when added to 1 returns a value different from 1. Compare your result with either MATLAB's built-in function eps or DBL_EPSILON, as defined in the C++ <float.h> header. [Computer]

26. Consider the Taylor expansion for the exponential

$$e^x = 1 + x + \frac{x^2}{2!} + \frac{x^3}{3!} + \ldots = \lim_{N \to \infty} S(x, N)$$

where $S(x, N)$ is the partial sum with $N+1$ terms. (a) Write a program that plots the absolute fractional error of the sum, $|S(x, N) - e^x|/e^x$, versus N (up to $N = 60$) for a given value of x. Test your program for $x = 10, 2, -2$, and -10. From the plots, explain why this is not a good way to evaluate e^x when $x < 0$.[49] (b) Modify your program so that it uses the identity $e^x = 1/e^{-x} = 1/S(-x, \infty)$ to evaluate the exponential when x is negative. Explain why this approach works better. [Computer]

BEYOND THIS CHAPTER

The Lagrange formulation for assembling an interpolating polynomial has only one advantage: It is easy to understand and remember. Algorithmically, it is not the best method for polynomial interpolation for a variety of reasons, including susceptibility to round-off error when fitting higher-order polynomials. A superior approach is to build a divided difference table and use the Newtonian formulation.[33]

The round-off error in a numerical scheme can be quantitatively estimated using backward error analysis.[133] It is possible to perform calculations of arbitrary precision by storing numbers as rational quotients (fraction with integer numerator and denominator). While a few calculations call for such accuracy (e.g., some orbital mechanics problems), the computations can be very slow.

Finally, you'll discover that most of the fundamental elements of numerical analysis were introduced long before the invention of the electronic computer. This is clear from the names of the basic algorithms; the litany includes Newton, Euler, Gauss, Jacobi, and many other famous physicists and mathematicians. For historical accounts of the development of numerical analysis, see Goldstine [58] and Nash [91].

APPENDIX A: MATLAB LISTINGS

Listing 1A.1 Program orthog. Determines if a pair of vectors is orthogonal by computing their dot product.

```
% orthog - Program to test if a pair of vectors
% is orthogonal.  Assumes vectors are in 3D space
clear all;  help orthog;   % Clear the memory and print header
%* Initialize the vectors a and b
a = input('Enter the first vector: ');
b = input('Enter the second vector: ');
%* Evaluate the dot product as sum over products of elements
a_dot_b = 0;
for i=1:3
  a_dot_b = a_dot_b + a(i)*b(i);
end
%* Print dot product and state whether vectors are orthogonal
if( a_dot_b == 0 )
  disp('Vectors are orthogonal');
else
  disp('Vectors are NOT orthogonal');
  fprintf('Dot product = %g \n',a_dot_b);
end
```

Listing 1A.2 Program interp. Uses the intrpf (Listing 1A.3) function to interpolate between data points.

```
% interp - Program to interpolate data using Lagrange
% polynomial to fit quadratic to three data points
clear all; help interp;  % Clear memory and print header
%* Initialize the data points to be fit by quadratic
disp('Enter data points as x,y pairs (e.g., [1 2])');
for i=1:3
  temp = input('Enter data point: ');
  x(i) = temp(1);
  y(i) = temp(2);
end
%* Establish the range of interpolation (from x_min to x_max)
```

```
xr = input('Enter range of x values as [x_min x_max]: ');
%* Find yi for the desired interpolation values xi using
%  the function intrpf
nplot = 100;      % Number of points for interpolation curve
for i=1:nplot
  xi(i) = xr(1) + (xr(2)-xr(1))*(i-1)/(nplot-1);
  yi(i) = intrpf(xi(i),x,y);  % Use intrpf function to interpolate
end
%* Plot the curve given by (xi,yi) and mark original data points
plot(x,y,'*',xi,yi,'-');
xlabel('x');
ylabel('y');
title('Three point interpolation');
legend('Data points','Interpolation');
```

Listing 1A.3 Function `intrpf`. Uses a quadratic to interpolate between three data points.

```
function yi = intrpf(xi,x,y)
% Function to interpolate between data points
% using Lagrange polynomial (quadratic)
% Inputs
%   x    Vector of x coordinates of data points (3 values)
%   y    Vector of y coordinates of data points (3 values)
%   xi   The x value where interpolation is computed
% Output
%   yi   The interpolation polynomial evaluated at xi

%* Calculate yi = p(xi) using Lagrange polynomial
yi = (xi-x(2))*(xi-x(3))/((x(1)-x(2))*(x(1)-x(3)))*y(1) ...
   + (xi-x(1))*(xi-x(3))/((x(2)-x(1))*(x(2)-x(3)))*y(2) ...
   + (xi-x(1))*(xi-x(2))/((x(3)-x(1))*(x(3)-x(2)))*y(3);
return;
```

APPENDIX B: C++ LISTINGS

Listing 1B.1 Program `orthog`. Determines if a pair of vectors is orthogonal by computing their dot product.

```
// orthog - Program to test if a pair of vectors
// is orthogonal.  Assumes vectors are in 3D space
#include <iostream.h>

void main() {

  //* Initialize the vectors a and b
```

```
  double a[3+1], b[3+1];
  cout << "Enter the first vector" << endl;
  int i;
  for( i=1; i<=3; i++ ) {
    cout << "  a[" << i << "] = ";
    cin >> a[i];
  }
  cout << "Enter the second vector" << endl;
  for( i=1; i<=3; i++ ) {
    cout << "  b[" << i << "] = ";
    cin >> b[i];
  }

  //* Evaluate the dot product as sum over products of elements
  double a_dot_b = 0.0;
  for( i=1; i<=3; i++ )
    a_dot_b += a[i]*b[i];


  //* Print dot product and state whether vectors are orthogonal
  if( a_dot_b == 0.0 )
    cout << "Vectors are orthogonal" << endl;
  else {
    cout << "Vectors are NOT orthogonal" << endl;
    cout << "Dot product = " << a_dot_b << endl;
  }
}
```

Listing 1B.2 Program interp. Uses the intrpf (Listing 1B.3) function to interpolate between data points.

```
// interp - Program to interpolate data using Lagrange
// polynomial to fit quadratic to three data points
#include "NumMeth.h"

double intrpf( double xi, double x[], double y[]);

void main() {

  //* Initialize the data points to be fit by quadratic
  double x[3+1], y[3+1];
  cout << "Enter data points:" << endl;
  int i;
  for( i=1; i<=3; i++ ) {
    cout << "x[" << i << "] = ";
    cin >> x[i];
    cout << "y[" << i << "] = ";
    cin >> y[i];
  }
```

```
//* Establish the range of interpolation (from x_min to x_max)
double x_min, x_max;
cout << "Enter minimum value of x: ";  cin >> x_min;
cout << "Enter maximum value of x: ";  cin >> x_max;

//* Find yi for the desired interpolation values xi using
//  the function intrpf
int nplot = 100;       // Number of points for interpolation curve
double *xi, *yi;
xi = new double [nplot+1];   // Allocate memory for these
yi = new double [nplot+1];   // arrays (nplot+1 elements)
for( i=1; i<=nplot; i++ ) {
  xi[i] = x_min + (x_max-x_min)*(i-1)/(nplot-1);
  yi[i] = intrpf(xi[i],x,y);  // Use intrpf function to interpolate
}

//* Print out the plotting variables: x, y, xi, yi
ofstream xOut("x.txt"), yOut("y.txt"), xiOut("xi.txt"),
         yiOut("yi.txt");
for( i=1; i<=3; i++ ) {
  xOut << x[i] << endl;
  yOut << y[i] << endl;
}
for( i=1; i<=nplot; i++ ) {
  xiOut << xi[i] << endl;
  yiOut << yi[i] << endl;
}

  delete [] xi, yi;  // Release memory allocated by "new"
}
/***** To plot in MATLAB; use the script below *******************
load x.txt; load y.txt; load xi.txt; load yi.txt;
plot(x,y,'*',xi,yi,'-');
xlabel('x');  ylabel('y');
title('Three point interpolation');
legend('Data points','Interpolation');
*****************************************************************/
```

Listing 1B.3 Function intrpf. Uses a quadratic to interpolate between three data points.

```
double intrpf( double xi, double x[], double y[]) {
// Function to interpolate between data points
// using Lagrange polynomial (quadratic)
// Inputs
//   xi    The x value where interpolation is computed
//   x     Vector of x coordinates of data points (3 values)
//   y     Vector of y coordinates of data points (3 values)
```

```
// Output
//   yi    The interpolation polynomial evaluated at xi

  //* Calculate yi = p(xi) using Lagrange polynomial
  double yi = (xi-x[2])*(xi-x[3])/((x[1]-x[2])*(x[1]-x[3]))*y[1]
    + (xi-x[1])*(xi-x[3])/((x[2]-x[1])*(x[2]-x[3]))*y[2]
    + (xi-x[1])*(xi-x[2])/((x[3]-x[1])*(x[3]-x[2]))*y[3];
  return (yi);
}
```

Listing 1B.4 Header NumMeth.h. Header file for this book's programs. Header file Matrix.h, which defines the Matrix object class, is listed in Appendix 4.C.

```
// General header file for C++ programs
// in "Numerical Methods for Physics"

#include <iostream.h>
#include <fstream.h>
#include <assert.h>
#include <math.h>
#include "Matrix.h"
```

Chapter 2

Ordinary Differential Equations I: Basic Methods

In this chapter we solve one of the first problems considered in freshman physics: the flight of a baseball. Without air resistance the problem is easy to solve. However, to include realistic drag, we need to compute the solution numerically. To analyze this problem we first have to define numerical differentiation. Before you studied physics, you had to learn calculus, so it should not be surprising that we start with this topic. In the latter half of the chapter we visit another old friend, the simple pendulum, but without the small angle approximation. Interestingly, oscillating systems, such as a pendulum, reveal a fatal flaw in some of the numerical methods for solving ordinary differential equations.

2.1 PROJECTILE MOTION

Basic Equations

Consider simple projectile motion, say the flight of a baseball. To describe the motion we must compute the vector position $\mathbf{r}(t)$ and vector velocity $\mathbf{v}(t)$ of the projectile. The basic equations of motion are

$$\frac{d\mathbf{v}}{dt} = \frac{1}{m}\mathbf{F}_{\mathrm{a}}(\mathbf{v}) - g\hat{\mathbf{y}}; \qquad \frac{d\mathbf{r}}{dt} = \mathbf{v} \tag{2.1}$$

where m is the mass of the projectile. The force due to air resistance is $\mathbf{F}_{\mathrm{a}}(\mathbf{v})$, the gravitational acceleration is g, and $\hat{\mathbf{y}}$ is the unit vector in the y-direction. The motion is two dimensional, so we may ignore the z-component and work in the xy plane.

Air resistance increases with the velocity of the object, and the precise form for $\mathbf{F}_{\mathrm{a}}$ depends on the flow around the projectile. Commonly, it is approximated as

$$\mathbf{F}_{\mathrm{a}} = -\frac{1}{2}C_{\mathrm{d}}\rho A|\mathbf{v}|\mathbf{v} \tag{2.2}$$

where C_d is the drag coefficient, ρ is the density of the air, and A is the cross-sectional area of the projectile. The drag coefficient is a dimensionless parameter that depends on the projectile's geometry—the more streamlined the object, the smaller the coefficient.

For a smooth sphere of radius R moving very slowly through a fluid, the drag coefficient is given by Stokes' law,

$$C_d = \frac{12\nu}{R\upsilon} = \frac{24}{Re} \tag{2.3}$$

where ν is the viscosity of the fluid ($\nu \approx 1.5 \times 10^{-5} \text{ m}^2/\text{s}$ for air) and $Re \equiv 2R\upsilon/\nu$ is the dimensionless *Reynolds number*. For an object the size of a baseball moving through air, Stokes' law is valid only if the velocity is less than about 0.2 mm/s ($Re \approx 1$).

At higher speeds (above 20 cm/s, $Re > 10^3$), the wake behind the sphere develops vortex rolls and the drag coefficient is approximately constant ($C_d \approx 0.5$) for a wide range of velocities. When the Reynolds number exceeds a critical value, the flow in the wake becomes turbulent and the drag coefficient *drops* dramatically. This reduction occurs because the turbulence disrupts the low-pressure region in the wake behind the sphere.[128] For a smooth sphere, this critical Reynolds number is approximately 3×10^5. For a baseball, the drag coefficient is usually smaller than that of a smooth sphere because the baseball's stitching disrupts the laminar flow, precipitating the onset of turbulence.* We take $C_d \approx 0.35$ as an average value for the typical range of velocities found in baseball (See Exercise 2.10).

Notice that the drag force, Equation (2.2), varies as the square of the magnitude of the velocity ($|\mathbf{F}_a| \propto v^2$) and, of course, acts in the direction opposite the velocity. A baseball's mass and diameter are 0.145 kg and 7.4 cm, almost exactly the same as for a cricket ball. For a baseball, the drag and gravitational forces are equal in magnitude when $v \approx 40$ m/s.

We know how to solve the equations of motion if air resistance is negligible. The trajectory is

$$\mathbf{r}(t) = \mathbf{r}_1 + \mathbf{v}_1 t - \frac{1}{2}gt^2\hat{\mathbf{y}} \tag{2.4}$$

where $\mathbf{r}_1 \equiv \mathbf{r}(t = 0)$ and $\mathbf{v}_1 \equiv \mathbf{v}(t = 0)$ are the initial position and velocity. If the projectile starts at the origin and the initial velocity is at an angle θ above the horizontal, then

$$x_{\max} = \frac{2v_1^2}{g}\sin\theta\cos\theta; \qquad y_{\max} = \frac{v_1^2}{2g}\sin^2\theta \tag{2.5}$$

are the horizontal range and the maximum height. The time of flight is

$$t_{fl} = \frac{2v_1}{g}\sin\theta \tag{2.6}$$

---

*Similarly, the dimples on a golf ball give it a lower drag coefficient.[78]

Again, these expressions only hold when there is no air resistance. It is easy to check that the maximum horizontal range is achieved when the initial velocity makes an angle of $\theta = 45°$ with the horizontal. We want to keep this information in mind when we build our simulation. If you know the exact solution for a special case, you should always check that the program works correctly for that case.

Forward Derivative

To solve the equations of motion (2.1) we need a numerical method for evaluating first derivatives. The formal definition of the derivative is,

$$f'(t) \equiv \lim_{\tau \to 0} \frac{f(t + \tau) - f(t)}{\tau} \qquad (2.7)$$

where τ is the time increment or time step. As discussed in Section 1.5, this formula must be treated with some care. Figure 1.3 illustrates that using an extremely small value for τ can cause large errors in the calculation of $[f(t + \tau) - f(t)]/\tau$. Specifically, round-off errors occur in the computation of $t + \tau$, in the evaluation of the function f and in the subtraction in the numerator. Given that τ cannot be taken to be arbitrarily small, we need to estimate the difference between $f'(t)$ and $[f(t + \tau) - f(t)]/\tau$ for finite τ.

To find this difference we'll use a Taylor expansion. As physicists, we usually see the Taylor series expressed as

$$f(t + \tau) = f(t) + \tau f'(t) + \frac{\tau^2}{2} f''(t) + \ldots \qquad (2.8)$$

where the symbol $(\ldots)$ means higher-order terms that are usually dropped from the derivation by the next line. An alternative, equivalent form of the Taylor series used in numerical analysis is

$$f(t + \tau) = f(t) + \tau f'(t) + \frac{\tau^2}{2} f''(\zeta) \qquad (2.9)$$

where ζ is a value between t and $t + \tau$. We have not dropped any terms; this expansion has a *finite* number of terms. Taylor's theorem guarantees that there exists *some* value ζ for which (2.9) is true, but it doesn't tell us what that value is.

The previous equation may be rewritten to give

$$f'(t) = \frac{f(t + \tau) - f(t)}{\tau} - \frac{1}{2} \tau f''(\zeta) \qquad (2.10)$$

where $t \le \zeta \le t + \tau$. This equation is known as the *right derivative* or *forward derivative* formula. The last term on the right-hand side is the *truncation error*; it is the error introduced by the truncation of the Taylor series.

In other words, if we keep the last term in (2.10), our expression for $f'(t)$ is exact. But we can't evaluate that term because we don't know ζ; all we know is that ζ lies somewhere between t and $t+\tau$. So we drop the $f''(\zeta)$ term (truncate) and say that the error we make by neglecting this term is the truncation error. Do not confuse this with the round-off error discussed in Section 1.5. Round-off error depends on hardware; truncation error depends on the approximations used in an algorithm.

Sometimes you will see Equation (2.10) written as

$$f'(t) = \frac{f(t+\tau) - f(t)}{\tau} + O(\tau) \tag{2.11}$$

where the truncation error term is now just specified by its order in τ; in this case the truncation error is linear in τ. In Figure 1.3 the predominant source of error in estimating $f'(x)$ as $[f(x+h) - f(x)]/h$ is round-off error when $h < 10^{-8}$ and truncation error when $h > 10^{-8}$. In the latter case, the absolute error is proportional to h, just as Equation (2.11) predicts.

Euler Method

The equations of motion that we want to solve numerically may be written as

$$\frac{d\mathbf{v}}{dt} = \mathbf{a}(\mathbf{r}, \mathbf{v}); \qquad \frac{d\mathbf{r}}{dt} = \mathbf{v} \tag{2.12}$$

where $\mathbf{a}$ is the acceleration. Notice that this is the more general form of the equations. In projectile motion the acceleration is only a function of $\mathbf{v}$ (because of drag); in later problems (e.g., orbits of comets) the acceleration will depend on position.

Using the forward derivative (2.11), our equations of motion are

$$\frac{\mathbf{v}(t+\tau) - \mathbf{v}(t)}{\tau} + O(\tau) = \mathbf{a}(\mathbf{r}(t), \mathbf{v}(t)) \tag{2.13}$$

$$\frac{\mathbf{r}(t+\tau) - \mathbf{r}(t)}{\tau} + O(\tau) = \mathbf{v}(t) \tag{2.14}$$

or

$$\mathbf{v}(t+\tau) = \mathbf{v}(t) + \tau\mathbf{a}(\mathbf{r}(t), \mathbf{v}(t)) + O(\tau^2) \tag{2.15}$$

$$\mathbf{r}(t+\tau) = \mathbf{r}(t) + \tau\mathbf{v}(t) + O(\tau^2) \tag{2.16}$$

Notice that $\tau O(\tau) = O(\tau^2)$. This numerical scheme is called the *Euler method*. Before discussing the relative merits of this approach, let's see how it would be used in practice.

First, we introduce the notation,

$$f_n = f(t_n); \quad t_n = (n-1)\tau; \quad n = 1, 2, \ldots \tag{2.17}$$

so $f_1 = f(t = 0)$. Our equations for the Euler method (dropping the error term) now take the form

$$\mathbf{v}_{n+1} = \mathbf{v}_n + \tau\mathbf{a}_n \tag{2.18}$$

$$\mathbf{r}_{n+1} = \mathbf{r}_n + \tau\mathbf{v}_n \tag{2.19}$$

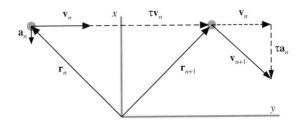

Figure 2.1: Trajectory of a particle after a single Euler time step. For illustrative purposes τ is large.

where $\mathbf{a}_n = \mathbf{a}(\mathbf{r}_n, \mathbf{v}_n)$. The calculation of the trajectory would proceed as follows:

1. Specify the initial conditions, $\mathbf{r}_1$ and $\mathbf{v}_1$.

2. Choose a time step τ.

3. Calculate the acceleration given the current $\mathbf{r}$ and $\mathbf{v}$.

4. Use equations (2.18) and (2.19) to compute the new $\mathbf{r}$ and $\mathbf{v}$.

5. Go to step 3 until enough trajectory points have been computed.

The method computes a set of values for $\mathbf{r}_n$ and $\mathbf{v}_n$ that gives us the trajectory, at least at a discrete set of points. Figure 2.1 illustrates the calculation of a trajectory for a single time step.

Euler-Cromer and Midpoint Methods

A simple (and for now unjustified) modification of the Euler method is to use the following equations:

$$\mathbf{v}_{n+1} = \mathbf{v}_n + \tau \mathbf{a}_n \qquad (2.20)$$

$$\mathbf{r}_{n+1} = \mathbf{r}_n + \tau \mathbf{v}_{n+1} \qquad (2.21)$$

Notice the subtle change: The updated velocity is used in the second equation. This formula is called the *Euler-Cromer method*.[36] The truncation error is still of order $O(\tau^2)$, so it doesn't look like we gain much. Interestingly, we will see that this form is markedly superior to the Euler method in some cases.

Our democratic nature makes us think of using the *midpoint method*,

$$\mathbf{v}_{n+1} = \mathbf{v}_n + \tau \mathbf{a}_n \qquad (2.22)$$

$$\mathbf{r}_{n+1} = \mathbf{r}_n + \tau \frac{\mathbf{v}_{n+1} + \mathbf{v}_n}{2} \qquad (2.23)$$

Notice that we average the two velocities. Plugging the velocity equation into the position equation, we see that

$$\mathbf{r}_{n+1} = \mathbf{r}_n + \tau \mathbf{v}_n + \frac{1}{2}\mathbf{a}_n \tau^2 \qquad (2.24)$$

which really makes this look appealing. The truncation error is still of order τ^2 in the velocity equation, but for position the truncation error is now τ^3. Indeed, for projectile motion this method works better than the other two. Unfortunately, we will later be disappointed to find that the midpoint method gives relatively poor results for other physical systems.

Local Error, Global Error, and Choosing a Time Step

To judge the accuracy of these methods we need to distinguish between local truncation error and global truncation error. So far, the truncation error we have discussed has been the local error, that is, the error made in a single time step. In a typical problem we want to evaluate a trajectory from $t = 0$ to $t = T$. The number of time steps is $N_\tau = T/\tau$; notice that if we reduce τ, we must take more steps. If the local error is $O(\tau^n)$, then we estimate the global error as

$$\text{global error} \quad \propto \quad N_\tau \times \text{(local error)}$$
$$= \quad N_\tau O(\tau^n) = (T/\tau)O(\tau^n) = TO(\tau^{n-1}) \qquad (2.25)$$

For example, the Euler method has a local truncation error of $O(\tau^2)$, but a global truncation error of $O(\tau)$. Of course, this analysis gives us only an estimate since we don't know if the local errors will accumulate or cancel (i.e., constructively or destructively interfere). The actual global error for a numerical scheme is highly dependent on the problem we are studying.

A question that is always raised is, "What do you pick for τ?", and the answer is often an inane comment such as, "A small number like 10^{-8}." Let's try to do better. First, let's assume that round-off error is negligible so we only have to worry about truncation error. From (2.10) and (2.16), the local truncation error in the Euler method's calculation of position is approximately $\tau^2 r'' = \tau^2 a$. Using only order of magnitude estimates, taking $a \approx 10 \text{ m/s}^2$, the single step error in position is 10^{-1} m, when $\tau = 10^{-1}$ s. If the time of flight is $T \approx 10^0$ s, then the global error is on the order of a meter. If an error of this magnitude is unacceptable then a smaller time step should be used. Finally, using a time step of 10^{-1} s should not introduce any significant round-off error given the magnitudes of the other parameters in the problem.

In the real world, we often don't do such a nice analysis for a variety of reasons (complicated equations, problems with round-off, laziness, etc.). However, we may often use physical intuition. Ask yourself, "On what time scale is the motion almost linear?" For example, for a baseball the entire trajectory is roughly parabolic, so if the time in the air is a few seconds, then the motion is approximately linear over a time scale of a few hundredths of a second. To check our intuition, we should compare the results obtained using $\tau = 10^{-1}$ s and $\tau = 10^{-2}$ s and, if they are sufficiently close, assume everything is fine. Sometimes we automate testing various values of τ; the program is then said to be "adaptive" (we will build such a program in Chapter 3). As with any numerical method, blind application of this technique is discouraged, although with just a bit of care it can be used successfully.

Table 2.1: Outline of program `balle`, which computes the trajectory of a baseball using the Euler method.

- Set initial position $\mathbf{r}_1$ and velocity $\mathbf{v}_1$ of the baseball.

- Set physical parameters (m, C_d, etc.).

- Loop until ball hits ground or maximum steps completed.

  - Record position (computed and theoretical) for plotting.
  - Compute acceleration of the baseball.
  - Calculate the new position and velocity, $\mathbf{r}_{n+1}$ and $\mathbf{v}_{n+1}$, using Euler method, (2.18) and (2.19).
  - If ball reaches ground ($y < 0$), break out of the loop.

- Print maximum range and time of flight.

- Graph the trajectory of the baseball.

See pages 58 and 61 for program listings.

Baseball Program

Table 2.1 outlines a simple program, called `balle`, that uses the Euler method to compute the trajectory of a baseball. Before running the program, let's establish some reasonable values to take as inputs. An initial speed $|\mathbf{v}_1| = 15$ m/s gives us a weakly hit ball (about 34 mph). Starting from the origin and neglecting air resistance, the time of flight is about 2.2 s, and the horizontal range is about 23 m when the initial angle is $\theta = 45°$. Here is what the output to the screen looks like when we run the MATLAB program under these conditions.

```
>>balle

  balle - Program to compute the trajectory of a baseball
          using the Euler method.

Enter initial height (meters): 0
Enter initial speed (m/s): 15
Enter initial angle (degrees): 45
Air resistance? (Yes:1, No:0): 0
Enter timestep, tau (sec): 0.1
Maximum range is 24.3952 meters
Time of flight is 2.3 seconds
```

The output from the C++ version is similar.

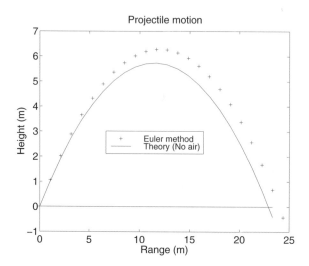

Figure 2.2: Output from `balle` for an initial height of 0 m, initial speed of 15 m/s, angle of $\theta = 45°$, and a time step of $\tau = 0.1$ s. There is no air resistance in this case; the difference between the theoretical curve and calculated points is due to the truncation error.

The trajectory computed by the program is shown in Figure 2.2. Using a time step of $\tau = 0.1$ s, the error in the horizontal range is about one meter, as expected from the truncation error. At this slow speed, the results are not much different when air resistance is included, since $|\mathbf{F}_a(\mathbf{v}_1)|/m \approx g/7$.

Next, let's try to hit a homerun. Consider a larger initial velocity, $|\mathbf{v}_1| = 50$ m/s (about 112 mph). Due to the air resistance, we find the range reduced to about 125 m, less than half of its theoretical maximum. The trajectory is shown in Figure 2.3; notice how it changes from a parabola to a sharply dropping curve. This trajectory shows why a ball driven deep into the outfield always appears to be caught as though it is falling almost straight down.

Our model equations for the flight of a baseball do not include all the factors in the problem. The drag coefficient is not really a constant but instead is a complicated function of velocity. Furthermore, the spin on the ball adds to the lift (Magnus effect). If you are interested in learning more, there are several good books on this fascinating subject.[4, 131]

EXERCISES

1. (a) Using Taylor expansion, derive the three-point forward difference formula

$$f'(t) = \frac{-3f(t) + 4f(t + \tau) - f(t + 2\tau)}{2\tau} + O(\tau^2)$$

and obtain an explicit expression for the error term. [Pencil]

2. Write a program that computes $f'(x)$ using the right derivative formula, Equation (2.11), and plots a graph of absolute error similar to Figure 1.3. Plot the error in the

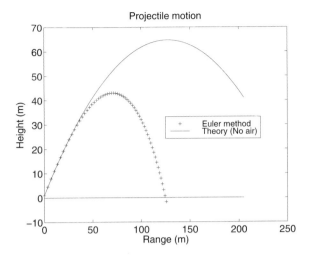

Figure 2.3: Output from `balle` for an initial height of 1 m, initial speed of 50 m/s, angle of $\theta = 45°$, and a time step of $\tau = 0.1$ s.

calculation of the derivatives of: (a) x^2 at $x = 1$; (b) x^5 at $x = 1$; (c) $\sin x$ at $x = 0$; (d) $\sin x$ at $x = \pi/4$; and (e) $\sin x$ at $x = \pi/2$. [Computer]

3. The `balle` program overestimates the range and time of flight (Figure 2.4). Fix this bit of sloppy programming: Compute a corrected maximum range and time of flight by interpolating between the last three values of **r** using the `intrpf` function from Section 1.4. Measure the improvement in the computed range and time of flight when there is no air resistance. Take an initial height of 0 m, initial speed of 50 m/s, angle of $\theta = 45°$, and try a variety of values for the time step τ. [Computer]

4. Take your program from the previous exercise and create two new versions that use the Euler-Cromer and midpoint methods. With no air resistance, find the largest value of τ that gives you a 1% error in the horizontal range (take $y_1 = 0$ m, $v_1 = 50$ m/s, and $\theta = 45°$). Comment on the performance of the three numerical methods. [Computer]

5. Suppose that a batter hits a ball and gives it an initial velocity of 50 m/s (take $y_1 = 1$ m). Modify `balle` so that it produces a plot of horizontal range as a function of angle for $10° < \theta < 50°$. Determine the angle (to within $1°$) at which the maximum range is achieved. [Computer]

6. In *Two New Sciences* [5, 52] Galileo claims that if a 100-lb iron ball and a 1-lb iron ball were dropped from a height of 100 braccia (about 50 m), then "when the larger one strikes the ground, the other is two inches behind it." (a) Modify `balle` to simultaneously compute the motion of two objects, and show that this statement is grossly inaccurate. Assume that $C_d = 0.5$ (smooth sphere); density of iron is 7.8 g/cm^3. [Computer] (b) Show that $y(t) = y(0) - b^{-1}\log(\cosh(\sqrt{bg}t))$ where $b = C_d\rho A/2m$. Use this result to check your answer in part (a). [Pencil] (c) What would C_d need to be for Galileo's statement to be accurate? [Computer]

7. Consider a pair of identical 1-lb iron balls dropped from a height of 50 m (see previous exercise). One ball has zero initial velocity, the other an initial velocity

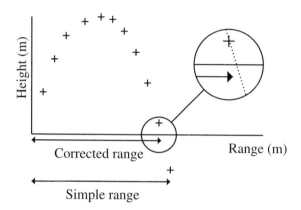

Figure 2.4: Improved calculation of horizontal range.

of 50 m/s in the horizontal direction. Modify `balle` to simultaneously compute the motion of two objects to determine the balls' separation, horizontal and vertical, when one strikes the ground. Which ball reaches the ground first? [Computer]

8. Suppose that an outfielder catches a fly ball 320 ft from home plate. The moment the ball is caught, a base runner on third base takes off for home plate to try to score on the sacrifice fly. The outfielder can throw the ball with a speed of 95 mph (initial height is 2 m).[†] At what angle should she throw? How much time does it take for the ball to arrive at the plate? A typical base runner will reach home in about 3.5 to 4.5 s. [Computer]

9. Modify `balle` to account for wind. Suppose that a batter hits a ball and gives it an initial velocity of 110 mph at an angle of $\theta = 35°$ from the horizontal (initial height is 1 m). Make a plot of horizontal range versus horizontal wind velocity for values between 40 mph and -40 mph. [Computer]

10. The drag coefficient for a baseball is really not a constant but rather varies with velocity.[51] Modify `balle` to use the values

v (mph)	0	25	50	75	100	125
C_d	0.5	0.5	0.5	0.4	0.28	0.23

using quadratic interpolation to estimate $C_d(v)$ (see Section 1.4). Plot horizontal range versus angle, as described in Exercise 2.5, and comment on the results. Does the range increase or decrease as compared to using a constant $C_d = 0.35$? [Computer]

2.2   SIMPLE PENDULUM

Basic Equations

The motion of pendula has fascinated physicists since Galileo was hypnotized by the lamp in the cathedral at Pisa. The problem is treated in the standard

---

[†]If this speed seems high, recall that an outfielder may throw on the run, unlike the restricted motion required of a pitcher.

mechanics texts, but before rushing to the computer let's review some basic results. For a simple pendulum it is more convenient to describe the position in terms of the angular displacement, $\theta(t)$. The equation of motion is

$$\frac{d^2\theta}{dt^2} = -\frac{g}{L}\sin\theta \tag{2.26}$$

where L is the length of the arm and g is the gravitational acceleration. In the small angle approximation, $\sin\theta \approx \theta$, Equation (2.26) simplifies to

$$\frac{d^2\theta}{dt^2} = -\frac{g}{L}\theta \tag{2.27}$$

This ordinary differential equation is easily solved to obtain

$$\theta(t) = C_1\cos(2\pi t/T_s + C_2) \tag{2.28}$$

where the constants C_1 and C_2 are determined by the initial values of θ and $\omega = d\theta/dt$. The small angle period, T_s, is

$$T_s = 2\pi\sqrt{\frac{L}{g}} \tag{2.29}$$

This approximation is reasonably good for oscillations with amplitudes of about $20°$ or less.

Without the small angle approximation, the equation of motion is more difficult to solve. However, we know from experience that the motion is still periodic. In fact, it is possible to obtain an expression for the period without explicitly solving for $\theta(t)$. The total energy is

$$E = \frac{1}{2}mL^2\omega^2 - mgL\cos\theta \tag{2.30}$$

where m is the mass of the bob. The total energy is conserved and equal to $E = -mgL\cos\theta_m$, where θ_m is the maximum angle. From the above, we have

$$\frac{1}{2}mL^2\omega^2 - mgL\cos\theta = -mgL\cos\theta_m \tag{2.31}$$

or

$$\omega^2 = \frac{2g}{L}(\cos\theta - \cos\theta_m) \tag{2.32}$$

Since $\omega = d\theta/dt$,

$$dt = \frac{d\theta}{\sqrt{\frac{2g}{L}(\cos\theta - \cos\theta_m)}} \tag{2.33}$$

In one period the pendulum swings from $\theta = \theta_m$ to $\theta = -\theta_m$ and back to $\theta = \theta_m$. Thus, in a half period the pendulum swings from $\theta = \theta_m$ to $\theta = -\theta_m$. Last, by the same argument, in a quarter period the pendulum swings from $\theta = \theta_m$ to $\theta = 0$, thus integrating both sides,

$$\frac{T}{4} = \sqrt{\frac{L}{2g}} \int_0^{\theta_m} \frac{d\theta}{\sqrt{\cos\theta - \cos\theta_m}} \tag{2.34}$$

This integral may be rewritten in terms of special functions by using the identity $\cos 2\theta = 1 - 2\sin^2\theta$, so

$$T = 2\sqrt{\frac{L}{g}} \int_0^{\theta_m} \frac{d\theta}{\sqrt{\sin^2(\theta_m/2) - \sin^2(\theta/2)}} \tag{2.35}$$

Introducing $K(x)$, the complete elliptic integral of the first kind, [62]

$$K(x) \equiv \int_0^{\pi/2} \frac{dz}{\sqrt{1 - x^2 \sin^2 z}} \tag{2.36}$$

we may write the period as

$$T = 4\sqrt{\frac{L}{g}} K\left(\sin\frac{1}{2}\theta_m\right) \tag{2.37}$$

using the change of variable $\sin z = \sin(\theta/2)/\sin(\theta_m/2)$. For small values of θ_m, we may expand $K(x)$ to obtain

$$T = 2\pi\sqrt{\frac{L}{g}}\left(1 + \frac{1}{16}\theta_m^2 + \cdots\right) \tag{2.38}$$

Notice that the leading term is the small angle approximation (2.29).

Centered Derivative Formulas

Before programming the pendulum problem, let's look at two other schemes for computing the motion of an object. The Euler method is based on the right derivative formulation for df/dt given by (2.7). An equivalent definition for the derivative is

$$f'(t) = \lim_{\tau \to 0} \frac{f(t+\tau) - f(t-\tau)}{2\tau} \tag{2.39}$$

This formula is said to be "centered" in t. While this formula looks very similar to (2.7), there is a big difference when τ is finite. Again, using the Taylor expansion,

$$f(t+\tau) = f(t) + \tau f'(t) + \frac{1}{2}\tau^2 f''(t) + \frac{1}{6}\tau^3 f^{(3)}(\zeta_+) \tag{2.40}$$

$$f(t-\tau) = f(t) - \tau f'(t) + \frac{1}{2}\tau^2 f''(t) - \frac{1}{6}\tau^3 f^{(3)}(\zeta_-) \tag{2.41}$$

where $f^{(3)}$ is the third derivative of $f(t)$ and $\zeta_{\pm}$ is a value between t and $t \pm \tau$. Subtracting Equation (2.41) from (2.40) and arranging terms gives,

$$f'(t) = \frac{f(t+\tau) - f(t-\tau)}{2\tau} - \frac{1}{6}\tau^2 f^{(3)}(\zeta) \qquad (2.42)$$

where $t - \tau \le \zeta \le t + \tau$. This is the *centered first derivative approximation*. The key point is that the truncation error is now quadratic in τ, which is a big improvement over the forward derivative approximation that has $O(\tau)$ truncation error.

Using the Taylor expansions for $f(t+\tau)$ and $f(t-\tau)$, we can also build a centered formula for the second derivative. It has the form

$$f''(t) = \frac{f(t+\tau) + f(t-\tau) - 2f(t)}{\tau^2} - \frac{1}{12}\tau^2 f^{(4)}(\zeta) \qquad (2.43)$$

where $t - \tau \le \zeta \le t + \tau$. Again, the truncation error is quadratic in τ. The best way to understand this formula is to think of the second derivative as being composed of a right derivative and left derivative, each with increment $\tau/2$.

You might think that the next step would be to cook up more involved formulas that have even smaller truncation error, maybe using both $f(t \pm \tau)$ and $f(t \pm 2\tau)$. While such formulas exist and are occasionally used, Equations (2.10), (2.42), and (2.43) serve as the workhorses for computing first and second derivatives.

Leap-Frog and Verlet Methods

For the pendulum, the generalized position and velocity are θ and ω, but to maintain the same notation as in Section 2.1, we'll work with $\mathbf{r}$ and $\mathbf{v}$. We start from the equations of motion written as

$$\frac{d\mathbf{v}}{dt} = \mathbf{a}(\mathbf{r}(t)) \qquad (2.44)$$

$$\frac{d\mathbf{r}}{dt} = \mathbf{v}(t) \qquad (2.45)$$

Note that we explicitly write the acceleration as depending only on position. Discretizing the time derivative using the centered derivative approximation gives,

$$\frac{\mathbf{v}(t+\tau) - \mathbf{v}(t-\tau)}{2\tau} + O(\tau^2) = \mathbf{a}(\mathbf{r}(t)) \qquad (2.46)$$

for the velocity equation. Notice that while the velocity values are evaluated at $t + \tau$ and $t - \tau$, the acceleration is evaluated at time t.

For reasons that will soon be apparent, the discretization of the position equation will be centered between $t + 2\tau$ and t,

$$\frac{\mathbf{r}(t+2\tau) - \mathbf{r}(t)}{2\tau} + O(\tau^2) = \mathbf{v}(t+\tau) \qquad (2.47)$$

Again we use the notation $f_n \equiv f(t = (n-1)\tau)$, in which (2.47) and (2.46) are written as,

$$\frac{\mathbf{v}_{n+1} - \mathbf{v}_{n-1}}{2\tau} + O(\tau^2) = \mathbf{a}(\mathbf{r}_n) \tag{2.48}$$

$$\frac{\mathbf{r}_{n+2} - \mathbf{r}_n}{2\tau} + O(\tau^2) = \mathbf{v}_{n+1} \tag{2.49}$$

Rearranging the terms to collect future values on the left-hand side,

$$\mathbf{v}_{n+1} = \mathbf{v}_{n-1} + 2\tau\mathbf{a}(\mathbf{r}_n) + O(\tau^3) \tag{2.50}$$

$$\mathbf{r}_{n+2} = \mathbf{r}_n + 2\tau\mathbf{v}_{n+1} + O(\tau^3) \tag{2.51}$$

which is the *leap-frog method*. Naturally, when the method is used in a program, the $O(\tau^3)$ terms must be left out and thus constitute the truncation error for the method.

The name "leap-frog" is used because the solution is advanced in steps of 2τ, with the position evaluated at odd values ($\mathbf{r}_1, \mathbf{r}_3, \mathbf{r}_5, \ldots$), while the velocity is computed at even values ($\mathbf{v}_2, \mathbf{v}_4, \mathbf{v}_6, \ldots$). This interlacing is necessary because the acceleration, which is a function of position, needs to be evaluated at a time that is centered between the new and old velocities. Sometimes the leap-frog scheme is formulated as

$$\mathbf{v}_{n+\frac{1}{2}} = \mathbf{v}_{n-\frac{1}{2}} + \tau\mathbf{a}(\mathbf{r}_n) \tag{2.52}$$

$$\mathbf{r}_{n+1} = \mathbf{r}_n + \tau\mathbf{v}_{n+\frac{1}{2}} \tag{2.53}$$

with $\mathbf{v}_{n\pm\frac{1}{2}} \equiv \mathbf{v}(t = (n-1\pm\frac{1}{2})\tau)$. In this form, the scheme is functionally equivalent to the Euler-Cromer method. Feynman uses the leap-frog scheme in his *Lectures on Physics* to calculate the oscillations of a spring and the orbit of a planet.[46]

For this chapter's last numerical scheme, let's take a different approach and start with,

$$\frac{d\mathbf{r}}{dt} = \mathbf{v}(t) \tag{2.54}$$

$$\frac{d^2\mathbf{r}}{dt^2} = \mathbf{a}(\mathbf{r}) \tag{2.55}$$

Using the central difference formulas for first and second derivatives, we have

$$\frac{\mathbf{r}_{n+1} - \mathbf{r}_{n-1}}{2\tau} + O(\tau^2) = \mathbf{v}_n \tag{2.56}$$

$$\frac{\mathbf{r}_{n+1} + \mathbf{r}_{n-1} - 2\mathbf{r}_n}{\tau^2} + O(\tau^2) = \mathbf{a}_n \tag{2.57}$$

where $\mathbf{a}_n \equiv \mathbf{a}(\mathbf{r}_n)$. Rearranging terms,

$$\mathbf{v}_n = \frac{\mathbf{r}_{n+1} - \mathbf{r}_{n-1}}{2\tau} + O(\tau^2) \tag{2.58}$$

$$\mathbf{r}_{n+1} = 2\mathbf{r}_n - \mathbf{r}_{n-1} + \tau^2\mathbf{a}_n + O(\tau^4) \tag{2.59}$$

These equations, known as the *Verlet method* [130], may look strange at first, but they are easy to use. Suppose that we know $\mathbf{r}_0$ and $\mathbf{r}_1$; using Equation (2.59), we get $\mathbf{r}_2$. Knowing $\mathbf{r}_1$ and $\mathbf{r}_2$, we may now compute $\mathbf{r}_3$, then using (2.58) obtain $\mathbf{v}_2$, and so forth.

The leap-frog and Verlet methods have the disadvantage that they are not "self-starting." Usually we have the initial conditions $\mathbf{r}_1 = \mathbf{r}(t = 0)$ and $\mathbf{v}_1 = \mathbf{v}(t = 0)$, but not $\mathbf{v}_0 = \mathbf{v}(t = -\tau)$ [needed by leap-frog in Equation (2.50)] or $\mathbf{r}_0 = \mathbf{r}(t = -\tau)$ [needed by Verlet in Equation (2.59)]. This is the price we pay for time-centered schemes.

To get these methods started, we have a variety of options. The Euler-Cromer method, using (2.53), takes $\mathbf{v}_{\frac{1}{2}} = \mathbf{v}_1$, which is simple but not very accurate. An alternative is to use another scheme to get things started, for example, in leap-frog one could take a backward Euler step, $\mathbf{v}_0 = \mathbf{v}_1 - \tau \mathbf{a}_1$. Some care should be taken in this first step to preserve a method's accuracy; using

$$\mathbf{r}_0 = \mathbf{r}_1 - \tau \mathbf{v}_1 + \frac{\tau^2}{2} \mathbf{a}(\mathbf{r}_1) \tag{2.60}$$

is a good way to start the Verlet method (see Exercise 2.22).

Besides its simplicity, the leap-frog method often has favorable properties (e.g., energy conservation) when solving certain problems. The Verlet method has several advantages. First, the position equation has a good truncation error. Second, if the force is only a function of position, and if we care only about the trajectory of the particle and not its velocity (as in many celestial mechanics problems), we can completely skip the velocity calculation. The method is popular for computing trajectories in systems with many particles, for example, the study of fluids at the microscopic level.

Simple Pendulum Program

The equations of motion for a simple pendulum are

$$\frac{d\omega}{dt} = \alpha(\theta); \qquad \frac{d\theta}{dt} = \omega \tag{2.61}$$

where the angular acceleration $\alpha(\theta) = -(g/L)\sin\theta$. The Euler method for solving these ordinary differential equations is to iterate the equations:

$$\theta_{n+1} = \theta_n + \tau \omega_n \tag{2.62}$$

$$\omega_{n+1} = \omega_n + \tau \alpha_n \tag{2.63}$$

If we are only interested in the angle and not the velocity, the Verlet method just uses the equation

$$\theta_{n+1} = 2\theta_n - \theta_{n-1} + \tau^2 \alpha_n \tag{2.64}$$

Instead of using SI units, we'll use the dimensionless units natural to the problem. There are only two parameters in the problem, g and L, and they always

Table 2.2: Outline of program `pendul`, which computes the time evolution of a simple pendulum using the Euler or Verlet method.

- Select the numerical method to use: Euler or Verlet.

- Set initial position θ_1 and velocity $\omega_1 = 0$ of the pendulum.

- Set the physical constants and other variables.

- Take one backward step to start Verlet; see Equation (2.60).

- Loop over desired number of steps with given time step and numerical method.

  - Record angle and time for plotting.
  - Compute new position and velocity using Euler or Verlet method.
  - Test if the pendulum has passed through $\theta = 0$; if yes, use time to estimate period.

- Estimate period of oscillation, including error bar.

- Graph the oscillations as θ versus t.

See pages 59 and 63 for program listings.

appear in the ratio g/L. Setting this ratio to unity, the small amplitude period is $T_s = 2\pi$. In other words, we need only one unit in the problem: a time scale. We set our unit of time such that the small amplitude period is 2π.

Table 2.2 outlines a program called `pendul`, which computes the motion of a simple pendulum using either the Euler or Verlet method. The program estimates the period by recording when the angle has changed sign; that is, it checks if θ_n and θ_{n+1} have opposite signs by testing if $\theta_n \theta_{n+1} < 0$. Each reversal after the first gives us an estimate for the period, $\tilde{T}_k = 2\tau(n_{k+1} - n_k)$, where n_k is the time step on which the kth reversal occurred. The estimated period from each reversal is recorded, and its average value is computed as

$$\langle \tilde{T} \rangle = \frac{1}{M} \sum_{k=1}^{M} \tilde{T}_k \tag{2.65}$$

where M is the number times $\tilde{T}$ is evaluated. The error bar for this measured period is estimated as $\sigma = s/\sqrt{M}$, where

$$s = \sqrt{\frac{1}{M-1} \sum_{k=1}^{M} (\tilde{T}_k - \langle \tilde{T} \rangle)^2} \tag{2.66}$$

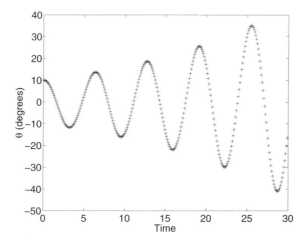

Figure 2.5: Output from `pendul` program using the Euler method. Initial angle is $\theta_m = 10°$, the time step $\tau = 0.1$, and 300 steps are computed.

is the sample standard deviation of $\tilde{T}$. Note that as the number of measurements increases, the sample standard deviation tends to a constant, while the estimated error bar decreases.

To check the `pendul` program, we first try a small value for the initial angle, θ_m, since we know the period $T \approx 2\pi$. Taking $\tau = 0.1$, we have about 60 data points per oscillation; taking 300 steps should give about five oscillations. For $\theta_m = 10°$, the Euler method computes an estimated period of $\langle \tilde{T} \rangle = 6.375 \pm 0.024$, about 1.5% larger than the expected $T = 2\pi(1.002)$ given by Equation (2.38). Our estimated error for the period is about $\pm\tau/2$ for each measurement. Five oscillations gives us nine measurements of $\tilde{T}$, so our estimated error for the period should be about $(\tau/2)/\sqrt{9} \approx 0.02$. Notice that this estimate is in good agreement with the result obtained using the sample standard deviation. So far everything looks reasonable.

Unfortunately, the graphic output (Figure 2.5) shows us that the Euler method has a problem. The amplitude of the oscillation is steadily growing in time. Since the energy is proportional to the maximum angle, this means that the total energy is also increasing in time. The global truncation error in the Euler method is, in this system, accumulating. By lowering the time step to $\tau = 0.05$ and increasing the number of steps to 600, we may improve the results, as shown in Figure 2.6, but not eliminate the accumulating error. The midpoint method, Equations (2.22) and (2.23), also suffers from this same numerical instability.

Using the Verlet method with $\theta_m = 10°$ and $\tau = 0.1$, we obtain the plot shown in Figure 2.7. These results are much better; the amplitude of the oscillation stays close to $10°$ and $\langle \tilde{T} \rangle = 6.289 \pm 0.033$. Fortunately, the Verlet, leap-frog, and Euler-Cromer methods do not suffer from the instability found using the Euler method.

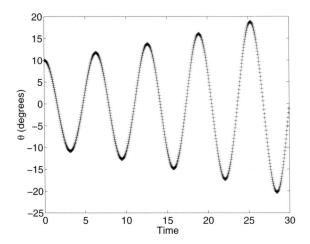

Figure 2.6: Output from `pendul` program using the Euler method. Initial angle is $\theta_m = 10°$, the time step $\tau = 0.05$, and 600 steps are computed. Compare with Figure 2.5; note difference in axes scales.

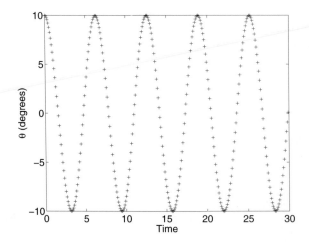

Figure 2.7: Output from `pendul` program using the Verlet method. Initial angle is $\theta_m = 10°$, the time step $\tau = 0.1$, and 300 steps are computed.

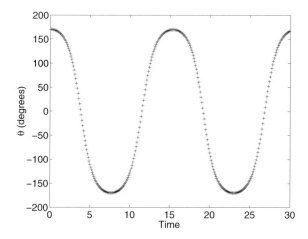

Figure 2.8: Output from **pendul** program using the Verlet method. Initial angle is $\theta_m = 170°$, the time step $\tau = 0.1$, and 300 steps are computed.

For $\theta_m = 90°$, the first correction to the small angle approximation, Equation (2.38), gives $T = 7.252$. Using the Verlet method, the program gives an estimated period of $\langle \tilde{T} \rangle = 7.429 \pm 0.027$, which indicates that (2.38) is a good approximation (about 2% error), even at this large angle. For the very large angle of $\theta_m = 170°$, we get the trajectory shown in Figure 2.8. Notice how the curve tends to flatten at the turning points. In this case the estimated period is $\langle \tilde{T} \rangle = 15.333 \pm 0.057$, while (2.38) gives $T = 9.740$, indicating that this approximation for (2.37) breaks down for this very large angle.

EXERCISES

11.   (a) Derive the centered second derivative formula (2.43). (b) Check that the centered formulas for $f'(x)$ and $f''(x)$, Equations (2.42) and (2.43), are exact for a quadratic (i.e., for $f(x) = ax^2 + bx + c$). Why is this true? [Pencil]

12.   Write a program that computes $f'(x)$ using the centered derivative formula (2.42) and plots a graph of absolute error similar to Figure 1.3. Plot the error in the calculation of the derivatives of: (a) x^2 at $x = 1$; (b) x^5 at $x = 1$; (c) $\sin x$ at $x = 0$; (d) $\sin x$ at $x = \pi/4$; and (e) $\sin x$ at $x = \pi/2$. [Computer]

13.   Write a program that computes $f''(x)$ using the centered second derivative formula (2.43) and produces a graph of absolute error similar to Figure 1.3. Plot the error in the calculation of the derivatives of: (a) x^2 at $x = 1$; (b) x^5 at $x = 1$; (c) $\sin x$ at $x = 0$; (d) $\sin x$ at $x = \pi/4$; and (e) $\sin x$ at $x = \pi/2$. [Computer]

14.   Using Taylor expansion, derive the centered difference formula for the third derivative

$$f^{(3)}(x) = \frac{f(x + 2h) - 2f(x + h) + 2f(x - h) - f(x - 2h)}{2h^3}$$

and obtain an explicit expression for the error term. [Pencil]

15. In the small angle approximation, the total energy of a simple pendulum is

$$E = \frac{1}{2}mL^2\omega^2 + \frac{1}{2}mgL\theta^2 - mgL$$

Show analytically that E monotonically increases with time when the Euler method is used to compute the motion. [Pencil]

16. Write a version of the **pendul** program that uses: (a) the Euler-Cromer method; (b) the leap-frog method; (c) the midpoint method. Run your program for the cases shown in Figures 2.5 to 2.8. Compare your results with those using Euler and Verlet. [Computer]

17. Obtain a plot of the period T as a function of the initial angle θ_m, using the Verlet method. Be sure to use a small enough value of τ to get at least 1% accuracy in T. On the same plot sketch the small angle approximation (2.29) and the approximation given by (2.38). Estimate the values of θ_m where the error in each approximation exceeds 10%. [Computer]

18. Modify the **pendul** program so that it plots $\omega(t)$ versus $\theta(t)$, that is, a phase space plot. Instead of running for a fixed number of steps, have your program halt the calculation when the pendulum completes one period. Using the Verlet method, plot the data for initial angles of $10°$, $45°$, $90°$, $120°$, and $170°$. Notice how the shape of the phase space orbit changes as a function of the initial angle. [Computer]

19. Consider a particle of mass m moving along the x-axis under the influence of the force

$$F = \begin{cases} F_0 & x < 0 \\ -F_0 & x > 0 \end{cases}$$

where F_0 is a constant. (a) Using the analysis presented in this section, show that the period is $T = 4\sqrt{2mx_m/F_0}$, where x_m is the maximum value for the particle's position. [Pencil] (b) Write a program to compute the trajectory of the particle and confirm the result from part (a). [Computer]

20. The **pendul** program computes the period in a rather crude fashion. Improve it by using interpolation to estimate when θ changes sign using its three most recent values. You may want to use the **intrpf** function from Section 1.4. Comment on the relative improvement in the error. [Computer]

21. Consider a pendulum with a harmonically driven pivot.[23, 83] The equation of motion is

$$\frac{d^2\theta}{dt^2} = -\frac{g + a_d(t)}{L}\sin\theta$$

where $a_d(t) = A_0\sin(2\pi t/T_d)$ is the time-varying acceleration of the pivot. Write a program that simulates this system; be sure to use a time step appropriate to the driving period, T_d. Show that when the amplitude of the driving acceleration is sufficiently high ($A_0 \gg g$), the pendulum is stable in the inverted position (i.e., if $\theta(t = 0) \approx 180°$, then the pendulum oscillates about the point $\theta = 180°$). [Computer]

22. The *velocity Verlet scheme* is defined as [9, 122]

$$\mathbf{r}_{n+1} = \mathbf{r}_n + \tau\mathbf{v}_n + \frac{1}{2}\tau^2\mathbf{a}_n$$

$$\mathbf{v}_{n+1} = \mathbf{v}_n + \frac{1}{2}\tau(\mathbf{a}_n + \mathbf{a}_{n+1})$$

Notice that this scheme is self-starting. Prove that the values of $\mathbf{r}_n$ computed by this scheme are the same as those obtained by the standard Verlet algorithm. [Pencil]

23. Show that for ordinary differential equations of the form $d^2x/dt^2 = f(t)x(t)$, where f is a known function, the Verlet algorithm may be improved as

$$x_{n+1} = \frac{2x_n - x_{n-1} + \tau^2 a_n + \frac{1}{12}\tau^2(a_{n-1} - 2a_n)}{1 - \frac{1}{12}\tau^2 f_{n+1}} + O(\tau^6)$$

where $a(t) \equiv f(t)x(t)$. This scheme is known as *Numerov's method*; notice its excellent local truncation error. Numerov's method is often used to solve the time-independent Schrödinger equation in one dimension. [Hint: Apply $\left(1 + \frac{\tau^2}{12}\frac{d^2}{dt^2}\right)$ to both sides of Equation (2.55).] [Pencil]

BEYOND THIS CHAPTER

This chapter introduced some basic techniques for solving ordinary differential equations and applied them in two fundamental physics problems, projectile motion and the simple pendulum. For many similar examples, see Giordano [55] and Gould and Tobochnik [61]. The next chapter covers some advanced techniques for solving ordinary differential equations. However, there are many instances for which we would want to stick with the basic methods. The most common scenario is the simulation of a large system of interacting particles (e.g., stars in a galaxy, electrons and ions in a plasma). In this case we are not interested in high-accuracy trajectories for individual particles. Instead, we want to measure the collective, statistical properties in the system, such as density and temperature. These statistical quantities are obtained from time averages, so computational efficiency is essential. The Verlet method is a popular algorithm for these types of simulations.[9, 67]

The basic formulas for estimating derivatives are presented in this chapter, and higher-order difference formulas are not difficult to construct using the Taylor expansion. One common use of specialized, high-accuracy formulas is for estimating derivatives at boundaries to compute the flux at the boundary. Partial derivatives (e.g., Laplacian operator) may be constructed by applying our standard formulas in each direction; specialized formulas also exist for partial derivatives. Tables of finite difference formulas are found in many references, for example Abramowitz and Stegun [2] and Anderson et al. [10].

The ordinary differential equations (ODEs) we consider are all initial value problems. That is, we have complete information as to the initial state of the system, and from it the future states are computed. An alternative type of ODE problem is a boundary value problem. Suppose that we are given incomplete state information for two points in time, say $t = 0$ and T. An example of such a problem would be if we knew the initial and final positions of a baseball (but not the velocities) and wished to compute the entire trajectory.

A common way of solving boundary value problems is to guess several initial conditions (e.g., initial velocities for the baseball). We then compute the solutions up to time T with the hope that some of the guesses will be close to the

specified boundary value at time T. We then refine our guesses and continue
until we find an acceptable result. This procedure is called a *shooting method*,
and of course there are systematic numerical methods for updating the guesses
(e.g., Newton's method). For more insight on how such iterative methods work,
see Section 4.3. An alternative way to solve boundary value problems is by
relaxation. This technique is described for linear partial differential equations
in Section 8.1. For a complete discussion of numerical techniques for solving
boundary value problems, see Ascher, et al..[12].

APPENDIX A: MATLAB LISTINGS

Listing 2A.1 Program `balle`. Computes the trajectory of a baseball, including air resistance, using the Euler method.

```
% balle - Program to compute the trajectory of a baseball
%          using the Euler method.
clear;  help balle;  % Clear memory and print header

%* Set initial position and velocity of the baseball
y1 = input('Enter initial height (meters): ');
r1 = [0, y1];     % Initial vector position
speed = input('Enter initial speed (m/s): ');
theta = input('Enter initial angle (degrees): ');
v1 = [speed*cos(theta*pi/180), ...
      speed*sin(theta*pi/180)];     % Initial velocity
r = r1;  v = v1;  % Set initial position and velocity

%* Set physical parameters (mass, Cd, etc.)
Cd = 0.35;       % Drag coefficient (dimensionless)
area = 4.3e-3;  % Cross-sectional area of projectile (m^2)
grav = 9.81;    % Gravitational acceleration (m/s^2)
mass = 0.145;   % Mass of projectile (kg)
airFlag = input('Air resistance? (Yes:1, No:0): ');
if( airFlag == 0 )
  rho = 0;       % No air resistance
else
  rho = 1.2;    % Density of air (kg/m^3)
end
air_const = -0.5*Cd*rho*area/mass;  % Air resistance constant

%* Loop until ball hits ground or max steps completed
tau = input('Enter timestep, tau (sec): ');  % (sec)
maxstep = 1000;   % Maximum number of steps
for istep=1:maxstep
```

```
%* Record position (computed and theoretical) for plotting
xplot(istep) = r(1);    % Record trajectory for plot
yplot(istep) = r(2);
t = (istep-1)*tau;      % Current time
xNoAir(istep) = r1(1) + v1(1)*t;
yNoAir(istep) = r1(2) + v1(2)*t - 0.5*grav*t^2;

%* Calculate the acceleration of the ball
accel = air_const*norm(v)*v;   % Air resistance
accel(2) = accel(2)-grav;      % Gravity

%* Calculate the new position and velocity using Euler method
r = r + tau*v;                 % Euler step
v = v + tau*accel;

%* If ball reaches ground (y<0), break out of the loop
if( r(2) < 0 )
  xplot(istep+1) = r(1);  % Record last values computed
  yplot(istep+1) = r(2);
  break;                  % Break out of the for loop
end
end

%* Print maximum range and time of flight
fprintf('Maximum range is %g meters\n',r(1));
fprintf('Time of flight is %g seconds\n',istep*tau);

%* Graph the trajectory of the baseball
clf;  figure(gcf);   % Clear figure window and bring it forward
% Mark the location of the ground by a straight line
xground = [0 max(xNoAir)];  yground = [0 0];
% Plot the computed trajectory and parabolic, no-air curve
plot(xplot,yplot,'+',xNoAir,yNoAir,'-',xground,yground,'-');
legend('Euler method','Theory (No air)');
xlabel('Range (m)');  ylabel('Height (m)');
title('Projectile motion');
```

Listing 2A.2 Program pendul. Computes the time evolution of a simple pendulum using the Euler or Verlet methods.

```
% pendul - Program to compute the motion of a simple pendulum
% using the Euler or Verlet method
clear all;  help pendul     % Clear the memory and print header
```

```
%* Select the numerical method to use: Euler or Verlet
NumericalMethod = menu('Choose a numerical method:', ...
                       'Euler','Verlet');

%* Set initial position and velocity of pendulum
theta0 = input('Enter initial angle (in degrees): ');
theta = theta0*pi/180;   % Convert angle to radians
omega = 0;               % Set the initial velocity

%* Set the physical constants and other variables
g_over_L = 1;            % The constant g/L
time = 0;                % Initial time
irev = 0;                % Used to count number of reversals
tau = input('Enter time step: ');

%* Take one backward step to start Verlet
accel = -g_over_L*sin(theta);    % Gravitational acceleration
theta_old = theta - omega*tau + 0.5*tau^2*accel;

%* Loop over desired number of steps with given time step
%     and numerical method
nstep = input('Enter number of time steps: ');
for istep=1:nstep

  %* Record angle and time for plotting
  t_plot(istep) = time;
  th_plot(istep) = theta*180/pi;   % Convert angle to degrees
  time = time + tau;

  %* Compute new position and velocity using
  %     Euler or Verlet method
  accel = -g_over_L*sin(theta);    % Gravitational acceleration
  if( NumericalMethod == 1 )
    theta_old = theta;                 % Save previous angle
    theta = theta + tau*omega;         % Euler method
    omega = omega + tau*accel;
  else
    theta_new = 2*theta - theta_old + tau^2*accel;
    theta_old = theta;                 % Verlet method
    theta = theta_new;
  end

  %* Test if the pendulum has passed through theta = 0;
  %     if yes, use time to estimate period
  if( theta*theta_old < 0 )  % Test position for sign change
    fprintf('Turning point at time t= %f \n',time);
```

```
    if( irev == 0 )            % If this is the first change,
      time_old = time;         % just record the time
    else
      period(irev) = 2*(time - time_old);
      time_old = time;
    end
    irev = irev + 1;           % Increment the number of reversals
  end
end

%* Estimate period of oscillation, including error bar
AvePeriod = mean(period);
ErrorBar = std(period)/sqrt(irev);
fprintf('Average period = %g +/- %g\n', AvePeriod,ErrorBar);

%* Graph the oscillations as theta versus time
clf;  figure(gcf);            % Clear and forward figure window
plot(t_plot,th_plot,'+');
xlabel('Time');  ylabel('\theta (degrees)');
```

APPENDIX B: C++ LISTINGS

Listing 2B.1 Program `balle`. Computes the trajectory of a baseball, including air resistance, using the Euler method.

```
// balle - Program to compute the trajectory of a baseball
//         using the Euler method.
#include "NumMeth.h"

void main() {

  //* Set initial position and velocity of the baseball
  double y1, speed, theta;
  double r1[2+1], v1[2+1], r[2+1], v[2+1], accel[2+1];
  cout << "Enter initial height (meters): "; cin >> y1;
  r1[1] = 0;  r1[2] = y1;     // Initial vector position
  cout << "Enter initial speed (m/s): "; cin >> speed;
  cout << "Enter initial angle (degrees): "; cin >> theta;
  const double pi = 3.141592654;
  v1[1] = speed*cos(theta*pi/180);   // Initial velocity (x)
  v1[2] = speed*sin(theta*pi/180);   // Initial velocity (y)
  r[1] = r1[1];  r[2] = r1[2];  // Set initial position and velocity
  v[1] = v1[1];  v[2] = v1[2];
```

```
//* Set physical parameters (mass, Cd, etc.)
double Cd = 0.35;       // Drag coefficient (dimensionless)
double area = 4.3e-3;   // Cross-sectional area of projectile (m^2)
double grav = 9.81;     // Gravitational acceleration (m/s^2)
double mass = 0.145;    // Mass of projectile (kg)
double airFlag, rho;
cout << "Air resistance? (Yes:1, No:0): "; cin >> airFlag;
if( airFlag == 0 )
  rho = 0;      // No air resistance
else
  rho = 1.2;    // Density of air (kg/m^3)
double air_const = -0.5*Cd*rho*area/mass;  // Air resistance constant

//* Loop until ball hits ground or max steps completed
double tau;
cout << "Enter timestep, tau (sec): "; cin >> tau;
int iStep, maxStep = 1000;   // Maximum number of steps
double *xplot, *yplot, *xNoAir, *yNoAir;
xplot = new double [maxStep+1];  yplot = new double [maxStep+1];
xNoAir = new double [maxStep+1]; yNoAir = new double [maxStep+1];
for( iStep=1; iStep<=maxStep; iStep++ ) {

  //* Record position (computed and theoretical) for plotting
  xplot[iStep] = r[1];   // Record trajectory for plot
  yplot[iStep] = r[2];
  double t = (iStep-1)*tau;     // Current time
  xNoAir[iStep] = r1[1] + v1[1]*t;
  yNoAir[iStep] = r1[2] + v1[2]*t - 0.5*grav*t*t;

  //* Calculate the acceleration of the ball
  double normV = sqrt( v[1]*v[1] + v[2]*v[2] );
  accel[1] = air_const*normV*v[1];   // Air resistance
  accel[2] = air_const*normV*v[2];   // Air resistance
  accel[2] -= grav;                  // Gravity

  //* Calculate the new position and velocity using Euler method
  r[1] += tau*v[1];                  // Euler step
  r[2] += tau*v[2];
  v[1] += tau*accel[1];
  v[2] += tau*accel[2];

  //* If ball reaches ground (y<0), break out of the loop
  if( r[2] < 0 )  {
    xplot[iStep+1] = r[1];  // Record last values computed
    yplot[iStep+1] = r[2];
```

```
      break;                          // Break out of the for loop
    }
  }


  //* Print maximum range and time of flight
  cout << "Maximum range is " << r[1] << " meters" << endl;
  cout << "Time of flight is " << iStep*tau << " seconds" << endl;

  //* Print out the plotting variables:
  //    xplot, yplot, xNoAir, yNoAir
  ofstream xplotOut("xplot.txt"), yplotOut("yplot.txt"),
           xNoAirOut("xNoAir.txt"), yNoAirOut("yNoAir.txt");
  int i;
  for( i=1; i<=iStep+1; i++ ) {
    xplotOut << xplot[i] << endl;
    yplotOut << yplot[i] << endl;
  }
  for( i=1; i<=iStep; i++ ) {
    xNoAirOut << xNoAir[i] << endl;
    yNoAirOut << yNoAir[i] << endl;
  }

  delete []  xplot, yplot, xNoAir, yNoAir; // Release memory

}
/***** To plot in MATLAB; use the script below *******************
load xplot.txt; load yplot.txt; load xNoAir.txt; load yNoAir.txt;
clf;  figure(gcf);   % Clear figure window and bring it forward
% Mark the location of the ground by a straight line
xground = [0 max(xNoAir)];  yground = [0 0];
% Plot the computed trajectory and parabolic, no-air curve
plot(xplot,yplot,'+',xNoAir,yNoAir,'-',xground,yground,'-');
legend('Euler method','Theory (No air)');
xlabel('Range (m)');   ylabel('Height (m)');
title('Projectile motion');
****************************************************************/
```

Listing 2B.2 Program pendul. Computes the time evolution of a simple pendulum using the Euler or Verlet methods.

```
// pendul - Program to compute the motion of a simple pendulum
// using the Euler or Verlet method
#include "NumMeth.h"

void main() {
```

```
//* Select the numerical method to use: Euler or Verlet
cout << "Choose a numerical method 1) Euler, 2) Verlet: ";
int method; cin >> method;

//* Set initial position and velocity of pendulum
cout << "Enter initial angle (in degrees): ";
double theta0; cin >> theta0;
const double pi = 3.141592654;
double theta = theta0*pi/180;   // Convert angle to radians
double omega = 0.0;             // Set the initial velocity

//* Set the physical constants and other variables
double g_over_L = 1.0;          // The constant g/L
double time = 0.0;              // Initial time
double time_old;                // Time of previous reversal
int irev = 0;                   // Used to count number of reversals
cout << "Enter time step: ";
double tau; cin >> tau;

//* Take one backward step to start Verlet
double accel = -g_over_L*sin(theta);   // Gravitational acceleration
double theta_old = theta - omega*tau + 0.5*tau*tau*accel;

//* Loop over desired number of steps with given time step
//     and numerical method
cout << "Enter number of time steps: ";
int nStep;  cin >> nStep;
double *t_plot, *th_plot, *period;   // Plotting variables
t_plot = new double [nStep+1]; th_plot = new double [nStep+1];
period = new double [nStep+1];
int iStep;
for( iStep=1; iStep<=nStep; iStep++ ) {

  //* Record angle and time for plotting
  t_plot[iStep] = time;
  th_plot[iStep] = theta*180/pi;   // Convert angle to degrees
  time += tau;

  //* Compute new position and velocity using
  //     Euler or Verlet method
  accel = -g_over_L*sin(theta);    // Gravitational acceleration
  if( method == 1 ) {
    theta_old = theta;             // Save previous angle
    theta += tau*omega;            // Euler method
    omega += tau*accel;
```

```
    }
    else {
      double theta_new = 2*theta - theta_old + tau*tau*accel;
      theta_old = theta;          // Verlet method
      theta = theta_new;
    }

    //* Test if the pendulum has passed through theta = 0;
    //   if yes, use time to estimate period
    if( theta*theta_old < 0 ) { // Test position for sign change
      cout << "Turning point at time t = " << time << endl;
      if( irev == 0 )           // If this is the first change,
        time_old = time;        // just record the time
      else {
        period[irev] = 2*(time - time_old);
        time_old = time;
      }
      irev++;          // Increment the number of reversals
    }
  }
  int nPeriod = irev-1;    // Number of times period is measured

  //* Estimate period of oscillation, including error bar
  double AvePeriod = 0.0, ErrorBar = 0.0;
  int i;
  for( i=1; i<=nPeriod; i++ ) {
    AvePeriod += period[i];
    ErrorBar += period[i]*period[i];
  }
  AvePeriod /= nPeriod;
  ErrorBar = sqrt(ErrorBar/(nPeriod*(nPeriod-1)));
  cout << "Average period = " << AvePeriod << " +/- " << ErrorBar << endl;

  //* Print out the plotting variables: t_plot, th_plot
  ofstream t_plotOut("t_plot.txt"), th_plotOut("th_plot.txt");
  for( i=1; i<=nStep; i++ ) {
    t_plotOut << t_plot[i] << endl;
    th_plotOut << th_plot[i] << endl;
  }

  delete [] t_plot, th_plot, period;

}
/***** To plot in MATLAB; use the script below ********************
load t_plot.txt; load th_plot.txt;
clf;  figure(gcf);          % Clear and forward figure window
```

```
plot(t_plot,th_plot,'+');
xlabel('Time');  ylabel('Theta (degrees)');
********************************************************/
```

Chapter 3

Ordinary Differential Equations II: Advanced Methods

In Chapter 2 we learned how to solve ordinary differential equations (ODEs) using some simple methods. In this chapter we do some basic celestial mechanics beginning with the Kepler problem. Computing the orbit of a small satellite about a large body (e.g., a comet orbiting the Sun), we discover that more sophisticated methods are needed to handle even this simple two-body system. The second problem we consider in this chapter is the Lorenz model. This nonlinear system of ODEs was one of the first in which chaotic dynamics was found.

3.1 ORBITS OF COMETS

Basic Equations

Consider the Kepler problem in which a small satellite, such as a comet, orbits the Sun. We use a Copernican coordinate system and fix the Sun at the origin. For now, consider only the gravitational force between the comet and the Sun, and neglect all other forces (e.g., forces due to the planets, solar wind). The force on the comet is

$$\mathbf{F} = -\frac{GmM}{|\mathbf{r}|^3}\mathbf{r} \tag{3.1}$$

where $\mathbf{r}$ is the position of the comet, m is its mass, M $(= 1.99 \times 10^{30}$ kg) is the mass of the Sun, and G $(= 6.67 \times 10^{-11}\,\mathrm{m^3/kg \cdot s^2})$ is the gravitational constant.

The natural units of length and time for this problem are not meters and seconds. As a unit of distance we will use the astronomical unit (AU; 1 AU = 1.496×10^{11} m), which equals the mean Earth-Sun distance. The unit of time will be the AU year (the period of a circular orbit of radius 1 AU). In these units, the product $GM = 4\pi^2 \text{AU}^3/\text{yr}^2$. We take the mass of the comet, m, as unity; in MKS units the typical mass of a comet is $10^{15\pm3}$ kg.

We now have enough to assemble our program, but before doing so let's quickly review what we know about orbits. For a complete treatment, see any of the standard mechanics texts, such as Symon [123] or Landau and Lifshitz [83]. The total energy of the satellite is

$$E = \frac{1}{2}mv^2 - \frac{GMm}{r} \tag{3.2}$$

where $r = |\mathbf{r}|$ and $v = |\mathbf{v}|$. This total energy is conserved, as is the angular momentum,

$$\mathbf{L} = \mathbf{r} \times (m\mathbf{v}) \tag{3.3}$$

Since this problem is two-dimensional, we will take the motion to be in the xy plane. The only nonzero component of the angular momentum is in the z-direction.

When the orbit is circular, the centripetal force is supplied by the gravitational force,

$$\frac{mv^2}{r} = \frac{GMm}{r^2} \tag{3.4}$$

or

$$v = \sqrt{GM/r} \tag{3.5}$$

To put in some values, in a circular orbit at $r = 1$ AU the orbital speed is $v = 2\pi$ AU/yr (about 30,000 km/h). Using (3.5) in (3.2), the total energy in a circular orbit is

$$E = -\frac{GMm}{2r} \tag{3.6}$$

In an elliptical orbit, the semimajor and semiminor axes, a and b, are unequal (Figure 3.1). The eccentricity, e, is defined as

$$e = \sqrt{1 - b^2/a^2} \tag{3.7}$$

Earth's eccentricity is $e = 0.017$, thus its orbit is nearly circular. The distance from the Sun at perihelion (closest approach) is $q = (1 - e)a$; the distance from the Sun at aphelion is $Q = (1 + e)a$.

Equation (3.6) also holds for elliptical orbits if we replace the radius with the semimajor axis; that is, the total energy is

$$E = -\frac{GMm}{2a} \tag{3.8}$$

Note that $E \leq 0$. From (3.2) and (3.8), we find that the orbital speed as a function of radial distance is

$$v = \sqrt{GM\left(\frac{2}{r} - \frac{1}{a}\right)} \tag{3.9}$$

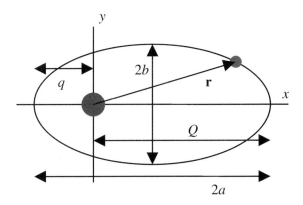

Figure 3.1: Elliptical orbit about the Sun.

Table 3.1: Orbital data for selected comets

Comet Name	T (yrs)	e	q (AU)	i	First Pass
Encke	3.30	0.847	0.339	12.4°	1786
Biela	6.62	0.756	0.861	12.6°	1772
Schwassmann-Wachmann 1	16.10	0.132	5.540	9.5°	1925
Halley	76.03	0.967	0.587	162.2°	239 B.C.
Grigg-Mellish	164.3	0.969	0.923	109.8°	1742
Hale-Bopp	2508.	0.995	0.913	89.4°	1995

The speed is maximum at perihelion and minimum at aphelion, the ratio of these speeds being Q/q. Finally, using conservation of angular momentum, we may derive Kepler's third law,

$$T^2 = \frac{4\pi^2}{GM}a^3 \qquad (3.10)$$

where T is the period of the orbit.

The orbital data for a few well-known comets are given in Table 3.1. The inclination, i, is the angle between the orbital plane of the comet and the ecliptic plane (the plane of the orbit of the planets). When the inclination is less than 90°, the orbit is said to be direct, when it is greater than 90°, the orbit is retrograde (i.e., orbits the Sun in the opposite direction from the planets).

Orbit Program

A simple program, called `orbit`, that computes orbits for the Kepler problem using various numerical methods is outlined in Table 3.2. The Euler method, described in Section 2.1, computes the comet's trajectory as

$$\mathbf{r}_{n+1} = \mathbf{r}_n + \tau\mathbf{v}_n \qquad (3.11)$$

$$\mathbf{v}_{n+1} = \mathbf{v}_n + \tau\mathbf{a}(\mathbf{r}_n) \qquad (3.12)$$

Table 3.2: Outline of program `orbit`, which computes the trajectory of a comet using various numerical methods.

- Set initial position and velocity of the comet.

- Set physical parameters (m, GM, etc.)

- Loop over desired number of steps using specified numerical method.

    - Record position and energy for plotting.
    - Calculate new position and velocity using:
        * Euler method (3.11), (3.12) **or**;
        * Euler-Cromer method (3.13), (3.14) **or**;
        * Fourth-order Runge-Kutta method (3.28), (3.29) **or**;
        * Adaptive Runge-Kutta method.

- Graph the trajectory of the comet.

- Graph the energy of the comet versus time.

See pages 91 and 96 for program listings.

where $\mathbf{a}$ is the gravitational acceleration. Again, we discretize in time and use the notation $f_n \equiv f(t = (n-1)\tau)$, where τ is the time step.

The simplest test case is a circular orbit. For an orbital radius of 1 AU, Equation (3.5) gives a tangential velocity of 2π AU/yr. Fifty data points per orbital revolution should give us a smooth curve, so $\tau = 0.02$ yr (or about one week) is a reasonable time step. With these values, the `orbit` program, using the Euler method, gives the results shown in Figure 3.2. We immediately see that the orbit is not a circle, but an outward spiral. The reason is clear from the energy graph; instead of being constant, the total energy is continuously increasing. This type of instability is also observed in the Euler method for the simple pendulum (see Section 2.2).

Fortunately, there is a simple solution to this problem—the Euler-Cromer method computes the trajectory as

$$\mathbf{v}_{n+1} = \mathbf{v}_n + \tau\mathbf{a}(\mathbf{r}_n) \tag{3.13}$$

$$\mathbf{r}_{n+1} = \mathbf{r}_n + \tau\mathbf{v}_{n+1} \tag{3.14}$$

Notice that the only change from the Euler method is that we first compute the new velocity, $\mathbf{v}_{n+1}$, and then use it in the calculation of the new position. For the same initial conditions and time step, the Euler-Cromer method gives much better results, as shown in Figure 3.3. The orbit is nearly circular, and the total energy is conserved. The kinetic and potential energies are not constant,

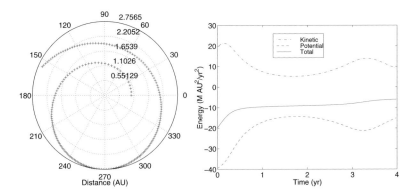

Figure 3.2: Graphs of trajectory and energy from the `orbit` program using the Euler method. Initial radial distance is 1 AU and the initial tangential velocity is 2π AU/yr. The time step is $\tau = 0.02$ yr; 200 time steps are computed. Results disagree with theoretical prediction of a circular orbit with constant total energy.

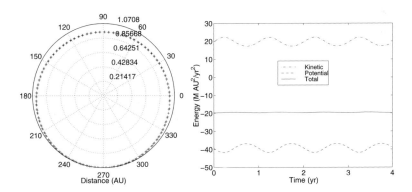

Figure 3.3: Graphs of trajectory and energy from the `orbit` program using the Euler-Cromer method. Parameters are given in Figure 3.2. The results are in qualitative agreement with theoretical prediction of a circular orbit with constant total energy.

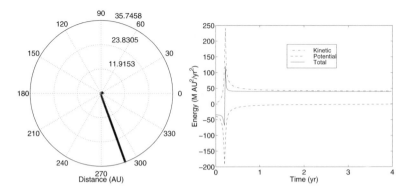

Figure 3.4: Graphs of trajectory and energy from the `orbit` program using the Euler-Cromer method. Initial radial distance is 1 AU and the initial tangential velocity is π AU/yr. The time step is $\tau = 0.02$ yr; 200 time steps are computed. Due to numerical error, the comet achieves escape velocity—final position is about 35 AU and the total energy is positive.

but this problem may be improved by using a smaller time step. The `orbit` program also gives you the option of using Runge-Kutta methods, which are described in the next two sections.

Although the Euler-Cromer method does a good job for low eccentricity orbits, it has problems with more elliptical orbits, as shown in Figure 3.4. Notice that the energy becomes positive; the satellite acquires escape velocity. If we lower the time step from $\tau = 0.02$ yr to 0.005 yr we obtain better results, as shown in Figure 3.5. These results are still not perfect; the orbit should be a closed ellipse, yet it has a noticeable spurious drift.

At this point you may be asking yourself, "Why are we studying this problem? The analytic solution is well known." It is true that there are more interesting celestial mechanics problems (e.g., the effect of perturbations on the orbit, the three-body problem). However, before doing the complicated cases we should always check our algorithms on known problems. Suppose that we introduced a small drag force on the comet. We might be fooled into believing that the precession in Figure 3.5 was a physical phenomenon rather than a numerical artifact.

Clearly, the Euler-Cromer method does an unacceptable job of tracking the more elliptical orbits. The results improve if we drop the time step, but then it takes forever to track a few orbits. Suppose that we wanted to track comets for possible Earth impacts. A comet striking Earth could be more destructive than nuclear war. Many comets have extremely elliptical orbits and periods of hundreds of years. This threat from outer space motivates our study of more advanced methods for solving ordinary differential equations.

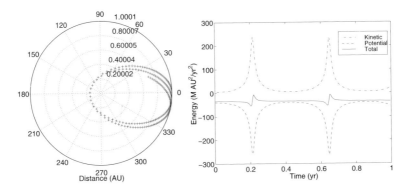

Figure 3.5: Graphs of trajectory and energy from the `orbit` program using the Euler-Cromer method. Parameters are as in Figure 3.4 except the time step is smaller ($\tau = 0.005$ yr). Results are better, yet the orbit has a spurious precession.

EXERCISES

1. Suppose that a planet suddenly lost all of its orbital velocity; of course, it would plunge directly into the Sun. Show that Earth would reach the core of the Sun in about 65 days. [Pencil]

2. Prove that for the Kepler problem the Euler-Cromer method conserves angular momentum exactly. [Pencil]

3. Modify the `orbit` program so that instead of running for a fixed number of time steps, the program stops when the satellite completes one orbit. (a) Have the program compute the period, eccentricity, semimajor axis, and perihelion distance of the orbit. Use the Euler-Cromer method and test the program with circular and slightly elliptical orbits. Compare the measured eccentricity with

$$\epsilon = \sqrt{1 + \frac{2EL^2}{G^2 M^2 m^3}}$$

(b) Show that your program confirms Kepler's third law. (c) Confirm that $\langle K \rangle = -\langle V \rangle /2$, where $\langle K \rangle$ and $\langle V \rangle$ are the time-average kinetic and potential energy (virial theorem). [Computer]

4. For an ellipse, the radial position varies with angle as

$$r(\theta) = \frac{a(1 - \epsilon^2)}{1 - \epsilon \cos \theta}$$

Modify the `orbit` program to compute and plot the absolute fractional error in $r(\theta)$ versus time. Using the Euler-Cromer method, obtain results for an initial radial distance of 1 AU, an initial tangential velocity of π AU/yr, and time steps of $\tau = 0.01$, 0.005, and 0.001 yr. [Computer]

5. Modify the `orbit` program to use the Verlet method. Run the modified program and produce graphs corresponding to Figures 3.2–3.5. [Computer]

6. The Euler-Cromer method must use a small time step for the more elliptic orbits. Using an initial radial distance of 35 AU (Halley's comet) and various values for the

aphelion velocity, find the largest value of τ for which the total energy is conserved to about 1% per orbit. Assemble a graph of τ versus initial velocity, and estimate the time step needed to track Halley's comet. [Computer]

7. The Lorentz force on a charged particle is $\mathbf{F} = q(\mathbf{E} + \mathbf{v} \times \mathbf{B})$ where $\mathbf{E}$ and $\mathbf{B}$ are the electric and magnetic fields acting on the particle and q is the particle's charge. Write a program to simulate the motion of an electron in uniform, perpendicular electric and magnetic fields. Show that the motion is helical in form, with a pitch that depends on the initial particle velocity and with a drift velocity $\mathbf{u}_{\mathrm{drift}} = \mathbf{E} \times \mathbf{B}/B^2$. [Computer]

3.2   RUNGE-KUTTA METHODS

Second Order Runge-Kutta

We now look at one of the most popular methods for numerically solving ODEs: Runge-Kutta. We will first work out the general Runge-Kutta formulas and then apply them specifically to our comet problem. In this way it will be easy to use the Runge-Kutta method for other physical systems. Our general ODE takes the form

$$\frac{d\mathbf{x}}{dt} = \mathbf{f}(\mathbf{x}(t), t) \tag{3.15}$$

where the state vector $x(t) = [x_1(t) \ldots x_N(t)]$ is the desired solution. In the Kepler problem we have

$$\mathbf{x}(t) = [r_x(t) \quad r_y(t) \quad v_x(t) \quad v_y(t)] \tag{3.16}$$

and

$$\begin{aligned} \mathbf{f}(\mathbf{x}(t), t) &= \left[\frac{dr_x}{dt} \quad \frac{dr_y}{dt} \quad \frac{dv_x}{dt} \quad \frac{dv_y}{dt} \right] \\ &= [v_x(t) \quad v_y(t) \quad F_x(t)/m \quad F_y(t)/m] \end{aligned} \tag{3.17}$$

where r_x, v_x and F_x are the x-components of position, velocity, and force, respectively (and similarly for the y-components). Notice that in the Kepler problem, the function $\mathbf{f}$ does not depend explicitly on time; rather, it only depends on $\mathbf{x}(t)$.

Our starting point is the simple Euler method; in vector form it may be written as

$$\mathbf{x}(t + \tau) = \mathbf{x}(t) + \tau \mathbf{f}(\mathbf{x}, t) \tag{3.18}$$

The first Runge-Kutta formula we consider is

$$\mathbf{x}(t + \tau) = \mathbf{x}(t) + \tau \mathbf{f}(\mathbf{x}^*(t + \tfrac{1}{2}\tau), t + \tfrac{1}{2}\tau) \tag{3.19}$$

where

$$\mathbf{x}^*(t + \tfrac{1}{2}\tau) \equiv \mathbf{x}(t) + \tfrac{1}{2}\tau \mathbf{f}(\mathbf{x}(t), t) \tag{3.20}$$

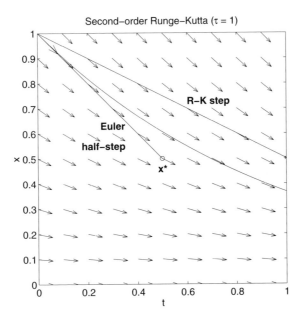

Figure 3.6: Graphical illustration of a simple, two-step Runge-Kutta formula. The arrows have slope $dx/dt = f(x(t), t)$. For this figure, $dx/dt = -x$ and $\tau = 1$.

To see where this formula comes from, consider for a moment the one-variable case. We know that the Taylor expansion

$$
\begin{aligned}
x(t + \tau) &= x(t) + \tau \frac{dx(\zeta)}{dt} \\
&= x(t) + \tau f(x(\zeta), \zeta)
\end{aligned}
\tag{3.21}
$$

is exact for some value of ζ between t and $t+\tau$, as seen in Equation (2.10). The Euler formula takes $\zeta = t$; Euler-Cromer uses $\zeta = t$ in the velocity equation and $\zeta = t+\tau$ in the position equation. Runge-Kutta tries to use $\zeta = t+\frac{1}{2}\tau$, since this is probably a better guess. However, $x(t+\frac{1}{2}\tau)$ is not known, so we approximate it in the simplest way possible: Use an Euler step to compute $x^*(t+\frac{1}{2}\tau)$ and use this as our estimate of $x(t+\frac{1}{2}\tau)$. Figure 3.6 illustrates this idea.

Let's walk through a simple example using the Runge-Kutta formula. Take the equation

$$
\frac{dx}{dt} = -x; \qquad x(t = 0) = 1
\tag{3.22}
$$

The solution of (3.22) is $x(t) = e^{-t}$. Using the Euler method with a time step of $\tau = 0.1$, we get

$$
\begin{aligned}
x(0.1) &= 1 + 0.1(-1) = 0.9 \\
x(0.2) &= 0.9 + (0.1)(-0.9) = 0.81
\end{aligned}
$$

$$\begin{aligned} x(0.3) &= 0.81 + 0.1(-0.81) = 0.729 \\ x(0.4) &= 0.729 + 0.1(-0.729) = 0.6561 \end{aligned}$$

Now let's try Runge-Kutta. To make a fair comparison, we use a larger time step of $\tau = 0.2$ for Runge-Kutta because it makes twice as many evaluations of $f(x)$. For the Runge-Kutta formula presented above,

$$\begin{aligned} x^*(0.1) &= 1 + 0.1(-1) = 0.9 \\ x(0.2) &= 1 + 0.2(-0.9) = 0.82 \\ x^*(0.3) &= 0.82 + 0.1(-0.82) = 0.738 \\ x(0.4) &= 0.82 + 0.2(-0.738) = 0.6724 \end{aligned}$$

Compare this with the exact solution $x(0.4) = \exp(-0.4) \approx 0.6703$. Clearly, Runge-Kutta does much better than Euler; the absolute percent errors are 0.3% and 2.1%, respectively.

General Runge-Kutta Formulas

The formula discussed above is not the only second-order Runge-Kutta formula. Here is an alternative one:

$$\mathbf{x}(t+\tau) = \mathbf{x}(t) + \frac{1}{2}\tau[\mathbf{f}(\mathbf{x}(t), t) + \mathbf{f}(\mathbf{x}^*(t+\tau), t+\tau)] \tag{3.23}$$

where

$$\mathbf{x}^*(t+\tau) \equiv \mathbf{x}(t) + \tau\mathbf{f}(\mathbf{x}(t), t) \tag{3.24}$$

To understand this scheme, again consider the one-variable case. In our original formula, we estimated $f(x(\zeta), \zeta)$ as $f(x^*(t + \frac{1}{2}\tau), t + \frac{1}{2}\tau)$. Our new formula is similar, but now we approximate $f(x(\zeta), \zeta)$ as $\frac{1}{2}[f(x, t) + f(x^*(t+\tau), t+\tau)]$.

These formulas were not pulled out of the air; you can work them out using the two-variable Taylor expansion,

$$f(x+h, t+\tau) = \sum_{i=0}^{\infty} \frac{1}{i!}\left(h\frac{\partial}{\partial x} + \tau\frac{\partial}{\partial t}\right)^i f(x, t) \tag{3.25}$$

where all derivatives are evaluated at (x, t). For a general second-order Runge-Kutta formula, we want to obtain a formula of the form

$$x(t+\tau) = x(t) + w_1\tau f(x(t), t) + w_2\tau f(x^*, t+\alpha\tau) \tag{3.26}$$

where

$$x^* \equiv x(t) + \beta\tau f(x(t), t) \tag{3.27}$$

There are four unspecified coefficients: a, b, w_1, and w_2. Notice that we recover (3.19) and (3.20) with the values

$$w_1 = 0; \quad w_2 = 1; \quad \alpha = \frac{1}{2}; \quad \beta = \frac{1}{2}$$

and (3.23) and (3.24) with

$$w_1 = \frac{1}{2}; \quad w_2 = \frac{1}{2}; \quad \alpha = 1; \quad \beta = 1$$

We want to pick these four coefficients such that we get second-order accuracy; that is, we want to match the Taylor series through the second derivative terms. The details of the calculation are left as an exercise, but any set of coefficients satisfying the relations $w_1 + w_2 = 1$, $\alpha w_2 = \frac{1}{2}$, and $\alpha = \beta$ will give a second-order Runge-Kutta scheme. The local truncation error is $O(\tau^3)$, but the explicit expression does not have a simple form (see Exercise 3.10). It is not clear that one scheme is superior to another since the truncation error, being a complicated function of $f(x, t)$, will vary from problem to problem.

Fourth-Order Runge-Kutta

I presented the second-order Runge-Kutta formulas because it is easy to understand their construction. In practice, however, the most commonly used method is the following fourth-order Runge-Kutta formula:

$$\mathbf{x}(t + \tau) = \mathbf{x}(t) + \frac{1}{6}\tau[\mathbf{F}_1 + 2\mathbf{F}_2 + 2\mathbf{F}_3 + \mathbf{F}_4] \qquad (3.28)$$

where

$$
\begin{aligned}
\mathbf{F}_1 &= \mathbf{f}(\mathbf{x}, t) \\
\mathbf{F}_2 &= \mathbf{f}\left(\mathbf{x} + \frac{1}{2}\tau\mathbf{F}_1, t + \frac{1}{2}\tau\right) \\
\mathbf{F}_3 &= \mathbf{f}\left(\mathbf{x} + \frac{1}{2}\tau\mathbf{F}_2, t + \frac{1}{2}\tau\right) \\
\mathbf{F}_4 &= \mathbf{f}\left(\mathbf{x} + \tau\mathbf{F}_3, t + \tau\right)
\end{aligned}
\qquad (3.29)
$$

The following excerpt from *Numerical Recipes* [104] best summarizes the status that the above formula holds in the world of numerical analysis:

> For many scientific users, fourth-order Runge-Kutta is not just the first word on ODE integrators, but the last word as well. In fact, you can get pretty far on this old workhorse especially if you combine it with an adaptive stepsize algorithm.... Bulirsch-Stoer or predictor-corrector methods can be very much more efficient for problems where very high accuracy is a requirement. Those methods are the high-strung racehorses. Runge-Kutta is for ploughing the fields.

You may wonder why fourth-order and not eighth- or twenty-third-order Runge-Kutta? Well, the higher-order methods have better truncation error but also require more computation, that is, more evaluations of $f(x, t)$. There is a trade-off between doing more steps with a smaller τ using a low-order method as opposed

Table 3.3: Outline of function rk4, which evaluates a single step using the fourth-order Runge-Kutta method.

- *Inputs*: $\mathbf{x}(t)$, t, τ, $\mathbf{f}(\mathbf{x}, t; \lambda)$, and λ.

- *Output*: $\mathbf{x}(t + \tau)$.

- Evaluate $\mathbf{F}_1$, $\mathbf{F}_2$, $\mathbf{F}_3$, and $\mathbf{F}_4$ using (3.29).

- Compute $\mathbf{x}(t + \tau)$ using fourth-order Runge-Kutta, (3.28).

See pages 92 and 99 for program listings.

Table 3.4: Outline of function gravrk, which is used by the Runge-Kutta routines to evaluate the equations of motion for the Kepler problem.

- *Inputs*: $\mathbf{x}(t)$, t (not used), GM.

- *Output*: $d\mathbf{x}(t)/dt$.

- Compute acceleration $\mathbf{a} = -(GM/|\mathbf{r}^3|)\mathbf{r}$.

- Return $d\mathbf{x}(t)/dt = [v_x,\ v_y,\ a_x,\ a_y]$.

See pages 93 and 100 for program listings.

to doing fewer steps with a larger τ using a high-order method. Because higher-order Runge-Kutta methods are quite complicated, the fourth-order scheme given above is favored. By the way, the local truncation error for fourth-order Runge-Kutta is $O(\tau^5)$.

To implement the fourth-order Runge-Kutta method for our orbit problem, we use the function rk4 (Table 3.3). This function takes as inputs: the current state of the system, $\mathbf{x}(t)$; the time step to be used, τ; the current time, t; the function $\mathbf{f}(\mathbf{x}(t), t; \lambda)$; and a list of parameters λ used by $\mathbf{f}$. The output is the new state of the system, $\mathbf{x}(t + \tau)$, as computed by the Runge-Kutta method. Using fourth-order Runge-Kutta gives the results shown in Figure 3.7, which are much better than those obtained using Euler-Cromer (Figure 3.5).

Passing Functions to Functions

The Runge-Kutta function rk4 is very simple, but introduces one programming element that we've not used before. The function $\mathbf{f}(\mathbf{x}, t; \lambda)$ is passed as an input parameter to rk4. This allows us to use rk4 to solve different problems by

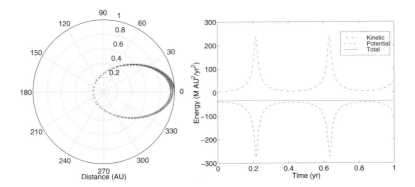

Figure 3.7: Graphs of trajectory and energy from the orbit program using fourth-order Runge-Kutta. Initial radial distance is 1 AU, and the initial tangential velocity is π AU/yr. The time step is $\tau = 0.005$ yr; 200 time steps are computed. Compare with Figure 3.5.

simply changing the definition of **f** (as we'll do in later sections). For the Kepler problem, the function gravrk (Table 3.4) defines the equations of motion by returning $d\mathbf{x}/dt$, Equation (3.17).

In the MATLAB version, a text string containing the name of the function $\mathbf{f}(\mathbf{x}, t; \lambda)$ is passed to rk4. The orbit program calls rk4 as

    state = rk4(state,time,tau,'gravrk',GM);

where the vector state is $\mathbf{x} = [\, r_x \ r_y \ v_x \ v_y \,]$. Within rk4, the variable derivsRK receives the input function name as a text string. MATLAB's feval (function evaluation) command is used by rk4 to call this function. For example, when derivsRK contains the string 'gravrk', then

    F1 = feval(derivsRK,x,t,param);

is equivalent to calling gravrk as

    F1 = gravrk(x,t,param);

Notice that **param** is used to pass any extra parameters (for the Kepler problem, the value of GM).

In C++, the pointer to the function $\mathbf{f}(\mathbf{x}, t; \lambda)$ is passed to rk4. The orbit program calls rk4 as

    rk4(state, nState, time, tau, gravrk, param);

where the vector state is $\mathbf{x} = [\, r_x \ r_y \ v_x \ v_y \,]$. At the top of the file, the function gravrk is declared with the prototype

    void gravrk(double x[], double t, double param[], double deriv[]);

The first line of rk4 is

```
void rk4(double x[], int nX, double t, double tau,
    void (*derivsRK)(double x[], double t, double param[],
    double deriv[]), double param[]) {
```

When called by `orbit`, this function receives a pointer to `gravrk` in the variable `derivsRK`. Within `rk4`, the statement

```
(*derivsRK)( x, t, param, F1 );
```

is equivalent to

```
gravrk( x, t, param, F1 );
```

since `derivsRK` points to `gravrk`.

EXERCISES

8. Prove that any nth-order ODE of the form

$$\frac{d^n z}{dt^n} = f\left(z, \frac{dz}{dt}, \ldots, \frac{d^{n-1} z}{dt^{n-1}}\right)$$

may be written as a system of first-order ODEs. [Pencil]

9. (a) Write a program to reproduce Figure 3.6 using the second-order Runge-Kutta formulas (3.19) and (3.20). Take $f(x, t) = -x$ and $\tau = 1$. (b) Write a program, as in part (a), but use the second-order Runge-Kutta formulas (3.23) and (3.24). (c) Write a program, as in part (a), but use the fourth-order Runge-Kutta formulas (3.28) and (3.29). [Computer]

10. (a) Use Equation (3.25) to show that a second-order Runge-Kutta formula requires that $w_1 + w_2 = 1$, $\alpha w_2 = \frac{1}{2}$, and $\alpha = \beta$. (b) Show that

$$\tau^3 \left[\left(\frac{1}{6} - \frac{\alpha}{4}\right)\left(\frac{\partial}{\partial t} + f\frac{\partial}{\partial x}\right)^2 f + \frac{1}{6}\frac{\partial f}{\partial x}\left(\frac{\partial f}{\partial t} + f\frac{\partial f}{\partial x}\right)\right]$$

is the truncation error for second-order Runge-Kutta. [Pencil]

11. Modify the program used in Exercise 3.6 to use the fourth-order Runge-Kutta method, and repeat that exercise. Compare the Euler-Cromer and Runge-Kutta methods. [Computer]

12. Suppose that our comet is subjected to a constant force in one direction (e.g., gravitational attraction of a large but distant object).[85] Modify the `orbit` program to simulate this system. Set the strength of the perturbing force to be 1% of the initial gravitational force. Using fourth-order Runge-Kutta, show that an initially circular orbit is transformed into an elliptical orbit with the semimajor axis perpendicular to the perturbing force. Produce a graph of the angular momentum as a function of time. [Computer]

13. The Wilberforce pendulum [17], a popular demonstration device, is illustrated in Figure 3.8. The pendulum has two modes of oscillation: vertical and torsional motion. The Lagrangian for this system is

$$L = \frac{1}{2}m\left(\frac{dz}{dt}\right)^2 + \frac{1}{2}I\left(\frac{d\theta}{dt}\right)^2 - \frac{1}{2}kz^2 - \frac{1}{2}\delta\theta^2 - \frac{1}{2}\epsilon z\theta$$

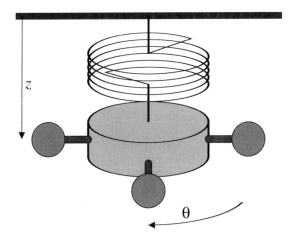

Figure 3.8: Wilberforce pendulum.

where m and I are the mass and rotational inertia of the bob, k and δ are the longitudinal and torsional spring constants, and ϵ is the coupling constant between the modes. Some typical values are $m = 0.5$ kg, $I = 10^{-4}$ kg $\cdot$m^2, $k = 5$ N/m, $\delta = 10^{-3}$ N $\cdot$ m, and $\epsilon = 10^{-2}$ N. (a) Find the equations of motion. [Pencil] (b) Write a program to compute $z(t)$ and $\theta(t)$ using fourth-order Runge-Kutta. Try the initial conditions $z(0) = 10$ cm, $\theta(0) = 0$ and $z(0) = 0$, $\theta(0) = 2\pi$. Show that when the longitudinal frequency, $f_z = (2\pi)^{-1}\sqrt{k/m}$, equals the torsional frequency, $f_\theta = (2\pi)^{-1}\sqrt{\delta/I}$, the motion periodically alternates between being purely longitudinal and purely torsional. [Computer]

3.3 ADAPTIVE METHODS

Adaptive Time Step Programs

Because the fourth-order Runge-Kutta method is more accurate (smaller truncation error), it does a better job with highly elliptical orbits. And yet, for an initial aphelion distance of 1 AU and an initial aphelion velocity of $\pi/2$ AU/yr using a time step as small as $\tau = 0.0005$ yr ($\approx 4\frac{1}{2}$ hr), the total energy varies by over 7% per orbit. If we think about the physics, we come to realize that the small time steps are only needed when the comet makes its closest approach, where its velocity is maximum. Any small error in the trajectory as it rounds the Sun causes a large deviation in the potential energy.

The idea now is to design a program that would use smaller time steps when the comet is near the Sun and larger time steps when it is far away. As it is, we normally have only a rough idea of what τ should be; now we have to select a $\tau_{\min}$ and $\tau_{\max}$ and a way to switch between them. If we have to do this by manual trial and error, it could be worse than just doing the brute force calculation with a small time step. Ideally, we wish to be completely freed of having to specify a time step. We want to have the trajectory computed from some initial position up to some final time with the assurance that the solution is correct to a specified accuracy.

Adaptive programs continuously monitor the solution and modify the time step to ensure that the user-specified accuracy is maintained. These programs may do some extra calculation to optimize the choice of τ, but in many cases this extra work is worth it. Here is one way to implement this idea: Given the current state $\mathbf{x}(t)$, the program computes $\mathbf{x}(t+\tau)$ as usual, and then it repeats the calculation by doing two steps, each with time step $\frac{1}{2}\tau$. Visually, this is

The difference between the two answers, $\mathbf{x}_b(t+\tau)$ and $\mathbf{x}_s(t+\tau)$, estimates the local truncation error. If the error is tolerable, then the computed value is accepted and a larger value of τ is used on the next iteration. On the other hand, if the error is too large, the answer is rejected, the time step is reduced, and the procedure is repeated until an acceptable answer is obtained. The estimated truncation error for the current time step can guide us in selecting a new time step for the next iteration.

Adaptive Runge-Kutta Function

Here is how such an adaptive iteration can be implemented for our fourth-order Runge-Kutta scheme: Call Δ the local truncation error; we know that $\Delta \propto \tau^5$ for fourth-order Runge-Kutta. Suppose that the current time step τ_{old} gave an error of $\Delta_c = |\mathbf{x}_b - \mathbf{x}_s|$; this is our estimate for the truncation error. Given that we want the error to be less than or equal to the user-specified ideal error, call it Δ_i; then, the estimate for the new time step is

$$\tau_{\text{est}} = \tau \left| \frac{\Delta_i}{\Delta_c} \right|^{1/5} \tag{3.30}$$

Since this is only an estimate, the new time step is $\tau_{\text{new}} = S_1 \tau_{\text{est}}$, where $S_1 < 1$. This makes us overestimate the change when we lower τ and underestimate the change when we raise it. We waste computer effort every time we reject an answer and need to reduce the time step, so it is better to set $\tau_{\text{new}} < \tau_{\text{est}}$.

We should also put in a second safety factor, $S_2 > 1$, to be sure that the program is not too enthusiastic about precipitously raising or lowering the time step. With both safeguards, the new time step is

$$\tau_{\text{new}} = \begin{cases} S_2 \tau_{\text{old}} & \text{if } S_1 \tau_{\text{est}} > S_2 \tau_{\text{old}} \\ \tau_{\text{old}}/S_2 & \text{if } S_1 \tau_{\text{est}} < \tau_{\text{old}}/S_2 \\ S_1 \tau_{\text{est}} & \text{otherwise} \end{cases} \tag{3.31}$$

Table 3.5: Outline of function `rka`, which evaluates a single step using the fourth-order adaptive Runge-Kutta method.

- *Inputs*: $\mathbf{x}(t)$, t, τ, Δ_i, $\mathbf{f}(\mathbf{x}, t; \lambda)$, and λ.

- *Outputs*: $\mathbf{x}(t')$, t', and τ_{new}.

- Set initial variables.

- Loop over maximum number of attempts to satisfy error bound.

  - Take the two small time steps.
  - Take the single big time step.
  - Compute the estimated truncation error.
  - Estimate new τ value (including safety factors).
  - If error is acceptable, return computed values.

- Issue error message if error bound never satisfied.

See pages 93 and 100 for program listings.

These constraints ensure that our new estimate for τ never increases or decreases by more than a factor of S_2. Of course, this new τ may be found to be insufficiently small, and we may have to continue reducing the time step; but at least we know it will not happen in an uncontrolled way.

This procedure is not bulletproof—round-off error becomes significant at very small time steps. For this reason the adaptive iteration may fail to find a time step that gives the desired accuracy. Keep this limitation in mind when you specify the ideal error.

An adaptive Runge-Kutta function, called `rka`, is outlined in Table 3.5. Notice that the inputs in the calling sequence are the same as for `rk4`, except for the addition of Δ_i, the specified ideal error. The outputs from `rka` are the new state of the system, $\mathbf{x}(t')$; the new time, t'; and the new time step, τ_{new}, which should be used the next time `rka` is called.

Using the adaptive Runge-Kutta method, the `orbit` program gives the results shown in Figure 3.9 for a highly elliptical orbit. Notice that the program takes many more steps at perihelion (closest approach) than at aphelion. Compare with the results using nonadaptive Runge-Kutta (Figure 3.7) in which the steps at perihelion are widely spaced. A plot of time step versus radial distance (Figure 3.10) shows that τ varies by nearly three orders of magnitude. Interestingly, this graph reveals an approximate power law relation of the form $\tau \propto r^{3/2}$. Of course this dependence reminds us of Kepler's third law, Equation (3.10). We expect some scatter in the points since our adaptive routine only

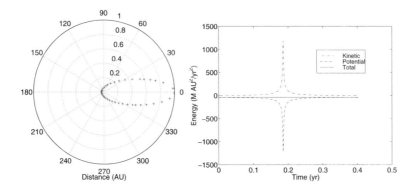

Figure 3.9: Graphs of trajectory and energy from the `orbit` program using adaptive Runge-Kutta. The initial radial distance is 1 AU, and the initial tangential velocity is $\pi/2$ AU/yr. The initial time step is $\tau = 0.1$ yr; 40 time steps are computed.

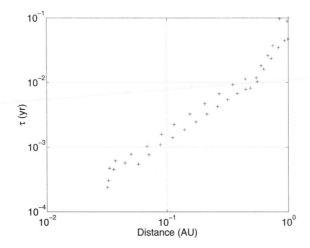

Figure 3.10: Time step, τ, as a function of radial distance from the `orbit` program, using adaptive Runge-Kutta. Parameters are the same as for Figure 3.9.

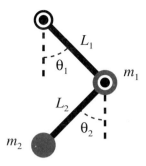

Figure 3.11: Double pendulum.

estimates the optimum time step.

EXERCISES

14. Consider the central force

$$\mathbf{F}(\mathbf{r}) = -\frac{GMm}{r^3}\left(1 - \frac{\alpha}{r}\right)\mathbf{r}$$

where α is a constant. Modify the `orbit` program to compute the motion of an object under this force law. Using adaptive Runge-Kutta, show that the orbit precesses $360(1-a)/a$ degrees per revolution, where $a = \sqrt{1 + GMm^2\alpha/L^2}$ and L is the angular momentum. [Computer]

15. Modify `orbit` to add a drag force on the comet, $\mathbf{F}_d = C|\mathbf{v}|\mathbf{v}$ (see Section 2.1). Take the drag force to be small relative to the gravitational force $\mathbf{F}_g$ by fixing the constant C such that $|\mathbf{F}_g(\mathbf{r}_1)| = 100|\mathbf{F}_d(\mathbf{v}_1)|$, where $\mathbf{r}_1$ and $\mathbf{v}_1$ are the initial position and velocity, respectively. Show that the average kinetic energy (averaged over an orbit) *increases* with time. [Computer]

16. In Rutherford scattering, an alpha particle is deflected as it passes near the nucleus of a heavy atom. Write a program using adaptive Runge-Kutta to simulate Rutherford scattering. Find the scattering angle for a 5-MeV alpha particle striking a gold nucleus at an impact parameter of 10 femtometers. [Computer]

17. The adaptive Runge-Kutta routine, `rka`, uses a generic method for estimating the error. Write a modified version of `rka` that accepts a user-specified function that computes Δ_c. For the comet problem, write a function that evaluates the absolute fractional error in the total energy. Test your routines and compare with the original version of `rka` for the case considered in Figures 3.9 and 3.10. [Computer]

18. Write an adaptive Runge-Kutta program to simulate a pendulum system consisting of a bob of mass m and a massless rod with rest length L. The rod acts like a stiff spring with spring constant k. Assume that the motion is in the xy plane. Obtain plots of the motion for the values $m = 0.1$ kg, $L = 1.0$ m, and spring constants in the range $k = 10^2$ N/m (rubber) to $k = 10^6$ N/m (metal wire). How does the average time step adopted by the algorithm vary with the spring constant? [Computer]

19. Consider a double pendulum, as shown in Figure 3.11. Its Lagrangian is

$$\frac{m_1 + m_2}{2} L_1^2 \dot{\theta}_1^2 + \frac{m_2}{2} L_2^2 \dot{\theta}_2^2 + m_2 g L_2 \cos \theta_2$$
$$+ m_2 L_1 L_2 \dot{\theta}_1 \dot{\theta}_2 \cos(\theta_1 - \theta_2) + (m_1 + m_2) g L_1 \cos \theta_1$$

where $\dot{\theta} \equiv d\theta/dt$. (a) Use the Lagrangian to find the equations of motion. [Pencil] (b) Write a program that uses adaptive Runge-Kutta to simulate the motion of the double pendulum. Take $g = 9.81$ m/s^2, $m_1 = m_2$, and $L_1 = L_2 = 0.1$ m; compute examples of the motion for various initial conditions. Show that in some cases, the lower mass spins completely around with an aperiodic motion. [Computer]

3.4 *CHAOS IN THE LORENZ MODEL

Optional sections, marked with an asterisk, may be omitted without loss of continuity.

Unwinding the Mechanical Universe

Newton's success in solving the Kepler problem had effects far beyond physics. It inspired the mechanistic picture of the universe, a philosophy developed by Laplace and others. The orbits of the planets had the regularity of a well-made clock. Even long-term events, such as solar eclipses and comet returns, were predictable to high accuracy. For centuries it was believed that other physical phenomena, such as weather, were only unpredictable due to the large number of variables in the problem. With the arrival of modern computers it was hoped that long-range weather prediction would soon be within our grasp.

In the early 1960s, however, an MIT meteorologist named Ed Lorenz saw that it would not be so. He found that the weather was intrinsically unpredictable, not because of its complexity, but because of the nonlinear nature of the governing equations. Lorenz formulated a simple model of the global weather, reducing the problem to a 12-variable system of nonlinear ODEs. What he observed was aperiodic behavior that was extremely sensitive to the initial conditions.[†]

To study this effect more easily, he introduced an even simpler model with only three variables. The Lorenz model [117] is

$$\begin{aligned}
\frac{dx}{dt} &= \sigma(y - x) \\
\frac{dy}{dt} &= rx - y - xz \\
\frac{dz}{dt} &= xy - bz
\end{aligned} \qquad (3.32)$$

where σ, r, and b are positive constants. These simple equations were originally developed as a model for buoyant convection in a fluid. Their derivation

---

[†]For a historical account of Lorenz's discovery, see Gleick [56].

Table 3.6: Outline of program `lorenz`, which computes the time series for the Lorenz model (3.32).

- Set initial state $[x,y,z]$ and parameters $[r,\sigma,b]$.

- Loop over the desired number of steps.

  - Record values of x, y, z, t, and τ for plotting.
  - Find new state using `rka`, the adaptive Runge-Kutta function.

- Print maximum and minimum time step returned by `rka`.

- Graph the time series $x(t)$.

- Graph the (x, y, z) phase space trajectory.

See pages 94 and 102 for program listings.

Table 3.7: Outline of function `lorzrk`, which is used by the Runge-Kutta routines to evaluate the Lorenz equations.

- *Inputs*: $\mathbf{x}(t)$, t (not used), $[r,\sigma,b]$.

- *Output*: $d\mathbf{x}(t)/dt$.

- Compute $d\mathbf{x}(t)/dt = [dx/dt \; dy/dt \; dz/dt]$ (see (3.32)).

See pages 96 and 104 for program listings.

is beyond the scope of this text, but, briefly, x measures the rate of convective overturning, and y and z measure the horizontal and vertical temperature gradients. The parameters σ and b depend on the fluid properties and the geometry of the container; commonly, the values $\sigma = 10$ and $b = 8/3$ are used. The parameter r is proportional to the applied temperature gradient.

Lorenz Model Program

A program, called `lorenz`, which solves the Lorenz model using our adaptive Runge-Kutta method is outlined in Table 3.6. This program does little more than repeatedly call `rka` and graph the results. The function `lorzrk` (see Table 3.7) specifies Equations (3.32) for use in the Runge-Kutta routines.

Although an adaptive scheme has many advantages, it may not always be the best method to use for a particular problem. Note that for the runs of the

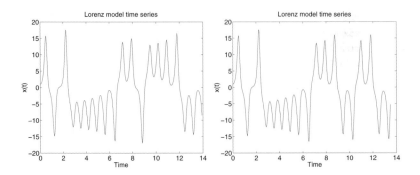

Figure 3.12: Time series $x(t)$ for the Lorenz model as computed by `lorenz`. The parameters are $\sigma = 10$, $b = 8/3$, and $r = 28$. The initial condition is $[x\ y\ z] = [1\ 1\ 20]$ for the plot on the left and $[x\ y\ z] = [1\ 1\ 20.01]$ for the plot on the right.

`lorenz` program described below, the value of the time step τ does not vary by much more than one order of magnitude. This is one argument for returning to our nonadaptive methods. Another is that nonadaptive methods automatically produce data points that are evenly spaced in time, the form required by most data analysis techniques. In an exercise, you are asked to make a comparison between simple and adaptive Runge-Kutta for the Lorenz problem and judge for yourself.

Two examples of time series obtained by the `lorenz` program are shown in Figure 3.12. The values of $x(t)$ oscillate in a fashion that does not seem much more complicated than simple harmonic motion; results for $y(t)$ and $z(t)$ are similar. However, in Chapter 5 we analyze the power spectra for these time series and find they have a complex structure. More importantly, Figure 3.12 shows that slightly different initial conditions will produce significantly different time series. Comparing the two plots of $x(t)$ shows that the evolution is initially very similar, but later the two time series are completely different. This extreme sensitivity to initial conditions led Lorenz to speculate that, if weather obeyed similar dynamics, long-term prediction was impossible. He termed this the butterfly effect: Even a single butterfly flapping its wings could, in the long run, influence the world's weather. Because the trajectories of the Lorenz model are extremely sensitive to initial conditions, the motion is considered chaotic.

Figure 3.13 shows the trajectory in the three dimensional space of the variables x, y, and z. Now the motion looks far more interesting. The trajectory is said to lie on an attractor; you may think of this motion as a sort of aperiodic orbit. This picture helps us understand the butterfly effect and the origin of the chaotic motion. The center portion of the attractor mixes trajectories, sending some to the left lobe, some to the right. Trajectories with nearly identical initial conditions are eventually separated in much the same way as adjacent particles of flour are separated in the kneading of bread.[63] The three points marked by asterisks in Figure 3.13 are the steady states of the Lorenz model;

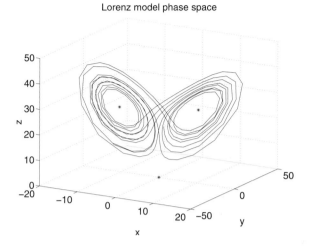

Figure 3.13: Phase space trajectory for the Lorenz model. The initial condition is $[x\ y\ z] = [1\ 1\ 20]$; parameters are the same as in Figure 3.12. Steady states are indicated by asterisks.

their definition is discussed in the next chapter.

Although many celestial mechanics problems are accurately modeled using two-body interactions, objects moving in our solar system experience a gravitational attraction to all the planets. Specifically, the orbits of highly elliptical comets can be significantly influenced by the gas giants, especially Jupiter, and, given these perturbations, their motion may actually be chaotic![32, 97]

EXERCISES

20. Try running the `lorenz` program with the following values for the parameter r: (a) 0, (b) 1, (c) 14, (d) 20, (e) 100. Use the initial condition $[x\ y\ z] = [1\ 1\ 20]$. Describe the different types of behavior found and compare with Figure 3.13. [Computer]

21. For $r = 28$, try the following initial conditions: $[x\ y\ z] = $ (a) $[0\ 0\ 0]$; (b) $[0\ 0\ 20]$; (c) $[0.01\ 0.01\ 0.01]$; (d) $[100\ 100\ 100]$; (e) $[8.5\ 8.5\ 27]$. Describe the different types of behavior found and compare with Figure 3.13. [Computer]

22. The following set of nonlinear ODEs is known as the Lotka-Volterra model:

$$\frac{dx}{dt} = (a - bx - cy)x; \qquad \frac{dy}{dt} = (-d + ex)y$$

where a, b, c, d, and e are positive constants. (a) These equations model a simple ecological system of predators and prey.[99] For example, the variables x and y could represent the number of hares and foxes in a forest. Describe the physical meaning of each of the five parameters. [Pencil] (b) Write a program using adaptive Runge-Kutta to compute the trajectory $(x(t), y(t))$ and plot $y(t)$ versus $x(t)$ for a variety of initial conditions using $a = 10$, $b = 10^{-5}$, $c = 0.1$, $d = 10$, and $e = 0.1$. Take $x(0) > 0$, $y(0) > 0$, since the number of animals should be positive. [Computer]

23. Consider the Hopf model, given by the nonlinear ODEs:

$$\frac{dx}{dt} = ax + y - x(x^2 + y^2); \qquad \frac{dy}{dt} = -x + ay - y(x^2 + y^2)$$

(a) By transforming these equations into polar coordinates show that when $a < 0$, trajectories spiral toward the origin, and when $a > 0$ they spiral toward a circle of radius $\sqrt{a}$ centered at the origin. [Pencil] (b) Write a program that uses the adaptive Runge-Kutta routine to compute the trajectories of the Hopf model. Plot these trajectories and confirm the result proven in part (a). [Computer]

24. Write a nonadaptive version of the `lorenz` program that uses `rk4`. Run the nonadaptive version using the minimum time step used by the adaptive version. Remember that `rka` is effectively using a time step of $\frac{1}{2}\tau$, since this is the step size for the small steps. Modify the main loop so that the iteration stops at $t = 10$. Determine the relative efficiency of the two methods (use the MATLAB `flops` command to count floating-point operations or the C++ timing routines in the `<time.h>` library). [Computer]

25. One characteristic of chaotic dynamics is sensitivity to initial conditions. Using `rk4`, write a nonadaptive version of the `lorenz` program that simultaneously computes the trajectories for two different initial conditions. Use initial conditions that are very close together (e.g., [1 1 20] and [1 1 20.001]). Plot the distance between these trajectories as a function of time, using both normal and logarithmic scales. What can you say about how the distance varies with time? [Computer]

26. Repeat the previous exercise using the: (a) Lotka-Volterra equations (see Exercise 3.22); (b) Hopf model (see Exercise 3.23). [Computer]

BEYOND THIS CHAPTER

While adaptive fourth-order Runge-Kutta is a good general-purpose algorithm, for some problems it is useful to employ more advanced methods. Specifically, if the solution is smooth and you want to minimize the number of evaluations of $f(x)$, you should consider trying Bulirsch-Stoer or predictor-corrector methods.[118] These are high-accuracy methods that, under the right conditions, allow you to use very large time steps. I especially recommend that you try Bulirsch-Stoer if your computational budget is limited and the routine is available in a library package.

On some problems you may find that the adaptive Runge-Kutta method demands an extremely small time step. For example, suppose that you wanted to simulate a pendulum consisting of bob of mass m at the end of a massless rod of stiffness k and rest length L (see Exercise 3.18). The period of oscillation for a simple pendulum is $T_p = 2\pi\sqrt{L_p/g}$, where $L_p \approx L$ is the length of the pendulum. The period of vibration for a spring is $T_s = 2\pi\sqrt{m/k}$. If the rod is very stiff (large k), then $T_s \ll T_p$. The time step will have to be less than the period of vibration so $\tau \ll T_p$. As you discover in Exercise 3.18, we may need to evaluate 10^4 time steps to simulate a single swing of the pendulum.

Systems of ordinary differential equations arising from physical problems with vastly different time scales, such as this spring-pendulum system, are said to be *stiff.* Another common example of such a system is a chemically reacting flow. The relaxation rates for the chemistry are often many orders of magnitude faster than the hydrodynamic time scales. Stiff ODEs are commonly solved using implicit schemes.[54] MATLAB has several routines (ode15s, ode23tb, etc.) for solving stiff ODEs.

APPENDIX A: MATLAB LISTINGS

Listing 3A.1 Program orbit. Computes the orbit of a comet about the Sun using the Euler, Euler-Cromer, fourth-order Runge-Kutta, or adaptive Runge-Kutta method. Uses rk4 (Listing 3A.2), gravrk (Listing 3A.3), and rka (Listing 3A.4).

```
% orbit - Program to compute the orbit of a comet.
clear all;  help orbit;  % Clear memory and print header

%* Set initial position and velocity of the comet.
r0 = input('Enter initial radial distance (AU): ');
v0 = input('Enter initial tangential velocity (AU/yr): ');
r = [r0 0];  v = [0 v0];
state = [ r(1) r(2) v(1) v(2) ];   % Used by R-K routines

%* Set physical parameters (mass, G*M)
GM = 4*pi^2;      % Grav. const. * Mass of Sun (au^3/yr^2)
mass = 1.;        % Mass of comet
adaptErr = 1.e-3; % Error parameter used by adaptive Runge-Kutta
time = 0;

%* Loop over desired number of steps using specified
%  numerical method.
nStep = input('Enter number of steps: ');
tau = input('Enter time step (yr): ');
NumericalMethod = menu('Choose a numerical method:', ...
       'Euler','Euler-Cromer','Runge-Kutta','Adaptive R-K');
for iStep=1:nStep

  %* Record position and energy for plotting.
  rplot(iStep) = norm(r);          % Record position for polar plot
  thplot(iStep) = atan2(r(2),r(1));
  tplot(iStep) = time;
  kinetic(iStep) = .5*mass*norm(v)^2;   % Record energies
  potential(iStep) = - GM*mass/norm(r);

  %* Calculate new position and velocity using desired method.
  if( NumericalMethod == 1 )
    accel = -GM*r/norm(r)^3;
    r = r + tau*v;              % Euler step
    v = v + tau*accel;
    time = time + tau;
```

```
  elseif( NumericalMethod == 2 )
    accel = -GM*r/norm(r)^3;
    v = v + tau*accel;
    r = r + tau*v;                % Euler-Cromer step
    time = time + tau;
  elseif( NumericalMethod == 3 )
    state = rk4(state,time,tau,'gravrk',GM);
    r = [state(1) state(2)];    % 4th order Runge-Kutta
    v = [state(3) state(4)];
    time = time + tau;
  else
    [state time tau] = rka(state,time,tau,adaptErr,'gravrk',GM);
    r = [state(1) state(2)];    % Adaptive Runge-Kutta
    v = [state(3) state(4)];
  end

end

%* Graph the trajectory of the comet.
figure(1); clf;  % Clear figure 1 window and bring forward
polar(thplot,rplot,'+');  % Use polar plot for graphing orbit
xlabel('Distance (AU)');  grid;
pause(1)    % Pause for 1 second before drawing next plot

%* Graph the energy of the comet versus time.
figure(2); clf;   % Clear figure 2 window and bring forward
totalE = kinetic + potential;   % Total energy
plot(tplot,kinetic,'-.',tplot,potential,'--',tplot,totalE,'-')
legend('Kinetic','Potential','Total');
xlabel('Time (yr)'); ylabel('Energy (M AU^2/yr^2)');
```

Listing 3A.2 Function rk4. Fourth-order Runge-Kutta routine.

```
function xout = rk4(x,t,tau,derivsRK,param)
%  Runge-Kutta integrator (4th order)
% Input arguments -
%   x = current value of dependent variable
%   t = independent variable (usually time)
%   tau = step size (usually timestep)
%   derivsRK = right hand side of the ODE; derivsRK is the
%              name of the function which returns dx/dt
%              Calling format derivsRK(x,t,param).
%   param = extra parameters passed to derivsRK
% Output arguments -
%   xout = new value of x after a step of size tau
half_tau = 0.5*tau;
F1 = feval(derivsRK,x,t,param);
t_half = t + half_tau;
xtemp = x + half_tau*F1;
```

```
F2 = feval(derivsRK,xtemp,t_half,param);
xtemp = x + half_tau*F2;
F3 = feval(derivsRK,xtemp,t_half,param);
t_full = t + tau;
xtemp = x + tau*F3;
F4 = feval(derivsRK,xtemp,t_full,param);
xout = x + tau/6.*(F1 + F4 + 2.*(F2+F3));
return;
```

Listing 3A.3 Function gravrk. Used by rk4 (Listing 3A.2) to define the equations of motion for the Kepler problem.

```
function deriv = gravrk(s,t,GM)
% Returns right-hand side of Kepler ODE; used by Runge-Kutta routines
% Inputs
%    s       State vector [r(1) r(2) v(1) v(2)]
%    t       Time (not used)
%    GM      Parameter G*M (gravitational const. * solar mass)
% Output
%    deriv   Derivatives [dr(1)/dt dr(2)/dt dv(1)/dt dv(2)/dt]

%* Compute acceleration
r = [s(1) s(2)];  % Unravel the vector s into position and velocity
v = [s(3) s(4)];
accel = -GM*r/norm(r)^3;  % Gravitational acceleration

%* Return derivatives [dr(1)/dt dr(2)/dt dv(1)/dt dv(2)/dt]
deriv = [v(1) v(2) accel(1) accel(2)];
return;
```

Listing 3A.4 Function rka. Adaptive Runge-Kutta routine. Uses rk4 (Listing 3A.2).

```
function [xSmall, t, tau] = rka(x,t,tau,err,derivsRK,param)
% Adaptive Runge-Kutta routine
% Inputs
%   x         Current value of the dependent variable
%   t         Independent variable (usually time)
%   tau       Step size (usually time step)
%   err       Desired fractional local truncation error
%   derivsRK  Right hand side of the ODE; derivsRK is the
%             name of the function which returns dx/dt
%             Calling format derivsRK(x,t,param).
%   param     Extra parameters passed to derivsRK
% Outputs
%   xSmall    New value of the dependent variable
%   t         New value of the independent variable
%   tau       Suggested step size for next call to rka
```

```
%* Set initial variables
tSave = t;   xSave = x;     % Save initial values
safe1 = .9;   safe2 = 4.;   % Safety factors

%* Loop over maximum number of attempts to satisfy error bound
maxTry = 100;
for iTry=1:maxTry

  %* Take the two small time steps
  half_tau = 0.5 * tau;
  xTemp = rk4(xSave,tSave,half_tau,derivsRK,param);
  t = tSave + half_tau;
  xSmall = rk4(xTemp,t,half_tau,derivsRK,param);

  %* Take the single big time step
  t = tSave + tau;
  xBig = rk4(xSave,tSave,tau,derivsRK,param);

  %* Compute the estimated truncation error
  scale = err * (abs(xSmall) + abs(xBig))/2.;
  xDiff = xSmall - xBig;
  errorRatio = max( abs(xDiff)./(scale + eps) );

  %* Estimate new tau value (including safety factors)
  tau_old = tau;
  tau = safe1*tau_old*errorRatio^(-0.20);
  tau = max(tau,tau_old/safe2);
  tau = min(tau,safe2*tau_old);

  %* If error is acceptable, return computed values
  if (errorRatio < 1)  return;   end
end

%* Issue error message if error bound never satisfied
error('ERROR: Adaptive Runge-Kutta routine failed');
return;
```

Listing 3A.5 Program `lorenz`. Computes the time evolution of the Lorenz model. Uses `rka` (Listing 3A.4) and `lorzrk` (Listing 3A.6).

```
% lorenz - Program to compute the trajectories of the Lorenz
% equations using the adaptive Runge-Kutta method.
clear;  help lorenz;

%* Set initial state x,y,z and parameters r,sigma,b
state = input('Enter the initial position [x y z]: ');
r = input('Enter the parameter r: ');
sigma = 10.;   % Parameter sigma
b = 8./3.;     % Parameter b
```

```
param = [r sigma b];  % Vector of parameters passed to rka
tau = 1;         % Initial guess for the timestep
err = 1.e-3;     % Error tolerance

%* Loop over the desired number of steps
time = 0;
nstep = input('Enter number of steps: ');
for istep=1:nstep

  %* Record values for plotting
  x = state(1);  y = state(2);  z = state(3);
  tplot(istep) = time;  tauplot(istep) = tau;
  xplot(istep) = x;  yplot(istep) = y;  zplot(istep) = z;
  if( rem(istep,50) < 1 )
    fprintf('Finished %g steps out of %g\n',istep,nstep);
  end

  %* Find new state using adaptive Runge-Kutta
  [state, time, tau] = rka(state,time,tau,err,'lorzrk',param);

end

%* Print max and min time step returned by rka
fprintf('Adaptive time step: Max = %g,  Min = %g \n', ...
            max(tauplot(2:nstep)), min(tauplot(2:nstep)));

%* Graph the time series x(t)
figure(1); clf;  % Clear figure 1 window and bring forward
plot(tplot,xplot,'-')
xlabel('Time');  ylabel('x(t)')
title('Lorenz model time series')
pause(1)  % Pause 1 second

%* Graph the x,y,z phase space trajectory
figure(2); clf;  % Clear figure 2 window and bring forward
% Mark the location of the three steady states
x_ss(1) = 0;              y_ss(1) = 0;        z_ss(1) = 0;
x_ss(2) = sqrt(b*(r-1));  y_ss(2) = x_ss(2);  z_ss(2) = r-1;
x_ss(3) = -sqrt(b*(r-1)); y_ss(3) = x_ss(3);  z_ss(3) = r-1;
plot3(xplot,yplot,zplot,'-',x_ss,y_ss,z_ss,'*')
view([30 20]);  % Rotate to get a better view
grid;           % Add a grid to aid perspective
xlabel('x'); ylabel('y'); zlabel('z');
title('Lorenz model phase space');
```

Listing 3A.6 Function `lorzrk`. Used by program `lorenz` (Listing 3A.5); defines equations of motion for the Lorenz model.

```
function deriv = lorzrk(s,t,param)
%  Returns right-hand side of Lorenz model ODEs
%  Inputs
%    s       State vector [x y z]
%    t       Time (not used)
%    param   Parameters [r sigma b]
%  Output
%    deriv   Derivatives [dx/dt dy/dt dz/dt]

%* For clarity, unravel input vectors
x = s(1); y = s(2); z = s(3);
r = param(1); sigma = param(2); b = param(3);

%* Return the derivatives [dx/dt dy/dt dz/dt]
deriv(1) = sigma*(y-x);
deriv(2) = r*x - y - x*z;
deriv(3) = x*y - b*z;
return;
```

APPENDIX B: C++ LISTINGS

Listing 3B.1 Program `orbit`. Computes the orbit of a comet about the Sun using the Euler, Euler-Cromer, fourth-order Runge-Kutta, or adaptive Runge-Kutta method. Uses `rk4` (Listing 3B.2), `gravrk` (Listing 3B.3), and `rka` (Listing 3B.4).

```cpp
// orbit - Program to compute the orbit of a comet.
#include "NumMeth.h"

void gravrk( double x[], double t, double param[], double deriv[] );
void rk4( double x[], int nX, double t, double tau,
   void (*derivsRK)(double x[], double t, double param[], double deriv[]),
   double param[]);
void rka( double x[], int nX, double& t, double& tau, double err,
   void (*derivsRK)(double x[], double t, double param[], double deriv[]),
   double param[]);

void main() {

   //* Set initial position and velocity of the comet.
   double r0, v0;
   cout << "Enter initial radial distance (AU): "; cin >> r0;
   cout << "Enter initial tangential velocity (AU/yr): "; cin >> v0;
```

```cpp
double r[2+1], v[2+1], state[4+1], accel[2+1];
r[1] = r0; r[2] = 0;  v[1] = 0; v[2] = v0;
state[1] = r[1]; state[2] = r[2];   // Used by R-K routines
state[3] = v[1]; state[4] = v[2];
int nState = 4;   // Number of elements in state vector

//* Set physical parameters (mass, G*M)
const double pi = 3.141592654;
double GM = 4*pi*pi;       // Grav. const. * Mass of Sun (au^3/yr^2)
double param[1+1];  param[1] = GM;
double mass = 1.;        // Mass of comet
double adaptErr = 1.e-3;  // Error parameter used by adaptive Runge-Kutta
double time = 0;

//* Loop over desired number of steps using specified
//  numerical method.
cout << "Enter number of steps: ";
int nStep;  cin >> nStep;
cout << "Enter time step (yr): ";
double tau;  cin >> tau;
cout << "Choose a numerical method:" << endl;
cout << "1) Euler,       2) Euler-Cromer, "   << endl
     << "3) Runge-Kutta, 4) Adaptive R-K: ";
int method;  cin >> method;
double *rplot, *thplot, *tplot, *kinetic, *potential;  // Plotting variables
rplot = new double [nStep+1];  thplot = new double [nStep+1];
tplot = new double [nStep+1];
kinetic = new double [nStep+1]; potential = new double [nStep+1];
int iStep;
for( iStep=1; iStep<=nStep; iStep++ ) {

  //* Record position and energy for plotting.
  double normR = sqrt( r[1]*r[1] + r[2]*r[2] );
  double normV = sqrt( v[1]*v[1] + v[2]*v[2] );
  rplot[iStep] = normR;                  // Record position for plotting
  thplot[iStep] = atan2(r[2],r[1]);
  tplot[iStep] = time;
  kinetic[iStep] = 0.5*mass*normV*normV;   // Record energies
  potential[iStep] = - GM*mass/normR;

  //* Calculate new position and velocity using desired method.
  if( method == 1 ) {
    accel[1] = -GM*r[1]/(normR*normR*normR);
    accel[2] = -GM*r[2]/(normR*normR*normR);
    r[1] += tau*v[1];             // Euler step
    r[2] += tau*v[2];
    v[1] += tau*accel[1];
    v[2] += tau*accel[2];
    time += tau;
  }
```

```
  else if( method == 2 ) {
    accel[1] = -GM*r[1]/(normR*normR*normR);
    accel[2] = -GM*r[2]/(normR*normR*normR);
    v[1] += tau*accel[1];
    v[2] += tau*accel[2];
    r[1] += tau*v[1];                    // Euler-Cromer step
    r[2] += tau*v[2];
    time += tau;
  }
  else if( method == 3 ) {
    rk4( state, nState, time, tau, gravrk, param );
    r[1] = state[1]; r[2] = state[2];    // 4th order Runge-Kutta
    v[1] = state[3]; v[2] = state[4];
    time += tau;
  }
  else {
    rka( state, nState, time, tau, adaptErr, gravrk, param );
    r[1] = state[1]; r[2] = state[2];    // Adaptive Runge-Kutta
    v[1] = state[3]; v[2] = state[4];
  }

}


//* Print out the plotting variables:
//    thplot, rplot, potential, kinetic
ofstream thplotOut("thplot.txt"), rplotOut("rplot.txt"),
    tplotOut("tplot.txt"), potentialOut("potential.txt"),
    kineticOut("kinetic.txt");
int i;
for( i=1; i<=nStep; i++ ) {
  thplotOut << thplot[i] << endl;
  rplotOut << rplot[i] << endl;
  tplotOut << tplot[i] << endl;
  potentialOut << potential[i] << endl;
  kineticOut << kinetic[i] << endl;
}

delete [] rplot, thplot, tplot, kinetic, potential;

}
/***** To plot in MATLAB; use the script below ********************
load thplot.txt; load rplot.txt; load tplot.txt;
load potential.txt; load kinetic.txt;
%* Graph the trajectory of the comet.
figure(1); clf;  % Clear figure 1 window and bring forward
polar(thplot,rplot,'+');  % Use polar plot for graphing orbit
xlabel('Distance (AU)');  grid;
pause(1)   % Pause for 1 second before drawing next plot
%* Graph the energy of the comet versus time.
figure(2); clf;   % Clear figure 2 window and bring forward
```

```
totalE = kinetic + potential;    % Total energy
plot(tplot,kinetic,'-.',tplot,potential,'--',tplot,totalE,'-')
legend('Kinetic','Potential','Total');
xlabel('Time (yr)'); ylabel('Energy (M AU^2/yr^2)');
********************************************************************/
```

Listing 3B.2 Function rk4. Fourth-order Runge-Kutta routine.

```
#include "NumMeth.h"

void rk4(double x[], int nX, double t, double tau,
  void (*derivsRK)(double x[], double t, double param[], double deriv[]),
  double param[]) {
// Runge-Kutta integrator (4th order)
// Inputs
//   x         Current value of dependent variable
//   nX        Number of elements in dependent variable x
//   t         Independent variable (usually time)
//   tau       Step size (usually time step)
//   derivsRK  Right hand side of the ODE; derivsRK is the
//             name of the function which returns dx/dt
//             Calling format derivsRK(x,t,param,dxdt).
//   param     Extra parameters passed to derivsRK
// Output
//   x         New value of x after a step of size tau

  double *F1, *F2, *F3, *F4, *xtemp;
  F1 = new double [nX+1];  F2 = new double [nX+1];
  F3 = new double [nX+1];  F4 = new double [nX+1];
  xtemp = new double [nX+1];

  //* Evaluate F1 = f(x,t).
  (*derivsRK)( x, t, param, F1 );

  //* Evaluate F2 = f( x+tau*F1/2, t+tau/2 ).
  double half_tau = 0.5*tau;
  double t_half = t + half_tau;
  int i;
  for( i=1; i<=nX; i++ )
    xtemp[i] = x[i] + half_tau*F1[i];
  (*derivsRK)( xtemp, t_half, param, F2 );

  //* Evaluate F3 = f( x+tau*F2/2, t+tau/2 ).
  for( i=1; i<=nX; i++ )
    xtemp[i] = x[i] + half_tau*F2[i];
  (*derivsRK)( xtemp, t_half, param, F3 );

  //* Evaluate F4 = f( x+tau*F3, t+tau ).
  double t_full = t + tau;
```

```
  for( i=1; i<=nX; i++ )
    xtemp[i] = x[i] + tau*F3[i];
  (*derivsRK)( xtemp, t_full, param, F4 );

  //* Return x(t+tau) computed from fourth-order R-K.
  for( i=1; i<=nX; i++ )
    x[i] += tau/6.*(F1[i] + F4[i] + 2.*(F2[i]+F3[i]));

  delete [] F1, F2, F3, F4, xtemp;
}
```

Listing 3B.3 Function gravrk. Used by rk4 (Listing 3B.2) to define the equations of motion for the Kepler problem.

```
#include "NumMeth.h"

void gravrk(double x[], double t, double param[], double deriv[]) {
//   Returns right-hand side of Kepler ODE; used by Runge-Kutta routines
//   Inputs
//     x       State vector [r(1) r(2) v(1) v(2)]
//     t       Time (not used)
//     param   Parameter G*M (gravitational const. * solar mass)
//   Output
//     deriv   Derivatives [dr(1)/dt dr(2)/dt dv(1)/dt dv(2)/dt]

  //* Compute acceleration
  double GM = param[1];
  double r1 = x[1], r2 = x[2];      // Unravel the vector s into
  double v1 = x[3], v2 = x[4];      // position and velocity
  double normR = sqrt( r1*r1 + r2*r2 );
  double accel1 = -GM*r1/(normR*normR*normR);   // Gravitational acceleration
  double accel2 = -GM*r2/(normR*normR*normR);

  //* Return derivatives [dr[1]/dt dr[2]/dt dv[1]/dt dv[2]/dt]
  deriv[1] = v1;      deriv[2] = v2;
  deriv[3] = accel1;  deriv[4] = accel2;
}
```

Listing 3B.4 Function rka. Adaptive Runge-Kutta routine. Uses rk4 (Listing 3B.2).

```
#include "NumMeth.h"

void rk4(double x[], int nX, double t, double tau,
  void (*derivsRK)(double x[], double t, double param[], double deriv[]),
  double param[]);

void rka( double x[], int nX, double& t, double& tau, double err,
```

```
   void (*derivsRK)(double x[], double t, double param[], double deriv[]),
   double param[]) {
// Adaptive Runge-Kutta routine
// Inputs
//   x          Current value of the dependent variable
//   nX         Number of elements in dependent variable x
//   t          Independent variable (usually time)
//   tau        Step size (usually time step)
//   err        Desired fractional local truncation error
//   derivsRK   Right hand side of the ODE; derivsRK is the
//              name of the function which returns dx/dt
//              Calling format derivsRK(x,t,param).
//   param      Extra parameters passed to derivsRK
// Outputs
//   x          New value of the dependent variable
//   t          New value of the independent variable
//   tau        Suggested step size for next call to rka

  //* Set initial variables
  double tSave = t;        // Save initial value
  double safe1 = 0.9, safe2 = 4.0;   // Safety factors

  //* Loop over maximum number of attempts to satisfy error bound
  double *xSmall, *xBig;
  xSmall = new double [nX+1];   xBig = new double [nX+1];
  int i, iTry, maxTry = 100;
  for( iTry=1; iTry<=maxTry; iTry++ ) {

    //* Take the two small time steps
    double half_tau = 0.5 * tau;
    for( i=1; i<=nX; i++ )
      xSmall[i] = x[i];
    rk4(xSmall,nX,tSave,half_tau,derivsRK,param);
    t = tSave + half_tau;
    rk4(xSmall,nX,t,half_tau,derivsRK,param);

    //* Take the single big time step
    t = tSave + tau;
    for( i=1; i<=nX; i++ )
      xBig[i] = x[i];
    rk4(xBig,nX,tSave,tau,derivsRK,param);

    //* Compute the estimated truncation error
    double errorRatio = 0.0, eps = 1.0e-16;
    for( i=1; i<=nX; i++ ) {
      double scale = err * (fabs(xSmall[i]) + fabs(xBig[i]))/2.0;
      double xDiff = xSmall[i] - xBig[i];
      double ratio = fabs(xDiff)/(scale + eps);
      errorRatio = ( errorRatio > ratio ) ? errorRatio:ratio;
    }
```

```
  //* Estimate new tau value (including safety factors)
  double tau_old = tau;
  tau = safe1*tau_old*pow(errorRatio, -0.20);
  tau = (tau > tau_old/safe2) ? tau:tau_old/safe2;
  tau = (tau < safe2*tau_old) ? tau:safe2*tau_old;

  //* If error is acceptable, return computed values
  if (errorRatio < 1)  {
    for( i=1; i<=nX; i++ )
      x[i] = xSmall[i];
    return;
  }
}

//* Issue error message if error bound never satisfied
cout << "ERROR: Adaptive Runge-Kutta routine failed" << endl;
}
```

Listing 3B.5 Program `lorenz`. Computes the time evolution of the Lorenz model. Uses `rka` (Listing 3B.4) and `lorzrk` (Listing 3B.6).

```
// lorenz - Program to compute the trajectories of the Lorenz
// equations using the adaptive Runge-Kutta method.
#include "NumMeth.h"

void lorzrk(double x[], double t, double param[], double deriv[]);
void rka( double x[], int nX, double& t, double& tau, double err,
  void (*derivsRK)(double x[], double t, double param[], double deriv[]),
  double param[]);

void main() {

  //* Set initial state x,y,z and parameters r,sigma,b
  cout << "Enter initial state (x,y,z)" << endl;
  double x; cout << "x = "; cin >> x;
  double y; cout << "y = "; cin >> y;
  double z; cout << "z = "; cin >> z;
  const int nState = 3;        // Number of elements in state
  double state[nState+1];
  state[1] = x;   state[2] = y;   state[3] = z;
  cout << "Enter the parameter r: ";
  double r;  cin >> r;
  double sigma = 10.;    // Parameter sigma
  double b = 8./3.;      // Parameter b
  double param[3+1];      // Vector of parameters passed to rka
  param[1] = r;  param[2] = sigma; param[3] = b;
  double tau = 1.0;      // Initial guess for the timestep
  double err = 1.e-3;    // Error tolerance
```

```
//* Loop over the desired number of steps
double time = 0;
cout << "Enter number of steps: ";
int iStep, nStep;  cin >> nStep;
double *tplot, *tauplot, *xplot, *yplot, *zplot;
tplot = new double [nStep+1];  tauplot = new double [nStep+1];
xplot = new double [nStep+1];  // Plotting variables
yplot = new double [nStep+1];  zplot = new double [nStep+1];
for( iStep=1; iStep<=nStep; iStep++ ) {

  //* Record values for plotting
  x = state[1]; y = state[2]; z = state[3];
  tplot[iStep] = time;  tauplot[iStep] = tau;
  xplot[iStep] = x;  yplot[iStep] = y;  zplot[iStep] = z;
  if( (iStep % 50) < 1 )
   cout << "Finished " << iStep << " steps out of "
        << nStep << endl;

  //* Find new state using adaptive Runge-Kutta
  rka(state,nState,time,tau,err,lorzrk,param);
}

//* Print max and min time step returned by rka
double maxTau = tauplot[2], minTau = tauplot[2];
int i;
for( i=3; i<=nStep; i++ ) {
  maxTau = (maxTau > tauplot[i]) ? maxTau:tauplot[i];
  minTau = (minTau < tauplot[i]) ? minTau:tauplot[i];
}
cout << "Adaptive time step: Max = " << maxTau <<
                        "  Min = " << minTau << endl;

// Find the location of the three steady states
double x_ss[3+1], y_ss[3+1], z_ss[3+1];
x_ss[1] = 0;                y_ss[1] = 0;        z_ss[1] = 0;
x_ss[2] = sqrt(b*(r-1));  y_ss[2] = x_ss[2]; z_ss[2] = r-1;
x_ss[3] = -sqrt(b*(r-1)); y_ss[3] = x_ss[3]; z_ss[3] = r-1;

//* Print out the plotting variables:
//    tplot, xplot, yplot, zplot, x_ss, y_ss, z_ss
ofstream tplotOut("tplot.txt"), xplotOut("xplot.txt"),
        yplotOut("yplot.txt"), zplotOut("zplot.txt"),
        x_ssOut("x_ss.txt"), y_ssOut("y_ss.txt"),
        z_ssOut("z_ss.txt");
for( i=1; i<=nStep; i++ ) {
  tplotOut << tplot[i] << endl;
  xplotOut << xplot[i] << endl;
  yplotOut << yplot[i] << endl;
  zplotOut << zplot[i] << endl;
```

```
  }
  for( i=1; i<=3; i++ ) {
    x_ssOut << x_ss[i] << endl;
    y_ssOut << y_ss[i] << endl;
    z_ssOut << z_ss[i] << endl;
  }

  delete [] tplot, tauplot, xplot, yplot, zplot; // Release memory

}
/***** To plot in MATLAB; use the script below ********************
load tplot.txt; load xplot.txt; load yplot.txt; load zplot.txt;
load x_ss.txt; load y_ss.txt; load z_ss.txt;
%* Graph the time series x(t)
figure(1); clf;  % Clear figure 1 window and bring forward
plot(tplot,xplot,'-')
xlabel('Time');   ylabel('x(t)')
title('Lorenz model time series')
pause(1)   % Pause 1 second
%* Graph the x,y,z phase space trajectory
figure(2); clf;  % Clear figure 2 window and bring forward
plot3(xplot,yplot,zplot,'-',x_ss,y_ss,z_ss,'*')
view([30 20]);   % Rotate to get a better view
grid;            % Add a grid to aid perspective
xlabel('x'); ylabel('y'); zlabel('z');
title('Lorenz model phase space');
****************************************************************/
```

Listing 3B.6 Function `lorzrk`. Used by program `lorenz` (Listing 3B.5); defines equations of motion for the Lorenz model.

```
#include "NumMeth.h"

void lorzrk(double X[], double t, double param[], double deriv[]) {
// Returns right-hand side of Lorenz model ODEs
// Inputs
//    X       State vector [x y z]
//    t       Time (not used)
//    param   Parameters [r sigma b]
// Output
//    deriv   Derivatives [dx/dt dy/dt dz/dt]

  //* For clarity, unravel input vectors
  double x = X[1]; double y = X[2]; double z = X[3];
  double r = param[1]; double sigma = param[2]; double b = param[3];

  //* Return the derivatives [dx/dt dy/dt dz/dt]
  deriv[1] = sigma*(y-x);
  deriv[2] = r*x - y - x*z;
```

```
  deriv[3] = x*y - b*z;
  return;
}
```

Chapter 4

Solving Systems of Equations

In this chapter we learn how to solve systems of equations, both linear and nonlinear. You already know the basic algorithm for linear systems: Eliminate variables until you have a single equation in a single unknown. For nonlinear problems we develop an iterative scheme that at each step solves a linearized version of the equations. To maintain continuity, the discussion is motivated by the calculation of steady states, an important topic in ordinary differential equations.

4.1 LINEAR SYSTEMS OF EQUATIONS

Steady States of ODEs

In the last chapter we saw how to solve ODEs of the form

$$\frac{d\mathbf{x}}{dt} = \mathbf{f}(\mathbf{x}, t) \tag{4.1}$$

where $\mathbf{x} = [\ x_1 \quad x_2 \quad \ldots \quad x_N\ ]$. Given the initial condition for the N variables, $x_i(t = 0)$, we can compute the time series $x_i(t)$ by a variety of methods (e.g., Runge-Kutta).

The examples we have studied so far have been autonomous systems where $\mathbf{f}(\mathbf{x}, t) = \mathbf{f}(\mathbf{x})$, that is, $\mathbf{f}$ does not depend explicitly on time. For autonomous systems, there often exists an important class of initial conditions for which $x_i(t) = x_i(0)$ for all i and t. These points in the N-dimensional space of our variables are called *steady states*. If we start at a steady state we stay there forever. Locating steady states for ODEs is important since they are used in bifurcation analysis.[115]

It is easy to see that $\mathbf{x}^* = [\ x_1^* \quad x_2^* \quad \ldots \quad x_N^*\ ]$ is a steady state if and only if

$$\mathbf{f}(\mathbf{x}^*) = 0 \tag{4.2}$$

or

$$f_i(x_1^*, \ldots, x_N^*) = 0; \quad \text{for all } i \tag{4.3}$$

since this implies that $d\mathbf{x}^*/dt = 0$. Locating steady states now reduces to the problem of solving N equations in the N unknowns x_i^*. This problem is also called "finding the roots of $f(x)$."

As an example, consider the simple pendulum; the state is described by the angle θ and the angular velocity ω (see Section 2.2). The steady states are found by solving the nonlinear equations

$$-\frac{g}{L}\sin\theta^* = 0; \quad \omega^* = 0 \tag{4.4}$$

The roots are $\theta^* = 0, \pm\pi, \pm 2\pi, \ldots$ and $\omega^* = 0$. Of course not all systems of equations are so easy to solve.

It should be clear that root finding has many more applications than the computation of steady states. In this chapter we consider a variety of ways to solve both linear and nonlinear systems. In this section and the next we consider linear systems, leaving nonlinear systems to the latter part of the chapter.

Gaussian Elimination

The problem of solving $f_i(\{x_j\}) = 0$ is divided into two important classes. In this section we consider the easier case of when $f_i(\{x_j\})$ is a linear function. The problem then reduces to solving a linear system of N equations with N unknowns

$$
\begin{array}{ccccccccc}
a_{11}x_1 & + & a_{12}x_2 & + & \ldots & + & a_{1N}x_N & - & b_1 & = & 0 \\
a_{21}x_1 & + & a_{22}x_2 & + & \ldots & + & a_{2N}x_N & - & b_2 & = & 0 \\
\vdots & & \vdots & & & & & & \vdots \\
a_{N1}x_1 & + & a_{N2}x_2 & + & \ldots & + & a_{NN}x_N & - & b_N & = & 0
\end{array}
\tag{4.5}
$$

or in matrix form

$$\mathbf{Ax} - \mathbf{b} = 0 \tag{4.6}$$

where

$$
\mathbf{A} = \begin{bmatrix} a_{11} & a_{12} & \ldots \\ a_{21} & a_{22} & \ldots \\ \vdots & \vdots & \ddots \end{bmatrix}; \quad
\mathbf{x} = \begin{bmatrix} x_1 \\ x_2 \\ \vdots \end{bmatrix}; \quad
\mathbf{b} = \begin{bmatrix} b_1 \\ b_2 \\ \vdots \end{bmatrix}
\tag{4.7}
$$

You learned how to solve linear sets of equations in grade school.* Combine equations to eliminate variables until you have an equation with only one unknown. Let's do a simple example to review how this procedure works. Take

---

*These problems usually start with something like, "Johnny has twice as many apples as Suzy, and ...."

the equations

$$\begin{array}{rcrcrcr} x_1 & + & x_2 & + & x_3 & = & 6 \\ -x_1 & + & 2x_2 & & & = & 3 \\ 2x_1 & & & + & x_3 & = & 5 \end{array} \tag{4.8}$$

We want to eliminate x_1 from the second and third equations. To accomplish this we add the first equation to the second and subtract twice the first equation from the third. This gives us

$$\begin{array}{rcrcrcr} x_1 & + & x_2 & + & x_3 & = & 6 \\ & & 3x_2 & + & x_3 & = & 9 \\ & & -2x_2 & - & x_3 & = & -7 \end{array} \tag{4.9}$$

Next, we eliminate x_2 from the last equation by multiplying the second equation by $-\frac{2}{3}$ (the ratio of the x_2 terms) and subtracting it from the third, giving

$$\begin{array}{rcrcrcr} x_1 & + & x_2 & + & x_3 & = & 6 \\ & & 3x_2 & + & x_3 & = & 9 \\ & & & & -\frac{1}{3}x_3 & = & -1 \end{array} \tag{4.10}$$

This procedure is called *forward elimination*. For N equations, we eliminate x_1 from equations 2 through N, eliminate x_1 and x_2 from equations 3 through N, and so on. The last equation will only contain the variable x_N.

Returning to the example, it is now trivial to solve the third equation for $x_3 = 3$. We can now substitute this value into the second equation to get $3x_2 + 3 = 9$ so $x_2 = 2$. Finally, plug the values of x_2 and x_3 into the first equation to get $x_1 = 1$. This second procedure is called *backsubstitution*. It should be clear how this works with larger systems of equations. Using the last equation to get x_N, this is plugged into the penultimate equation to obtain x_{N-1} and so forth.

This method of solving systems of linear equations by forward elimination and backsubstitution is called *Gaussian elimination*.[50] It is a rote sequence of steps that is simple for a computer to perform systematically. For N equations in N unknowns, the computation time for Gaussian elimination goes as N^3. Fortunately, if the system is sparse (most coefficients are zero), this calculation time can be greatly reduced (see Section 9.3).

Pivoting

Gaussian elimination is a simple procedure, yet you should be aware of its pitfalls. To illustrate the first possible source of problems, consider the set of equations

$$\begin{array}{rcrcrcr} \epsilon x_1 & + & x_2 & + & x_3 & = & 5 \\ x_1 & + & x_2 & & & = & 3 \\ x_1 & & & + & x_3 & = & 4 \end{array} \tag{4.11}$$

In the limit $\epsilon \to 0$, the solution is $x_1 = 1, x_2 = 2, x_3 = 3$. For these equations, the forward elimination step would start by multiplying the first equation by

$(1/\epsilon)$ and subtracting it from the second and third equations, giving

$$
\begin{array}{rcrcrcr}
\epsilon x_1 & + & x_2 & + & x_3 & = & 5 \\
 & & (1 - 1/\epsilon)x_2 & - & (1/\epsilon)x_3 & = & 3 - 5/\epsilon \\
 & & -(1/\epsilon)x_2 & + & (1 - 1/\epsilon)x_3 & = & 4 - 5/\epsilon
\end{array}
\tag{4.12}
$$

Of course, if $\epsilon = 0$ we have big problems, since the $1/\epsilon$ factors blow up. Even if $\epsilon \neq 0$, but is small, we are going to have serious round-off problems. Suppose that $1/\epsilon$ is so large that $(C - 1/\epsilon) \to -1/\epsilon$, where C is of the order of unity. Our equations, after round-off, become

$$
\begin{array}{rcrcrcr}
\epsilon x_1 & + & x_2 & + & x_3 & = & 5 \\
 & & -(1/\epsilon)x_2 & - & (1/\epsilon)x_3 & = & -5/\epsilon \\
 & & -(1/\epsilon)x_2 & - & (1/\epsilon)x_3 & = & -5/\epsilon
\end{array}
\tag{4.13}
$$

At this point it is clear that we cannot proceed since the second and third equations in (4.13) are now identical; we no longer have three independent equations. The next step of forward elimination would transform the third equation in (4.13) into the tautology $0 = 0$.

Fortunately, there is a simple fix: Interchange the order of the equations before performing the forward elimination. Exchanging the first and second equations in (4.11),

$$
\begin{array}{rcrcrcr}
x_1 & + & x_2 & & & = & 3 \\
\epsilon x_1 & + & x_2 & + & x_3 & = & 5 \\
x_1 & + & & & x_3 & = & 4
\end{array}
\tag{4.14}
$$

The first step of forward elimination gives us the equations

$$
\begin{array}{rcrcrcr}
x_1 & + & x_2 & & & = & 3 \\
 & & (1 - \epsilon)x_2 & + & x_3 & = & 5 - 3\epsilon \\
 & & -x_2 & + & x_3 & = & 4 - 3
\end{array}
\tag{4.15}
$$

Round-off eliminates the ϵ terms, giving

$$
\begin{array}{rcrcrcr}
x_1 & + & x_2 & & & = & 3 \\
 & & x_2 & + & x_3 & = & 5 \\
 & & -x_2 & + & x_3 & = & 1
\end{array}
\tag{4.16}
$$

The second step of forward elimination removes x_2 from the third equation in (4.16) using the second equation,

$$
\begin{array}{rcrcrcr}
x_1 & + & x_2 & & & = & 3 \\
 & & x_2 & + & x_3 & = & 5 \\
 & & & & 2x_3 & = & 6
\end{array}
\tag{4.17}
$$

You can easily check that backsubstitution gives $x_1 = 1, x_2 = 2$ and $x_3 = 3$, which is the correct answer in the limit $\epsilon \to 0$.

Algorithms that rearrange the equations when they spot small diagonal elements are said to *pivot*. Even if all the elements of a matrix are initially of comparable magnitude, the forward elimination procedure may produce small elements on the main diagonal. The price of pivoting is just a little extra book-keeping in the program, but it is essential to use pivoting for all but the smallest matrices. Even with pivoting, you cannot guarantee being safe from round-off problems when dealing with very large matrices.

Determinants

It is easy to obtain the determinant of a matrix using Gaussian elimination. After completing forward elimination, one simply computes the product of the coefficients of the diagonal elements. Take our original example, Equation (4.8); the matrix is

$$\mathbf{A} = \begin{bmatrix} 1 & 1 & 1 \\ -1 & 2 & 0 \\ 2 & 0 & 1 \end{bmatrix} \tag{4.18}$$

At the completion of forward elimination, Equation (4.10), the product of the coefficients of the diagonal elements is $(1)(3)(-\frac{1}{3}) = -1$, which, you can check to confirm, is the determinant of $\mathbf{A}$. This method is slightly more complicated when pivoting is used. If the number of pivots is odd, the determinant is the negative of the product of the coefficients of the diagonal elements. It should now be obvious that Cramer's rule is a computationally inefficient way to solve sets of linear equations.

Gaussian Elimination in MATLAB

We do not need to write a MATLAB program to perform Gaussian elimination with pivoting. Instead we can use MATLAB's built-in matrix manipulation capabilities. In MATLAB, Gaussian elimination is a primitive routine, much like the sine and square root functions. As with any "canned" routine, you should understand, in general, how it works and recognize possible pitfalls, especially computational ones (e.g., does `sqrt(-1)` return an imaginary number or an error?).

MATLAB implements Gaussian elimination using the slash, / , and back-slash, \ , operators. The linear system of equations, $\mathbf{xA} = \mathbf{b}$, where $\mathbf{x}$ and $\mathbf{b}$ are row vectors, is solved using the slash operator as $\mathbf{x} = \mathbf{b}/\mathbf{A}$. The linear system of equations, $\mathbf{Ax} = \mathbf{b}$, where $\mathbf{x}$ and $\mathbf{b}$ are column vectors, is solved using the backslash operator as $\mathbf{x} = \mathbf{A}\backslash\mathbf{b}$. As an example, take Equation (4.11) with $\epsilon = 0$, written in matrix form

$$\begin{bmatrix} 0 & 1 & 1 \\ 1 & 1 & 0 \\ 1 & 0 & 1 \end{bmatrix} \begin{bmatrix} x_1 \\ x_2 \\ x_3 \end{bmatrix} = \begin{bmatrix} 5 \\ 3 \\ 4 \end{bmatrix} \tag{4.19}$$

Using MATLAB interactively, the solution is illustrated below:

```
>>A=[0 1 1;1 1 0;1 0 1];
```

```
>>b=[5; 3; 4];
>>x=A\b;
>>disp(x);
     1
     2
     3
```

Clearly, MATLAB uses pivoting in this case. The slash and backslash operators may be used in the same way in programs. If MATLAB "thinks" that the computation is of questionable accuracy (for example, due to round-off), a warning message is issued. The MATLAB command `det(A)` returns the determinant of a matrix.

Gaussian Elimination with C++ Matrix Objects

Using multi-dimensional arrays in C++ is awkward. The standard ways to declare an $M \times N$ array of double precision floating-point numbers are

```
    const int M = 3, N = 3;
    double A[M][N];
```

for static allocation and

```
    int i, M, N;
    ... // Assign values to M and N
    double **A;
    A = new double *[M];       // Allocate vector of pointers
    for( i=0; i<M; i++ )
      A[i] = new double [N]; // Allocate memory for each row
```

for dynamic allocation (don't forget to deallocate each row with a `delete []`). Static allocation is simple but rigid, since the dimensions are fixed constants. When a static array is passed to a function, that function must declare an array with the same number of columns in order for the array to be indexed properly. Dynamic allocation is flexible but clumsy, although the details can be hidden within separate functions. Accessing elements outside the array bounds is a common programming bug and one that is difficult to track down with dynamic arrays.

C++ allows us to correct these deficiencies by creating our own variable type. These user-defined variables are called *object classes*. From here on we'll use the `Matrix` class for declaring one- and two-dimensional arrays of floating-point numbers. This class is entirely defined within the `Matrix.h` header file (see Appendix 4.C). Some examples of declaring `Matrix` objects are

```
    int M = 3, N = 3;
    Matrix A(M,N), b(N), x(3);
```

Although this resembles static array allocation notice that the dimensions are *not* fixed constants. Both one-dimensional vectors and two-dimensional matrices can be declared; the former are treated as single column matrices. The values in these variables can be set by the assignment statements

```
A(1,1) = 0;  A(1,2) = 1;  A(1,3) = 1;
A(2,1) = 1;  A(2,2) = 1;  A(2,3) = 0;
A(3,1) = 1;  A(3,2) = 0;  A(3,3) = 1;
b(1) = 5;  b(2) = 3;  b(3) = 4;
```

The format for `Matrix` objects is `A(i,j)`, rather than `A[i][j]`, to distinguish them from conventional C++ arrays.

A `Matrix` object knows its dimensions, and you can get them by using the `nRow()` and `nCol()` member functions. For example

```
int m = A.nRow(), n = A.nCol();
```

sets m and n to the dimensions of `A`. Bounds checking is performed whenever a `Matrix` object is indexed. The lines

```
Matrix newA(3,7); // Non-square matrix (3 by 7)
newA(4,5) = 0;    // Out-of-bounds error
```

produce the error message[†]

```
Assertion failed: i > 0 && i <= nRow_
```

when the program is run. This means that at least one index i did not satisfy the condition $0 < i \le N$. Matrix objects automatically deallocate their memory when they go out of scope, so it is not necessary to invoke `delete`.

To set all the elements of a `Matrix` object to a given value use the `set(double x)` member function, for example `A.set(1.0)`. An entire matrix can be assigned to equal another of the same size (e.g., `Matrix C(3,3); C=A;`). However, unlike MATLAB matrices, arithmetic operations (`A+C`, `2*A`, etc.) are *not* allowed. These operations must be carried out element by element, typically using `for` loops.

The Gaussian elimination routine `ge`, which uses `Matrix` objects, is outlined in Table 4.1. Declaring and assigning the matrix `A` and the vectors `b` and `x` as above, a program can call this routine as

```
double determ = ge(A,b,x); // Gaussian elimination
cout << x(1) << ", " << x(2) << ", " << x(3) << endl;
cout << "Determinant = " << determ << endl;
```

to solve the linear system $\mathbf{Ax} = \mathbf{b}$ and compute the determinant of $\mathbf{A}$.

[†]Depending on your C++ compiler, the wording of this error message may differ slightly.

Table 4.1: Outline of function **ge**, which solves a system of linear equations $\mathbf{Ax} = \mathbf{b}$ by Gaussian elimination. The function also returns the determinant of $\mathbf{A}$.

- *Inputs*: $\mathbf{A}$, $\mathbf{b}$.

- *Outputs*: $\mathbf{x}$, det $\mathbf{A}$.

- Set scale factor, $s_i = \max_j(|A_{i,j}|)$, for each row.

- Loop over rows $k = 1, \ldots, (N-1)$.

  - Select pivot row from $\max_j(|A_{j,k}|/s_j)$.
  - Perform pivoting using row index list.
  - Perform forward elimination.

- Compute determinant, det $\mathbf{A}$, as product of diagonal elements.

- Perform backsubstitution.

See page 134 for the program listing.

EXERCISES

1. Find the steady states of the one-variable Ginzburg-Landau equation,

$$\frac{dx}{dt} = -x + \lambda x^3$$

where x is a real number and λ is a real parameter. Sketch the right-hand side of this equation as a function of x for positive and negative values of λ. Notice that the number of steady states varies with λ. [Pencil]

2. Show that the three steady states of the Lorenz model [Equation (3.32)] are: $x^* = y^* = z^* = 0$, and $x^* = y^* = \pm\sqrt{b(r-1)}$, $z^* = r - 1$ if $\sigma \neq 0$. What are the steady states when $\sigma = 0$? [Pencil]

3. (a) Find the steady states of the Lotka-Volterra equations (see Exercise 3.22). [Pencil] (b) The trajectories in the Lotka-Volterra model are periodic cycles called *limit cycles*. Modify your program from Exercise 3.22 to compute the time-averaged values of x and y as,

$$\langle x \rangle = \frac{1}{T} \int_0^T x(t)\, dt \approx \frac{1}{N} \sum_{n=1}^N x_n$$

and similarly for $\langle y \rangle$. Show that $\langle x \rangle = x^*$, $\langle y \rangle = y^*$ as $N \to \infty$. [Computer]

4. The Brusselator is a simple model for oscillatory chemical systems such as the Belousov-Zhabotinski reaction.[92] The time evolution of the concentration of two chemical species, x and y, is described by the ODEs,

$$\frac{dx}{dt} = A + x^2 y - (B+1)x$$

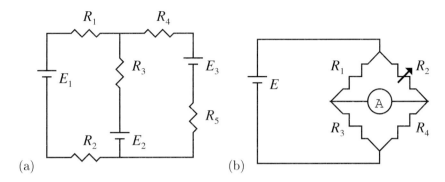

Figure 4.1: (a) A simple resistor network. (b) Wheatstone bridge.

$$\frac{dy}{dt} \quad = \quad Bx - x^2 y$$

where $A > 0, B > 0$ are constants. (a) Find the single steady state of this model. [Pencil] (b) Write a program to compute $x(t)$ and $y(t)$ for a given initial condition $x(0) \geq 0$ and $y(0) \geq 0$. Plot a few trajectories in the xy plane, and mark the location of the steady state. Investigate cases where $B/(1 + A^2)$ is less than, greater than, and equal to one. [Computer]

5. The best way to understand an algorithm is to work out an example by hand. (a) Using Gaussian elimination solve

$$\begin{bmatrix} 1 & 1 & 1 \\ 3 & 1 & 0 \\ -1 & 0 & 1 \end{bmatrix} \begin{bmatrix} x_1 \\ x_2 \\ x_3 \end{bmatrix} = \begin{bmatrix} 6 \\ 11 \\ -2 \end{bmatrix}$$

Show the intermediate steps. Compute the determinant of the matrix using your forward elimination results. (b) Interchange the second and third equations and repeat part (a). [Pencil]

6. Using Kirchhoff's laws in circuit problems involves solving a set of simultaneous equations. Consider the simple circuit illustrated in Figure 4.1a. Write a program that computes the currents given the resistances and voltages as inputs. Be sure to check your program by working out a simple case by hand. Have your program produce a graph of the power delivered to resistor 5 as a function of E_2 for the range of values $E_2 = 0$ V to $E_2 = 20$ V. For the other values, use $R_1 = R_2 = 1\Omega$, $R_3 = R_4 = 2\Omega$, $R_5 = 5\Omega$, $E_1 = 2$ V, $E_3 = 5$ V. [Computer]

7. Consider the Wheatstone bridge illustrated in Figure 4.1b. There is no current flow through the ammeter when $R_1 = R_2 R_3 / R_4$, allowing us to measure R_1 if the other resistances are known (R_2 is a variable resistor). At first glance this suggests that it makes no difference whether $R_3 = R_4 = 1\Omega$, 100Ω, or $10^4\Omega$. Graph the current through the ammeter as a function of R_2 for each of these cases. Take $E = 6$V, $R_1 = 1\Omega$, and the internal resistance of the ammeter to be $10^{-3}\Omega$. Given that the sensitivity of the ammeter is 10^{-4} amps, approximately how accurate is each bridge? [Computer]

8. A problem you probably remember from freshman physics is the resistor cube (Figure 4.2). If the resistances are all equal, then the equivalent resistance of the

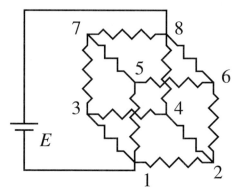

Figure 4.2: Resistor cube.

cube may be obtained by making use of the symmetry. (a) Write a program that uses Kirchhoff's laws to solve the resistor cube problem for the case where all the resistors are 1Ω except the resistor between vertices 5 and 7. Plot the equivalent resistance as a function of this variable resistor. (b) Repeat using 1–3 as the variable resistor. (c) Repeat using 3–7 as the variable resistor. [Computer]

4.2   MATRIX INVERSE

Matrix Inverse and Gaussian Elimination

In the previous section we reviewed how to solve a set of simultaneous equations by Gaussian elimination. However, if you are familiar with linear algebra, you would probably write the solution of

$$\mathbf{Ax} = \mathbf{b} \tag{4.20}$$

as

$$\mathbf{x} = \mathbf{A}^{-1}\mathbf{b} \tag{4.21}$$

where $\mathbf{A}^{-1}$ is the matrix inverse of $\mathbf{A}$. It should not be surprising that the calculation of a matrix inverse is related to the algorithm for solving a set of linear equations. Usually the inverse of a matrix is computed by repeated applications of Gaussian elimination (or a variant called LU decomposition).

The inverse of a matrix is defined by the equation

$$\mathbf{AA}^{-1} = \mathbf{I} \tag{4.22}$$

where $\mathbf{I}$ is the identity matrix

$$\mathbf{I} = \begin{bmatrix} 1 & 0 & 0 & \cdots \\ 0 & 1 & 0 & \cdots \\ 0 & 0 & 1 & \cdots \\ \vdots & \vdots & \vdots & \ddots \end{bmatrix} \tag{4.23}$$

Defining the column vectors,

$$\mathbf{e}_1 = \begin{bmatrix} 1 \\ 0 \\ 0 \\ \vdots \end{bmatrix} ; \quad \mathbf{e}_2 = \begin{bmatrix} 0 \\ 1 \\ 0 \\ \vdots \end{bmatrix} ; \quad \ldots ; \quad \mathbf{e}_N = \begin{bmatrix} \vdots \\ 0 \\ 0 \\ 1 \end{bmatrix} \qquad (4.24)$$

we may write the identity matrix as a row vector of column vectors,

$$\mathbf{I} = \begin{bmatrix} \mathbf{e}_1 & \mathbf{e}_2 & \ldots & \mathbf{e}_N \end{bmatrix} \qquad (4.25)$$

If we solve the linear set of equations,

$$\mathbf{A}\mathbf{x}_1 = \mathbf{e}_1 \qquad (4.26)$$

The solution vector $\mathbf{x}_1$ is the first column of the inverse $\mathbf{A}^{-1}$. If we proceed this way with the other $\mathbf{e}$'s we will compute all the columns of $\mathbf{A}^{-1}$. In other words, our matrix inverse equation $\mathbf{A}\mathbf{A}^{-1} = \mathbf{I}$ is solved by writing it as

$$\mathbf{A} \begin{bmatrix} \mathbf{x}_1 & \mathbf{x}_2 & \ldots & \mathbf{x}_N \end{bmatrix} = \begin{bmatrix} \mathbf{e}_1 & \mathbf{e}_2 & \ldots & \mathbf{e}_N \end{bmatrix} \qquad (4.27)$$

After computing the $\mathbf{x}$'s, we build $\mathbf{A}^{-1}$ as

$$\mathbf{A}^{-1} = \begin{bmatrix} \mathbf{x}_1 & \mathbf{x}_2 & \ldots & \mathbf{x}_N \end{bmatrix} = \begin{bmatrix} (\mathbf{x}_1)_1 & (\mathbf{x}_2)_1 & \cdots & (\mathbf{x}_N)_1 \\ (\mathbf{x}_1)_2 & (\mathbf{x}_2)_2 & \cdots & (\mathbf{x}_N)_2 \\ \vdots & \vdots & \ddots & \vdots \\ (\mathbf{x}_1)_N & (\mathbf{x}_2)_N & \cdots & (\mathbf{x}_N)_N \end{bmatrix} \qquad (4.28)$$

where $(\mathbf{x}_i)_j$ is the jth element of $\mathbf{x}_i$.

Table 4.2 outlines the function `inv` for computing the inverse of a matrix; a C++ version of it is given in the appendices. In MATLAB, `inv(A)` is a built-in function that returns the inverse of matrix `A`. It is possible to solve a system of linear equations using the matrix inverse, but doing so is usually overkill. An exception would be the case where you want to solve a number of similar problems in which the matrix $\mathbf{A}$ is fixed but the vector $\mathbf{b}$ takes many different values. Finally, here's a handy formula to keep around: The inverse of a 2×2 matrix is

$$\mathbf{A}^{-1} = \frac{1}{a_{11}a_{22} - a_{12}a_{21}} \begin{bmatrix} a_{22} & -a_{12} \\ -a_{21} & a_{11} \end{bmatrix} \qquad (4.29)$$

For larger matrices the formulas very quickly become very messy.

Singular and Ill-Conditioned Matrices

Before getting back to physics, let's discuss another possible pitfall in solving linear systems of equations. Consider the equations

$$x_1 + x_2 = 1 \qquad (4.30)$$
$$2x_1 + 2x_2 = 2$$

Table 4.2: Outline of function `inv`, which computes the inverse of a matrix and its determinant.

- *Inputs*: **A**.

- *Outputs*: $\mathbf{A}^{-1}$, det **A**.

- Matrix **b** is initialized to the identity matrix.

- Set scale factor, $s_i = \max_j(|A_{i,j}|)$, for each row.

- Loop over rows $k = 1, \ldots, (N-1)$.

  - Select pivot row from $\max_j(|A_{j,k}|/s_j)$.
  - Perform pivoting, using row index list.
  - Perform forward elimination.

- Compute determinant as product of diagonal elements.

- Perform backsubstitution.

See page 135 for the program listing.

Notice that we really don't have two independent equations, since the second is just twice the first. These equations do not have a unique solution. If we try to do forward elimination, we get

$$x_1 + x_2 = 1 \tag{4.31}$$
$$0 = 0$$

and are stuck.

Another way to look at this problem is to see that the matrix

$$\mathbf{A} = \begin{bmatrix} 1 & 1 \\ 2 & 2 \end{bmatrix} \tag{4.32}$$

has no inverse. A matrix without an inverse is said to be *singular*. A singular matrix also has a determinant of zero. Singular matrices are not always trivially spotted; would you have guessed that the matrix

$$\begin{bmatrix} 1 & 2 & 3 \\ 4 & 5 & 6 \\ 7 & 8 & 9 \end{bmatrix}$$

was singular?

Here is what happens in MATLAB when we try to solve (4.30)

```
>>A = [1 1;2 2];
>>b = [1; 2];
>>x = A\b;
Warning: Matrix is singular to working precision.
```

Depending on your compiler, the C++ routine `inv` will probably return infinity or issue an error message. In some cases the routine calculates an inverse for a singular matrix, but naturally the answer is spurious.

Sometimes a matrix is not singular but is so close to being singular that round-off may "push it over the edge." A trivial example would be

$$\begin{bmatrix} 1+\epsilon & 1 \\ 2 & 2 \end{bmatrix} \tag{4.33}$$

where ϵ is a very small number. The condition of a matrix indicates how close it is to being singular; a matrix is said to be ill-conditioned if it is almost singular. If you suspect that you are dealing with an ill-conditioned matrix when solving $\mathbf{Ax} = \mathbf{b}$, then compute the absolute error, $|\mathbf{Ax} - \mathbf{b}|/|\mathbf{b}|$, to check if $\mathbf{x}$ is an accurate solution.

Formally, the condition number is defined as the normalized "distance" between a matrix and the nearest singular matrix.[33] There are a variety of ways to define this distance, depending on the kind of norm used. The MATLAB function `cond(A)` returns the two-norm condition number of a matrix `A`. The MATLAB function `rcond(A)` returns an estimate of the reciprocal of the one-norm condition number of a matrix `A`. The latter function is more efficient but less reliable. A matrix with a large condition number is ill-conditioned. As a rule of thumb, $\log_{10}(\text{cond(A)})$ is the number of significant (decimal) digits that you can expect to lose in Gaussian elimination. A small determinant can sometimes tip us off that a matrix might be ill-conditioned, but the condition number is the real criterion.[59]

Coupled Harmonic Oscillators

At the beginning of this chapter, I discussed the problem of finding the steady states of ODEs. A canonical example of a system with linear interactions is the case of coupled harmonic oscillators. Consider the system shown in Figure 4.3; the spring constants are $k_1, \ldots, k_4$. The positions of the blocks, relative to the left wall, are x_1, x_2, and x_3. The distance between the walls is L_{w}, and the unstretched lengths of the springs are $L_1, \ldots, L_4$. The blocks are of negligible width.

The equation of motion for block i is

$$\frac{dx_i}{dt} = v_i; \qquad \frac{dv_i}{dt} = \frac{1}{m_i} F_i \tag{4.34}$$

where F_i is the net force on block i. At the steady state, the velocities, v_i, are zero and the net forces, F_i, are zero. This is just static equilibrium. Our job

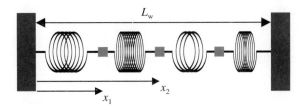

Figure 4.3: System of blocks coupled by springs anchored between walls.

now is to find the rest positions of the masses. Explicitly, the net forces are

$$
\begin{aligned}
F_1 &= -k_1(x_1 - L_1) + k_2(x_2 - x_1 - L_2) \\
F_2 &= -k_2(x_2 - x_1 - L_2) + k_3(x_3 - x_2 - L_3) \\
F_3 &= -k_3(x_3 - x_2 - L_3) + k_4(L_{\mathrm{w}} - x_3 - L_4)
\end{aligned}
\tag{4.35}
$$

or in matrix form,

$$
\begin{bmatrix} F_1 \\ F_2 \\ F_3 \end{bmatrix}
=
\begin{bmatrix}
-k_1 - k_2 & k_2 & 0 \\
k_2 & -k_2 - k_3 & k_3 \\
0 & k_3 & -k_3 - k_4
\end{bmatrix}
\begin{bmatrix} x_1 \\ x_2 \\ x_3 \end{bmatrix}
$$
$$
-
\begin{bmatrix}
-k_1 L_1 + k_2 L_2 \\
-k_2 L_2 + k_3 L_3 \\
-k_3 L_3 + k_4 (L_4 - L_{\mathrm{w}})
\end{bmatrix}
\tag{4.36}
$$

For convenience, we abbreviate the above equation as $\mathbf{F} = \mathbf{Kx} - \mathbf{b}$. In matrix form the symmetries are clear, and we see that it would not be difficult to extend the problem to larger systems of coupled oscillators. At static equilibrium the net forces are zero, so we obtain the rest positions of the masses by solving $\mathbf{Kx} = \mathbf{b}$, which you are asked to do in the exercises.

EXERCISES

9. To help you understand how the matrix inversion algorithm works, find $\mathbf{K}^{-1}$ by hand [see Equation (4.36)]. Take $k_1 = k_2 = k_3 = k_4 = 1$. Check your result by showing that $\mathbf{KK}^{-1} = \mathbf{I}$. [Pencil]

10. Write a program to solve for the rest positions of the masses in the harmonic oscillator system described above. Try your program with the following values:

(a) $\mathbf{k} = [1\ 2\ 3\ 4]$; $\mathbf{L} = [1\ 1\ 1\ 1]$; $L_{\mathrm{w}} = 4$
(b) $\mathbf{k} = [1\ 2\ 3\ 4]$; $\mathbf{L} = [1\ 1\ 1\ 1]$; $L_{\mathrm{w}} = 10$
(c) $\mathbf{k} = [1\ 1\ 1\ 1]$; $\mathbf{L} = [2\ 2\ 1\ 1]$; $L_{\mathrm{w}} = 4$
(d) $\mathbf{k} = [1\ 1\ 1\ 0]$; $\mathbf{L} = [2\ 2\ 1\ 1]$; $L_{\mathrm{w}} = 4$
(e) $\mathbf{k} = [0\ 1\ 1\ 0]$; $\mathbf{L} = [2\ 2\ 1\ 1]$; $L_{\mathrm{w}} = 4$

Using general physical arguments, explain the results in each case. [Computer]

11. The force on the right wall is $F_{\mathrm{rw}} = -k_4(L_{\mathrm{w}} - x_3 - L_4)$. Write a program to solve $\mathbf{Kx} = \mathbf{b}$, evaluate F_{rw}, and plot it as a function of L_{w}. For the other parameters,

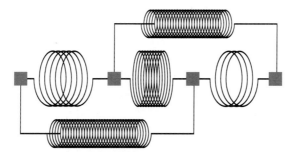

Figure 4.4: Spring-mass system with next-nearest neighbor couplings.

select any nontrivial values. Verify numerically that the force on the right wall is

$$F_{\mathrm{rw}} = -k_0(L_{\mathrm{w}} - L_0)$$

where $L_0 = L_1 + L_2 + L_3 + L_4$ and

$$\frac{1}{k_0} = \frac{1}{k_1} + \frac{1}{k_2} + \frac{1}{k_3} + \frac{1}{k_4}$$

This is the law of equivalent springs. Since the matrix $\mathbf{K}$ is fixed, it is more efficient to use matrix inverse rather than Gaussian elimination. [Computer]

12.   Gaussian elimination is not the only way to compute the inverse of a matrix. Consider the iterative scheme,

$$\mathbf{X}_{n+1} = 2\mathbf{X}_n - \mathbf{X}_n \mathbf{A} \mathbf{X}_n$$

where $\mathbf{X}_1$ is the initial guess for $\mathbf{A}^{-1}$. Write a computer program that uses this scheme to compute the inverse of a matrix. Test your program with a few matrices, including some that are singular, and comment on your results. How good does your initial guess have to be? When might this scheme be preferable to Gaussian elimination? For more details, see Exercise 4.22. [Computer]

13.   Consider the spring-mass system in Figure 4.4 (a simple model of a short polymer molecule). The blocks are free to move but only along the x-axis. The springs connecting adjacent blocks have spring constant k_1, while the two outer springs have stiffness k_2. All the springs have a rest length of one. (a) Write the matrix equation for the equilibrium positions of the blocks. [Pencil] (b) Write a program that plots the total length of the system as a function of k_1/k_2. [Computer]

14.   Consider a system of coupled masses (such as in Figure 4.3) with $N - 1$ blocks. The spring constants are

(a) $k_1 = k_2 = k_3 = \ldots = k_N = 1$
(b) $k_1 = 2k_2 = 3k_3 = \ldots = Nk_N = 1$
(c) $k_1 = 4k_2 = 9k_3 = \ldots = N^2 k_N = 1$
(d) $k_1 = 2k_2 = 4k_3 = \ldots = 2^{(N-1)} k_N = 1$

Compute the condition number of $\mathbf{K}$ using MATLAB's cond function, and plot it as a function of N. Estimate the value of N for which cond($\mathbf{K}$) exceeds 10^{12}. [MATLAB]

15. For a set of data points (x_i, y_i) with $i = 1, \ldots, N$, one can find the polynomial

$$p(x) = a_1 + a_2 x + \ldots + a_N x^{N-1}$$

that passes through these points (i.e., $p(x_i) = y_i$) by solving the linear system

$$
\begin{bmatrix}
1 & x_1 & x_1^2 & \ldots & x_1^{N-1} \\
1 & x_2 & x_2^2 & \ldots & x_2^{N-1} \\
\vdots & \vdots & \ddots & \vdots \\
1 & x_N & x_N^2 & \ldots & x_N^{N-1}
\end{bmatrix}
\begin{bmatrix}
a_1 \\
a_2 \\
\vdots \\
a_N
\end{bmatrix}
=
\begin{bmatrix}
y_1 \\
y_2 \\
\vdots \\
y_N
\end{bmatrix}
$$

or $\mathbf{Va} = \mathbf{y}$ where $\mathbf{V}$ is the *Vandermonde matrix*. Write a program to compute $\mathbf{V}^{-1}$ taking $x_i = i$ (evenly spaced data). Plot the error $E = \max\{|D_{ij}|\}$ versus N where $\mathbf{D} \equiv \mathbf{VV}^{-1} - \mathbf{I}$. Vandermonde matrices are very ill-conditioned, so the error will grow quickly with N. [Computer]

4.3 *NONLINEAR SYSTEMS OF EQUATIONS

One-Variable Newton's Method

Now that we know how to solve systems of linear equations, we proceed to the more general (and more challenging) case of solving systems of nonlinear equations. This problem is difficult enough that it is worthwhile to first consider the single variable case. We want to solve for x^* such that

$$f(x^*) = 0 \tag{4.37}$$

where $f(x)$ is now some general function. There are a number of different methods available for one-variable root finding. If you've had a numerical analysis course you are probably familiar with bisection, the secant method, and perhaps other algorithms. There are also specialized algorithms for when $f(x)$ is a polynomial (e.g., MATLAB's `roots` function). Instead of going through all of these schemes, we will concentrate on the single most useful method for the general N-variable case.

Newton's method [3] is based on the Taylor expansion of $f(x)$ around the root x^*. Suppose that we make an initial guess as to the location of the root; call this guess x_1. Our error may be written as $\delta x = x_1 - x^*$ or $x^* = x_1 - \delta x$. Writing out the Taylor expansion of $f(x^*)$,

$$f(x^*) = f(x_1 - \delta x) = f(x_1) - \delta x \frac{df(x_1)}{dx} + O(\delta x^2) \tag{4.38}$$

Notice that since x^* is a root, $f(x^*) = 0$, so we may solve for δx as

$$\delta x = \frac{f(x_1)}{f'(x_1)} + O(\delta x^2) \tag{4.39}$$

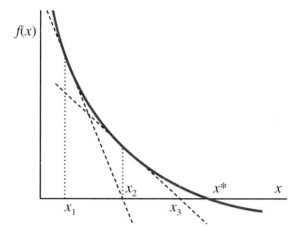

Figure 4.5: Graphical representation of Newton's method.

We drop the $O(\delta x^2)$ term (this will be our truncation error) and use the resulting expression for δx to "correct" our initial guess. The new guess is

$$x_2 = x_1 - \delta x = x_1 - \frac{f(x_1)}{f'(x_1)} \tag{4.40}$$

This procedure may be iterated as

$$x_{n+1} = x_n - \frac{f(x_n)}{f'(x_n)} \tag{4.41}$$

to improve our guess further until the desired accuracy is obtained.

The iterative procedure described above may best be understood graphically (Figure 4.5). Notice that at each step we use the derivative of $f(x)$ to draw the tangent line of the function. Where this tangent line intersects the x-axis is our next guess for the root. Effectively, we are linearizing $f(x)$ and solving the linear problem. If the function is well behaved, then it will be approximately linear in some neighborhood near the root x^*.

A few notes about Newton's method: First, when it converges, it finds a root very quickly; but, unfortunately, it sometimes diverges (e.g., $f'(x_n) \approx 0$) and fails. For well-behaved functions, Newton's method is guaranteed to converge if we get "close enough" to the root. For this reason it is sometimes combined with a slower but surer root-finding algorithm, such as bisection. Second, if there are multiple roots, the root to which the method converges depends on the initial guess (and it may not be the root you want). There are procedures (e.g., "deflation") for finding multiple roots using Newton's method. Finally, the method is slower when finding tangent roots, such as for $f(x) = x^2$.

Multivariable Newton's Method

It is not difficult to generalize Newton's method to N-variable problems. Now our unknown $\mathbf{x} = [\ x_1 \quad x_2 \quad \ldots \quad x_N\ ]$ is a row vector, and we want to find the zeros (roots) of the row vector function

$$\mathbf{f}(\mathbf{x}) = [\ f_1(\mathbf{x}) \quad f_2(\mathbf{x}) \quad \ldots \quad f_N(\mathbf{x})\ ] \tag{4.42}$$

Again, we make an initial guess as to the location of the root, calling this guess $\mathbf{x}_1$. Our error may be written as $\delta\mathbf{x} = \mathbf{x}_1 - \mathbf{x}^*$ or $\mathbf{x}^* = \mathbf{x}_1 - \delta\mathbf{x}$. Using the Taylor expansion of $\mathbf{f}(\mathbf{x}_1)$,

$$\mathbf{f}(\mathbf{x}^*) = \mathbf{f}(\mathbf{x}_1 - \delta\mathbf{x}) = \mathbf{f}(\mathbf{x}_1) - \delta\mathbf{x}\,\mathbf{D}(\mathbf{x}_1) + O(\delta\mathbf{x}^2) \tag{4.43}$$

where the Jacobian matrix, $\mathbf{D}$, is defined as

$$D_{ij}(\mathbf{x}) = \frac{\partial f_j(\mathbf{x})}{\partial x_i} \tag{4.44}$$

Since $\mathbf{x}^*$ is a root, $f(\mathbf{x}^*) = 0$, we may solve for $\delta\mathbf{x}$ as before. Dropping the error term, we may write (4.43) as

$$\mathbf{f}(\mathbf{x}_1) = \delta\mathbf{x}\,\mathbf{D}(\mathbf{x}_1) \tag{4.45}$$

or

$$\delta\mathbf{x} = \mathbf{f}(\mathbf{x}_1)\mathbf{D}^{-1}(\mathbf{x}_1) \tag{4.46}$$

Our new guess is

$$\mathbf{x}_2 = \mathbf{x}_1 - \delta\mathbf{x} = \mathbf{x}_1 - \mathbf{f}(\mathbf{x}_1)\mathbf{D}^{-1}(\mathbf{x}_1) \tag{4.47}$$

This procedure may be iterated to improve our guess further until the desired accuracy is obtained. Since $\mathbf{D}$ changes at each iteration, it would be wasteful to compute its inverse. Instead, use Gaussian elimination on (4.45) to solve for $\delta\mathbf{x}$, and compute the new guess as $\mathbf{x}_2 = \mathbf{x}_1 - \delta\mathbf{x}$.

Newton's Method Program

To demonstrate Newton's method, we'll use it to compute the steady states of the Lorenz model (3.32). A program that finds the roots of a system of equations using Newton's method, called `newtn`, is outlined in Table 4.3. This program calls the function `fnewt` (Table 4.4), which given $\mathbf{x} = [x\ y\ z]$ returns

$$\mathbf{f} = \begin{bmatrix} \sigma(y - x) \\ rx - y - xz \\ xy - bz \end{bmatrix} ; \qquad \mathbf{D} = \begin{bmatrix} -\sigma & r - z & y \\ \sigma & -1 & x \\ 0 & -x & -b \end{bmatrix} \tag{4.48}$$

For $r = 28, \sigma = 10$, and $b = 8/3$, the three roots are $[x\ y\ z] = [0\ 0\ 0]$, $[6\sqrt{2}\ 6\sqrt{2}\ 27]$, and $[-6\sqrt{2}\ -6\sqrt{2}\ 27]$.

An example of the output from the MATLAB version of `newtn` is given below; notice that the program obtains the root $[6\sqrt{2}\ 6\sqrt{2}\ 27]$.

Table 4.3: Outline of program `newtn`, which finds a root for a set of equations.

- Set initial guess $\mathbf{x}_1$ and parameters $\{\lambda_k\}$.

- Loop over desired number of steps.

    - Evaluate function $\mathbf{f}(\mathbf{x}_n; \{\lambda_k\})$ and its Jacobian matrix $\mathbf{D}$.
    - Find $\delta\mathbf{x}$ by Gaussian elimination [see (4.45)].
    - Update the estimate for the root as $\mathbf{x}_{n+1} = \mathbf{x}_n - \delta\mathbf{x}$.

- Print the final estimate for the root.

- Plot the iterations from initial guess to final estimate.

See pages 129 and 131 for program listings.

```
>>newtn

  newtn - Program to solve a system of nonlinear equations
  using Newton's method.  Equations defined by function fnewt.

Enter the initial guess (row vector): [50 50 50]
Enter the parameter a: [28 10 8/3]
After 10 iterations the root is
    8.4853     8.4853    27.0000
```

The graph showing the convergence to the root for this run is illustrated in Figure 4.6. Notice the difference between the iterative approach to the root and the trajectory for the Lorenz ODEs. Other initial conditions converge to other roots. For example, starting from [2 2 2], we converge to [0 0 0]; starting from [5 5 5], we converge to $[-6\sqrt{2} \ -6\sqrt{2} \ 27]$. Interestingly, starting from [4 4 15], the method converges to a root only after making an incredibly distant excursion away from the origin.

Continuation

The primary difficulty with Newton's method is the necessity of providing a good initial guess for the root. Often our problem is of the form

$$\mathbf{f}(\mathbf{x}^*; \lambda) = 0 \tag{4.49}$$

where λ is some parameter in the problem. Suppose that we know a root $\mathbf{x}_o^*$ for the value λ_o but need to find a root for a different value λ_a. Intuitively, if $\lambda_a \approx \lambda_o$, then $\mathbf{x}_o^*$ would be a good initial guess for finding $\mathbf{x}_o^*$ using Newton's method. But what if $\lambda_a \not\approx \lambda_o$; is there any way to make use of our known root?

Table 4.4: Outline of function `fnewt`, which is used by `newtn` to find the steady states of the Lorenz equations.

- *Inputs*: $\mathbf{x} = [x, y, z]$, $\lambda = [r, \sigma, b]$.

- *Outputs*: $\mathbf{f}$, $\mathbf{D}$.

- Evaluate $\mathbf{f}$ for the Lorenz model [see (4.48)].

- Evaluate the Jacobian matrix $\mathbf{D}$ for the Lorenz model.

See pages 131 and 133 for program listings.

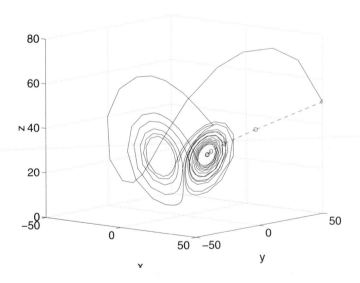

Figure 4.6: Graph of successive estimates of the root as obtained by `newtn` using the initial guess $[x\ y\ z] = [50\ 50\ 50]$ and the parameters $[r\ \sigma\ b] = [28\ 10\ 8/3]$. Also shown is the trajectory from the `lorenz` program.

The answer is yes, and the technique is known as *continuation*. The idea is to sneak up on λ_a by defining the following sequence of λ's:

$$\lambda_i = \lambda_o + (\lambda_a - \lambda_o)\frac{i}{N} \tag{4.50}$$

for $i = 1, \ldots, N$. Using Newton's method, we solve $f(\mathbf{x}_1^*; \lambda_1) = 0$ with $\mathbf{x}_o^*$ as the initial guess. If N is sufficiently large, then $\lambda_1 \approx \lambda_o$, and the method should converge quickly. We then use $\mathbf{x}_1^*$ as an initial guess to solve $f(\mathbf{x}_2^*; \lambda_2) = 0$; the sequence continues until we reach our desired value of λ_a. Continuation has the added benefit that we can use it when we are interested in knowing not just a single root, but knowing how $\mathbf{x}^*$ varies with λ.

EXERCISES

16. Write a program that uses Newton's method to find the roots of functions. Test your program on the following cases:

   (a) $f(x) = \sin(x)$; $x_1 = 1$ (b) $f(x) = \sin(x)$; $x_1 = 2$
   (c) $f(x) = x^{10}$; $x_1 = 1$ (d) $f(x) = \tanh(x)$; $x_1 = 1$
   (e) $f(x) = \tanh(x)$; $x_1 = 3$ (f) $f(x) = \ln(x)$; $x_1 = 3$

Have the program make a plot of x_i versus i. Think carefully about how you want the program to decide when to stop the iteration process. [Computer]

17.   One of the fundamental problems in celestial mechanics is solving the Kepler equation [37],

$$E - e\sin(E) = M$$

where E is the eccentric anomaly, M is the mean anomaly, and e is the eccentricity. Write a program to find E using Newton's method. Run your program for a variety of values $0 < e < 1$, and plot E as a function of M for $0 < M < 2\pi$. [Computer]

18.   Consider a particle in a quantum square well potential of depth $V < 0$ and half-width a. The energy eigenvalues, $E > V$, are given by the transcendental equation

$$\sqrt{-E} = \sqrt{E - V} \tan\left(\frac{a}{\hbar}\sqrt{2m(E - V)}\right)$$

for the even states and

$$\sqrt{-E} = -\sqrt{E - V} \operatorname{ctn}\left(\frac{a}{\hbar}\sqrt{2m(E - V)}\right)$$

for the odd states.[111] Write a program to obtain the first 10 energy eigenvalues of an electron for $V = -13.6$ eV and $a = 20a_0$, where a_0 is the Bohr radius. [Computer]

19.   For blackbody radiation, the radiant energy per unit volume in the wavelength range λ to $\lambda + d\lambda$ is [108]

$$u(\lambda)\,d\lambda = \frac{8\pi}{\lambda^5}\frac{hc}{\exp(hc/\lambda kT) - 1}\,d\lambda$$

where T is the temperature of the body, c is the speed of light, h is Planck's constant, and k is Boltzmann's constant. Show that the wavelength at which $u(\lambda)$ is maximum may be written as $\lambda_{\max} = \alpha hc/kT$, where α is a constant. Determine the value of α numerically from the resulting transcendental equation. [Computer]

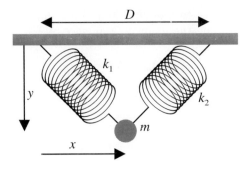

Figure 4.7: Mass hanging from two springs.

20.   (a) Modify `fnewt` to solve for the steady states of the Lotka-Volterra model (see Exercise 3.22). Try a variety of initial conditions. (b) Modify `fnewt` to solve for the steady state of the Brusselator model (see Exercise 4.4). Try a variety of initial conditions. [Computer]

21.   The program `newtn` is not very sophisticated because it always performs the same number of iterations. Modify the program so that it stops when the answer is within some user-specified tolerance or if the procedure appears to be diverging hopelessly. [Computer]

22.   Newton's method gives us an iterative technique for finding the inverse of a matrix. Consider the function $\mathbf{F}(\mathbf{X}) = \mathbf{A} - \mathbf{X}^{-1}$; the root is $\mathbf{X}^* = \mathbf{A}^{-1}$. Show that Newton's method gives us the iterative scheme

$$\mathbf{X}_{n+1} = 2\mathbf{X}_n - \mathbf{X}_n \mathbf{A} \mathbf{X}_n$$

where $\mathbf{X}_1$ is the initial guess for $\mathbf{A}^{-1}$. When might this scheme be preferable to Gaussian elimination? [Pencil]

23.   Write a version of `newtn` that does not require the user to supply the matrix $\mathbf{D}$. Instead, the program estimates it from $\mathbf{f}(\mathbf{x})$ by centered finite difference. The program should determine the appropriate value for the grid spacing h (possibly with the user supplying an initial estimate). [Computer]

24. For the simple, two-dimensional spring-mass system illustrated in Figure 4.7, the potential energy may be written as

$$V(x,y) = \frac{1}{2}k_1\left(\sqrt{x^2 + y^2} - L_1\right)^2 + \frac{1}{2}k_2\left(\sqrt{(x - D)^2 + y^2} - L_2\right)^2 - mgy$$

where k_1 and k_2 are the spring constants, L_1 and L_2 are the rest lengths of the springs, m is the mass of the object, and $g = 9.81\mathrm{m/s}^2$. At static equilibrium, $\mathbf{F} = -\nabla V = 0$. Write a program to solve for the positions x and y at static equilibrium. What is the equilibrium position for $k_1 = 10$ N/m, $k_2 = 20$ N/m, $L_1 = L_2 = 0.1$ m, $D = 0.1$ m, $m = 0.1$ kg, and $g = 9.81\mathrm{m/s}^2$? [Computer]

25.   Modify your program from the previous exercise to use continuation. Using the spring constant k_2 as the variable parameter ($k_2 = 0$ to 20 N/m), obtain a graph of the equilibrium position for $k_1 = 10$ N/m, $L_1 = L_2 = 0.1$ m, $D = 0.1$ m, $m = 0.1$ kg, and $g = 9.81\mathrm{m/s}^2$. [Computer]

BEYOND THIS CHAPTER

As you will see in the latter half of this book, many numerical schemes make use of linear algebra. For this reason it is one of the richest branches of numerical analysis. Many facets of matrix computations are covered by Golub and Van Loan [59]. Gaussian elimination and pivoting strategies are discussed in detail by Forsythe and Moler [50]. Three principal concerns in numerical linear algebra are storage, speed, and singularity. In computational physics we often employ very large matrices and memory allocation can be a concern. Often these matrices are sparse (that is, most of the elements are zero), and full storage can be avoided. The computational expense of Gaussian elimination increases quickly with the size of the matrix. Again, if a matrix is sparse, the computation cost can often be reduced significantly. Sparse matrix techniques are discussed in Section 9.3.

For solving very large systems of equations, iterative techniques, such as Gauss-Seidel, provide alternatives to Gaussian elimination. These iterative techniques are described in the context of solving elliptic partial differential equations in Section 8.1. For further discussion, see Varga [129].

Ill-conditioned matrices are common in numerical analysis (e.g., Vandermonde matrices in least squares curve fitting). Singular value decomposition (SVD) is a general technique for solving ill-conditioned problems.[49] It may also be used to solve overdetermined (more equations than unknowns) or underdetermined (more unknowns than equations) problems.

There are many schemes besides Newton's method for finding roots; you'll find them described in practically any numerical analysis textbook. If you are finding the roots of the characteristic polynomial of a matrix to get the eigenvalues, you're barking up the wrong tree. There are much better ways to get eigenvalues and eigenvectors. One complication in using Newton's method is the necessity of supplying the derivative, $f'(x)$. A natural solution is to evaluate this derivative numerically; the secant method is a variant based on this idea. For multidimensional problems, secant methods are not always suitable, since the resulting estimated Jacobian matrix can be singular. An alternative is a set of schemes known as quasi-Newton methods; see Broyden [28] for a survey.

APPENDIX A: MATLAB LISTINGS

Listing 4A.1 Program `newtn`. Finds steady states of the Lorenz model using Newton's method. Uses `fnewt` (Listing 4A.2).

```
% newtn - Program to solve a system of nonlinear equations
% using Newton's method.  Equations defined by function fnewt.
clear all;  help newtn;  % Clear memory and print header

%* Set initial guess and parameters
x0 = input('Enter the initial guess (row vector): ');
```

```
x = x0;  % Copy initial guess
xp(:,1) = x(:); % Record initial guess for plotting
a = input('Enter the parameter a: ');

%* Loop over desired number of steps
nStep = 10;    % Number of iterations before stopping
for iStep=1:nStep

  %* Evaluate function f and its Jacobian matrix D
  [f D] = fnewt(x,a);       % fnewt returns value of f and D
  %* Find dx by Gaussian elimination
  dx = f/D;
  %* Update the estimate for the root
  x = x - dx;                % Newton iteration for new x
  xp(:,iStep+1) = x(:); % Save current estimate for plotting

end
%* Print the final estimate for the root
fprintf('After %g iterations the root is\n',nStep);
disp(x);

%* Plot the iterations from initial guess to final estimate
figure(1); clf;  % Clear figure 1 window and bring forward
subplot(1,2,1) % Left plot
  plot3(xp(1,:),xp(2,:),xp(3,:),'o-',...
      x(1),x(2),x(3),'*');
  xlabel('x');  ylabel('y'); zlabel('z');
  view([-37.5, 30]);  % Viewing angle
  title(sprintf('Initial guess is %g  %g  %g',x0(1),x0(2),x0(3)));
  grid; drawnow;
subplot(1,2,2) % Right plot
  plot3(xp(1,:),xp(2,:),xp(3,:),'o-',...
      x(1),x(2),x(3),'*');
  xlabel('x');  ylabel('y'); zlabel('z');
  view([-127.5, 30]);  % Viewing angle
  title(sprintf('After %g iterations, root is %g  %g  %g',...
                          nStep,x(1),x(2),x(3)));
  grid; drawnow;
% Plot data from lorenz (if available). To write lorenz data, use:
% >>save xplot; save yplot; save zplot;
% after running the lornez program.
flag = input('Plot data from lorenz program? (1=Yes/0=No): ');
if( flag == 1 )
  figure(2); clf;  % Clear figure 1 window and bring forward
  load xplot; load yplot; load zplot;
  plot3(xplot,yplot,zplot,'-',xp(1,:),xp(2,:),xp(3,:),'o--');
  xlabel('x'); ylabel('y'); zlabel('z');
  view([40 10]);  % Rotate to get a better view
  grid;           % Add a grid to aid perspective
end
```

Listing **4A.2** Function `fnewt`. Used by program `newtn`; defines the equations of the Lorenz model along with the Jacobian matrix.

```
function [f,D] = fnewt(x,a)
%  Function used by the N-variable Newton's method
%  Inputs
%    x      State vector [x y z]
%    a      Parameters [r sigma b]
%  Outputs
%    f      Lorenz model r.h.s. [dx/dt dy/dt dz/dt]
%    D      Jacobian matrix, D(i,j) = df(j)/dx(i)

% Evaluate f(i)
f(1) = a(2)*(x(2)-x(1));
f(2) = a(1)*x(1)-x(2)-x(1)*x(3);
f(3) = x(1)*x(2)-a(3)*x(3);

% Evaluate D(i,j)
D(1,1) = -a(2);          % df(1)/dx(1)
D(1,2) = a(1)-x(3);      % df(2)/dx(1)
D(1,3) = x(2);           % df(3)/dx(1)
D(2,1) = a(2);           % df(1)/dx(2)
D(2,2) = -1;             % df(2)/dx(2)
D(2,3) = x(1);           % df(3)/dx(2)
D(3,1) = 0;              % df(1)/dx(3)
D(3,2) = -x(1);          % df(2)/dx(3)
D(3,3) = -a(3);          % df(3)/dx(3)
return;
```

APPENDIX B: C++ LISTINGS

Listing **4B.1** Program `newtn`. Finds steady states of the Lorenz model using Newton's method. Uses `fnewt` (Listing 4B.2) and `ge` (Listing 4B.3).

```
// newtn - Program to solve a system of nonlinear equations
// using Newton's method.  Equations defined by function fnewt.
#include "NumMeth.h"

void ge(Matrix a, Matrix b, Matrix& x);
void fnewt(Matrix x, Matrix a, Matrix& f, Matrix& D);

void main() {

  //* Set initial guess and parameters
  int iStep, nStep = 10;   // Number of iterations before stopping
```

```
int nVars = 3, nParams = 3;   // Number of variables and parameters
Matrix x(nVars), xp(nVars,nStep+1);
cout << "Enter the initial guess: " << endl;
int i,j;
for( i=1; i<=nVars; i++ ) {
  cout << " x(" << i << ") = "; cin >> x(i);
  xp(i,1) = x(i); // Record initial guess for plotting
}
Matrix a(nParams);
cout << "Enter the parameters: " << endl;
for( i=1; i<=nParams; i++ ) {
  cout << "a(" << i << ") = "; cin >> a(i);
}

//* Loop over desired number of steps
Matrix f(nVars), D(nVars,nVars), dx(nVars);
for( iStep=1; iStep<=nStep; iStep++ )  {

  //* Evaluate function f and its Jacobian matrix D
  fnewt(x,a,f,D);        // fnewt returns value of f and D
  for( i=1; i<=nVars; i++ )
    for( j=i+1; j<=nVars; j++ )  {
      double temp = D(i,j);
      D(i,j) = D(j,i);       // Transpose of matrix D
      D(j,i) = temp;
    }

  //* Find dx by Gaussian elimination
  ge(D,f,dx);

  //* Update the estimate for the root
  for( i=1; i<=nVars; i++ ) {
    x(i) -= dx(i);             // Newton iteration for new x
    xp(i,iStep+1) = x(i); // Save current estimate for plotting
  }
}

//* Print the final estimate for the root
cout << "After " << nStep << " iterations the root is:" << endl;
for( i=1; i<=nVars; i++ )
  cout << "x(" << i << ") = " << x(i) << endl;

//* Print out the plotting variable: xp
ofstream xpOut("xp.txt");
for( i=1; i<=nVars; i++ ) {
  for( int j=1; j<=nStep; j++ )
    xpOut << xp(i,j) << ", ";
  xpOut << xp(i,nStep+1) << endl;
}
}
```

```
/***** To plot in MATLAB; use the script below ********************
load xp.txt;
%* Plot the iterations from initial guess to final estimate
figure(1); clf;  % Clear figure 1 window and bring forward
subplot(1,2,1) % Left plot
  plot3(xp(1,:),xp(2,:),xp(3,:),'o-');
  xlabel('x');  ylabel('y'); zlabel('z');
  view([-37.5, 30]);  % Viewing angle
  grid; drawnow;
subplot(1,2,2) % Right plot
  plot3(xp(1,:),xp(2,:),xp(3,:),'o-');
  xlabel('x');  ylabel('y'); zlabel('z');
  view([-127.5, 30]);  % Viewing angle
  grid; drawnow;
% Plot data from lorenz (if available).
flag = input('Plot data from lorenz program? (1=Yes/0=No): ');
if( flag == 1 )
  figure(2); clf;  % Clear figure 1 window and bring forward
  load xplot.txt; load yplot.txt; load zplot.txt;
  plot3(xplot,yplot,zplot,'-',xp(1,:),xp(2,:),xp(3,:),'o--');
  xlabel('x'); ylabel('y'); zlabel('z');
  view([40 10]);  % Rotate to get a better view
  grid;           % Add a grid to aid perspective
end
********************************************************************/
```

Listing 4B.2 Function `fnewt`. Used by program `newtn`; defines the equations of the Lorenz model along with the Jacobian matrix.

```cpp
#include "NumMeth.h"

void fnewt(Matrix x, Matrix a, Matrix& f, Matrix& D) {
// Function used by the N-variable Newton's method
// Inputs
//   x    State vector [x y z]
//   a    Parameters [r sigma b]
// Outputs
//   f    Lorenz model r.h.s. [dx/dt dy/dt dz/dt]
//   D    Jacobian matrix, D(i,j) = df(j)/dx(i)

  // Evaluate f(i)
  f(1) = a(2)*(x(2)-x(1));
  f(2) = a(1)*x(1)-x(2)-x(1)*x(3);
  f(3) = x(1)*x(2)-a(3)*x(3);

  // Evaluate D(i,j)
  D(1,1) = -a(2);          // df(1)/dx(1)
  D(1,2) = a(1)-x(3);      // df(2)/dx(1)
  D(1,3) = x(2);           // df(3)/dx(1)
```

```
    D(2,1) = a(2);          // df(1)/dx(2)
    D(2,2) = -1;            // df(2)/dx(2)
    D(2,3) = x(1);          // df(3)/dx(2)
    D(3,1) = 0;             // df(1)/dx(3)
    D(3,2) = -x(1);         // df(2)/dx(3)
    D(3,3) = -a(3);         // df(3)/dx(3)
}
```

Listing 4B.3 Function ge. Performs Gaussian elimination with pivoting.

```
#include "NumMeth.h"

// ge - Function to perform Gaussian elimination to solve A*x = b
//      using scaled column pivoting
// Inputs
//    A    -     Matrix A (N by N)
//    b    -     Vector b (N by 1)
// Outputs
//    x    -     Vector x (N by 1)
//   determ -   Determinant of matrix A   (return value)
double ge(Matrix A, Matrix b, Matrix& x) {

  int N = A.nRow();
  assert( N == A.nCol() && N == b.nRow() && N == x.nRow() );

  int i, j, k;
  Matrix scale(N);  // Scale factor
  int *index;  index = new int [N+1];   // Row index list

  //* Set scale factor, scale(i) = max( |A(i,j)| ), for each row
  for( i=1; i<=N; i++ ) {
    index[i] = i;            // Initialize row index list
    double scaleMax = 0.0;
    for( j=1; j<=N; j++ )
      scaleMax = (scaleMax > fabs(A(i,j))) ? scaleMax : fabs(A(i,j));
    scale(i) = scaleMax;
  }

  //* Loop over rows k = 1, ..., (N-1)
  int signDet = 1;
  for( k=1; k<=(N-1); k++ ) {
    //* Select pivot row from max( |A(j,k)/s(j)| )
    double ratiomax = 0.0;
    int jPivot = k;
    for( i=k; i<=N; i++ ) {
      double ratio = fabs(A(index[i],k))/scale(index[i]);
      if( ratio > ratiomax ) {
        jPivot = i;
        ratiomax = ratio;
```

```cpp
    }
  }
  //* Perform pivoting using row index list
  int indexJ = index[k];
  if( jPivot != k ) {                // Pivot
    indexJ = index[jPivot];
    index[jPivot] = index[k];      // Swap index jPivot and k
    index[k] = indexJ;
    signDet *= -1;                 // Flip sign of determinant
  }
  //* Perform forward elimination
  for( i=k+1; i<=N; i++ ) {
    double coeff = A(index[i],k)/A(indexJ,k);
    for( j=k+1; j<=N; j++ )
      A(index[i],j) -= coeff*A(indexJ,j);
    A(index[i],k) = coeff;
    b(index[i]) -= A(index[i],k)*b(indexJ);
  }
}
//* Compute determinant as product of diagonal elements
double determ = signDet;       // Sign of determinant
for( i=1; i<=N; i++ )
  determ *= A(index[i],i);

//* Perform backsubstitution
x(N) = b(index[N])/A(index[N],N);
for( i=N-1; i>=1; i-- ) {
  double sum = b(index[i]);
  for( j=i+1; j<=N; j++ )
    sum -= A(index[i],j)*x(j);
  x(i) = sum/A(index[i],i);
}

delete [] index;   // Release allocated memory
return( determ );
}
```

Listing 4B.4 Function inv. Computes the inverse of a matrix with pivoting.

```cpp
#include "NumMeth.h"

// Compute inverse of matrix
double inv(Matrix A, Matrix& Ainv)
// Input
//    A    -    Matrix A (N by N)
// Outputs
//    Ainv  -    Inverse of matrix A (N by N)
//    determ -    Determinant of matrix A (return value)
{
```

```
int N = A.nRow();
assert( N == A.nCol() );

Ainv = A;  // Copy matrix to ensure Ainv is same size

int i, j, k;
Matrix scale(N), b(N,N);    // Scale factor and work array
int *index;   index = new int [N+1];

//* Matrix b is initialized to the identity matrix
b.set(0.0);
for( i=1; i<=N; i++ )
  b(i,i) = 1.0;

//* Set scale factor, scale(i) = max( |a(i,j)| ), for each row
for( i=1; i<=N; i++ ) {
  index[i] = i;                 // Initialize row index list
  double scalemax = 0.;
  for( j=1; j<=N; j++ )
    scalemax = (scalemax > fabs(A(i,j))) ? scalemax : fabs(A(i,j));
  scale(i) = scalemax;
}

//* Loop over rows k = 1, ..., (N-1)
int signDet = 1;
for( k=1; k<=N-1; k++ ) {
  //* Select pivot row from max( |a(j,k)/s(j)| )
  double ratiomax = 0.0;
  int jPivot = k;
  for( i=k; i<=N; i++ ) {
    double ratio = fabs(A(index[i],k))/scale(index[i]);
    if( ratio > ratiomax ) {
      jPivot=i;
      ratiomax = ratio;
    }
  }
  //* Perform pivoting using row index list
  int indexJ = index[k];
  if( jPivot != k ) {            // Pivot
    indexJ = index[jPivot];
    index[jPivot] = index[k];   // Swap index jPivot and k
    index[k] = indexJ;
    signDet *= -1;              // Flip sign of determinant
  }
  //* Perform forward elimination
  for( i=k+1; i<=N; i++ ) {
    double coeff = A(index[i],k)/A(indexJ,k);
    for( j=k+1; j<=N; j++ )
      A(index[i],j) -= coeff*A(indexJ,j);
```

```
      A(index[i],k) = coeff;
      for( j=1; j<=N; j++ )
        b(index[i],j) -= A(index[i],k)*b(indexJ,j);
   }
 }
 //* Compute determinant as product of diagonal elements
 double determ = signDet;      // Sign of determinant
 for( i=1; i<=N; i++ )
   determ *= A(index[i],i);

 //* Perform backsubstitution
 for( k=1; k<=N; k++ ) {
   Ainv(N,k) = b(index[N],k)/A(index[N],N);
   for( i=N-1; i>=1; i--) {
     double sum = b(index[i],k);
     for( j=i+1; j<=N; j++ )
       sum -= A(index[i],j)*Ainv(j,k);
     Ainv(i,k) = sum/A(index[i],i);
   }
 }

 delete [] index;  // Release allocated memory
 return( determ );
}
```

APPENDIX C: C++ MATRIX CLASS

Listing 4C.1 Header file `Matrix.h`. Defines the C++ `Matrix` class.

```
#include <assert.h>  // Defines the assert function.

class Matrix {

public:

// Default Constructor. Creates a 1 by 1 matrix; sets value to zero.
Matrix () {
  nRow_ = 1; nCol_ = 1;
  data_ = new double [1];  // Allocate memory
  set(0.0);                // Set value of data_[0] to 0.0
}

// Regular Constructor. Creates an nR by nC matrix; sets values to zero.
// If number of columns is not specified, it is set to 1.
Matrix(int nR, int nC = 1) {
  assert(nR > 0 && nC > 0);    // Check that nC and nR both > 0.
```

```
    nRow_ = nR; nCol_ = nC;
    data_ = new double [nR*nC];   // Allocate memory
    assert(data_ != 0);           // Check that memory was allocated
    set(0.0);                     // Set values of data_[] to 0.0
}


// Copy Constructor.
// Used when a copy of an object is produced
// (e.g., passing to a function by value)
Matrix(const Matrix& mat) {
  this->copy(mat);   // Call private copy function.
}


// Destructor. Called when a Matrix object goes out of scope.
~Matrix() {
  delete [] data_;   // Release allocated memory
}


// Assignment operator function.
// Overloads the equal sign operator to work with
// Matrix objects.
Matrix& operator=(const Matrix& mat) {
  if( this == &mat ) return *this;  // If two sides equal, do nothing.
  delete [] data_;                  // Delete data on left hand side
  this->copy(mat);                  // Copy right hand side to l.h.s.
  return *this;
}


// Simple "get" functions. Return number of rows or columns.
int nRow() const { return nRow_; }
int nCol() const { return nCol_; }


// Parenthesis operator function.
// Allows access to values of Matrix via (i,j) pair.
// Example: a(1,1) = 2*b(2,3);
// If column is unspecified, take as 1.
double& operator() (int i, int j = 1) {
  assert(i > 0 && i <= nRow_);          // Bounds checking for rows
  assert(j > 0 && j <= nCol_);          // Bounds checking for columns
  return data_[ nCol_*(i-1) + (j-1) ];  // Access appropriate value
}


// Parenthesis operator function (const version).
const double& operator() (int i, int j = 1) const{
  assert(i > 0 && i <= nRow_);          // Bounds checking for rows
  assert(j > 0 && j <= nCol_);          // Bounds checking for columns
  return data_[ nCol_*(i-1) + (j-1) ];  // Access appropriate value
}


// Set function. Sets all elements of a matrix to a given value.
```

```
void set(double value) {
  int i, iData = nRow_*nCol_;
  for( i=0; i<iData; i++ )
    data_[i] = value;
}


//*****************************************************************
private:

// Matrix data.
int nRow_, nCol_;  // Number of rows, columns
double* data_;     // Pointer used to allocate memory for data.

// Private copy function.
// Copies values from one Matrix object to another.
void copy(const Matrix& mat) {
  nRow_ = mat.nRow_;
  nCol_ = mat.nCol_;
  int i, iData = nRow_*nCol_;
  data_ = new double [iData];
  for(i = 0; i<iData; i++ )
    data_[i] = mat.data_[i];
}

}; // Class Matrix
```

Chapter 5

Analysis of Data

It is often remarked that simulating physical systems on a computer is similar to experimental work. The reason this analogy is made is because computer simulations produce data in much the same way as laboratory experiments. We know that in experimental work one often needs to analyze the output, and it is the same with some numerical simulations. This chapter covers several topics in data analysis, including curve fitting and Fourier transforms.

5.1 CURVE FITTING

Global Warming

At present, it appears that accurate long-range weather prediction will never be achieved. The reason is because the governing equations are highly nonlinear and their solutions are extremely sensitive to initial conditions (see the Lorenz model discussed in Section 3.4). On the other hand, general predictions of Earth's climate are still possible. Forecasters can predict whether or not there will be drought conditions in Africa next year, although not the amount of precipitation on any given day.

Global warming is an important and hotly debated topic in climate research. The warming is blamed on greenhouse gases, such as carbon dioxide, in the atmosphere. These gases warm Earth by being transparent to the short-wave radiation arriving from the Sun but opaque to the infrared radiation from the ground. Scientists and policy makers are still debating the threat of global warming.[60] However, no one questions that concentrations of greenhouse gases are increasing. Specifically, carbon dioxide levels have been rising steadily since the Industrial Revolution. Figure 5.1 shows the increase in the carbon dioxide concentration during the 1980s, as measured in Mauna Loa, Hawaii.

The study of global warming has produced vast amounts of data, from both measurements in the field and computer simulations of the world's climate. In this chapter we study some basic techniques for analyzing and reducing such data sets. For example, for the data shown in Figure 5.1, what is the estimated

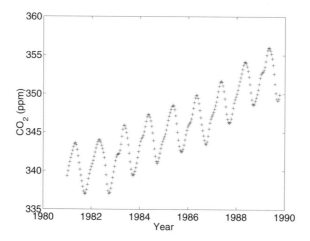

Figure 5.1: Carbon dioxide (in parts per million) measured at Mauna Loa, Hawaii from 1981 to 1990. Estimated error bar is $\sigma_o = 0.16$ ppm.

rate of increase in CO_2 concentration per year? This first question motivates our study of curve fitting.

General Theory

The simplest type of data analysis is curve fitting. Suppose that we have a data set of N points (x_i, y_i). We wish to fit this data to a function $Y(x; \{a_j\})$, where $\{a_j\}$ is a set of M adjustable parameters. Our objective is to find the values of these parameters for which the function best "fits" the data. Intuitively, we expect that if our curve fit is good, then a graph of the data set (x_i, y_i) and the function $Y(x; \{a_j\})$ will show the curve passing "near" the points (see Figure 5.2). We can quantify this statement by measuring the distance between a data point and the curve

$$\Delta_i = Y(x_i; \{a_j\}) - y_i \tag{5.1}$$

Our curve fitting criterion will be that the sum of the square of the errors be a minimum; that is, we need to find $\{a_j\}$ that minimizes the function

$$D(\{a_j\}) = \sum_{i=1}^{N} \Delta_i^2 = \sum_{i=1}^{N} [Y(x_i; \{a_j\}) - y_i]^2 \tag{5.2}$$

This technique will give us the *least squares fit*; it is not the only way to obtain a curve fit, but it is the most common. The least squares method was first used by Gauss to determine the orbits of comets from observational data.

Often, our data points have an estimated error bar (or confidence interval), which we write as $y_i \pm \sigma_i$. In this case we should modify our fit criterion so as

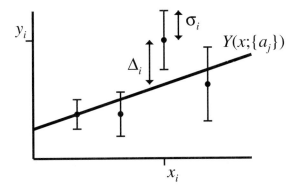

Figure 5.2: Fitting data to a curve.

to give less weight to the points with the most error. In this spirit we define

$$\chi^2(\{a_j\}) = \sum_{i=1}^{N} \left(\frac{\Delta_i}{\sigma_i}\right)^2 = \sum_{i=1}^{N} \frac{[Y(x_i; \{a_j\}) - y_i]^2}{\sigma_i^2} \tag{5.3}$$

The chi-square function is the most commonly used fitting function because, if the errors are Gaussian distributed, we can make statistical statements concerning the goodness of the fit.

Before continuing, I should remark that we will only briefly discuss the validation of our curve fit. You can fit any curve to any data set, but this does not mean that the results are meaningful. To establish significance we have to ask the following statistical question: What is the probability that the data, given the experimental error associated with each data point, are described by the curve? Unfortunately, hypothesis testing occupies a significant portion of a statistics course and is outside the scope of this book.[88]

Linear Regression

We first consider fitting the data set with a straight line,

$$Y(x; \{a_1, a_2\}) = a_1 + a_2 x \tag{5.4}$$

This type of curve fit is also known as linear regression. We want to determine a_1 and a_2 such that

$$\chi^2(a_1, a_2) = \sum_{i=1}^{N} \frac{1}{\sigma_i^2} (a_1 + a_2 x_i - y_i)^2 \tag{5.5}$$

is minimized. The minimum is found by differentiating (5.5) and setting the derivatives to zero:

$$\frac{\partial \chi^2}{\partial a_1} = 2 \sum_{i=1}^{N} \frac{1}{\sigma_i^2} (a_1 + a_2 x_i - y_i) = 0 \tag{5.6}$$

$$\frac{\partial \chi^2}{\partial a_2} = 2 \sum_{i=1}^{N} \frac{1}{\sigma_i^2} (a_1 + a_2 x_i - y_i) x_i = 0 \tag{5.7}$$

or

$$a_1 S + a_2 \Sigma x - \Sigma y = 0 \tag{5.8}$$

$$a_1 \Sigma x + a_2 \Sigma x^2 - \Sigma xy = 0 \tag{5.9}$$

where

$$S \equiv \sum_{i=1}^{N} \frac{1}{\sigma_i^2}; \quad \Sigma x \equiv \sum_{i=1}^{N} \frac{x_i}{\sigma_i^2}; \quad \Sigma y \equiv \sum_{i=1}^{N} \frac{y_i}{\sigma_i^2}; \tag{5.10}$$

$$\Sigma x^2 \equiv \sum_{i=1}^{N} \frac{x_i^2}{\sigma_i^2}; \quad \Sigma xy \equiv \sum_{i=1}^{N} \frac{x_i y_i}{\sigma_i^2}$$

Since the sums may be computed directly from the data, they are known constants. We thus have a linear set of two simultaneous equations in the unknowns a_1 and a_2. These equations are easy to solve:

$$a_1 = \frac{\Sigma y \Sigma x^2 - \Sigma x \Sigma xy}{S \Sigma x^2 - (\Sigma x)^2}; \quad a_2 = \frac{S \Sigma xy - \Sigma y \Sigma x}{S \Sigma x^2 - (\Sigma x)^2} \tag{5.11}$$

Notice that if σ_i is a constant, that is, if the error is the same for all data points, then the σ's cancel out in Equations (5.11). In this case, the parameters, a_1 and a_2, are independent of the error bar. It is not uncommon that a data set will not include the associated error bars. We may still use Equations (5.11) to fit the data if we take σ_i to be constant ($\sigma_i = 1$ being the simplest choice).

Next, we want to obtain an associated error bar, σ_{a_j}, for the curve fit parameter a_j. Using the law of the propagation of errors, [18]

$$\sigma_{a_j}^2 = \sum_{i=1}^{N} \left(\frac{\partial a_j}{\partial y_i} \right)^2 \sigma_i^2 \tag{5.12}$$

and inserting Equations (5.11), after a bit of algebra we obtain

$$\sigma_{a_1} = \sqrt{\frac{\Sigma x^2}{S \Sigma x^2 - (\Sigma x)^2}}; \quad \sigma_{a_2} = \sqrt{\frac{S}{S \Sigma x^2 - (\Sigma x)^2}} \tag{5.13}$$

Notice that σ_{a_j} is independent of y_i. If the error bars on the data are constant ($\sigma_i = \sigma_0$), the error in the parameters is

$$\sigma_{a_1} = \frac{\sigma_0}{\sqrt{N}} \sqrt{\frac{\langle x^2 \rangle}{\langle x^2 \rangle - \langle x \rangle^2}}; \quad \sigma_{a_2} = \frac{\sigma_0}{\sqrt{N}} \sqrt{\frac{1}{\langle x^2 \rangle - \langle x \rangle^2}} \tag{5.14}$$

where

$$\langle x \rangle = \frac{1}{N} \sum_{i=1}^{N} x_i; \quad \langle x^2 \rangle = \frac{1}{N} \sum_{i=1}^{N} x_i^2 \tag{5.15}$$

Finally, if our data set does not have an associated set of error bars, we may estimate σ_o from the sample variance of the data,

$$\sigma_o^2 \approx s^2 = \frac{1}{N-2} \sum_{i=1}^{N} [y_i - (a_1 + a_2 x_i)]^2 \tag{5.16}$$

where s is the sample standard deviation. Notice that this sample variance is normalized by $N-2$, since we have already extracted two parameters, a_1 and a_2, from the data.

Many nonlinear curve-fitting problems may be transformed into linear problems by a simple change of variable. For example,

$$Z(x; \{\alpha, \beta\}) = \alpha e^{\beta x} \tag{5.17}$$

may be written as Equation (5.4) using the change of variable

$$\ln Z = Y; \quad \ln \alpha = a_1; \quad \beta = a_2 \tag{5.18}$$

Similarly, to fit a power law of the form

$$Z(t; \{\alpha, \beta\}) = \alpha t^{\beta} \tag{5.19}$$

we use the change of variable

$$\ln Z = Y; \quad \ln t = x; \quad \ln \alpha = a_1; \quad \beta = a_2 \tag{5.20}$$

These transformations should be familiar because you are using them whenever you plot data using semilog or log–log scales.

General Linear Least Squares Fit

The least squares fit procedure is easy to generalize to functions of the form

$$\begin{aligned} Y(x; \{a_j\}) &= a_1 Y_1(x) + a_2 Y_2(x) + \ldots + a_M Y_M(x) \tag{5.21} \\ &= \sum_{j=1}^{M} a_j Y_j(x) \end{aligned}$$

To find the optimum parameters we proceed as before by finding the minimum of χ^2,

$$\frac{\partial \chi^2}{\partial a_j} = \frac{\partial}{\partial a_j} \sum_{i=1}^{N} \frac{1}{\sigma_i^2} \left\{ \sum_{k=1}^{M} a_k Y_k(x) - y_i \right\}^2 = 0 \tag{5.22}$$

or

$$\sum_{i=1}^{N} \frac{1}{\sigma_i^2} Y_j(x_i) \left\{ \sum_{k=1}^{M} a_k Y_k(x) - y_i \right\} = 0 \tag{5.23}$$

so

$$\sum_{i=1}^{N} \sum_{k=1}^{M} \frac{Y_j(x_i) Y_k(x_i)}{\sigma_i^2} a_k = \sum_{i=1}^{N} \frac{Y_j(x_i) y_i}{\sigma_i^2} \tag{5.24}$$

for $j = 1, \ldots, M$. This set of equations is known as the *normal equations* of the least squares problem.

The normal equations are easier to work with in matrix form. First, we define the design matrix, $\mathbf{A}$, as

$$\mathbf{A} = \begin{bmatrix} Y_1(x_1)/\sigma_1 & Y_2(x_1)/\sigma_1 & \cdots \\ Y_1(x_2)/\sigma_2 & Y_2(x_2)/\sigma_2 & \cdots \\ \vdots & \vdots & \ddots \end{bmatrix} ; \qquad A_{ij} = \frac{Y_j(x_i)}{\sigma_i} \qquad (5.25)$$

Notice that the design matrix does not depend on y_i, the data values, but does depend on x_i, that is, on the design of the experiment (where the measurements are taken). Using the design matrix, we may write (5.24) as

$$\sum_{i=1}^{N} \sum_{k=1}^{M} A_{ij} A_{ik} a_k = \sum_{i=1}^{N} A_{ij} \frac{y_i}{\sigma_i} \qquad (5.26)$$

or in matrix form,

$$(\mathbf{A}^\mathrm{T} \mathbf{A}) \mathbf{a} = \mathbf{A}^\mathrm{T} \mathbf{b} \qquad (5.27)$$

where the vector $\mathbf{b}$ is defined as $b_i = y_i/\sigma_i$ and $\mathbf{A}^\mathrm{T}$ is the transpose of the design matrix. This equation is easy to solve for the parameter vector $\mathbf{a}$,

$$\mathbf{a} = (\mathbf{A}^\mathrm{T} \mathbf{A})^{-1} \mathbf{A}^\mathrm{T} \mathbf{b} \qquad (5.28)$$

Using this result and the law of the propagation of errors, Equation (5.12), we find the estimated error in the parameter a_j to be

$$\sigma_{a_j} = \sqrt{C_{jj}} \qquad (5.29)$$

where $\mathbf{C} = (\mathbf{A}^\mathrm{T} \mathbf{A})^{-1}$.

A common application of this general linear least squares fit formulation is the fitting of data to polynomials,

$$Y(x; \{a_j\}) = a_1 + a_2 x + a_3 x^2 + \ldots + a_M x^{M-1} \qquad (5.30)$$

The design matrix has elements $A_{ij} = a_j x_i^{j-1}/\sigma_i$, which is a type of Vandermonde matrix (see Exercise 4.15). Unfortunately these matrices are notoriously ill-conditioned, so be careful if $M > 10$.

Goodness of Fit

We can easily fit every data point if the number of parameters, M, equals the number of data points, N. In this case we have either built a Rube Goldberg* theory or have not taken enough data. Instead, let's assume the more common scenario in which $N \gg M$. Because each data point has an error, we don't

---

*As a cartoonist, Rube Goldberg created absurdly elaborate machines that performed trivial tasks.

expect the curve to pass exactly through the data. However, we ask, "With the given error bars, how likely is it that the curve actually describes the data?" Of course, if we are not given any error bars there is nothing we can say concerning the goodness of the fit.

Common sense suggests that if the fit is good, then on average the difference should be approximately equal to the error bar,

$$|y_i - Y(x_i)| \approx \sigma_i \tag{5.31}$$

Putting this into our definition for χ^2, Equation (5.3), gives $\chi^2 \approx N$. Yet we know that the more parameters we use, the easier it is to get the curve to match the data; the fit can be perfect if $M = N$. This suggests that we take our rule of thumb for a good fit to be

$$\chi^2 \approx N - M \tag{5.32}$$

Of course, this is only a crude indicator, but it is better than just "eye-balling" the curve. A complete analysis would use the χ-statistic to assign a probability that the data are fit by the curve.

If we find that $\chi^2 \gg N - M$, then either we are not using an appropriate function, $Y(x)$, for our curve fit or the error bars, σ_i, are too small. On the other hand, if $\chi^2 \ll N - M$, then the fit is so spectacularly good that we may suspect that the error bars are actually too large.

Curve Fit Routines

Having worked out the general least squares problem, let's step back for a moment to the special case of fitting a straight line. Linear regression is such a common task that it is worth having a function especially designed to perform it. The function `linreg`, which fits a straight line to a data set, is outlined in Table 5.1. To demonstrate this routine, we'll use the program `lsfdemo`, outlined in Table 5.2. A data set is generated by `lsfdemo` using the equations

$$
\begin{aligned}
x_i &= i; & \sigma_i &= \alpha \\
y_i &= c_1 + c_2 x_i + c_3 x_i^2 + \alpha \Re_i^{\mathrm{G}}
\end{aligned}
\tag{5.33}
$$

where $\Re^{\mathrm{G}}$ is a Gaussian distributed random number with unit variance (see Chapter 11). Note that all the data points have the same estimated error, α.

Figures 5.3 and 5.4 show some typical curve fits for linear and quadratic curves. The data is marked by the circles; the **I**-bars on the data points indicate the estimated error bars. The solid line is the curve fit to the data. In the former figure the curve fit is good, and $\chi^2 \approx N - 2$. In Figure 5.4 the function is attempting to fit a quadratic; the fit is poor and $\chi^2 \gg N - 2$. Notice that the estimated error in the parameters, σ_{a_j}, is the same in the two cases. Looking at Equations (5.13), you will see that σ_{a_j} is independent of the values of the data vector y_i. The moral of the story is to use χ^2 to judge the fit and not the estimated errors, σ_{a_j}.

Table 5.1: Outline of function `linreg`, which performs linear regression (i.e., fits a straight line).

- *Inputs*: $\{x_i\}$, $\{y_i\}$, and $\{\sigma_i\}$.

- *Outputs*: $\{a_1, a_2\}$, $\{\sigma_{a_1}, \sigma_{a_2}\}$, $\{Y_i\}$, and χ^2.

- Evaluate various sums (5.10).

- Compute intercept a_1 and slope a_2 using (5.11).

- Compute error bars for intercept and slope using (5.13).

- Evaluate curve fit at each data point, $Y_i = Y(x_i)$, and compute χ^2 using (5.5).

See pages 171 and 177 for program listings.

Table 5.2: Outline of program `lsfdemo`, which computes the least squares fit of a randomly generated data set.

- Initialize data to be fit using (5.33).

- Fit the data to:

  - Straight line using `linreg` function **or**;
  - Polynomial using `pollsf` function.

- Print out the fit parameters, including their error bars.

- Graph the data, with error bars and fitting function.

See pages 172 and 178 for program listings.

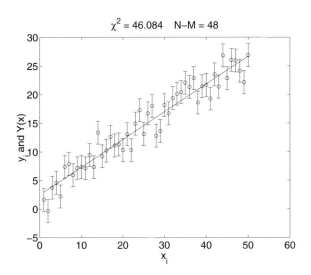

Figure 5.3: Curve fit result from `lsfdemo` using `linreg` (straight line curve fit). Input values are $c = [2.0, \ 0.5, \ 0.0]$, $\alpha = 2.0$. The fit gave the parameters $a = [2.46 \pm 0.57, \ 0.485 \pm 0.020]$ with $\chi^2 = 46.1$. The fit is good since $\chi^2 \approx N - 2 = 48$.

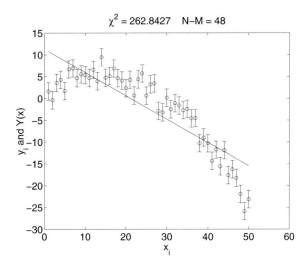

Figure 5.4: Curve fit result from `lsfdemo` using `linreg` (straight line curve fit). Input values are $c = [2.0, \ 0.5, \ -0.02]$, $\alpha = 2.0$. The fit gave the parameters $a = [11.30 \pm 0.57, \ -0.535 \pm 0.020]$ with $\chi^2 = 262.8$. The fit is poor since $\chi^2 \gg N - 2 = 48$.

Table 5.3: Outline of function `pollsf`, which performs polynomial least squares fit.

- *Inputs:* $\{x_i\}$, $\{y_i\}$, $\{\sigma_i\}$, and M.

- *Outputs:* $\{a_j\}$, $\{\sigma_{a_j}\}$, $\{Y_i\}$, and χ^2.

- Form the vector **b** and design matrix **A** using (5.27).

- Compute the correlation matrix $\mathbf{C} = (\mathbf{A}^T\mathbf{A})^{-1}$.

- Compute the least squares polynomial coefficients, $\mathbf{a} = \mathbf{C}\mathbf{A}^T\mathbf{b}$.

- Compute the estimated error bars, $\sigma_{a_j} = \sqrt{C_{jj}}$.

- Evaluate curve fit at each data point, $Y_i = Y(x_i)$, and compute χ^2 using (5.3).

See pages 173 and 179 for program listings.

The function `pollsf`, which uses the general formulation [Equations (5.27) to (5.29)] to fit a polynomial to a data set, is outlined in Table 5.3. Figure 5.5 illustrates that `pollsf` produces a good fit to the data generated by `lsfdemo`.

Power corrupts; having a function like `pollsf` tempts us to fit data with all sorts of functions. However, we should not be too ambitious using too many parameters. First, the matrices encountered in curve fitting are notoriously ill-conditioned. The problem is rapidly aggravated if we try to fit a large number of parameters (e.g., a high-order polynomial). Second, although the function may pass near the data points, it may oscillate wildly between the data points (Figure 5.6). Finally, can you really justify a theory that has 30 free parameters? In brief, you have better ways to spend your time.

EXERCISES

1. Derive Equations (5.13) using (5.11) and (5.12). [Pencil]
2. Two scientists want to measure the resistivity, $R(T)$, of a material as a function of temperature. They assume that $R(T) = a_1 + a_2T$, where a_1 and a_2 are the constants to be determined. The first scientist measures R for temperatures $T = 0°, 10°, 20°, \ldots, 100°$. The second performs the measurement at $T = 0°, 100°, \ldots, 400°$. Assuming that they use the same instruments and that the measurement error is constant, which scientist will obtain the more accurate estimate for the intercept? For the slope? [Pencil]
3. Given a set of measurements $y_i \pm \sigma_i$, find the least squares fit for the constant function $Y = \alpha$ and the error bar σ_α for the fit parameter α. Since the fitting function is a constant, the values of x_i are irrelevant. What is the relation between this least

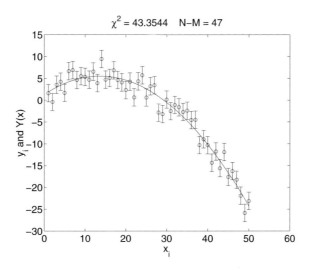

Figure 5.5: Curve fit result from `lsfdemo` using `pollsf` (polynomial curve fit). Input values are $c = [2.0, \ 0.5, \ -0.02]$, $\alpha = 2.0$. The fit gave the parameters $a = [1.35 \pm 0.88, \ 0.613 \pm 0.080, \ -0.0225 \pm 0.0015]$ with $\chi^2 = 43.4$. The fit is good since $\chi^2 \approx N - 3 = 47$.

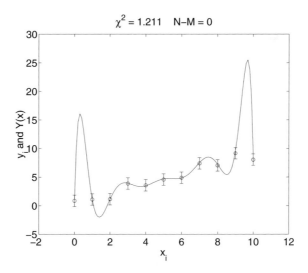

Figure 5.6: Curve fit of a 10th-order polynomial to 11 data points. Notice that the fit is good at the data points but oscillates wildly between the points. The data were generated as $y_i = x_i + \Re$, where $\Re$ is a Gaussian distributed random number with unit variance.

squares fit and the sample average $\langle y \rangle_s = \sum_{i=1}^{N} y_i/N$? [Pencil]

4. Suppose that we want to fit a data set to the function $Y(x;\alpha) = \alpha x$, that is, a straight line that passes through the origin. Using the method of least squares, obtain an expression for α and its estimated error, σ_α. [Pencil]

5. Write a version of `linreg` that fits data sets that do not include error bars. What value do you get for χ^2? Have the function also return the sample standard deviation. Testing your function with `lsfdemo`, compare this standard deviation with the errors in the data. [Computer]

6. Consider the following stock market data of Dow Jones Averages:

Day	1	2	3	4	5
DJA	2470	2510	2410	2350	2240

Assuming constant error bars, fit this data to polynomials from a straight line to a quartic (which will exactly fit the five data points). Plot these polynomials from day 1 to 6; the sixth day is October 19, 1987, when the market dropped 500 points. [Computer]

7. (a) Repeat Exercise 2.2 using linear regression to confirm numerically that the truncation errors for the right first derivative goes as h. (b) Repeat Exercise 2.12 using linear regression to confirm numerically that the truncation errors for the centered first derivative goes as h^2. (c) Repeat Exercise 2.13 using linear regression to confirm numerically that the truncation error for the centered second derivative goes as h^2. [Computer]

8. Repeat Exercise 2.17 and fit a quadratic to $T(\theta)$ for angles in the range $0 < \theta < 90°$. Compare your results with Equation (2.38). [Computer]

9. In Figure 3.10 we see that the time step selected by the adaptive Runge-Kutta routine varies with distance roughly as $\tau \propto r^{3/2}$. Use linear regression to fit this data to obtain a numerical estimate for the exponent, including its estimated error. [Computer]

10. In some problems we know, from physical grounds, that the curve must intercept the origin. Write a function that fits a data set to the equation

$$Y(x;a_1,a_2) = a_1 x + a_2 x^2$$

Use it to fit the trajectories obtained from `balle` for the initial condition $y_1 = 0$ (see Section 2.1). Try a variety of values for the initial velocity, keeping the initial angle equal to $45°$; include cases where air resistance is significant (see Figure 2.3). What is the largest velocity for which a parabola accurately fits the data? [Computer]

11. Polynomial approximations are often used to evaluate special functions. For example, the Bessel function $J_0(x)$ in the interval $0 \le x \le 3$ is accurately approximated as, [2]

$$\begin{aligned} J_0(x) = 1 \quad &- \quad 2.2499997(x/3)^2 + 1.2656208(x/3)^4 - 0.3163866(x/3)^6 \\ &+ \quad 0.0444479(x/3)^8 - 0.0039444(x/3)^{10} + 0.0002100(x/3)^{12} \end{aligned}$$

Generate 300 points in the interval $0 \le x \le 3$ using this equation, and fit this data to polynomials from quadratic up to 12th order (i.e., $M = 3$ to 13). Tabulate the estimated maximum error, $\max(Y(x_i) - y_i)$, versus the number of fitting parameters, M. You will encounter some interesting effects in computing the high-order polynomials. [Computer]

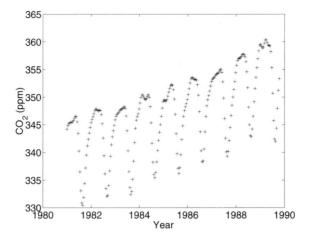

Figure 5.7: Carbon dioxide (in parts per million) measured at Barrow, Alaska, from 1981 to 1990. Estimated error bar is $\sigma_\mathrm{o} = 0.27$ ppm.

12. Carbon dioxide concentration in parts per million (ppm) as measured in Mauna Loa, Hawaii (Figure 5.1), and Barrow, Alaska (Figure 5.7), is tabulated in Appendix 5B. The data were taken every 14 days, starting in 1981. (a) Using linear regression, find the rate of increase of CO_2 in ppm per year at the two locations. (b) Approximately when will the carbon dioxide concentration be 10% above its 1981 level? [Computer]

5.2 SPECTRAL ANALYSIS

Discrete Fourier Transform

The carbon dioxide time series shown in Figure 5.1 has a general upward trend but also a significant periodicity due to the annual seasonal cycle. If our data set exhibits periodic oscillations, we probably want to fit it using trigonometric functions. This class of problems moves us from the regime of curve fitting to that of spectral analysis. Spectral analysis is a rich field that can easily fill a semester course (usually offered by engineers under the title "signal processing"). This section introduces some of the basic concepts, including the discrete Fourier transform and the power spectrum. For a more complete treatment, see Jenkins and Watts [77].

Take a vector of N data points, $\mathbf{y} = [\ y_1 \quad y_2 \quad \dots \quad y_N\ ]$; we call this data set a time series because transform methods are often used in signal analysis. The data is evenly spaced in time, so $t_{j+1} = \tau j$, where τ is the sampling interval, that is, the time increment between data points, and $j = 0, \dots, N-1$. We define the vector $\mathbf{Y}$, the discrete Fourier transform of $\mathbf{y}$, as

$$Y_{k+1} = \sum_{j=0}^{N-1} y_{j+1} e^{-2\pi i j k/N} \tag{5.34}$$

where $i = \sqrt{-1}$ and $k = 0, \ldots, N-1$. The inverse transform is

$$y_{j+1} = \frac{1}{N} \sum_{k=0}^{N-1} Y_{k+1} e^{2\pi i j k/N} \tag{5.35}$$

Note that texts (and numerical libraries) will vary slightly in how they define this transform, especially how it is normalized. If you use a library function from a numerical analysis package to evaluate a Fourier transform, check carefully how the transform is defined by that routine.

Each point Y_{k+1} of the transform has an associated frequency,

$$f_{k+1} = \frac{k}{\tau N} \tag{5.36}$$

The lowest (nonzero) frequency is $f_2 = 1/\tau N = 1/T$, where T is the length of the time series. To measure very low frequencies, we need to analyze long time series. The highest frequency is $f_N \approx 1/\tau$, so to measure very high frequencies we need to use a short sampling rate.[†]

The program `ftdemo` (Fourier transform demonstration) is outlined in Table 5.4. The program creates a time series

$$y_{j+1} = \sin(2\pi f_{\mathrm{s}} j\tau + \phi_{\mathrm{s}}) \tag{5.37}$$

This signal is a sine wave of frequency f_{s} and phase ϕ_{s}. The program evaluates the transform Y_{k+1} and plots both the signal and its transform. Note that although y is real, Y is complex, so we separately consider its real and imaginary parts.

Let's walk through a few examples using `ftdemo`; in each case the sampling interval $\tau = 1$. For $N = 50$ data points, a signal frequency of $f_{\mathrm{s}} = 0.2$, and phase of $\phi_{\mathrm{s}} = 0$, we obtain the sine wave and transform shown in Figure 5.8. The discrete sampling of the sine wave is evident from its jaggedness in the time series plot. Notice that the real part of the transform is zero and that the imaginary part has spikes at the frequencies $f = 0.2$ and 0.8 ($k = 10$ and 40). Using $N = 50$ data points, a signal frequency of $f_{\mathrm{s}} = 0.2$, and phase of $\phi_{\mathrm{s}} = \pi/2$, we obtain the cosine wave (because of the phase) and transform shown in Figure 5.9. Notice that the imaginary part of the transform is zero and that the real part has spikes at the frequencies $f = 0.2$ and $f = 0.8$.

Next, let's try a frequency that does not fall on a grid point; that is, $f_{\mathrm{s}} \neq f_{k+1}$ for all k. Using the values $N = 50$, $f_{\mathrm{s}} = 0.2123$, and $\phi_{\mathrm{s}} = 0$, we obtain the results

---

[†]For a real time series, the highest frequency is actually $1/(2\tau)$; see the discussion in this section on the Nyquist frequency.

Table 5.4: Outline of program `ftdemo`, which computes the Fourier transform of a sine wave time series.

- Initialize the sine wave time series $y_{j+1} = \sin(2\pi f_s j\tau + \phi_s)$.

- Compute the transform using desired method:
    - Direct summation using (5.34) **or**;
    - Fast Fourier transform (FFT) algorithm.

- Graph the time series, y_{j+1}, and its transform, Y_{k+1}.

- Compute and graph the power spectrum $P_{k+1} = |Y_{k+1}|^2$.

See pages 174 and 180 for program listings.

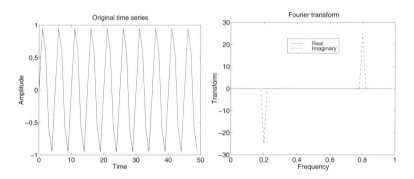

Figure 5.8: Time series and its Fourier transform from `ftdemo` for $N = 50$ data points, signal frequency $f_s = 0.2$, and phase $\phi_s = 0$.

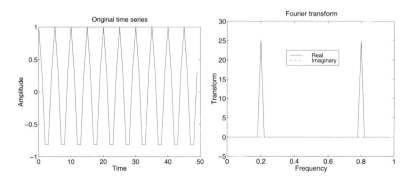

Figure 5.9: Time series and its Fourier transform from `ftdemo` for $N = 50$ data points, signal frequency $f_s = 0.2$, and phase $\phi_s = \pi/2$.

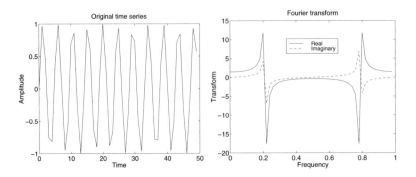

Figure 5.10: Time series and its Fourier transform from ftdemo for $N = 50$ data points, signal frequency $f_s = 0.2123$, and phase $\phi_s = 0$.

shown in Figure 5.10. Notice that we still have a peak around the frequency of the sine wave, but the structure is more complicated. In this example, because the frequency of the signal is not equal to a multiple of $1/\tau N = 1/50$, our Fourier transform is not a simple spike. For this reason, it is often useful to compute the (unnormalized) power spectrum,

$$P_{k+1} = |Y_{k+1}|^2 = Y_{k+1}Y^*_{k+1} \tag{5.38}$$

where Y^* is the complex conjugate of Y. The power spectrum from our previous example ($N = 50$, $f_s = 0.2123$, and $\phi_s = 0$) is shown in Figure 5.11. This spectrum shows two well-defined spikes; the first peak in the spectrum is between $f = 0.20$ and $f = 0.22$. If you are wondering about the second spike at $f = 1 - f_s$, read on.

Aliasing and Nyquist Frequency

For our next example let's try a higher signal frequency, say $f_s = 0.8$. Using $N = 50$ data points and $\phi_s = 0$, we obtain the results shown in Figure 5.12. Comparing these results with Figure 5.8, we see that the results for $f_s = 0.2$ and $f_s = 0.8$ are almost identical; the time series differ only by a phase shift of π. But how is this possible since these sine waves have completely different frequencies?

To help you understand why we obtain similar Fourier transforms, consider Figure 5.13. The two sine waves have frequencies $f_s = 0.2$ and $f_s = 0.8$; the former is shifted by $\phi = \pi$. When the sampling interval is $\tau = 1$, the two data sets for these sine waves (the circles in Figure 5.13) are identical. This phenomenon is known as *aliasing*.

Not surprisingly, because of aliasing there is a limit as to how high a frequency we may resolve for a given sampling interval τ. This upper bound, called the *Nyquist frequency*, is

$$f_{Ny} = \frac{1}{2\tau} \tag{5.39}$$

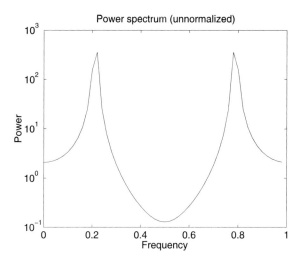

Figure 5.11: Plot of the power spectrum for $N = 50$ data points, signal frequency $f_s = 0.2123$, and phase $\phi_s = 0$. Compare with the Fourier transform shown in Figure 5.10.

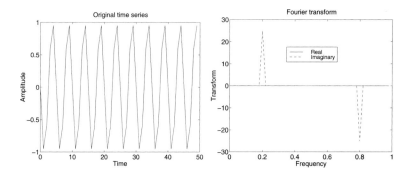

Figure 5.12: Time series and its Fourier transform from ftdemo for $N = 50$ data points, signal frequency $f_s = 0.8$, and phase $\phi_s = 0$. Compare with Figure 5.8, where $f_s = 0.2$.

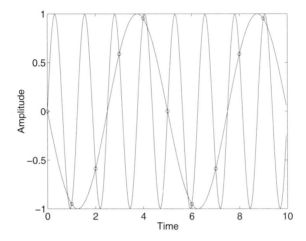

Figure 5.13: Illustration of aliasing. The two sine waves have frequencies $f_s =$ 0.2 and $f_s = 0.8$; the former is shifted by $\phi = \pi$. When the sampling interval is $\tau = 1$, the two data sets (circles) are identical.

For our examples above, $f_{Ny} = 1/2$, since $\tau = 1$. Truncating our Fourier transform at this upper bound means that we discard the upper half of the vector $\mathbf{Y}$.

Another way to understand this upper bound is to consider the following "information" argument. The (real) time series $\mathbf{y}$ contains N data points, but its Fourier transform contains N complex data points. However, the information content of the signal and its transform must be the same. Since the transform contains twice as many data values (a real and an imaginary value for each point), it must contain a duplicate of the signal. This is why the Nyquist frequency cutoff truncates the transform vector by half.

Fast Fourier Transform

Consider again the definition of the discrete Fourier transform, as given by Equation (5.34). The number of operations required to compute Y_{k+1} for a single value of k is $O(N)$, where N is the number of data points in our time series. To compute $\mathbf{Y}$ for all values of k (from 0 to $N - 1$), thus requires $O(N^2)$ operations. For many years spectral work was hobbled because it was computationally prohibitive to analyze large data sets.

In 1965, Cooley and Tukey introduced an algorithm that later became known as the fast Fourier transform (or FFT).[34] They showed that by cleverly rearranging the order in which the calculation was performed, the number of operations could be reduced to $O(N \log_2 N)$. Their original algorithm was limited to the case where $N = 2^n$; that is, the number of data points in the time series is a power of two. Sophisticated implementations of the FFT (such as MATLAB's built-in version) can handle any value of N but are still most efficient when N

is a power of two. If N is a prime number, the number of operations returns to $O(N^2)$.

We won't write an FFT routine in MATLAB because there is a powerful, built-in version. Given a data vector y,

```
Y = fft(y);    % MATLAB's built-in FFT routine
```

gives the transform vector Y. For C++, we will use the function fft outlined in Table 5.5. In the ftdemo program, this function is called as

```
ytReal = y;
ytImag.set(0.0);     // Copy data for input to fft
fft(ytReal, ytImag);
```

where y is a Matrix object containing the time series. The Matrix objects ytReal and ytImag contain the time series on entering the fft function and the real and imaginary parts of the transform on exiting the function. This FFT function requires the number of data points to be a power of two.

Comparing the results obtained using the direct summation with those from the FFT algorithm you should notice that the outputs are identical but the run time is significantly shorter using the FFT. As long as you understand that the FFT does nothing more than evaluate the discrete Fourier transform in an efficient way, you don't really need to know how it works. If you're satisfied knowing what it does and don't care how, go on and skip to the next section. On the other hand, if you're one of those who can't stand using a black box without having some idea of what's inside, read on. The rest of this section works through an example illustrating the fast Fourier transform algorithm. The discussion is adapted from Brigham [27]; see that excellent reference for a complete coverage of the FFT algorithm.

How the FFT Works

The discrete Fourier transform is defined as

$$Y_{k+1} = \sum_{j=0}^{N-1} y_{j+1} W^{kj} \tag{5.40}$$

where $W \equiv e^{-2\pi i/N}$. The easiest way to understand the FFT algorithm is to work through a simple example; we take $N = 8$, so $j, k = 0, \ldots, 7$. It is useful to decompose j and k into binary form,

$$j = 4j_2 + 2j_1 + j_0 \tag{5.41}$$
$$k = 4k_2 + 2k_1 + k_0 \tag{5.42}$$

where $j_2, j_1, \ldots, k_1, k_0 = 0$ or 1. To make the notation easier to read, define

$$y_{j+1} = y(j_2, j_1, j_0); \qquad Y_{k+1} = Y(k_2, k_1, k_0) \tag{5.43}$$

Table 5.5: Outline of function `fft`, which computes the Fourier transform of a data vector.

- *Inputs*: Real($\mathbf{y}$) and Imag($\mathbf{y}$).

- *Outputs*: Real($\mathbf{Y}$) and Imag($\mathbf{Y}$).

- Determine size of input data, and check that it is power of 2.

- Bit-scramble the input data by swapping elements.

- Loop over number of layers, $M = \log_2(N)$.

    - Compute lowest, nonzero power of W for this layer.
    - Loop over elements in binary order (outer loop).
        * Loop over elements in binary order (inner loop).
            · Compute the $y(\cdot)W^\bullet$ factor for this element.
            · Update the current element and its binary pair.
        * Increment the power of W for next set of elements.

See page 185 for program listing.

Table 5.6: Outline of function `ifft`, which computes the inverse Fourier transform of a data vector using (5.53).

- *Inputs*: Real($\mathbf{Y}$) and Imag($\mathbf{Y}$).

- *Outputs*: Real($\mathbf{y}$) and Imag($\mathbf{y}$).

- Take complex conjugate of input transform $\mathbf{Y}$.

- Evaluate the fast fourier transform of $\mathbf{Y}^*$.

- Take complex conjugate and normalize by N.

See page 186 for program listing.

Using the binary notation defined above, the discrete Fourier transform may be written as

$$Y(k_2, k_1, k_0) = \sum_{j_0=0}^{1} \sum_{j_1=0}^{1} \sum_{j_2=0}^{1} y(j_2, j_1, j_0) W^{(4k_2+2k_1+k_0)(4j_2+2j_1+j_0)} \quad (5.44)$$

The first simplification comes from noticing that $W^8 = W^{16} = \ldots = 1$, since $e^{-i(2\pi n)} = 1$; so

$$W^{(4k_2+2k_1+k_0)4j_2} = W^{4k_0 j_2} \quad (5.45)$$
$$W^{(4k_2+2k_1+k_0)2j_1} = W^{(2k_1+k_0)2j_1} \quad (5.46)$$

and

$$Y(k_2, k_1, k_0) = \sum_{j_0=0}^{1} W^{(4k_2+2k_1+k_0)j_0} \sum_{j_1=0}^{1} W^{(2k_1+k_0)2j_1}$$

$$\times \sum_{j_2=0}^{1} y(j_2, j_1, j_0) W^{4k_0 j_2} \quad (5.47)$$

The sums may be further simplified by using $W^0 = 1$.

The nested sums are usually processed in layers. The inner sum over j_2 is evaluated in the first layer as

$$y_1(k_0, j_1, j_0) = y(0, j_1, j_0) + y(1, j_1, j_0) W^{4k_0} \quad (5.48)$$

for k_0, j_1, and $j_0 = 0, 1$. The subsequent layers are

$$y_2(k_0, k_1, j_0) = y_1(k_0, 0, j_0) + y_1(k_0, 1, j_0) W^{(4k_1+2k_0)} \quad (5.49)$$

for k_0, k_1, and $j_0 = 0, 1$, and

$$y_3(k_0, k_1, k_2) = y_2(k_0, k_1, 0) + y_2(k_0, k_1, 1) W^{(4k_2+2k_1+k_0)} \quad (5.50)$$

for k_0, k_1, and $k_2 = 0, 1$. Finally, the vector y_3 is "bit unscrambled" to give,

$$Y(k_2, k_1, k_0) = y_3(k_0, k_1, k_2) \quad (5.51)$$

where Y is the desired Fourier transform of y.

Note that processing each layer requires eight complex multiplications and eight complex additions. Since there are three $[= \log_2(8)]$ layers, the total number of operations is 24 multiplications and additions. It is not difficult to extend the above example to any value N that is a power of 2. The number of layers will be $\log_2(N)$ so the number of operations will be $O[N \log_2(N)]$. Another attractive feature of the FFT is that the operations may be performed "in place"; that is, the vector $\mathbf{Y}$ may be created in the same space in memory originally occupied by the time series $\mathbf{y}$. This feature can be important if memory is constrained.

The inverse transform can be defined in terms of the direct transform as,

$$
\begin{aligned}
y_{j+1} &= \frac{1}{N} \sum_{k=0}^{N-1} Y_{k+1} e^{2\pi i k j/N} \\
&= \frac{1}{N} \left(\sum_{k=0}^{N-1} \left(Y_{k+1} e^{2\pi i k j/N} \right)^* \right)^* \\
&= \frac{1}{N} \left(\sum_{k=0}^{N-1} Y_{k+1}^* e^{-2\pi i k j/N} \right)^*
\end{aligned}
\tag{5.52}
$$

where asterisk denotes complex conjugate. This result allows us to compute the inverse transform by applying a complex conjugate before and after calling the direct transform FFT routine. MATLAB has a built-in inverse tranform function, `ifft`, and a C++ version, with the same name, is outlined in Table 5.6.

EXERCISES

13. Consider the time series $y_{j+1} = \cos(2\pi f_\ell j\tau)$ with $f_\ell = \ell/\tau N$ and $\ell = 0, \dots, N-1$. Show that the discrete Fourier transform is

$$
Y_{k+1} = \begin{cases} N/2 & \ell = k \text{ or } \ell = N - k \\ 0 & \text{otherwise} \end{cases}
$$

by using the definition (5.34). [Pencil]

14.   Show that $\sin(\frac{2\pi}{5}j + \pi) = \sin(\frac{8\pi}{5}j)$, which is the result illustrated in Figure 5.12. [Pencil]

15.   Watching a Western on television, you may have noticed that sometimes the wheels on a fast stagecoach appear to be rotating backward. Explain how aliasing causes this effect. [Pencil]

16. A good way to understand how an algorithm works is to work a small example by hand. Evaluate the discrete Fourier transform of $\mathbf{y} = [0\ 1\ 0\ -1]$ using: (a) the direct summation (5.34); (b) the FFT algorithm. Be sure to show the intermediate steps in the calculation. [Pencil]

17.   Modify `ftdemo` to compute the Fourier transform and power spectrum for the function:

$$
\begin{aligned}
(a) \quad y_j &= \theta_j/2\pi & \text{(sawtooth wave)} \\[2mm]
(b) \quad y_j &= \begin{cases} 1 & 0 \le \theta_j < \pi \\ -1 & \text{otherwise} \end{cases} & \text{(square wave)} \\[2mm]
(c) \quad y_j &= \begin{cases} 1 & 0 \le \theta_j < \pi \\ 0 & \text{otherwise} \end{cases} & \text{(square pulses)} \\[2mm]
(d) \quad y_j &= \begin{cases} \theta_j/\pi & 0 \le \theta_j < \pi \\ (2\pi - \theta_j)/\pi & \text{otherwise} \end{cases} & \text{(triangle wave)}
\end{aligned}
$$

where $\theta_j = 2\pi f_s j\tau$ modulo 2π. Find the transform and spectrum for $f_s = 0.2$, 0.2123, and 0.8, taking $\tau = 1$ for $N = 50$, 512, and 4096 data points. [Computer]

18.   The fast Fourier transform is most efficient when the number of data points is a power of two. Unfortunately, we cannot always control the number of points in our time series. A common workaround is to "pad" the time series with zeros; that is, add to the end of the data extra points whose value is zero. Write a program to demonstrate the effect of padding a time series, comparing the spectra from padded and nonpadded data. Use the time series $y_{j+1} = \sin(2\pi f_s j\tau)$ with $f_s = 0.2$ and $\tau = 1$. Evaluate the time series for $N = 150$, 200, and 251 points, and in each case pad it to 256 points. [Computer]

19.   The `ftdemo` program prints the number of flops (floating-point operations) executed in computing the Fourier transform. Modifying the program to graph flop count versus N, the number of points in the time series. Show that using the FFT the lower bound goes as $N \log_2(N)$ while the upper bound goes as N^2. [MATLAB]

20.   (a) Consider the following simple digital filter.[69] We may smooth our time series y_i by averaging adjacent data points to create a new time series z_j,

$$z_j = \frac{1}{2}(y_j + y_{j+1})$$

where $y_{N+1} \equiv y_1$. Write a program that applies this simple smoothing to a signal composed of a sum of sine waves of various frequencies. Show that the averaging serves as a digital low-pass filter by plotting the power spectra of both y and z. (b) Repeat part (a), but use the difference filter

$$z_j = \frac{1}{2}(y_j - y_{j+1})$$

Show that this is a high-pass filter. [Computer]

21.   Carbon dioxide concentration (in parts per million) as measured in Barrow, Alaska, and Mauna Loa, Hawaii, is tabulated in Appendix 5C. Besides the linear trend, the data shows an annual cycle in CO_2 concentration. (a) Write a program that removes the annual cycle from the data. Remove the cycle by transforming into the frequency domain, zeroing the appropriate values, and transforming back. For comparison, plot the filtered and unfiltered data together on one graph. (b) Repeat part (a), but remove the linear trend from the data before filtering, and then replace it after filtering. Compare and comment with your results from part (a). [Computer]

5.3 *NORMAL MODES

Coupled Mass System

In this section we use Fourier transforms to study oscillations in a simple spring-mass system. Recall the system introduced in Section 4.2 (see Figure 4.3). It consists of three blocks (of mass m) coupled together and to opposite walls by four springs. To simplify the analysis, we assume the springs are identical and take the spring constants and rest lengths of the springs equal to k and L, respectively. Given the distance between the walls as L_w, the rest position of the masses are $x_j^* = \frac{1}{4}jL_w$. In Chapter 4 we studied the more general problem for which finding x^* was more complicated.

We now want to analyze the oscillatory motion when the masses are not at rest. The equation of motion is

$$m\frac{d^2}{dt^2}\mathbf{x}(t) = \mathbf{K}\mathbf{x}(t) - \mathbf{b} \tag{5.53}$$

where

$$\mathbf{K} = -k \begin{bmatrix} 2 & -1 & 0 \\ -1 & 2 & -1 \\ 0 & -1 & 2 \end{bmatrix}; \qquad \mathbf{b} = -kL_w \begin{bmatrix} 0 \\ 0 \\ 1 \end{bmatrix} \tag{5.54}$$

Physical intuition suggests the periodic trial solution,

$$\mathbf{x}(t) = \mathbf{a}e^{i\omega t} + \mathbf{x}^* \tag{5.55}$$

where $\mathbf{a}$ is the (complex) amplitude vector. Inserting this trial solution into (5.53) gives us

$$-m\omega^2 \mathbf{a} = \mathbf{K}\mathbf{a} \tag{5.56}$$

This is an *eigenvalue* problem; Equation (5.56) will have solutions only for certain values of ω.

We may write equation (5.56) as

$$\begin{bmatrix} 2 & -1 & 0 \\ -1 & 2 & -1 \\ 0 & -1 & 2 \end{bmatrix} \mathbf{a} - \lambda \mathbf{a} = 0 \tag{5.57}$$

where $\lambda = m\omega^2/k$. If we further rearrange it as

$$\begin{bmatrix} 2-\lambda & -1 & 0 \\ -1 & 2-\lambda & -1 \\ 0 & -1 & 2-\lambda \end{bmatrix} \mathbf{a} = 0 \tag{5.58}$$

it is clear that we have a nontrivial solution (i.e., $\mathbf{a} \neq 0$) only if the matrix has no inverse.

The matrix is singular if its determinant is zero,

$$\begin{vmatrix} 2-\lambda & -1 & 0 \\ -1 & 2-\lambda & -1 \\ 0 & -1 & 2-\lambda \end{vmatrix} = 0 \tag{5.59}$$

or

$$(2-\lambda)\{(2-\lambda)^2 - 1\} - (2-\lambda) = 0 \tag{5.60}$$

This equation is easy to factor,

$$[2-\lambda][(2+\sqrt{2}) - \lambda][(2-\sqrt{2}) - \lambda] = 0 \tag{5.61}$$

The three eigenvalues are thus $\lambda = 2, 2 + \sqrt{2}$, and $2 - \sqrt{2}$. I should point out that while this analysis is suitable for small matrices, it is not the recommended way of computing eigenvalues numerically.

Our spring-mass system has three normal modes of oscillation; their angular frequencies are

$$\omega_0 = \sqrt{2\frac{k}{m}}; \qquad \omega_\pm = \sqrt{(2 \pm \sqrt{2})\frac{k}{m}} \tag{5.62}$$

Some further calculation gives us the associated eigenvectors,

$$\mathbf{a}_0 = \begin{bmatrix} 1/\sqrt{2} \\ 0 \\ -1/\sqrt{2} \end{bmatrix}; \qquad \mathbf{a}_\pm = \begin{bmatrix} 1/2 \\ \mp 1/\sqrt{2} \\ 1/2 \end{bmatrix} \tag{5.63}$$

Notice that the three vectors are orthogonal and normalized to unit length. Our final solution

$$\mathbf{x}(t) = c_0 \mathbf{a}_0 e^{i\omega_0 t} + c_+ \mathbf{a}_+ e^{i\omega_+ t} + c_- \mathbf{a}_- e^{i\omega_- t} + \mathbf{x}^* \tag{5.64}$$

is a linear combination of the three normal modes. The constants, c_0, c_+, and c_-, are specified by the initial condition $\mathbf{x}(t = 0)$.

Numerical Results

Now that we have done the problem analytically, let's solve the equations of motion numerically and compare the results. The program sprfft (Table 5.7) simulates the coupled mass-spring system using fourth-order Runge-Kutta. Since we want our time series to have a constant time increment, I chose not to use the adaptive routine.[‡] The equations of motion are defined in the function sprrk (Table 5.8). Notice that the program computes the displacements from the steady states, which are zero when the system is at rest.

If the initial displacement is one of the normal modes, then we have a simple uniform oscillation with a single frequency (Figure 5.14). On the other hand, for an arbitrary initial displacement of the masses we have a linear combination of the three modes (Figure 5.15). To the untrained eye, the masses appear to oscillate in a chaotic fashion with no discernible pattern.

While the time series in Figure 5.15 may appear chaotic, the power spectrum (Figure 5.16) clearly reveals the three eigenfrequencies of the system. The peaks are not sharp because the length of our time series, $T = N\tau$, is not equal to an integer number of periods of any of the modes. This effect is called *leakage*. Figure 5.17 illustrates how leakage is produced by the discontinuity in the periodic extension of the time series. We saw the same phenomenon in Figure 5.11; although the input is a pure tone, the output is a broad spike.

[‡]However, with just a bit of extra coding, you can modify the adaptive routine to deliver data that is evenly spaced in time.

Table 5.7: Outline of program `sprfft`, which computes the evolution of a coupled mass-spring system; uses Fourier transforms to obtain the eigenfrequencies.

- Set parameters for the system (initial positions, etc.).

- Loop over the desired number of time steps.

    - Use Runge-Kutta to find new displacements of the masses.
    - Record the positions for graphing and to compute spectra.

- Graph the displacements, $x_i(t) - x^*$, of the three masses.

- Calculate the power spectrum of $x_1(t) - x^*$.

- Apply the Hanning window (5.65) to the time series and calculate the resulting power spectrum.

- Graph the power spectra for original and windowed data.

See pages 175 and 182 for program listings.

Table 5.8: Outline of function `sprrk`, which is used by the Runge-Kutta routines to evaluate the spring-mass equations of motion (5.53).

- *Inputs*: $\mathbf{x}(t)$, t (not used), k/m.

- *Output*: $d\mathbf{x}(t)/dt$.

- Set $dx_i/dt = v_i$.

- Evaluate dv_i/dt from (5.53).

- Return state vector $\mathbf{x} = [dx_1/dt, \; dx_2/dt, \; \dots, \; dv_3/dt]$

See pages 176 and 184 for program listings.

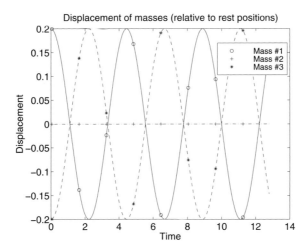

Figure 5.14: Displacement of masses, $\mathbf{x} - \mathbf{x}^*$, in the coupled spring system as a function of time as computed by `sprfft`. The initial displacement is $[0.2, 0, -0.2]$, which is the normal mode with frequency $\omega_0 = \sqrt{2k/m}$. The time step is $\tau = 0.05$.

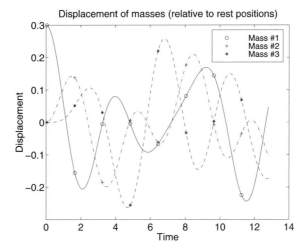

Figure 5.15: Displacement of masses, $\mathbf{x} - \mathbf{x}^*$, in the coupled spring system as a function of time as computed by `sprfft`. The initial displacement was $[0.3\ 0\ 0]$; all three normal modes are excited. The time step used was $\tau = 0.05$.

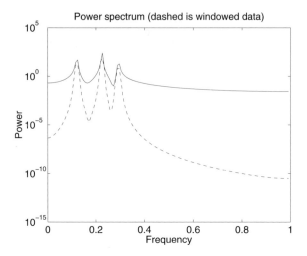

Figure 5.16: Power spectrum for the coupled spring system as computed by `sprfft`. The initial displacement is [0.3, 0, 0], which gives a combination of the three normal modes (notice the three spikes). The time step is $\tau = 0.5$; frequencies are truncated at the Nyquist frequency. Dashed line is the spectrum of windowed data.

One way to compensate for our time series being finite is to apply a window. The `sprfft` program uses the Hanning window,

$$\bar{y}_{j+1} = \left[\frac{1}{2} - \frac{1}{2}\cos\left(2\pi\frac{j}{N}\right)\right] y_{j+1}; \qquad j = 0, 1, \ldots, N-1 \tag{5.65}$$

where $\mathbf{y}$ is the original time series and $\bar{\mathbf{y}}$ is the windowed time series. This window smoothly tapers the data at the ends, reducing spurious leakage effects. Notice in Figure 5.16 that the spikes in the windowed data (dashed line) are significantly more pronounced. The peaks become even narrower if we add more data points to the time series.

The results from this coupled oscillator problem may remind you of the Lorenz model. Looking back on the time series from that model (Figure 3.12) we recall that they appear periodic. It is a simple matter to modify `sprfft` to compute the Lorenz model. Although in Chapter 3 we used the adaptive Runge-Kutta routine, we found that the time step, τ, did not vary significantly. Using `rk4` with a fixed time step gives us a time series we can easily analyze. The resulting power spectrum for $z(t)$ is shown in Figure 5.18 (the results are similar for the other two variables in the Lorenz model). While there is a peak around $f \approx 1.5$, on the whole, the spectrum is quite complicated. A signal whose spectrum contains all frequencies in equal amplitude is called *white noise*, an analogy to the spectrum of white light. Spectra such as that in Figure 5.18 are commonly referred to as *red noise*, since all frequencies are present but have more power in the lower frequencies.

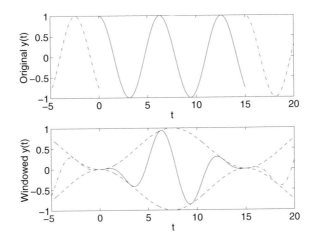

Figure 5.17: Illustration of leakage and windowing. The upper graph shows the time series $y(t) = \cos(t)$ in the interval $0 \leq t \leq 15$ as a solid line and its periodic extensions outside the interval as dot-dashed lines. The lower graph shows the same time series after applying the Hanning window (5.65), indicated by the dashed line.

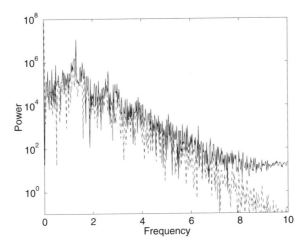

Figure 5.18: Power spectrum of $z(t)$ from the Lorenz model; dashed line is spectrum of windowed data. The parameters used are the same as in Figure 3.13, with time step, $\tau = 0.05$, and $N = 1024$ data points.

For a long time it was believed that a noisy spectrum indicated that a physical system contained many degrees of freedom. For example, a coupled oscillator system with many masses (e.g., atoms in a crystal) has a spectrum with many eigenfrequencies. The Lorenz model, however, is a simple, *nonlinear* system with only three degrees of freedom that produces a red noise spectrum. These results in nonlinear dynamics have revolutionized time series analysis and forecasting.

EXERCISES

22. Derive the eigenvectors (5.63) for the coupled spring-mass system. Also show that they are orthogonal and normalized to unit length. [Pencil]

23. (a) Find the normal mode frequencies for the Wilberforce pendulum (see Exercise 3.13). [Pencil] (b) Modify `sprfft` to evaluate the time series for the Wilberforce pendulum. Compute the power spectrum and confirm your results from part (a). [Computer]

24. Modify `sprfft` to evaluate the time series for the Lorenz model. Plot the resulting power spectrum, as shown in Figure 5.18. Take $\sigma = 10$, $b = 8/3$, and try $r = 10$, 28, and 222.

25. (a) Modify `sprfft` to evaluate the time series for the Lotka-Voltera model (Exercise 3.22) and plot the resulting power spectrum. (b) Repeat part (a) for the Brusselator model (see Exercise 4.4). [Computer]

26. (a) Find the normal mode frequencies for the spring-mass system in Exercise 4.13; assume $k_1 = k_2$. [Pencil] (b) Modify `sprfft` to evaluate the time series for the this system. Compute the power spectrum and confirm your results from part (a). [Computer]

27. Compute the power spectrum of the angular displacement $\theta(t)$ for the simple pendulum (see Section 2.2). Show that for small initial displacements, for example $\theta(0) = 10°$, the spectrum only has a single peak, but for large displacements, for example $\theta(0) = 170°$, multiple peaks appear. What is the relation between the frequencies of these multiple peaks? [Computer]

BEYOND THIS CHAPTER

Curve fitting is such an important topic in scientific data analysis that entire books are dedicated to the subject.[18, 26] Even linear least squares analysis can be complicated since the matrices in the normal equations are often ill-conditioned. Gaussian elimination can fail, and the best approach is to use singular value decomposition (SVD).[49]

In this chapter we only consider fitting data to functions that are linear in the coefficients. In general, to fit nonlinear functions requires an iterative procedure for finding the minimum of χ^2. In some cases, the problem is notoriously difficult; the function

$$Y(x; \{a_1, \ldots, a_4\}) = a_1 e^{-a_2 x} + a_3 e^{-a_4 x} \tag{5.66}$$

is a famous example. There are, however, specialized algorithms for tackling these problems.[14, 113]

Least squares analysis can give poor results when the data contains outliers or if the errors are not Gaussian distributed. So-called robust techniques have been developed to provide alternative ways to fit data.[74, 109] It is often useful to apply both least squares and a robust algorithm to a data set; if the fit parameters differ significantly, you might want to investigate why. Robust techniques are also useful for identifying outliers.

Sometimes we want to draw a smooth curve through a data set, but don't really care to specify the function. In this case it's simplest to assemble the curve using a piecewise function, the *cubic spline* being the most popular choice.[40, 82] This is also a good approach when we want to interpolate between data points.

The Fourier transform has many applications besides that of estimating power spectra. Computing convolutions and correlations of data sets is most efficiently performed using FFTs. Section 8.2 covers spectral methods for solving partial differential equations. Specifically, the Fourier transform is used to numerically solve the Poisson equation. See Brigham [27] for an extensive summary of other applications.

An alternative technique for power spectrum estimation is the maximum entropy method (MEM).[31] This algorithm is useful when a data set has sharp peaks in the power spectrum, especially when trying to resolve peaks that are close together. Unfortunately, careless use of the method leads to spurious features (e.g., false peaks) in the spectrum. MEM can be significantly improved when combined with an adaptive filter.[95]

APPENDIX A: MATLAB LISTINGS

Listing 5A.1 Function `linreg`. Fits a straight line to a data set.

```
function [a_fit, sig_a, yy, chisqr] = linreg(x,y,sigma)
% Function to perform linear regression (fit a line)
% Inputs
%   x       Independent variable
%   y       Dependent variable
%   sigma   Estimated error in y
% Outputs
%   a_fit   Fit parameters; a(1) is intercept, a(2) is slope
%   sig_a   Estimated error in the parameters a()
%   yy      Curve fit to the data
%   chisqr  Chi squared statistic

%* Evaluate various sigma sums
sigmaTerm = sigma .^ (-2);
s = sum(sigmaTerm);
sx = sum(x .* sigmaTerm);
```

```
sy = sum(y .* sigmaTerm);
sxy = sum(x .* y .* sigmaTerm);
sxx = sum((x .^ 2) .* sigmaTerm);
denom = s*sxx - sx^2;

%* Compute intercept a_fit(1) and slope a_fit(2)
a_fit(1) = (sxx*sy - sx*sxy)/denom;
a_fit(2) = (s*sxy - sx*sy)/denom;

%* Compute error bars for intercept and slope
sig_a(1) = sqrt(sxx/denom);
sig_a(2) = sqrt(s/denom);

%* Evaluate curve fit at each data point and compute Chi^2
yy = a_fit(1)+a_fit(2)*x;       % Curve fit to the data
chisqr = sum( ((y-yy)./sigma).^2 );  % Chi square
return;
```

Listing 5A.2 Program lsfdemo. Generates a data set and fits a curve to the data; may be used to test the linreg (Listing 5A.1) and pollsf (Listing 5A.3) functions.

```
% lsfdemo - Program for demonstrating least squares fit routines
clear all; help lsfdemo; % Clear memory and print header

%* Initialize data to be fit. Data is quadratic plus random number.
fprintf('Curve fit data is created using the quadratic\n');
fprintf('   y(x) = c(1) + c(2)*x + c(3)*x^2 \n');
c = input('Enter the coefficients as [c(1) c(2) c(3)]: ');
N = 50;                  % Number of data points
x = 1:N;                 % x = [1, 2, ..., N]
randn('state',0);        % Initialize random number generator
alpha = input('Enter estimated error bar: ');
r = alpha*randn(1,N);    % Gaussian distributed random vector
y = c(1) + c(2)*x + c(3)*x.^2 + r;
sigma = alpha*ones(1,N);    % Constant error bar

%* Fit the data to a straight line or a more general polynomial
M = input('Enter number of fit parameters (=2 for line): ');
if( M == 2 )
  %* Linear regression (Straight line) fit
  [a_fit sig_a yy chisqr] = linreg(x,y,sigma);
else
  %* Polynomial fit
  [a_fit sig_a yy chisqr] = pollsf(x,y,sigma,M);
end

%* Print out the fit parameters, including their error bars.
fprintf('Fit parameters:\n');
for i=1:M
```

```
    fprintf(' a(%g) = %g +/- %g \n',i,a_fit(i),sig_a(i));
end

%* Graph the data, with error bars, and fitting function.
figure(1); clf;              % Bring figure 1 window forward
errorbar(x,y,sigma,'o');     % Graph data with error bars
hold on;                     % Freeze the plot to add the fit
plot(x,yy,'-');              % Plot the fit on same graph as data
xlabel('x_i'); ylabel('y_i and Y(x)');
title(['\chi^2 = ',num2str(chisqr),'    N-M = ',num2str(N-M)]);
```

Listing 5A.3 Function pollsf. Fits a polynomial to a data set.

```
function [a_fit, sig_a, yy, chisqr] = pollsf(x, y, sigma, M)
% Function to fit a polynomial to data
% Inputs
%   x       Independent variable
%   y       Dependent variable
%   sigma   Estimate error in y
%   M       Number of parameters used to fit data
% Outputs
%   a_fit   Fit parameters; a(1) is intercept, a(2) is slope
%   sig_a   Estimated error in the parameters a()
%   yy      Curve fit to the data
%   chisqr  Chi squared statistic

%* Form the vector b and design matrix A
b = y./sigma;
N = length(x);
for i=1:N
 for j=1:M
  A(i,j) = x(i)^(j-1)/sigma(i);
 end
end

%* Compute the correlation matrix C
C = inv(A.' * A);

%* Compute the least squares polynomial coefficients a_fit
a_fit = C * A.' * b.';

%* Compute the estimated error bars for the coefficients
for j=1:M
  sig_a(j) = sqrt(C(j,j));
end

%* Evaluate curve fit at each data point and compute Chi^2
yy = zeros(1,N);
for j=1:M
```

```
    yy = yy + a_fit(j)*x.^(j-1);  % yy is the curve fit
end
chisqr = sum( ((y-yy)./sigma).^2 );
return;
```

Listing 5A.4 Program `ftdemo`. Demonstrates the discrete Fourier transform using the direct summation or the Fast Fourier transform method.

```
% ftdemo - Discrete Fourier transform demonstration program
clear all; help ftdemo; % Clear memory and print header

%* Initialize the sine wave time series to be transformed.
N = input('Enter the number of points: ');
freq = input('Enter frequency of the sine wave: ');
phase = input('Enter phase of the sine wave: ');
tau = 1;  % Time increment
t = (0:(N-1))*tau;          % t = [0, tau, 2*tau, ... ]
y = sin(2*pi*t*freq + phase);  % Sine wave time series
f = (0:(N-1))/(N*tau);      % f = [0, 1/(N*tau), ... ]

%* Compute the transform using desired method: direct summation
%  or fast Fourier transform (FFT) algorithm.
flops(0);  % Reset the flops counter to zero
Method = menu('Compute transform by','Direct summation','FFT');
if( Method == 1 );                % Direct summation
  twoPiN = -2*pi*sqrt(-1)/N;
  for k=0:N-1
    expTerm = exp(twoPiN*(0:N-1)*k);
    yt(k+1) = sum(y .* expTerm);
  end
else                              % Fast Fourier transform
  yt = fft(y);
end
fprintf('Number of floating point operations = %g\n',flops);

%* Graph the time series and its transform.
figure(1); clf;  % Clear figure 1 window and bring forward
plot(t,y);
title('Original time series');
ylabel('Amplitude');   xlabel('Time');
figure(2); clf;  % Clear figure 2 window and bring forward
plot(f,real(yt),'-',f,imag(yt),'--');
legend('Real','Imaginary');
title('Fourier transform');
ylabel('Transform');   xlabel('Frequency');

%* Compute and graph the power spectrum of the time series.
figure(3); clf;  % Clear figure 3 window and bring forward
powspec = abs(yt).^2;
```

```
semilogy(f,powspec,'-');
title('Power spectrum (unnormalized)');
ylabel('Power');  xlabel('Frequency');
```

Listing 5A.5 Program `sprfft`. Computes the evolution of a coupled mass-spring system; uses Fourier transforms to obtain the eigenfrequencies. Uses `rk4` (Listing 3A.2) and `sprrk` (Listing 5A.6).

```
% sprfft - Program to compute the power spectrum of a
% coupled mass-spring system.
clear; help sprfft;  % Clear memory and print header

%* Set parameters for the system (initial positions, etc.).
x = input('Enter initial displacement [x1 x2 x3]: ');
v = [0 0 0];        % Masses are initially at rest
state = [x v];      % Positions and velocities; used by rk4
tau = input('Enter timestep: ');
k_over_m = 1;       % Ratio of spring const. over mass

%* Loop over the desired number of time steps.
time = 0;           % Set initial time
nstep = 256;        % Number of steps in the main loop
nprint = nstep/8;   % Number of steps between printing progress
for istep=1:nstep   %%% MAIN LOOP %%%

  %* Use Runge-Kutta to find new displacements of the masses.
  state = rk4(state,time,tau,'sprrk',k_over_m);
  time = time + tau;

  %* Record the positions for graphing and to compute spectra.
  xplot(istep,1:3) = state(1:3);   % Record positions
  tplot(istep) = time;
  if( rem(istep,nprint) < 1 )
    fprintf('Finished %g out of %g steps\n',istep,nstep);
  end
end

%* Graph the displacements of the three masses.
figure(1); clf;  % Clear figure 1 window and bring forward
ipr = 1:nprint:nstep;  % Used to graph limited number of symbols
plot(tplot(ipr),xplot(ipr,1),'o',tplot(ipr),xplot(ipr,2),'+',...
     tplot(ipr),xplot(ipr,3),'*',...
     tplot,xplot(:,1),'-',tplot,xplot(:,2),'-.',...
     tplot,xplot(:,3),'--');
legend('Mass #1','Mass #2','Mass #3');
title('Displacement of masses (relative to rest positions)');
xlabel('Time'); ylabel('Displacement');
drawnow;
```

```
%* Calculate the power spectrum of the time series for mass #1
f(1:nstep) = (0:(nstep-1))/(tau*nstep);      % Frequency
x1 = xplot(:,1);                % Displacement of mass 1
x1fft = fft(x1);                % Fourier transform of displacement
spect = abs(x1fft).^2;          % Power spectrum of displacement


%* Apply the Hanning window to the time series and calculate
%  the resulting power spectrum
window = 0.5*(1-cos(2*pi*((1:nstep)-1)/nstep)); % Hanning window
x1w = x1 .* window';            % Windowed time series
x1wfft = fft(x1w);              % Fourier transf. (windowed data)
spectw = abs(x1wfft).^2;        % Power spectrum (windowed data)


%* Graph the power spectra for original and windowed data
figure(2); clf;  % Clear figure 2 window and bring forward
semilogy(f(1:(nstep/2)),spect(1:(nstep/2)),'-',...
         f(1:(nstep/2)),spectw(1:(nstep/2)),'--');
title('Power spectrum (dashed is windowed data)');
xlabel('Frequency'); ylabel('Power');
```

Listing 5A.6 Function sprrk. Defines the equations of motion for coupled spring-mass system. Used by sprfft.

```
function deriv = sprrk(s,t,param)
%  Returns right-hand side of 3 mass-spring system
%  equations of motion
%  Inputs
%    s          State vector [x(1) x(2) ... v(3)]
%    t          Time (not used)
%    param      (Spring constant)/(Block mass)
%  Output
%    deriv      [dx(1)/dt dx(2)/dt ... dv(3)/dt]
deriv(1) = s(4);
deriv(2) = s(5);
deriv(3) = s(6);
param2 = -2*param;
deriv(4) = param2*s(1) + param*s(2);
deriv(5) = param2*s(2) + param*(s(1)+s(3));
deriv(6) = param2*s(3) + param*s(2);
return;
```

APPENDIX B: C++ LISTINGS

Listing 5B.1 Function `linreg`. Fits a straight line to a data set.

```cpp
#include "NumMeth.h"

void linreg(Matrix x, Matrix y, Matrix sigma,
            Matrix &a_fit, Matrix &sig_a, Matrix &yy, double &chisqr) {
// Function to perform linear regression (fit a line)
// Inputs
//   x        Independent variable
//   y        Dependent variable
//   sigma    Estimated error in y
// Outputs
//   a_fit    Fit parameters; a(1) is intercept, a(2) is slope
//   sig_a    Estimated error in the parameters a()
//   yy       Curve fit to the data
//   chisqr   Chi squared statistic

  //* Evaluate various sigma sums
  int i, nData = x.nRow();
  double sigmaTerm;
  double s = 0.0, sx = 0.0, sy = 0.0, sxy = 0.0, sxx = 0.0;
  for( i=1; i<=nData; i++ ) {
    sigmaTerm = 1.0/(sigma(i)*sigma(i));
    s += sigmaTerm;
    sx += x(i) * sigmaTerm;
    sy += y(i) * sigmaTerm;
    sxy += x(i) * y(i) * sigmaTerm;
    sxx += x(i) * x(i) * sigmaTerm;
  }
  double denom = s*sxx - sx*sx;

  //* Compute intercept a_fit(1) and slope a_fit(2)
  a_fit(1) = (sxx*sy - sx*sxy)/denom;
  a_fit(2) = (s*sxy - sx*sy)/denom;

  //* Compute error bars for intercept and slope
  sig_a(1) = sqrt(sxx/denom);
  sig_a(2) = sqrt(s/denom);

  //* Evaluate curve fit at each data point and compute Chi^2
  chisqr = 0.0;
  for( i=1; i<=nData; i++ ) {
    yy(i) = a_fit(1)+a_fit(2)*x(i);      // Curve fit to the data
    double delta = (y(i)-yy(i))/sigma(i);
    chisqr += delta*delta;  // Chi square
  }
}
```

Listing 5B.2 Program `lsfdemo`. Generates a data set and fits a curve to the data; may be used to test the `linreg` (Listing 5B.1) and `pollsf` (Listing 5B.3) functions. Also uses the random number generator `randn` (Listing 11B.8).

```
// lsfdemo - Program for demonstrating least squares fit routines
#include "NumMeth.h"

void linreg( Matrix x, Matrix y, Matrix sigma,
             Matrix &a_fit, Matrix &sig_a, Matrix &yy, double &chisqr );
void pollsf( Matrix x, Matrix y, Matrix sigma, int M,
             Matrix& a_fit, Matrix& sig_a, Matrix& yy, double& chisqr );
double randn( long& iseed );

void main() {

  //* Initialize data to be fit. Data is quadratic plus random number.
  Matrix c(3);
  cout << "Curve fit data is created using the quadratic" << endl;
  cout << "  y(x) = c(1) + c(2)*x + c(3)*x^2" << endl;
  cout << "Enter the coefficients:" << endl;
  cout << "c(1) = "; cin >> c(1);
  cout << "c(2) = "; cin >> c(2);
  cout << "c(3) = "; cin >> c(3);
  double alpha;
  cout << "Enter estimated error bar: "; cin >> alpha;
  int i, N = 50;         // Number of data points
  long seed = 1234;      // Seed for random number generator
  Matrix x(N), y(N), sigma(N);
  for( i=1; i<=N; i++ ) {
    x(i) = i;                        // x = [1, 2, ..., N]
    y(i) = c(1) + c(2)*x(i) + c(3)*x(i)*x(i) + alpha*randn(seed);
    sigma(i) = alpha;                // Constant error bar
  }

  //* Fit the data to a straight line or a more general polynomial
  cout << "Enter number of fit parameters (=2 for line): ";
  int M;  cin >> M;
  Matrix a_fit(M), sig_a(M), yy(N);  double chisqr;
  if( M == 2 )  //* Linear regression (Straight line) fit
    linreg( x, y, sigma, a_fit, sig_a, yy, chisqr);
  else          //* Polynomial fit
    pollsf( x, y, sigma, M, a_fit, sig_a, yy, chisqr);

  //* Print out the fit parameters, including their error bars.
  cout << "Fit parameters:" << endl;
  for( i=1; i<=M; i++ )
    cout << " a(" << i << ") = " << a_fit(i) <<
            " +/- " << sig_a(i) << endl;
```

```
  cout << "Chi square = " << chisqr << "; N-M = " << N-M << endl;

  //* Print out the plotting variables: x, y, sigma, yy
  ofstream xOut("x.txt"), yOut("y.txt"),
           sigmaOut("sigma.txt"), yyOut("yy.txt");
  for( i=1; i<=N; i++ ) {
    xOut << x(i) << endl;
    yOut << y(i) << endl;
    sigmaOut << sigma(i) << endl;
    yyOut << yy(i) << endl;
  }
}
/***** To plot in MATLAB; use the script below *******************
load x.txt; load y.txt; load sigma.txt; load yy.txt
%* Graph the data, with error bars, and fitting function.
figure(1); clf;          % Bring figure 1 window forward
errorbar(x,y,sigma,'o'); % Graph data with error bars
hold on;                 % Freeze the plot to add the fit
plot(x,yy,'-');          % Plot the fit on same graph as data
xlabel('x_i'); ylabel('y_i and Y(x)');
*****************************************************************/
```

Listing 5B.3 Function `pollsf`. Fits a polynomial to a data set. Uses `inv` (Listing 4B.4).

```
#include "NumMeth.h"

void inv(Matrix a, Matrix& aInv);

void pollsf( Matrix x, Matrix y, Matrix sigma, int M,
             Matrix& a_fit, Matrix& sig_a, Matrix& yy, double& chisqr) {
// Function to fit a polynomial to data
// Inputs
//   x       Independent variable
//   y       Dependent variable
//   sigma   Estimate error in y
//   M       Number of parameters used to fit data
// Outputs
//   a_fit   Fit parameters; a(1) is intercept, a(2) is slope
//   sig_a   Estimated error in the parameters a()
//   yy      Curve fit to the data
//   chisqr  Chi squared statistic

  //* Form the vector b and design matrix A
  int i, j, k, N = x.nRow();
  Matrix b(N), A(N,M);
  for( i=1; i<=N; i++ ) {
    b(i) = y(i)/sigma(i);
    for( j=1; j<=M; j++ )
```

```
      A(i,j) = pow(x(i),(double)(j-1))/sigma(i);
    }


    //* Compute the correlation matrix C
    Matrix C(M,M), Cinv(M,M);
    for( i=1; i<=M; i++ ) {   // (C inverse) = (A transpose) * A
      for( j=1; j<=M; j++ ) {
        Cinv(i,j) = 0.0;
        for( k=1; k<=N; k++ )
          Cinv(i,j) += A(k,i)*A(k,j);
      }
    }
    inv( Cinv, C );   // C = ( (C inverse) inverse)

    //* Compute the least squares polynomial coefficients a_fit
    for( k=1; k<=M; k++ ) {
      a_fit(k) = 0.0;
      for( j=1; j<=M; j++ )
       for( i=1; i<=N; i++ )
         a_fit(k) += C(k,j) * A(i,j) * b(i);
    }

    //* Compute the estimated error bars for the coefficients
    for( j=1; j<=M; j++ )
      sig_a(j) = sqrt(C(j,j));

    //* Evaluate curve fit at each data point and compute Chi^2
    chisqr = 0.0;
    for( i=1; i<=N; i++ ) {
      yy(i) = 0.0;        // yy is the curve fit
      for( j=1; j<=M; j++ )
        yy(i) += a_fit(j) * pow( x(i), (double)(j-1) );
      double delta = (y(i)-yy(i))/sigma(i);
      chisqr += delta*delta;   // Chi square
    }
}
```

Listing 5B.4 Program `ftdemo`. Demonstrates the discrete Fourier transform using the direct summation or the Fast Fourier transform method. Uses `fft` function (Listing 5B.7).

```
// ftdemo - Discrete Fourier transform demonstration program
#include "NumMeth.h"
// Defines timing routines time() and difftime()
#include <time.h>

void fft( Matrix& RealA, Matrix& ImagA);
```

```cpp
void main() {

  //* Initialize the sine wave time series to be transformed.
  cout << "Enter the number of points: ";
  int N; cin >> N;
  cout << "Enter frequency of the sine wave: ";
  double freq; cin >> freq;
  cout << "Enter phase of the sine wave: ";
  double phase; cin >> phase;
  double tau = 1;  // Time increment
  const double pi = 3.141592654;
  Matrix t(N), y(N), f(N);
  int i,j,k;
  for( i=1; i<=N; i++ ) {
    t(i) = (i-1)*tau;                    // t = [0, tau, 2*tau, ... ]
    y(i) = sin(2*pi*t(i)*freq + phase);  // Sine wave time series
    f(i) = (i-1)/(N*tau);                // f = [0, 1/(N*tau), ... ]
  }

  //* Compute the transform using desired method: direct summation
  //  or fast Fourier transform (FFT) algorithm.
  Matrix ytReal(N), ytImag(N);
  cout << "Compute transform by, 1) Direct summation; 2) FFT: ";
  int method; cin >> method;
  time_t startTime = time(NULL);
  if( method == 1 ) {              // Direct summation
    double twoPiN = -2*pi/N;
    for( k=0; k<N; k++ ) {
      ytReal(k+1) = 0.0;
      ytImag(k+1) = 0.0;
      for( j=0; j<N; j++ ) {
        ytReal(k+1) += y(j+1)*cos(twoPiN*j*k);
        ytImag(k+1) += y(j+1)*sin(twoPiN*j*k);
      }
    }
  }
  else  {                         // Fast Fourier transform
    ytReal = y;
    ytImag.set(0.0);       // Copy data for input to fft
    fft(ytReal, ytImag);
  }
  time_t stopTime = time(NULL);
  double totalSec = difftime( stopTime, startTime );
  cout << "Computation time = " << totalSec << " seconds" << endl;
  // Compute the power spectrum
  Matrix powSpec(N);
  for( k=1; k<=N; k++ )
    powSpec(k) = ytReal(k)*ytReal(k) + ytImag(k)*ytImag(k);

  //* Print out the plotting variables:
```

```
//    t, y, f, ytReal, ytImag, powspec
ofstream tOut("t.txt"), yOut("y.txt"), fOut("f.txt"),
    ytRealOut("ytReal.txt"), ytImagOut("ytImag.txt"),
    powSpecOut("powSpec.txt");
for( i=1; i<=N; i++ ) {
  tOut << t(i) << endl;
  yOut << y(i) << endl;
  fOut << f(i) << endl;
  ytRealOut << ytReal(i) << endl;
  ytImagOut << ytImag(i) << endl;
  powSpecOut << powSpec(i) << endl;
  }
}
/***** To plot in MATLAB; use the script below ********************
load t.txt; load y.txt; load f.txt;
load ytReal.txt; load ytImag.txt; load powSpec.txt;
%* Graph the time series and its transform.
figure(1); clf;  % Clear figure 1 window and bring forward
plot(t,y);
title('Original time series');
ylabel('Amplitude');  xlabel('Time');
figure(2); clf;  % Clear figure 2 window and bring forward
plot(f,ytReal,'-',f,ytImag,'--');
legend('Real','Imaginary');
title('Fourier transform');
ylabel('Transform');  xlabel('Frequency');
%* Compute and graph the power spectrum of the time series.
figure(3); clf;  % Clear figure 3 window and bring forward
semilogy(f,powSpec,'-');
title('Power spectrum (unnormalized)');
ylabel('Power');  xlabel('Frequency');
*****************************************************************/
```

Listing 5B.5 Program `sprfft`. Computes the evolution of a coupled mass-spring system; uses Fourier transforms to obtain the eigenfrequencies. Uses `rk4` (Listing 3B.2), `sprrk` (Listing 5B.6) and `fft` (Listing 5B.7).

```
// sprfft - Program to compute the power spectrum of a
// coupled mass-spring system.
#include "NumMeth.h"

void sprrk(double x[], double t, double param[], double deriv[]);
void rk4( double x[], int nX, double t, double tau,
  void (*derivsRK)(double x[], double t, double param[], double deriv[]),
  double param[]);
void fft( Matrix& RealA, Matrix& ImagA);

void main() {
```

```cpp
//* Set parameters for the system (initial positions, etc.).
const int nState = 6;
Matrix x(3), v(3); double state[nState+1];
cout << "Enter initial displacement of:" << endl;
cout << "  Mass #1 = "; cin >> x(1);
cout << "  Mass #2 = "; cin >> x(2);
cout << "  Mass #3 = "; cin >> x(3);
v(1) = 0.0; v(2) = 0.0; v(3) = 0.0; // Masses are initially at rest
state[1] = x(1);  state[2] = x(2);  state[3] = x(3);
state[4] = v(1);  state[5] = v(2);  state[6] = v(3);
cout << "Enter timestep: "; double tau; cin >> tau;
double k_over_m = 1;      // Ratio of spring const. over mass
double param[1+1]; param[1] = k_over_m;

//* Loop over the desired number of time steps.
double time = 0;          // Set initial time
int nStep = 256;          // Number of steps in the main loop
int nprint = nStep/8;     // Number of steps between printing progress
Matrix xplot(nStep,3), tplot(nStep);  // Plotting variables
int i, iStep;
for( iStep=1; iStep<=nStep; iStep++ ) {

  //* Use Runge-Kutta to find new displacements of the masses.
  rk4(state,nState,time,tau,sprrk,param);
  time = time + tau;

  //* Record the positions for graphing and to compute spectra.
  xplot(iStep,1) = state[1];   // Record positions
  xplot(iStep,2) = state[2];  xplot(iStep,3) = state[3];
  tplot(iStep) = time;
  if( (iStep%nprint) < 1 )
    cout << "Finished " << iStep << " out of " <<
                     nStep << " steps" << endl;
}

//* Calculate the power spectrum of the time series for mass #1
Matrix f(nStep), x1fftR(nStep), x1fftI(nStep), spect(nStep);
for( i=1; i<=nStep; i++ ) {
  f(i) = (i-1)/(tau*nStep);       // Frequency
  double x1 = xplot(i,1);         // Displacement of mass 1
  x1fftR(i) = x1;
  x1fftI(i) = 0.0;     // Copy data for input to fft
}
fft(x1fftR, x1fftI);             // Fourier transform of displacement
for( i=1; i<=nStep; i++ )       // Power spectrum of displacement
  spect(i) = x1fftR(i)*x1fftR(i) + x1fftI(i)*x1fftI(i);

//* Apply the Hanning window to the time series and calculate
//  the resulting power spectrum
double window, pi = 3.141592654;
```

```
  Matrix x1fftRw(nStep), x1fftIw(nStep), spectw(nStep);
  for( i=1; i<=nStep; i++ ) {
    window = 0.5*(1.0-cos(2.0*pi*(i-1.0)/nStep)); // Hanning window
    double x1w = xplot(i,1) * window;       // Windowed time series
    x1fftRw(i) = x1w;
    x1fftIw(i) = 0.0;      // Copy data for input to fft
  }
  fft(x1fftRw, x1fftIw);                  // Fourier transf. (windowed data)
  for( i=1; i<=nStep; i++ )     // Power spectrum (windowed data)
    spectw(i) = x1fftRw(i)*x1fftRw(i) + x1fftIw(i)*x1fftIw(i);

  //* Print out the plotting variables:
  //    tplot, xplot, f, spect, spectw
  ofstream tplotOut("tplot.txt"), xplotOut("xplot.txt"), fOut("f.txt"),
           spectOut("spect.txt"), spectwOut("spectw.txt");
  for( i=1; i<=nStep; i++ ) {
    tplotOut << tplot(i) << endl;
    xplotOut << xplot(i,1) << ", " << xplot(i,2) << ", "
             << xplot(i,3) << endl;
    fOut << f(i) << endl;
    spectOut << spect(i) << endl;
    spectwOut << spectw(i) << endl;
  }
}
/***** To plot in MATLAB; use the script below ********************
load tplot.txt; load xplot.txt; load f.txt;
load spect.txt; load spectw.txt
nstep = length(tplot);  nprint = nstep/8;
%* Graph the displacements of the three masses.
figure(1); clf;  % Clear figure 1 window and bring forward
ipr = 1:nprint:nstep;  % Used to graph limited number of symbols
plot(tplot(ipr),xplot(ipr,1),'o',tplot(ipr),xplot(ipr,2),'+',...
     tplot(ipr),xplot(ipr,3),'*',...
     tplot,xplot(:,1),'-',tplot,xplot(:,2),'-.',...
     tplot,xplot(:,3),'--');
legend('Mass #1','Mass #2','Mass #3');
title('Displacement of masses (relative to rest positions)');
xlabel('Time'); ylabel('Displacement');
%* Graph the power spectra for original and windowed data
figure(2); clf;  % Clear figure 2 window and bring forward
semilogy(f(1:(nstep/2)),spect(1:(nstep/2)),'-',...
         f(1:(nstep/2)),spectw(1:(nstep/2)),'--');
title('Power spectrum (dashed is windowed data)');
xlabel('Frequency'); ylabel('Power');
****************************************************************/
```

Listing 5B.6 Function sprrk. Defines the equations of motion for coupled spring-mass system. Used by sprfft.

```
void sprrk(double x[], double t, double param[], double deriv[]) {
```

```
//  Returns right-hand side of 3 mass-spring system
//  equations of motion
//  Inputs
//    x         State vector [x(1) x(2) ... v(3)]
//    t         Time (not used)
//    param     (Spring constant)/(Block mass)
//  Output
//    deriv     [dx(1)/dt dx(2)/dt ... dv(3)/dt]
  deriv[1] = x[4];
  deriv[2] = x[5];
  deriv[3] = x[6];
  double param2 = -2*param[1];
  deriv[4] = param2*x[1] + param[1]*x[2];
  deriv[5] = param2*x[2] + param[1]*(x[1]+x[3]);
  deriv[6] = param2*x[3] + param[1]*x[2];
  return;
}
```

Listing 5B.7 Function fft. Computes the discrete Fourier transform using the FFT algorithm.

```
#include "NumMeth.h"

void fft( Matrix& RealA, Matrix& ImagA) {
// Routine to compute discrete Fourier transform using FFT algorithm
// Inputs
//    RealA, ImagA        Real and imaginary parts of data vector
// Outputs
//    RealA, ImagA        Real and imaginary parts of transform

  double RealU, RealW, RealT, ImagU, ImagW, ImagT;

  //* Determine size of input data and check that it is power of 2
  int N = RealA.nRow();  // Number of data points
  int M = (int)(log( (double)N )/log(2.0) + 0.5);   // N = 2^M
  int NN = (int)(pow(2.0,(double)M) + 0.5);
  if( N != NN ) {
    cerr << "ERROR in fft(): Number of data points not power of 2" << endl;
    return;
  }
  const double pi = 3.141592654;
  int N_half = N/2;
  int Nm1 = N-1;

  //* Bit-scramble the input data by swapping elements
  int i,k,j=1;
  for( i=1; i<=Nm1; i++ ) {
    if( i < j ) {
      RealT = RealA(j);     ImagT = ImagA(j);     // Swap elements i and j
```

```
      RealA(j) = RealA(i);   ImagA(j) = ImagA(i);  // of RealA and ImagA
      RealA(i) = RealT;      ImagA(i) = ImagT;
    }
    k = N_half;
    while( k < j ) {
      j -= k;
      k /= 2;
    }
    j += k;
  }

  //* Loop over number of layers, M = log_2(N)
  for( k=1; k<=M; k++ ) {
    int ke = (int)(pow(2.0,(double)k) + 0.5);
    int ke1 = ke/2;
    //* Compute lowest, non-zero power of W for this layer
    RealU = 1.0;  ImagU = 0.0;
    double angle = -pi/ke1;
    RealW = cos(angle);  ImagW = sin(angle);
    //* Loop over elements in binary order (outer loop)
    for( j=1; j<=ke1; j++ ) {
      //* Loop over elements in binary order (inner loop)
      for( i=j; i<=N; i+=ke ) {
        int ip = i + ke1;
        //* Compute the y(.)*W^. factor for this element
        RealT = RealA(ip)*RealU - ImagA(ip)*ImagU;  // T = A(ip)*U
        ImagT = RealA(ip)*ImagU + ImagA(ip)*RealU;
        //* Update the current element and its binary pair
        RealA(ip) = RealA(i)-RealT;
        ImagA(ip) = ImagA(i)-ImagT;     // A(ip) = A(i) - T
        RealA(i) += RealT;
        ImagA(i) += ImagT;              // A(i) = A(i) + T
      }
      //* Increment the power of W for next set of elements
      double temp = RealU*RealW - ImagU*ImagW;
      ImagU = RealU*ImagW + ImagU*RealW;        // U = U * W
      RealU = temp;
    }
  }
}
```

Listing 5B.8 Function ifft. Computes the discrete inverse Fourier transform using the FFT algorithm. Uses fft (Listing 5B.7).

```
#include "NumMeth.h"

void fft( Matrix& RealA, Matrix& ImagA);

void ifft( Matrix& RealA, Matrix& ImagA) {
```

```
// Routine to compute inverse Fourier transform using FFT algorithm
// Inputs
//    RealA, ImagA          Real and imaginary parts of transform
// Outputs
//    RealA, ImagA          Real and imaginary parts of time series

  int i, N = RealA.nRow();    // Number of data points

  //* Take complex conjugate of input transform
  for( i=1; i<=N; i++ )
    ImagA(i) *= -1.0;          // Complex conjugate

  //* Evaluate fast fourier transform
  fft( RealA, ImagA );

  //* Take complex conjugate and normalize by N
  double invN = 1.0/N;
  for( i=1; i<=N; i++ ) {
    RealA(i) *= invN;
    ImagA(i) *= -invN;      // Normalize and complex conjugate
  }
}
```

APPENDIX C: CARBON DIOXIDE DATA

Table 5.9: Carbon dioxide (in parts per million) measured at Mauna Loa, Hawaii.

339.35	339.96	340.59	341.17	341.67	342.13	342.61	343.10
343.49	343.60	343.34	342.72	341.90	341.01	340.18	339.41
338.66	337.93	337.32	337.00	337.07	337.52	338.21	338.96
339.60	340.10	340.51	340.89	341.32	341.84	342.39	342.92
343.40	343.78	343.99	343.96	343.69	343.28	342.85	342.36
341.68	340.69	339.45	338.24	337.36	337.01	337.17	337.69
338.37	339.11	339.84	340.56	341.28	341.79	342.07	342.15
342.25	342.64	343.43	344.46	345.37	345.86	345.87	345.51
344.95	344.23	343.34	342.27	341.16	340.21	339.60	339.40
339.54	339.91	340.40	341.00	341.71	342.48	343.26	343.81
344.15	344.36	344.61	345.06	345.70	346.41	346.99	347.28
347.25	346.96	346.46	345.77	344.91	343.91	342.85	341.89
341.22	340.98	341.19	341.69	342.30	342.89	343.39	343.79
344.14	344.42	344.78	345.30	345.93	346.55	347.07	347.53
347.96	348.34	348.53	348.41	347.93	347.14	346.12	345.01
343.99	343.19	342.69	342.47	342.52	342.83	343.36	344.02
344.69	345.26	345.71	345.97	346.15	346.36	346.74	347.35
348.11	348.88	349.48	349.80	349.79	349.43	348.75	347.85
346.90	346.01	345.24	344.56	343.97	343.54	343.43	343.78
344.53	345.45	346.23	346.74	347.05	347.30	347.62	348.01
348.46	348.98	349.61	350.32	351.00	351.48	351.66	351.52
351.07	350.33	349.38	348.34	347.40	346.70	346.31	346.20
346.35	346.77	347.42	348.17	348.83	349.29	349.65	350.02
350.52	351.09	351.63	352.12	352.63	353.19	353.72	354.07
354.14	353.95	353.55	352.98	352.21	351.25	350.19	349.26
348.68	348.54	348.75	349.11	349.51	349.96	350.55	351.27
352.07	352.55	352.77	352.87	353.07	353.51	354.22	355.02
355.66	355.97	355.92	355.63	355.19	354.59	353.74	352.60
351.30	350.12	349.36	349.13	349.37	349.91		

Notes: Measurements were taken every 14 days, starting in 1981. Values in table are ordered left to right and then down (i.e., the second value is 339.96). Estimated error is $\sigma_0 = 0.16$ ppm.

Table 5.10: Carbon dioxide (in parts per million) measured at Barrow, Alaska.

344.20	344.83	345.20	345.37	345.41	345.42	345.52	345.79
346.21	346.56	346.47	345.51	343.42	340.24	336.50	333.06
330.85	330.45	331.84	334.40	337.20	339.52	341.17	342.39
343.49	344.52	345.39	345.95	346.44	347.01	347.57	347.88
347.82	347.62	347.56	347.67	347.60	346.87	345.18	342.59
339.41	336.15	333.46	332.02	332.24	334.01	336.66	339.31
341.39	342.83	343.91	344.91	345.89	346.55	346.89	347.08
347.29	347.55	347.76	347.86	347.93	348.12	348.30	347.98
346.60	343.92	340.29	336.55	333.67	332.37	332.93	335.17
338.43	341.78	344.35	345.82	346.48	346.99	347.87	348.96
349.92	350.41	350.38	350.05	349.69	349.57	349.77	350.19
350.45	349.98	348.29	345.33	341.66	338.24	336.01	335.45
336.40	338.28	340.36	342.16	343.62	345.01	346.53	348.04
349.23	349.53	349.38	349.29	349.57	350.19	350.92	351.57
352.05	352.30	352.15	351.36	349.66	346.92	343.38	339.78
337.13	336.24	337.24	339.58	342.34	344.78	346.52	347.60
348.28	348.85	349.59	350.48	351.54	352.56	353.29	353.57
353.47	353.26	353.19	353.23	353.07	352.24	350.37	347.40
343.72	340.30	338.30	338.47	340.61	343.70	346.52	348.44
349.53	350.29	351.11	352.02	352.82	353.25	353.44	353.61
353.87	354.12	354.27	354.36	354.57	354.89	355.03	354.46
352.76	349.83	346.14	342.57	340.10	339.33	340.20	342.16
344.50	346.69	348.52	350.02	351.40	352.83	354.41	355.73
356.60	356.95	357.01	357.10	357.36	357.65	357.77	357.65
357.27	356.38	354.58	351.72	348.20	344.98	343.04	342.84
344.22	346.56	349.18	351.57	353.58	355.32	356.92	358.35
359.40	359.55	359.18	358.86	359.07	359.75	360.34	360.37
359.90	359.43	359.33	359.26	358.23	355.34	350.71	345.74
342.40	342.01	344.35	347.96	351.22	353.33		

Notes: Measurements were taken every 14 days, starting in 1981. Values in table are ordered left to right and then down (i.e., the second value is 344.83). Estimated error is $\sigma_0 = 0.27$ ppm.

Chapter 6

Partial Differential Equations I: Foundations and Basic Explicit Methods

Up to now, most of the physical systems we have simulated were formulated using ordinary differential equations. However, much of physics involves working with partial differential equations (PDEs). We have the Schrödinger equation in quantum mechanics, Maxwell's equations in electricity and magnetism, and the wave equation in optics and acoustics. The next four chapters cover techniques used to treat such equations numerically. This chapter starts by discussing the various types of PDEs and describing how to solve parabolic PDEs, such as the diffusion equation, using an explicit marching method.

6.1   INTRODUCTION TO PDEs

Classification of PDEs

In solving ordinary differential equations we developed some general methods, such as Runge-Kutta, that could be applied to any problem. The situation is different with partial differential equations (PDEs). The classification of the equation is a guide to the type of method that should be used.

Instead of introducing the classification of PDEs in the abstract, let's discuss some familiar, concrete examples. There are three PDEs that serve as model equations for our classification scheme and, fortunately, you have already seen them in your other physics courses. The first is the one-dimensional diffusion equation:

$$\frac{\partial}{\partial t} T(x,t) = \kappa \frac{\partial^2}{\partial x^2} T(x,t) \tag{6.1}$$

This equation is used to describe many different diffusion processes. Here it is written as the Fourier equation from the theory of heat transport. The variable $T(x,t)$ is the temperature at position x and time t. The constant κ is the thermal diffusion coefficient. This first equation is an example of a *parabolic equation*. The time-dependent Schrödinger equation is another example (see Section 9.2).

The second important PDE that we study is the one-dimensional wave equation

$$\frac{\partial^2 A}{\partial t^2} = c^2 \frac{\partial^2 A}{\partial x^2} \tag{6.2}$$

where $A(x,t)$ is the wave amplitude and c is the wave speed. This equation is classified as a *hyperbolic equation*.

Our third partial differential equation is Poisson's equation used in electrostatics. In two dimensions, it takes the form

$$\frac{\partial^2 \Phi}{\partial x^2} + \frac{\partial^2 \Phi}{\partial y^2} = -\frac{1}{\epsilon_0} \rho(x,y) \tag{6.3}$$

where $\Phi(x,y)$ is the electrostatic potential, $\rho(x,y)$ is the charge density, and ϵ_0 is the permittivity of free space. If $\rho = 0$, then we have Laplace's equation. The Poisson and Laplace equations are classified as *elliptic equations*.

Notice that in each of these examples we have two independent variables, either (x,t) or (x,y). All the methods we discuss are extendable to higher-dimensional systems, but are much easier to understand when first used with only two variables. Formally, a second-order PDE in two independent variables of the form

$$a\frac{\partial^2 A}{\partial x^2} + b\frac{\partial^2 A}{\partial x \partial y} + c\frac{\partial^2 A}{\partial y^2} + d\frac{\partial A}{\partial x} + e\frac{\partial A}{\partial y} + f A(x,y) + g = 0 \tag{6.4}$$

was classified as hyperbolic if $b^2 - 4ac > 0$, parabolic if $b^2 - 4ac = 0$, and elliptic if $b^2 - 4ac < 0$.

Initial Value Problems

The diffusion equation and the wave equation are similar in that they are usually solved as initial value problems. For the diffusion equation, we might be given an initial temperature distribution $T(x,t=0)$ and want to find $T(x,t)$ for all $t > 0$. Similarly, for the wave equation, we could start with the initial amplitude $A(x,t=0)$ and velocity $dA(x,t=0)/dt$ of a wave pulse and be asked to find the shape of the wave pulse, $A(x,t)$, for all $t > 0$.

Besides initial conditions, we also need to specify boundary conditions. Say our solution is constrained to the region of space between $x = -L/2$ and $x =$

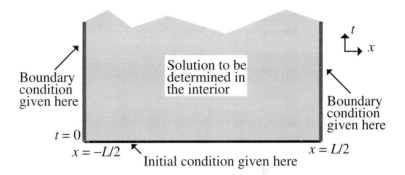

Figure 6.1: Schematic representation for an initial value problem.

$L/2$. Boundary conditions are imposed at these end points. For the diffusion equation we could fix the temperature at the boundaries,

$$T(x = -L/2, t) = T_a; \qquad T(x = L/2, t) = T_b \qquad (6.5)$$

This is an example of *Dirichlet boundary conditions*. An alternative would be to fix the heat flux at the boundaries

$$-\kappa \frac{dT}{dx}\bigg|_{x=-L/2} = F_a; \qquad -\kappa \frac{dT}{dx}\bigg|_{x=L/2} = F_b \qquad (6.6)$$

If the boundaries are insulated, then $F_a = F_b = 0$. In this case we have *Neumann boundary conditions*. A third type of boundary condition is common in numerical simulations. We can equate the function at the two ends,

$$T(x = -L/2, t) = T(x = L/2, t) \qquad (6.7)$$

$$\frac{dT}{dx}\bigg|_{x=-L/2} = \frac{dT}{dx}\bigg|_{x=L/2} \qquad (6.8)$$

This is called a *periodic boundary condition*. In one dimension, using periodic boundary conditions is equivalent to transforming our coordinates from a line to a circle.

A useful way to picture initial value problems is to view them on the xt plane, as shown in Figure 6.1. Notice that the interior region is open ended; we may compute $T(x, t)$ or $A(x, t)$ as far into the future as we want.

As with ODEs, we discretize the time as $t_n = (n - 1)\tau$, where τ is the time step and $n = 1, 2, \ldots$. Similarly we discretize space as $x_i = (i - 1)h - L/2$, where h is the grid spacing and $i = 1, 2, \ldots$. A schematic of an initial value problem in discretized form is shown in Figure 6.2. Our job is to determine the unknown values in the interior (open circles) given the initial conditions (gray circles) and the boundary conditions (filled circles).

Initial value problems are often solved using *marching methods*. Starting from the initial condition, we compute the solution one time step into the future.

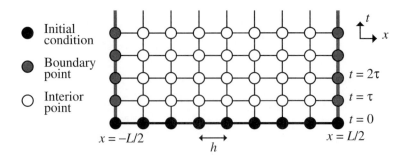

Figure 6.2: Schematic representation for a discretized initial value problem.

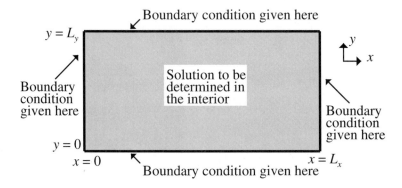

Figure 6.3: Schematic representation for a boundary value problem.

Using this result, the solution at $t = 2\tau$ is computed. The algorithm proceeds in this manner and marches forward in time. Initial value problems are solved both analytically and numerically in this chapter and the next.

Boundary Value Problems

Elliptic equations, such as Laplace's equation in electrostatics, are not initial value problems but rather boundary value problems. For example, we may be told the potential on the four sides of a rectangle,

$$\Phi(x = 0, y) = \Phi_1; \qquad \Phi(x = L_x, y) = \Phi_2;$$
$$\Phi(x, y = 0) = \Phi_3; \qquad \Phi(x, y = L_y) = \Phi_4 \qquad (6.9)$$

and be asked to solve for $\Phi(x, y)$ at all points inside the rectangle (Figure 6.3). We discretize space as $x_i = (i - 1)h_x$, $y_j = (j - 1)h_y$ where h_x and h_y are the x and y grid spacings. Now our task is to determine Φ at the interior points, given the constraints specified by the boundary conditions (Figure 6.4).

Algorithms for solving boundary value problems are sometimes called *jury methods*. The potential at an interior point is influenced by all the bound-

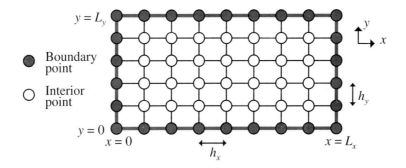

Figure 6.4: Schematic representation for a discretized boundary value problem.

ary points; the solution in the interior is a weighted result that reconciles all the demands (constraints) imposed by the boundary. The methods for solving boundary value problems are covered in Chapter 8.

I don't want to dwell too much on the classification of equations. We could go on to discuss the uniqueness of solutions; instead, let's start looking at algorithms for solving our three model equations. One last note: Most equations encountered in real research do not fall neatly into one of our three categories. Instead, they are often hybrids. For example, consider acoustic wave propagation with attenuation. The equations are in part hyperbolic and in part parabolic. Still, the methods we develop here will be applicable to such hybrid problems.

6.2 DIFFUSION EQUATION

Method of Images

We'll start with the most cooperative of the three PDEs introduced in the previous section, the diffusion equation:

$$\frac{\partial}{\partial t}T(x,t) = \kappa\frac{\partial^2}{\partial x^2}T(x,t) \tag{6.10}$$

where $T(x,t)$ is the temperature at location x and time t; the constant κ is the thermal diffusion coefficient. Before solving this equation numerically, let's obtain the analytical solutions to some simple initial value problems. There are several ways to solve the diffusion equation (e.g., separation of variables, integral transforms). In this section we use one of the lesser known techniques, the *method of images*.[86]

An important solution of this PDE is a Gaussian of the form

$$T_G(x,t) = \frac{1}{\sigma(t)\sqrt{2\pi}}\exp\left[\frac{-(x-x_0)^2}{2\sigma^2(t)}\right] \tag{6.11}$$

where x_0 is the location of the maximum. The standard deviation, $\sigma(t)$, increases in time as

$$\sigma(t) = \sqrt{2\kappa t} \tag{6.12}$$

Notice that as $t \to 0$, $\sigma(t) \to 0$, so the width of the Gaussian tends to zero. Since the Gaussian is normalized,

$$\int_{-\infty}^{\infty} T_G(x,t)dx = 1 \tag{6.13}$$

then

$$\lim_{t \to 0} T_G(x,t) = \delta(x - x_0) \tag{6.14}$$

where $\delta(x)$ is the Dirac delta function. In fact, this Gaussian is one of the definitions of a delta function.[11] This Gaussian solution is important since it is also the Green's function for the infinite domain.[89]

The problem we want to solve is the following: Given the initial condition $T(x, t = 0) = \delta(x)$ and the Dirichlet boundary conditions,

$$T(x = -L/2, t) = T(x = L/2, t) = 0 \tag{6.15}$$

find $T(x,t)$ for all x and t. Physically, this problem corresponds to the diffusion of heat in a bar of length L whose ends are held at temperature $T = 0$. If this zero temperature bothers you, remember that we may add an arbitrary constant to the solution. At time $t = 0$, an infinitesimal spot at the center of the bar is instantaneously heated to a very high (infinite) temperature. The total heat (or energy) in the bar remains finite since the integral of the temperature is finite.

By the method of images, we may construct an analytical solution as

$$T(x,t) = \sum_{n=-\infty}^{\infty} (-1)^n T_G(x + nL, t) \tag{6.16}$$

To understand the construction, consider the schematic shown in Figure 6.5. The initial condition has images at $-L$ and L. But the image at L has an image of itself at $-2L$; similarly, the image at $-L$ has an image at $2L$. Of course, there are an infinity of images of images. The images are initially all delta functions of alternating signs. In time each spreads as a Gaussian, yet the sum maintains the boundary conditions at $x = \pm L/2$ (Figure 6.6). Notice that the solution looks somewhat like a Gaussian, except that the values at $x = \pm L/2$ are fixed at zero by the boundary conditions.

The method of images is most useful when we are interested in the solution for small t. The solution is an infinite sum, but for short times only the images near the origin contribute significantly. As t increases, more and more images contribute; in the case of large t it is better to use the solution obtained by separation of variables (see Sections 6.3 and 8.1). That solution is also an infinite sum, but the contributions from the higher-order terms decrease with time.

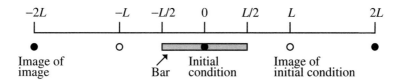

Figure 6.5: Method of images solution for the diffusion of a delta function initial condition. The images are positive or negative as indicated by the solid or open circles, respectively. There is an infinity of images at $\pm L, \pm 2L, \ldots$..

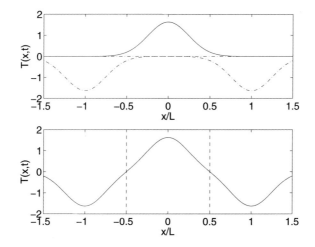

Figure 6.6: Plot of $T(x,t)$ as given by Equation (6.16) at $t = 0.03$ for $\kappa = 1$, $L = 1$. The original pulse and one image on each side are plotted in the top graph and their sum in the lower graph. Only the solution between $-L/2$ and $L/2$ has physical meaning.

Forward Time Centered Space Scheme

Now let's try to numerically solve the diffusion equation. As mentioned earlier in the chapter, we discretize time and space, so it is useful to introduce the shorthand

$$T_i^n = T(x_i, t_n) \tag{6.17}$$

where $x_i = (i-1)h - L/2$ and $t_n = (n-1)\tau$ (see Figure 6.2). The index i denotes the spatial location of a grid point, while the index n indicates the temporal step. Note that the boundary points are T_1^n and T_N^n, so the grid spacing is $h = L/(N-1)$.

The time derivative, discretized using the forward derivative form, becomes

$$\frac{\partial T(x,t)}{\partial t} \Rightarrow \frac{T(x_i, t_n + \tau) - T(x_i, t_n)}{\tau} = \frac{T_i^{n+1} - T_i^n}{\tau} \tag{6.18}$$

The space derivative is discretized using the centered derivative form,

$$
\begin{aligned}
\frac{\partial^2 T(x,t)}{\partial x^2} &\Rightarrow \frac{T(x_i + h, t_n) + T(x_i - h, t_n) - 2T(x_i, t_n)}{h^2} \\
&= \frac{T_{i+1}^n + T_{i-1}^n - 2T_i^n}{h^2}
\end{aligned} \tag{6.19}
$$

From the way we discretized the derivatives, this method takes the name forward time centered space (FTCS) scheme.

Using the above, our discretized diffusion equation is

$$\frac{T_i^{n+1} - T_i^n}{\tau} = \kappa \frac{T_{i+1}^n + T_{i-1}^n - 2T_i^n}{h^2} \tag{6.20}$$

The future value of temperature (at step $n + 1$) is explicitly determined from the current value, as is most apparent by arranging the terms as

$$T_i^{n+1} = T_i^n + \frac{\kappa\tau}{h^2}(T_{i+1}^n + T_{i-1}^n - 2T_i^n) \tag{6.21}$$

Given that everything that depends on time step n is on the right-hand side, while only the future value of temperature is on the left, the FTCS scheme is an example of an *explicit* method (implicit methods are discussed in Section 9.2). Because of the way the time derivative is discretized, the FTCS scheme may remind you of the Euler scheme for ODEs (see Chapter 2).

FTCS Program

A program called `dftcs`, which solves the diffusion equation using the FTCS method, is outlined in Table 6.1. The temperature at the ends is fixed at $T = 0$, so the boundary conditions are

$$T_1^n = T_N^n = 0 \tag{6.22}$$

Table 6.1: Outline of program `dftcs`, which computes the diffusion of a delta function using the FTCS method.

- Initialize parameters (τ, h, etc.).

- Set initial conditions (6.25) and boundary conditions (6.22) .

- Set up loop and plot variables.

- Loop over the desired number of time steps.

  - Compute new temperature using FTCS scheme, (6.21).
  - Periodically record temperature for plotting.

- Plot temperature versus x and t as wire-mesh and contour plots.

See pages 208 and 210 for program listings.

for all n. The initial condition we want to use is $T(x,0) = \delta(x)$, but we cannot put a delta function in the program. To best represent the delta function numerically, we use

$$\Delta(x) = \begin{cases} (x+h)/h^2 & \text{for } -h < x \le 0 \\ (h-x)/h^2 & \text{for } 0 \le x < h \\ 0 & \text{otherwise} \end{cases} \tag{6.23}$$

Notice that

$$\lim_{h \to 0} \Delta(x) = \delta(x) \tag{6.24}$$

The function $\Delta(x)$ is just a triangular spike with unit area. When we discretize $\Delta(x)$ we have

$$\Delta_i = \begin{cases} 1/h & \text{for } i = N/2 \\ 0 & \text{otherwise} \end{cases} \tag{6.25}$$

Note that

$$\int_{-L/2}^{L/2} \Delta(x)\, dx \to \sum_{i=1}^{N} \Delta_i h = 1 \tag{6.26}$$

so Δ_i also has unit area.

Before running the program, we should have some idea as to how to specify the time step. From Equation (6.12), we know the width of our Gaussian will spread in time as

$$\sigma(t) = \sqrt{2\kappa t} \tag{6.27}$$

Call t_σ the time it takes the width σ to increase from zero to h (i.e., by one grid spacing). From the above, we may write

$$t_\sigma = \frac{h^2}{2\kappa} \tag{6.28}$$

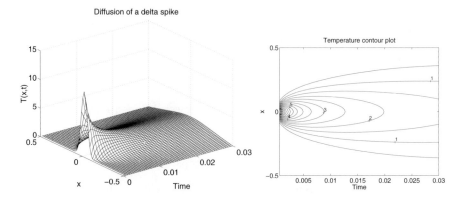

Figure 6.7: Mesh and contour plots of $T(x,t)$ from `dftcs`. Number of grid points is $N = 61$, time step $\tau = 1.0 \times 10^{-4}$.

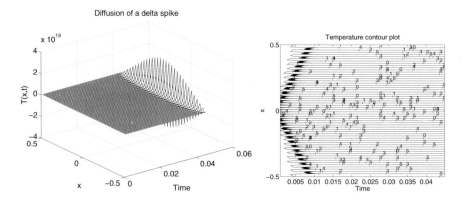

Figure 6.8: Mesh and contour plots of $T(x,t)$ from `dftcs`. Number of grid points is $N = 61$, time step $\tau = 1.5 \times 10^{-4}$. In this case, because $\tau > t_\sigma$, the FTCS scheme is numerically unstable.

Notice that the FTCS scheme, Equation (6.21), may be written in terms of t_σ as

$$T_i^{n+1} = T_i^n + \frac{\tau}{2t_\sigma}(T_{i+1}^n + T_{i-1}^n - 2T_i^n) \tag{6.29}$$

Our physical intuition tells us that we probably don't want to use a time step much larger than t_σ.

In running the `dftcs` program for $N = 61$ and $\tau = 1.0 \times 10^{-4}$, we obtain the results shown in Figure 6.7. In this case $h = L/(N-1) = 1/60$ and $\kappa = 1$, so $t_\sigma = 1.389 \times 10^{-4}$. Qualitatively, the profile looks correct; in the exercises you are asked to compare it quantitatively with the analytical solution.

The FTCS method is not stable for all values of τ and N. Specifically, it is unstable when $\tau > t_\sigma$ (Figure 6.8). In Chapter 9 we analyze why this happens and discuss some more advanced numerical methods that don't suffer from numerical instabilities.

EXERCISES

1. Show that Equation (6.11) is a solution to the diffusion PDE, Equation (6.10). [Pencil]
2. Show that the solution of the diffusion PDE, Equation (6.10), for the initial condition $T(x, t = 0) = T_0(x)$ $(-\infty < x < \infty)$ is

$$T(x, t) = \int_{-\infty}^{\infty} T_0(x')T_G(x - x', t)\, dx'$$

where T_G is given by (6.11). [Pencil]
3. Run the dftcs program with $N = 61$ and a variety of values for τ between 10^{-3} and 10^{-5}. For $\tau = 1.0 \times 10^{-4}$, try a variety of values for N. What do you observe? [Computer]
4. (a) Write a function to evaluate Equation (6.16) numerically for $T(x, t)$ and reproduce Figure 6.6. (b) Use the function from part (a) in the dftcs program to produce a graph of $|T_a(x, t) - T_c(x, t)|$, the absolute difference between the analytical temperature profile, T_a, and the profile obtained by the FTCS scheme, T_c. [Computer]
5. (a) Using the method of images, find the solution of the diffusion equation with Dirichlet boundary conditions $T(x = -L/2) = T(x = L/2) = 0$ and initial condition $T(x, t = 0) = \delta(x - L/4)$. [Pencil] (b) Write a program to graph the solution obtained in part (a) at $t = 0.25t_L, 0.50t_L, \ldots, 5t_L$, where $t_L = L^2/8\kappa$ is the time it takes the width of the Gaussian to spread a distance $L/2$. How many images are needed to obtain 1% accuracy in the boundary condition at each of these times? [Computer]
6. Suppose that we replace our Dirichlet boundary conditions with the following Neumann boundary conditions:

$$\left.\frac{\partial T}{\partial x}\right|_{x=-L/2} = \left.\frac{\partial T}{\partial x}\right|_{x=L/2} = 0$$

(a) Using the method of images, find the solution $T(x, t)$ for the initial condition, $T(x, 0) = \delta(x)$. [Pencil] (b) Using the method of images, find the solution $T(x, t)$ for the initial condition, $T(x, 0) = \delta(x - L/4)$. [Pencil] (c) Modify dftcs to implement these boundary conditions by setting $T_1^n = T_2^n$ and $T_N^n = T_{N-1}^n$. Compare the program's output with the results from parts (a) and (b). Explain why the spatial discretization is $x_i = (i - \frac{3}{2})h - L/2$ with $h = L/(N-2)$ for these boundary conditions. [Computer]
7. Consider the periodic boundary conditions:

$$T(x = -L/2, t) = T(x = L/2, t); \qquad \left.\frac{\partial T}{\partial x}\right|_{x=-L/2} = \left.\frac{\partial T}{\partial x}\right|_{x=L/2}$$

(a) Using the method of images, find the solution $T(x, t)$ for the initial condition, $T(x, 0) = \delta(x)$. [Pencil] (b) Using the method of images, find the solution $T(x, t)$ for the initial condition, $T(x, 0) = \delta(x - L/4)$. [Pencil] (c) Compare the results from parts (a) and (b) of this exercise with those of the previous exercise. In what ways are they similar and how are they different? [Pencil] (d) Modify dftcs to implement these boundary conditions by setting $T_1^n = T_{N-1}^n$ and $T_N^n = T_2^n$. Compare the program's output with the results from parts (a) and (b). Explain why the spatial discretization is $x_i = (i - \frac{3}{2})h - L/2$ with $h = L/(N-2)$ for these boundary conditions. [Computer]

8.   The Richardson scheme for solving the diffusion equation uses the following discretization:

$$\frac{T_i^{n+1} - T_i^{n-1}}{2\tau} = \kappa \frac{T_{i+1}^n + T_{i-1}^n - 2T_i^n}{h^2}$$

Note that this is a three time-level scheme, that is, the method uses T^{n+1}, T^n, and T^{n-1}, so the scheme is not self-starting. Write a program that uses this scheme to solve the diffusion problem discussed in this section. Use the FTCS scheme on the first step to get it started. Try a variety of values for τ, and show that the method is *always* unstable. [Computer]

9.   The DuFort-Frankel scheme for solving the diffusion equation uses the following discretization:

$$\frac{T_i^{n+1} - T_i^{n-1}}{2\tau} = \kappa \frac{T_{i+1}^n + T_{i-1}^n - (T_i^{n+1} + T_i^{n-1})}{h^2}$$

Note that this is a three time-level scheme, that is, the method uses T^{n+1}, T^n, and T^{n-1}, so the scheme is not self-starting. Write a program that uses this scheme to solve the diffusion problem discussed in this section. Use the FTCS scheme on the first step to get it started. Try a variety of values for τ and show that the method is unconditionally stable but that the accuracy of the solution decreases with increasing τ. [Computer]

6.3   *CRITICAL MASS

Manhattan Project

In the spring of 1943, as global war raged, physicists were gathering at a secret facility in the New Mexico desert. Had you been among them, on arriving you would have received the *Los Alamos Primer*, twenty-four mimeographed pages that described the essential theoretical principles behind the Manhattan Project.[114] The *Primer*'s first sentence clearly stated the project's goal: "to produce a practical military weapon in the form of a bomb in which the energy is released by a fast neutron chain reaction...."

Though the technical difficulties were staggering, the basic principles outlined in the *Primer* are simple. If a thermal neutron collides with a fissionable nucleous, say of uranium 235, a significant amount of energy is released when the nucleus splits. More significantly, several neutrons are produced in the reaction and, as these neutrons cause other nuclei to fission, a *chain reaction* occurs. Yet neutrons are also lost by escaping at the surface of the material. The first question to be answered is "Under what conditions can a chain reaction be sustained?"

Neutron Diffusion

We assume the neutron density, $n(\mathbf{r}, t)$, obeys ordinary diffusion theory,

$$\frac{\partial}{\partial t} n(\mathbf{r}, t) = D\nabla^2 n + Cn \qquad (6.30)$$

where D is the diffusion constant and C is the creation rate for neutrons. For U^{235}, $D \approx 10^5$ m^2/s and $C \approx 10^8$ s^{-1}. To simplify the analysis, consider a one-dimensional system of length L, so (6.30) is,

$$\frac{\partial}{\partial t} n(x, t) = D\frac{\partial^2 n}{\partial x^2} + Cn \qquad (6.31)$$

with $-L/2 \leq x \leq L/2$. If all neutrons that reach the boundary escape from the system, then
$$n(x = -L/2, t) = 0; \qquad n(x = L/2, t) = 0 \qquad (6.32)$$
are the (Dirichlet) boundary conditions.

Our analysis of Equation (6.31) will *not* take the usual approach of explicitly solving for $n(x, t)$ for a given initial condition. Instead, we simply want to find the criterion under which the neutron density increases in time (i.e., chain reaction occurs).

Separation of Variables

We start by using the *separation of variables* trial solution,

$$n(x, t) = X(x)T(t) \qquad (6.33)$$

where X and T are unknown functions of x and t, respectively. Inserting this trial solution into the neutron diffusion PDE, Equation (6.31),

$$X\frac{\partial T}{\partial t} = DT\frac{\partial^2 X}{\partial x^2} + CXT \qquad (6.34)$$

or

$$\frac{1}{T}\frac{\partial T}{\partial t} = \frac{D}{X}\frac{\partial^2 X}{\partial x^2} + C \qquad (6.35)$$

Now comes the key step that simplifies our partial differential equation into a pair of ordinary differential equations. Since the left-hand side can depend only on t and the right-hand side only on x, they cannot depend on either variable. In other words, each side of (6.35) equals a constant.

Calling this constant α, the left hand side is

$$\frac{1}{T}\frac{dT}{dt} = \alpha \qquad (6.36)$$

The general solution of this ODE is simply

$$T(t) = T(0)e^{\alpha t} \qquad (6.37)$$

where $T(0)$ is determined by the initial condition.

The right-hand side of (6.35) is

$$\frac{D}{X}\frac{d^2 X}{dx^2} + C = \alpha \tag{6.38}$$

or

$$\frac{d^2 X}{dx^2} = \frac{\alpha - C}{D}X \tag{6.39}$$

Given the boundary conditions (6.32), the general solution of this ODE is,

$$X(x) = \sum_{j=1}^{\infty} a_j \sin\left(\frac{j\pi}{L}\left(x + \frac{L}{2}\right)\right) \tag{6.40}$$

where

$$-\left(\frac{j\pi}{L}\right)^2 = \frac{\alpha - C}{D} \tag{6.41}$$

and the a_n's are determined by the initial condition.

Finally, to establish if a chain reaction occurs, we need to determine if $\alpha > 0$ so that (6.37) gives exponential growth. From Equation (6.41), $\alpha > 0$ if

$$C - D\left(\frac{j\pi}{L}\right)^2 > 0 \tag{6.42}$$

for any j. This inequality is satisfied when $L > L_c$ where

$$L_c = \pi\sqrt{D/C} \tag{6.43}$$

is the critical length. For our one-dimensional geometry, this relation establishes the *critical mass* for a chain reaction. If the system's length is smaller than L_c, then the flux of neutrons at the boundary will damp out the neutron density. However, if $L > L_c$, then the density (and energy) will increase exponentially, with dramatic consequences.

Neutron Diffusion Program

Using the FTCS scheme, the one-dimensional neutron diffusion equation, (6.31), is discretized as

$$\frac{n_i^{n+1} - n_i^n}{\tau} = D\frac{n_{i+1}^n + n_{i-1}^n - 2n_i^n}{h^2} + Cn_i^n \tag{6.44}$$

or

$$n_i^{n+1} = n_i^n + \frac{D\tau}{h^2}\left(n_{i+1}^n + n_{i-1}^n - 2n_i^n\right) + C\tau n_i^n \tag{6.45}$$

As before, space and time are discretized as $x_i = (i-1)h - L/2$ and $t_n = (n-1)\tau$ with $h = L/(N-1)$. The boundary conditions $n(\pm L/2, t) = 0$ are discretized as $n_1^n = n_N^n = 0$, that is, the endpoint values are fixed to zero.

Table 6.2: Outline of program `neutrn`, which computes the neutron diffusion of a delta function using the FTCS method.

- Initialize parameters (τ, h, etc.).

- Set initial and boundary conditions.

- Loop over desired number of time steps.

  - Compute the new density using FTCS scheme, (6.45).
  - Periodically record density for plotting.

- Plot density versus x and t as wire-mesh plot.

- Plot average neutron density versus time.

See pages 209 and 212 for program listings.

Again the criterion for stability is $\tau \leq t_\sigma = h^2/2D$. Here we must be careful not to confuse numerical instability with the exponential growth produced by a chain reaction. It helps to be familiar with the signature of a numerical instability—the exponential growth of short wavelength oscillations (see Figure 6.8).

The program `neutrn`, which solves the neutron diffusion equation as an initial value problem using the FTCS scheme, is outlined in Table 6.2. The initial condition is a delta function at the center of the system [see Equation (6.25)]. The physical constants are set to $C = D = 1$, which is equivalent to defining the length scale as L_c/π and the time scale as C^{-1}.

Figure 6.9 shows the diffusive decay of the neutron density in a subcritical system ($L/L_c = 2/\pi$). The average density,

$$\bar{n}(t) = \frac{1}{L} \int_{-L/2}^{L/2} n(x,t)\, dx \quad \Rightarrow \quad \bar{n}^n = \frac{1}{N} \sum_{i=1}^{N} n_i^n \qquad (6.46)$$

approximately decays as $\bar{n}(t) \sim e^{\alpha_1 t}$, where $\alpha_1 = C - D\pi^2/L^2 = C(1 - L_c^2/L^2)$. A supercritical system, with $L/L_c = 4/\pi$, is shown in Figure 6.10. In this case, $\alpha_1 = 0.38C$, so the time it takes for the average density to increase by a factor of 10 is about $6.1/C$, in agreement with the growth rate shown in Figure 6.10.

Exercises

10. From the neutron diffusion PDE, Equation (6.30), in three dimensions, find the critical volume for a rectangular system with sides of length L_x, L_y, and L_z. Show

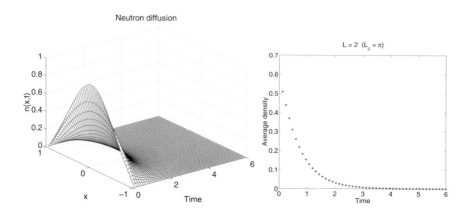

Figure 6.9: Mesh plot of $n(x,t)$ and plot $\bar{n}(t)$ from **neutrn**. System length is $L = 2$ (subcritical), number of grid points is $N = 61$, the number of steps is $12,000$, and time step $\tau = 5.0 \times 10^{-4}$.

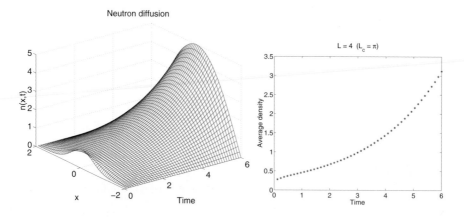

Figure 6.10: Mesh plot of $n(x,t)$ and plot $\bar{n}(t)$ from **neutrn**. System length is $L = 4$ (supercritical), number of grid points is $N = 61$, the number of steps is $12,000$, and time step $\tau = 5.0 \times 10^{-4}$.

that this volume is minimum when the system is a cube. [Hint: Use the trial solution $n(x, y, z, t) = X(x)Y(y)Z(z)T(t)$]. [Pencil]

11. (a) Modify **neutrn** to add the curve $\bar{n}(t = 0)e^{\alpha_1 t}$ to the graph of $\bar{n}(t)$ versus t. Plot your results for the cases shown in Figures 6.9 and 6.10. (b) Repeat part (a) but graph $\bar{n}(t)$ versus t using a log scale on the vertical axis; increase the number of steps to 5×10^4. [Computer]

12. Consider the Neumann boundary conditions:

$$\left.\frac{\partial n}{\partial x}\right|_{x=-L/2} = \left.\frac{\partial n}{\partial x}\right|_{x=L/2} = 0$$

(a) Using separation of variables show that this system is always supercritical. [Pencil] (b) Modify **neutrn** to implement these boundary conditions by setting $n_1^n = n_2^n$ and $n_N^n = n_{N-1}^n$. In this case the spatial discretization is $x_i = (i - \frac{3}{2})h - L/2$ with $h = L/(N - 2)$ for these boundary conditions. Compare the program's output with the result predicted in part (a). [Computer]

13. Consider the mixed boundary conditions:

$$n(x = -L/2, t) = 0 \quad ; \quad \left.\frac{\partial n}{\partial x}\right|_{x=L/2} = 0$$

(a) Show that $L_c = \frac{1}{2}\pi\sqrt{D/C}$ (Hint: Think symmetry). [Pencil] (b) Modify **neutrn** to implement these boundary conditions by setting $n_1^n = 0$ and $n_N^n = n_{N-1}^n$. Explain why the spatial discretization is $x_i = (i - 1)h - L/2$ with $h = L/(N - \frac{3}{2})$ for these boundary conditions. Compare the program's output with the result predicted in part (a). [Computer]

14. The critical mass can be reduced by surrounding the fissionable material with a tamper, an inactive material that diffuses neutrons. Modify **neutrn** to have the system extend from $-aL/2$ to $aL/2$, but with $C = 0$ for $|x| > L/2$. By trial and error, find the critical length for this system when $a = 2, 4,$ and 10. [Computer]

BEYOND THIS CHAPTER

The most complete reference on the analytical treatment of partial differential equations is still Courant and Hilbert.[35] On the other hand, the standard mathematical physics texts [11, 24, 86] also present the important material in a more easily digestible format. The physics behind most of the PDEs we'll consider is discussed in Morse and Feshbach [89].

The FTCS method introduced in Section 6.2 is just one scheme for solving the diffusion equation. Fletcher [47] catalogues and compares many schemes for solving both the one-dimensional and the multidimensional diffusion equation. Numerical instability is the FTCS method's Achilles heel, but in Section 9.2 we introduce implicit methods that are unconditionally stable.

APPENDIX A: MATLAB LISTINGS

Listing 6A.1 Program `dftcs`. Solves the Fourier heat diffusion equation using the FTCS scheme.

```
% dftcs - Program to solve the diffusion equation
% using the Forward Time Centered Space (FTCS) scheme.
clear; help dftcs;  % Clear memory and print header

%* Initialize parameters (time step, grid spacing, etc.).
tau = input('Enter time step: ');
N = input('Enter the number of grid points: ');
L = 1.;  % The system extends from x=-L/2 to x=L/2
h = L/(N-1);  % Grid size
kappa = 1.;   % Diffusion coefficient
coeff = kappa*tau/h^2;
if( coeff < 0.5 )
  disp('Solution is expected to be stable');
else
  disp('WARNING: Solution is expected to be unstable');
end

%* Set initial and boundary conditions.
tt = zeros(N,1);         % Initialize temperature to zero at all points
tt(round(N/2)) = 1/h;    % Initial cond. is delta function in center
%% The boundary conditions are tt(1) = tt(N) = 0

%* Set up loop and plot variables.
xplot = (0:N-1)*h - L/2;  % Record the x scale for plots
iplot = 1;                % Counter used to count plots
nstep = 300;              % Maximum number of iterations
nplots = 50;              % Number of snapshots (plots) to take
plot_step = nstep/nplots; % Number of time steps between plots

%* Loop over the desired number of time steps.
for istep=1:nstep  %% MAIN LOOP %%

  %* Compute new temperature using FTCS scheme.
  tt(2:(N-1)) = tt(2:(N-1)) + ...
      coeff*(tt(3:N) + tt(1:(N-2)) - 2*tt(2:(N-1)));

  %* Periodically record temperature for plotting.
  if( rem(istep,plot_step) < 1 )   % Every plot_step steps
    ttplot(:,iplot) = tt(:);       % record tt(i) for plotting
    tplot(iplot) = istep*tau;      % Record time for plots
    iplot = iplot+1;
  end
end
```

```
%* Plot temperature versus x and t as wire-mesh and contour plots.
figure(1); clf;
mesh(tplot,xplot,ttplot);  % Wire-mesh surface plot
xlabel('Time');  ylabel('x');  zlabel('T(x,t)');
title('Diffusion of a delta spike');
pause(1);
figure(2); clf;
contourLevels = 0:0.5:10;  contourLabels = 0:5;
cs = contour(tplot,xplot,ttplot,contourLevels);  % Contour plot
clabel(cs,contourLabels);  % Add labels to selected contour levels
xlabel('Time'); ylabel('x');
title('Temperature contour plot');
```

Listing 6A.2 Program `neutrn`. Solves the neutron diffusion equation using the FTCS scheme.

```
% neutrn - Program to solve the neutron diffusion equation
% using the Forward Time Centered Space (FTCS) scheme.
clear; help neutrn;  % Clear memory and print header

%* Initialize parameters (time step, grid points, etc.).
tau = input('Enter time step: ');
N = input('Enter the number of grid points: ');
L = input('Enter system length: ');
% The system extends from x=-L/2 to x=L/2
h = L/(N-1);  % Grid size
D = 1.;   % Diffusion coefficient
C = 1.;   % Generation rate
coeff = D*tau/h^2;
coeff2 = C*tau;
if( coeff < 0.5 )
  disp('Solution is expected to be stable');
else
  disp('WARNING: Solution is expected to be unstable');
end

%* Set initial and boundary conditions.
nn = zeros(N,1);         % Initialize density to zero at all points
nn_new = zeros(N,1);     % Initialize temporary array used by FTCS
nn(round(N/2)) = 1/h;    % Initial cond. is delta function in center
%% The boundary conditions are nn(1) = nn(N) = 0

%* Set up loop and plot variables.
xplot = (0:N-1)*h - L/2;  % Record the x scale for plots
iplot = 1;                % Counter used to count plots
nstep = input('Enter number of time steps: ');
nplots = 50;              % Number of snapshots (plots) to take
plot_step = nstep/nplots; % Number of time steps between plots
```

```
%* Loop over the desired number of time steps.
for istep=1:nstep  %% MAIN LOOP %%

  %* Compute the new density using FTCS scheme.
  nn_new(2:(N-1)) = nn(2:(N-1)) + ...
      coeff*(nn(3:N) + nn(1:(N-2)) - 2*nn(2:(N-1))) + ...
      coeff2*nn(2:(N-1));
  nn = nn_new;           % Reset temperature to new values

  %* Periodically record the density for plotting.
  if( rem(istep,plot_step) < 1 )   % Every plot_step steps
    nnplot(:,iplot) = nn(:);       % record nn(i) for plotting
    tplot(iplot) = istep*tau;      % Record time for plots
    nAve(iplot) = mean(nn);        % Record average density
     iplot = iplot+1;
     fprintf('Finished %g of %g steps\n',istep,nstep);
  end
end

%* Plot density versus x and t as a 3D-surface plot
figure(1); clf;
surf(tplot,xplot,nnplot);
xlabel('Time');  ylabel('x');  zlabel('n(x,t)');
title('Neutron diffusion');

%* Plot average neutron density versus time
figure(2); clf;
plot(tplot,nAve,'*');
xlabel('Time'); ylabel('Average density');
title(['L = ',num2str(L),'  (L_c = \pi)']);
```

APPENDIX B: C++ LISTINGS

Listing 6B.1 Program dftcs. Solves the Fourier heat diffusion equation using the FTCS scheme.

```
// dftcs - Program to solve the diffusion equation
// using the Forward Time Centered Space (FTCS) scheme.
#include "NumMeth.h"

void main() {

  //* Initialize parameters (time step, grid spacing, etc.).
  cout << "Enter time step: "; double tau; cin >> tau;
  cout << "Enter the number of grid points: "; int N; cin >> N;
  double L = 1.;  // The system extends from x=-L/2 to x=L/2
```

```cpp
double h = L/(N-1);   // Grid size
double kappa = 1.;    // Diffusion coefficient
double coeff = kappa*tau/(h*h);
if( coeff < 0.5 )
  cout << "Solution is expected to be stable" << endl;
else
  cout << "WARNING: Solution is expected to be unstable" << endl;

//* Set initial and boundary conditions.
Matrix tt(N), tt_new(N);
tt.set(0.0);     // Initialize temperature to zero at all points
tt(N/2) = 1/h;   // Initial cond. is delta function in center
//// The boundary conditions are tt(1) = tt(N) = 0
tt_new.set(0.0);  // End points are unchanged during iteration

//* Set up loop and plot variables.
int iplot = 1;                      // Counter used to count plots
int nStep = 300;                    // Maximum number of iterations
int plot_step = 6;                  // Number of time steps between plots
int nplots = nStep/plot_step + 1;   // Number of snapshots (plots)
Matrix xplot(N), tplot(nplots), ttplot(N,nplots);
int i,j;
for( i=1; i<=N; i++ )
  xplot(i) = (i-1)*h - L/2;   // Record the x scale for plots

//* Loop over the desired number of time steps.
int iStep;
for( iStep=1; iStep<=nStep; iStep++ ) {

  //* Compute new temperature using FTCS scheme.
  for( i=2; i<=(N-1); i++ )
    tt_new(i) = tt(i) + coeff*(tt(i+1) + tt(i-1) - 2*tt(i));

  tt = tt_new;      // Reset temperature to new values

  //* Periodically record temperature for plotting.
  if( (iStep%plot_step) < 1 ) { // Every plot_step steps
    for( i=1; i<=N; i++ )        // record tt(i) for plotting
      ttplot(i,iplot) = tt(i);
    tplot(iplot) = iStep*tau;      // Record time for plots
    iplot++;
  }
}
nplots = iplot-1;  // Number of plots actually recorded

//* Print out the plotting variables: tplot, xplot, ttplot
ofstream tplotOut("tplot.txt"), xplotOut("xplot.txt"),
        ttplotOut("ttplot.txt");
for( i=1; i<=nplots; i++ )
  tplotOut << tplot(i) << endl;
```

```
  for( i=1; i<=N; i++ ) {
    xplotOut << xplot(i) << endl;
    for( j=1; j<nplots; j++ )
      ttplotOut << ttplot(i,j) << ", ";
    ttplotOut << ttplot(i,nplots) << endl;
  }
}
/***** To plot in MATLAB; use the script below ********************
load tplot.txt; load xplot.txt; load ttplot.txt;
%* Plot temperature versus x and t as wire-mesh and contour plots.
figure(1); clf;
mesh(tplot,xplot,ttplot);  % Wire-mesh surface plot
xlabel('Time');   ylabel('x');   zlabel('T(x,t)');
title('Diffusion of a delta spike');
pause(1);
figure(2); clf;
contourLevels = 0:0.5:10;   contourLabels = 0:5;
cs = contour(tplot,xplot,ttplot,contourLevels);   % Contour plot
clabel(cs,contourLabels);   % Add labels to selected contour levels
xlabel('Time'); ylabel('x');
title('Temperature contour plot');
****************************************************************/
```

Listing 6B.2 Program `neutrn`. Solves the neutron diffusion equation using the FTCS scheme.

```
// neutrn - Program to solve the neutron diffusion equation
// using the Forward Time Centered Space (FTCS) scheme.
#include "NumMeth.h"

void main() {

  //* Initialize parameters (time step, grid spacing, etc.).
  cout << "Enter time step: "; double tau; cin >> tau;
  cout << "Enter the number of grid points: "; int N; cin >> N;
  cout << "Enter system length: "; double L; cin >> L;
  // The system extends from x=-L/2 to x=L/2
  double h = L/(N-1);  // Grid size
  double D = 1.;        // Diffusion coefficient
  double C = 1.;        // Generation rate
  double coeff = D*tau/(h*h);
  double coeff2 = C*tau;
  if( coeff < 0.5 )
    cout << "Solution is expected to be stable" << endl;
  else
    cout << "WARNING: Solution is expected to be unstable" << endl;

  //* Set initial and boundary conditions.
  Matrix nn(N), nn_new(N);
```

```
nn.set(0.0);       // Initialize density to zero at all points
nn(N/2) = 1/h;     // Initial cond. is delta function in center
//// The boundary conditions are nn(1) = nn(N) = 0
nn_new.set(0.0);   // End points are unchanged during iteration

//* Set up loop and plot variables.
int iplot = 1;                     // Counter used to count plots
cout << "Enter number of time steps: "; int nStep; cin >> nStep;
int plot_step = 200;               // Number of time steps between plots
int nplots = nStep/plot_step + 1;  // Number of snapshots (plots)
Matrix xplot(N), tplot(nplots), nnplot(N,nplots), nAve(nplots);
int i,j;
for( i=1; i<=N; i++ )
  xplot(i) = (i-1)*h - L/2;   // Record the x scale for plots

//* Loop over the desired number of time steps.
int iStep;
for( iStep=1; iStep<=nStep; iStep++ ) {

  //* Compute new density using FTCS scheme.
  for( i=2; i<=(N-1); i++ )
    nn_new(i) = nn(i) + coeff*(nn(i+1) + nn(i-1) - 2*nn(i))
                      + coeff2*nn(i);

  nn = nn_new;      // Reset density to new values

  //* Periodically record density for plotting.
  if( (iStep%plot_step) < 1 ) { // Every plot_step steps ...
    double nSum = 0;
    for( i=1; i<=N; i++ ) {
      nnplot(i,iplot) = nn(i);  // Record tt(i) for plotting
      nSum += nn(i);
    }
    nAve(iplot) = nSum/N;
    tplot(iplot) = iStep*tau;   // Record time for plots
    iplot++;
  }
}
nplots = iplot-1;  // Number of plots actually recorded

//* Print out the plotting variables: tplot, xplot, nnplot, nAve
ofstream tplotOut("tplot.txt"), xplotOut("xplot.txt"),
         nnplotOut("nnplot.txt"), nAveOut("nAve.txt");
for( i=1; i<=nplots; i++ ) {
  tplotOut << tplot(i) << endl;
  nAveOut << nAve(i) << endl;
}
for( i=1; i<=N; i++ ) {
  xplotOut << xplot(i) << endl;
  for( j=1; j<nplots; j++ )
```

```
      nnplotOut << nnplot(i,j) << ", ";
    nnplotOut << nnplot(i,nplots) << endl;
  }
}
/***** To plot in MATLAB; use the script below *******************
load tplot.txt; load xplot.txt; load nnplot.txt; load nAve.txt;
%* Plot density versus x and t as a 3D-surface plot
figure(1); clf;
surf(tplot,xplot,nnplot);
xlabel('Time');  ylabel('x');  zlabel('n(x,t)');
title('Neutron diffusion');
%* Plot average neutron density versus time
figure(2); clf;
plot(tplot,nAve,'*');
xlabel('Time'); ylabel('Average density');
****************************************************************/
```

Chapter 7

Partial Differential Equations II: Advanced Explicit Methods

This chapter introduces more advanced marching methods and applies them to solving hyperbolic PDEs. In the first section we consider the linear advection equation that, despite its simplicity, is challenging to solve numerically and serves as a good test case for our explicit schemes. In Section 7.2 these schemes are applied to a more interesting nonlinear PDE with shock wave solutions: the continuity equation for traffic flow.

7.1 ADVECTION EQUATION

Wave and Advection Equations

We now look at hyperbolic equations, the paradigm of which is the familiar wave equation,

$$\frac{\partial^2 A}{\partial t^2} = c^2 \frac{\partial^2 A}{\partial x^2} \tag{7.1}$$

where $A(x, t)$ is the wave amplitude and c is the wave speed. In Chapters 2 and 3 the equations of motion for a particle were ODEs of the form

$$\frac{d^2 \mathbf{r}}{dt^2} = f(\mathbf{r}, \mathbf{v}) \tag{7.2}$$

where $\mathbf{r}$ and $\mathbf{v}$ are the position and velocity of the particle. To solve the equations numerically, we usually rewrite (7.2) as a pair of first-order equations,

$$\frac{d\mathbf{v}}{dt} = f(\mathbf{r}, \mathbf{v}); \qquad \frac{d\mathbf{r}}{dt} = \mathbf{v} \tag{7.3}$$

215

For the wave equation, we use a similar trick and introduce the variables

$$P = \frac{\partial A}{\partial t}; \qquad Q = c\frac{\partial A}{\partial x} \tag{7.4}$$

The wave equation may now be written as the pair of equations

$$\frac{\partial P}{\partial t} = c\frac{\partial Q}{\partial x}; \qquad \frac{\partial Q}{\partial t} = c\frac{\partial P}{\partial x} \tag{7.5}$$

or

$$\frac{\partial \mathbf{a}}{\partial t} = c\mathbf{B}\frac{\partial}{\partial x}\mathbf{a} \tag{7.6}$$

where $\mathbf{a} = \begin{bmatrix} P \\ Q \end{bmatrix}$ and $\mathbf{B} = \begin{bmatrix} 0 & 1 \\ 1 & 0 \end{bmatrix}$.

This suggests that even though the wave equation is the most familiar hyperbolic equation, it is not the simplest possible hyperbolic equation. When formulating and studying numerical methods, it is best to first use them with the simplest, nontrivial problem. We will thus use as our model hyperbolic equation the *advection equation*,

$$\frac{\partial a}{\partial t} = -c\frac{\partial a}{\partial x} \tag{7.7}$$

Physically, this equation describes the evolution of the passive scalar field, $a(x,t)$, carried along by a flow with constant velocity c. This equation is also known as the linear convection equation. In the wave equation we have left- and right-moving waves; with the advection equation, waves move only in one direction (to the right if $c > 0$). Of course, left- and right-moving waves may be described using (7.6), the vector advection equation.

The advection equation is the simplest example of a flux-conservation equation,

$$\frac{\partial p}{\partial t} = -\nabla \cdot \mathbf{F}(p) \tag{7.8}$$

which in one dimension is

$$\frac{\partial p}{\partial t} = -\frac{\partial}{\partial x}F(p) \tag{7.9}$$

Equations of this form are ubiquitous in physics because if p is any conserved quantity (such as mass or energy), then $F(p)$ is the flux. For example, in electrodynamics if p is charge density, then F is current density. Note that if F goes as $\partial p/\partial x$ instead of p, then (7.9) becomes the diffusion equation.

Solution of the Advection Equation

The analytical solution of the advection equation is easy to obtain. For the initial condition

$$a(x, t = 0) = f_0(x) \tag{7.10}$$

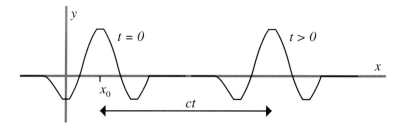

Figure 7.1: Linear advection of a wave pulse.

where f_0 is an arbitrary function, the solution is

$$a(x,t) = f_0(x - ct) \tag{7.11}$$

For example, suppose that our initial condition is a cosine-modulated Gaussian pulse,

$$a(x, t = 0) = \cos[k(x - x_0)] \exp\left[-\frac{(x - x_0)^2}{2\sigma^2}\right] \tag{7.12}$$

where the constants x_0 and σ give the location of the peak and the width of the pulse. The wave number $k = 2\pi/\lambda$, where λ is the wavelength of the modulation. The solution is

$$
\begin{aligned}
a(x,t) &= \cos[k((x - ct) - x_0)] \exp\left[-\frac{((x - ct) - x_0)^2}{2\sigma^2}\right] \\
&= \cos[k(x - (x_0 + ct))] \exp\left[-\frac{(x - (x_0 + ct))^2}{2\sigma^2}\right]
\end{aligned}
\tag{7.13}
$$

Notice that the solution $a(x,t)$ exactly preserves its shape, but with the location of the peak displaced to $x_0 + ct$ (Figure 7.1). Although the advection equation is simple to solve analytically, it makes an excellent test case for our numerical methods for hyperbolic equations. We will discover that even this simple equation is nontrivial to compute numerically.

FTCS Method for Advection Equation

Let's try to solve the advection equation numerically using the FTCS method from the previous section. The time derivative is replaced by its forward (right) discretized form

$$\frac{\partial a}{\partial t} \Rightarrow \frac{a(x_i, t_n + \tau) - a(x_i, t_n)}{\tau} = \frac{a_i^{n+1} - a_i^n}{\tau} \tag{7.14}$$

where $x_i = (i-1)h - L/2$ and $t_n = (n-1)\tau$ (see Figure 6.2). The index i denotes the spatial location of a grid point, while the index n indicates the temporal step.

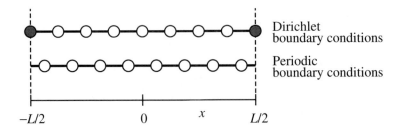

Figure 7.2: Grids used by Dirichlet and periodic boundary conditions. With periodic boundary conditions, the boundary lies between the first and last grid points.

The space derivative is replaced by its centered discretized form,

$$\frac{\partial a}{\partial x} \Rightarrow \frac{a(x_i + h, t_n) - a(x_i - h, t_n)}{2h} = \frac{a_{i+1}^n - a_{i-1}^n}{2h} \qquad (7.15)$$

We'll use periodic boundary conditions, so grid points x_1 and x_N are adjacent; the grid spacing is $h = L/N$ (Figure 7.2). The discretized advection equation is

$$\frac{a_i^{n+1} - a_i^n}{\tau} = -c\frac{a_{i+1}^n - a_{i-1}^n}{2h} \qquad (7.16)$$

The FTCS scheme is obtained by solving for a_i^{n+1},

$$a_i^{n+1} = a_i^n - \frac{c\tau}{2h}(a_{i+1}^n - a_{i-1}^n) \qquad (7.17)$$

A program, called advect, that implements the FTCS scheme for the advection equation, is outlined in Table 7.1. The initial condition is a cosine-modulated Gaussian pulse [Equation (7.12)].

The number of iterations performed equals $L/(c\tau)$. With periodic boundary conditions, the pulse should move across and around the system once, returning to its starting point. Since the wave speed is c, the time it takes a wave to move a distance equal to the grid spacing, h, is $t_w = h/c$. This gives us a characteristic time scale for the problem. Figure 7.3 shows the initial and final values for the wave amplitude, $a(x,t)$. The solid line is the initial condition; the dashed line shows the pulse after it evolves long enough to circle the system once. Clearly, the FTCS method failed; the pulse does not maintain its shape. The mesh plot shown in Figure 7.4 illustrates how the pulse distorts in time.

Lax Method for Advection Equation

Now for the bad news: For the advection equation, the FTCS method is numerically unstable for all values of τ! As will be shown in Section 9.1 for a smaller value of τ, we can delay but not escape it. Fortunately, the

Table 7.1: Outline of program `advect`, which computes the advection of a cosine-modulated Gaussian pulse using various numerical methods.

- Select numerical parameters (τ, h, etc.).

- Set initial and boundary conditions.

- Initialize plotting variables.

- Loop over desired number of steps.

  - Compute new values of wave amplitude using FTCS (7.17), Lax (7.18), or Lax-Wendroff (7.28) method.

  - Periodically record $a(x,t)$ for plotting.

- Plot the initial and final amplitude profiles.

- Plot the wave amplitude $a(x,t)$ versus x and t.

See pages 239 and 242 for program listings.

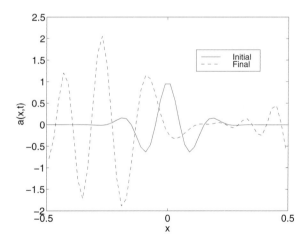

Figure 7.3: Initial and final shapes of the wave pulse as obtained by the `advect` program using the FTCS method. Notice that the wave does not correctly retain its shape. The number of grid points is $N = 50$, and the time step is $\tau = 0.002$ ($\tau < t_{\mathrm{w}} = 0.02$).

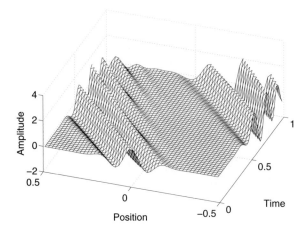

Figure 7.4: Output from the `advect` program using the FTCS method. Notice how the wave pulse moves in the positive direction but incorrectly distorts with time. The parameters are as in Figure 7.3.

stability problem is simple to fix. We introduce the *Lax method*, defined by the following iteration equation:

$$a_i^{n+1} = \frac{1}{2}(a_{i+1}^n + a_{i-1}^n) - \frac{c\tau}{2h}(a_{i+1}^n - a_{i-1}^n) \tag{7.18}$$

Notice that the Lax method simply replaces the a_i^n term in the FTCS method with the average value of the left and right neighbors. The Lax method is stable if

$$\frac{c\tau}{h} \leq 1 \tag{7.19}$$

The maximum usable value for τ is thus

$$\tau_{\max} = \frac{h}{c} = t_{\mathrm{w}} \tag{7.20}$$

This criterion is known as the *Courant-Friedrichs-Lewy* (CFL) condition. It commonly appears as a stability criterion for numerical schemes that solve hyperbolic equations. Notice that if we use a finer grid (smaller h), we are forced to use a smaller τ. The CFL stability condition is derived in Section 9.1.

Using Lax's method with a grid of $N = 50$ points and a time step of $\tau = \tau_{\max} = 0.02$, we find that the pulse exactly preserves its shape. The mesh plot of the solution is shown in Figure 7.5. From (7.18), we know that if $\tau = \tau_{\max}$, then $a_i^{n+1} = a_{i-1}^n$, which is the exact solution of the advection equation.

Lax's method has an interesting property. For values of τ above $\tau_{\max}$, you will have problems because the method is numerically unstable. However, for τ significantly less than $\tau_{\max}$, the numerical solution is also wrong. If τ is too small, we find that the pulse dies out as it moves (Figure 7.6). We get the

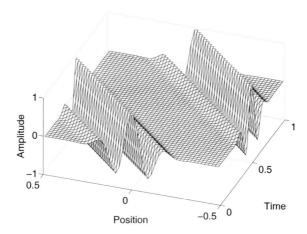

Figure 7.5: Mesh plot obtained by the **advect** program using the Lax method. Parameters used are $N = 50$ grid points and time step $\tau = t_{\mathrm{w}} = 0.02$. The wave pulse correctly retains its shape.

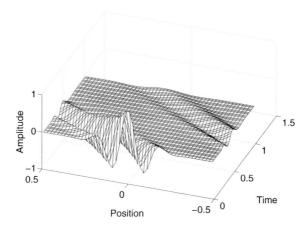

Figure 7.6: Mesh plot obtained by the **advect** program using the Lax method. Parameters used are $N = 50$ grid points and time step $\tau = 0.015$. Notice how the pulse amplitude dies out since $\tau < t_{\mathrm{w}} = 0.02$.

best results when $\tau = \tau_{\mathrm{max}}$. This example should dismiss a popular misconception about numerical methods: The smaller the time step, the better the solution. While it is usually true that the truncation error for many schemes is proportional to τ, this is not a universal property for all methods.

The averaging term in the Lax method serves to stabilize the numerical solution by introducing an *artificial diffusion* (or artificial viscosity). The magnitude of this artificial diffusion is inversely proportional to the time step τ. When the time step is too large ($\tau > \tau_{\mathrm{max}}$), the artificial diffusion is too weak to stabilize the solution. When the time step is too small ($\tau < \tau_{\mathrm{max}}$), the diffusion is too strong and it damps out the true solution. Many hyperbolic PDE schemes besides the Lax method incorporate some form of numerical diffusion.

Lax-Wendroff Scheme

Let's look at one more scheme for solving hyperbolic PDEs. The Lax-Wendroff scheme is a second-order finite difference scheme; the idea is that we want to take the Taylor expansion

$$a(x, t + \tau) = a(x, t) + \tau \left(\frac{\partial a}{\partial t} \right) + \frac{\tau^2}{2} \left(\frac{\partial^2 a}{\partial t^2} \right) + O(\tau^3) \qquad (7.21)$$

and keep the terms through τ^2. The term that is linear in τ is easy to represent using the original equation, which we now write in the more general form

$$\frac{\partial a}{\partial t} = -\frac{\partial}{\partial x} F(a) \qquad (7.22)$$

where the flux $F(a) = ca$ for the advection equation.

To obtain an expression for the second-order term, we differentiate the equation above:

$$\frac{\partial^2 a}{\partial t^2} = -\frac{\partial}{\partial t}\frac{\partial}{\partial x} F(a) = -\frac{\partial}{\partial x}\frac{\partial F}{\partial t} \qquad (7.23)$$

Yet we may write

$$\frac{\partial F}{\partial t} = \frac{dF}{da}\frac{\partial a}{\partial t} = F'(a)\frac{\partial a}{\partial t} = -F'(a)\frac{\partial F}{\partial x} \qquad (7.24)$$

where $F'(a) = c$ for the advection equation.

Inserting (7.24) into Equation (7.23),

$$\frac{\partial^2 a}{\partial t^2} = \frac{\partial}{\partial x} F'(a)\frac{\partial F}{\partial x} \qquad (7.25)$$

Putting it all together in our Taylor expansion, we get

$$a(x, t + \tau) \approx a(x, t) - \tau \left(\frac{\partial}{\partial x} F(a) \right) + \frac{\tau^2}{2} \left(\frac{\partial}{\partial x} F'(a)\frac{\partial F}{\partial x} \right) \qquad (7.26)$$

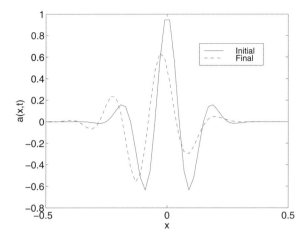

Figure 7.7: Initial (solid) and final (dashed) amplitudes obtained by the `advect` program using the Lax-Wendroff method. Parameters used are $N = 50$ grid points and time step $\tau = 0.015$. Note how the amplitude decreases since $\tau < t_{\mathrm{w}} = 0.02$.

After discretizing the derivatives, we obtain the *Lax-Wendroff scheme*,

$$
\begin{aligned}
a_i^{n+1} &= a_i^n - \tau \frac{F_{i+1} - F_{i-1}}{2h} + \frac{\tau^2}{2} \frac{\left[F' \frac{\partial F}{\partial x} \right]_{i+\frac{1}{2}} - \left[F' \frac{\partial F}{\partial x} \right]_{i-\frac{1}{2}}}{h} \qquad (7.27) \\
&= a_i^n - \tau \frac{F_{i+1} - F_{i-1}}{2h} + \frac{\tau^2}{2} \frac{1}{h} \left(F'_{i+\frac{1}{2}} \frac{F_{i+1} - F_i}{h} - F'_{i-\frac{1}{2}} \frac{F_i - F_{i-1}}{h} \right)
\end{aligned}
$$

where $F_i \equiv F(a_i^n)$ and $F'_{i\pm\frac{1}{2}} \equiv F'[(a_{i\pm1}^n + a_i^n)/2]$. For the advection equation this expression simplifies considerably, since $F_i = ca_i^n$ and $F'_{i\pm\frac{1}{2}} = c$, and Equation (7.27) reduces to

$$
a_i^{n+1} = a_i^n - \frac{c\tau}{2h}(a_{i+1}^n - a_{i-1}^n) + \frac{c^2\tau^2}{2h^2}(a_{i+1}^n + a_{i-1}^n - 2a_i^n) \qquad (7.28)
$$

Notice that the last term is a discretized second derivative in $a(x,t)$. This term give us an artificial diffusion that stabilizes the numerical solution. The CFL condition (7.20) is also the criterion for stability for the Lax-Wendroff scheme. Notice that if $\tau = \tau_{\mathrm{max}} = h/c$, the Lax-Wendroff scheme is identical to the Lax scheme. This is good news, since we know that Lax is exact when $\tau = \tau_{\mathrm{max}}$.

The Lax scheme is flawed because when $\tau < \tau_{\mathrm{max}}$, the solution is rapidly damped out by the artificial viscosity (see Figure 7.6). The Lax-Wendroff scheme also has artificial viscosity to control instability, but it does not increase as rapidly with decreasing τ. Figure 7.7 illustrates the use of the Lax-Wendroff scheme for the same parameters as those in Figure 7.6. Comparing the two results, you see that the Lax-Wendroff scheme is still useful even when $\tau < \tau_{\mathrm{max}}$.

I want to emphasize again that the one-dimensional advection equation makes a useful test case but is of little interest since the analytical solution is trivial. In the next section we consider a much more interesting hyperbolic equation that (1) is nonlinear, (2) has solutions that develop discontinuities (shocks) even if the initial conditions are smooth and continuous, and (3) is a model for the flow of automobile traffic.

EXERCISES

1.   By direct substitution into the advection equation, (7.7), check that Equation (7.11) is a solution. [Pencil]

2. Modify **advect** to use the Dirichlet boundary conditions

$$a(x = -L/2, t) = \sin(\omega t)$$
$$a(x = L/2, t) = 0$$

Have the program run long enough for the wave generated at $x = -L/2$ to reach the opposite side of the system. Using $N = 50$ grid points and a frequency of $\omega = 10\pi$, what do you observe for time steps of $\tau = 0.015$, 0.02, and 0.03? How do your results change when you vary the frequency? Test each case using the FTCS, Lax, and Lax-Wendroff schemes. [Computer]

3.   The advection and diffusion of a passive scalar in a one-dimensional flow is commonly described by the transport equation,

$$\frac{\partial T}{\partial t} = -c\frac{\partial T}{\partial x} + \kappa\frac{\partial^2 T}{\partial x^2}$$

Find the solution of this PDE for the initial condition $T(x, t = 0) = \delta(x)$ and periodic boundary conditions at $x = \pm L/2$. [Pencil]

4. Write a program that uses the FTCS scheme to solve the one-dimensional transport equation in the previous problem. (a) Empirically show that the numerical solution is stable if

$$\left(\frac{c\tau}{h}\right)^2 \le \frac{2\kappa\tau}{h^2} \le 1$$

In this case, physical diffusion can serve to stabilize the numerical scheme. (b) Compare the results from your program with the solution for the delta function initial condition of the previous exercise. [Computer]

5. The "upwind" scheme for solving the advection equation uses a left derivative for the $\partial/\partial x$ term,

$$\frac{a_i^{n+1} - a_i^n}{\tau} = -c\frac{a_i^n - a_{i-1}^n}{h}$$

Modify the **advect** program to use this scheme, and compare it with the others discussed in this section for the cases shown in Figures 7.3–7.7. For what values of τ is it stable? [Computer]

6. The leap-frog scheme for solving the advection equation uses centered derivatives for both terms,

$$\frac{a_i^{n+1} - a_i^{n-1}}{2\tau} = -c\frac{a_{i+1}^n - a_{i-1}^n}{2h}$$

Notice that this is a three time-level scheme, that is, it uses a_i^{n+1}, a_i^n, and a_i^{n-1}. To get it started, we need to use one of the other schemes (e.g., Lax). Modify the **advect** program to use this scheme and compare it with the others discussed in this section for the cases shown in Figures 7.3–7.7. For what values of τ is it stable? [Computer]

7.2 *PHYSICS OF TRAFFIC FLOW

Fluid Mechanics

In fluid mechanics the equations of motion are obtained by constructing equations of the form

$$\frac{\partial p}{\partial t} = -\nabla \cdot \mathbf{F}(p) \tag{7.29}$$

or in one dimension,

$$\frac{\partial p}{\partial t} = -\frac{\partial}{\partial x} F(p) \tag{7.30}$$

Here p is any one of the conserved quantities

$$p = \begin{cases} \text{mass density} \\ x, y \text{ or } z-\text{momentum density} \\ \text{energy density} \end{cases} \tag{7.31}$$

and F is

$$F(p) = \begin{cases} \text{mass flux} \\ x, y \text{ or } z-\text{momentum flux} \\ \text{energy flux} \end{cases} \tag{7.32}$$

that is, the corresponding flux.

While the equations for the momentum and energy are somewhat complicated, the equation for the mass density, ρ, is quite simple. The mass flux equals the mass density times the fluid velocity, v, so

$$\frac{\partial \rho(x,t)}{\partial t} = -\frac{\partial}{\partial x}\{\rho(x,t)v(x,t)\} \tag{7.33}$$

This equation is known as the *equation of continuity*. The equation for the momentum density may be rewritten as an equation for the velocity. This velocity equation involves the energy density (the coupling is in the pressure term), so we must solve the entire set of equations simultaneously.

The full set of hydrodynamics equations is called the *Navier-Stokes equations*. For a variety of reasons, these equations are usually not solved in their full form but rather with a number of approximations. Of course the approximations used depend on the problem at hand. For example, air is incompressible to a good approximation in many subsonic flows.

Traffic Flow

One of the simplest, nontrivial flows that may be studied involves fluids for which the velocity is only a function of density,

$$v(x,t) = v(\rho) \tag{7.34}$$

For example, suppose that the velocity of the fluid decreased linearly with increasing density as

$$v(\rho) = v_{\mathrm{m}}(1 - \rho/\rho_{\mathrm{m}}) \tag{7.35}$$

where $v_{\mathrm{m}} > 0$ is the maximum velocity and $\rho_{\mathrm{m}} > 0$ is the maximum density. What type of fluid behaves this way? One flow you are probably very familiar with is automobile traffic. The maximum velocity is the speed limit; if the density is near zero (few cars on the road), then the traffic moves at this speed. The maximum density, ρ_{m}, is achieved when the traffic is bumper-to-bumper. While on real highways the flow may not exactly obey Equation (7.35), it turns out to be a good first approximation.[65]

Our equation for the evolution of the density may be written as

$$\frac{\partial \rho}{\partial t} = -\frac{\partial}{\partial x}\left\{ \left(\alpha + \frac{1}{2}\beta\rho\right)\rho \right\} \tag{7.36}$$

where $\alpha = v_{\mathrm{m}}$ and $\beta = -2v_{\mathrm{m}}/\rho_{\mathrm{m}}$. This equation is called the generalized inviscid Burger's equation. We obtain the standard inviscid Burger's equation when $\alpha = 0$ and $\beta = 1$. This equation has been studied extensively because it is the simplest nonlinear PDE with wave solutions.[16] Equations of this type appear frequently in nonlinear acoustics and shock wave theory.

Returning to our traffic model, we want to develop a method to solve the nonlinear PDE,

$$\frac{\partial \rho}{\partial t} = -\frac{\partial}{\partial x}\left\{ \rho v(\rho) \right\} \tag{7.37}$$

Rewrite this equation as

$$\frac{\partial \rho}{\partial t} = -\left(\frac{d}{d\rho}\rho v(\rho)\right)\frac{\partial \rho}{\partial x} \tag{7.38}$$

or

$$\frac{\partial \rho}{\partial t} = -c(\rho)\frac{\partial \rho}{\partial x} \tag{7.39}$$

where $c(\rho) \equiv d(\rho v)/d\rho$. Using our linear function for $v(\rho)$ as given by Equation (7.35), we have

$$c(\rho) = v_{\mathrm{m}}(1 - 2\rho/\rho_{\mathrm{m}}) \tag{7.40}$$

Notice that $c(\rho)$ is also linear in ρ and takes the values $c(0) = v_{\mathrm{m}}$ and $c(\rho_{\mathrm{m}}) = -v_{\mathrm{m}}$. The function $c(\rho)$ is not the speed of the traffic, but rather is the speed at which disturbances (or waves) in the flow will travel. Since $c(\rho)$ may be both positive or negative, the waves may move in either direction. Note, however, that $c(\rho) \leq v(\rho)$, so the waves may never move faster than the cars.

Method of Characteristics

For $c(\rho) = $ constant, we have the advection equation for which we already know the solution. We may build an analytical solution to (7.39) from our knowledge of the solution of the advection equation by using the *method of*

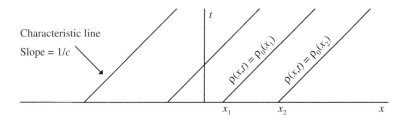

Figure 7.8: Sketch of the characteristic lines for the advection equation.

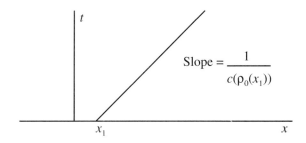

Figure 7.9: Sketch of a single characteristic line for the nonlinear traffic equation.

characteristics.[1] If you are not interested in learning this method, skim through the introduction to the stoplight problem (see Figures 7.11 and 7.12), and skip to its solution, Equation (7.46).

For a moment let's return to our solution of the linear advection PDE, Equation (7.11). We know that, with time, the initial condition, $\rho(x, t = 0) = \rho_0(x)$, is translated with speed c. Consider the sketch of the xt plane shown in Figure 7.8. Suppose that we draw a line with slope $dt/dx = 1/c$ from a point x_1 on the x-axis. This line will be a contour of constant ρ in the xt plane because the solution of the advection equation is just the initial condition displaced by a distance $\Delta x = c\Delta t$.

Now let's return to the nonlinear problem, Equation (7.39). In Figure 7.9 we draw the characteristic line from the point x_1; this line has slope $dt/dx = 1/c(\rho_0(x_1))$. Even in the nonlinear problem, the density is constant along this line. Here is the proof: For any function of two variables, the chain rule tells us that

$$\frac{d}{dt}f(x(t), t) = \frac{\partial}{\partial t}f(x(t), t) + \frac{dx}{dt}\frac{\partial}{\partial x}f(x(t), t) \tag{7.41}$$

Suppose that we vary x with t such that we move along the characteristic line. This means that $dt/dx = 1/c(\rho_0)$ or $dx/dt = c(\rho_0)$. Using the previous equation with $f(x, t) = \rho(x, t)$,

$$\frac{d}{dt}\rho(x(t), t) = \frac{\partial}{\partial t}\rho(x(t), t) + c(\rho_0(x))\frac{\partial}{\partial x}\rho(x(t), t) \tag{7.42}$$

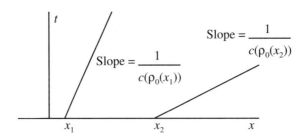

Figure 7.10: Sketch of various characteristic lines for the nonlinear traffic equation.

Yet from our original PDE, the right-hand side is zero, so

$$\frac{d}{dt}\rho(x(t), t) = 0 \qquad \text{(on the characteristic line)} \qquad (7.43)$$

which completes the proof.

To use the method of characteristics to construct our solution, we draw a characteristic line from each point on the x-axis (Figure 7.10). You should think of these lines as forming a contour map of $\rho(x, t)$, since each line is a line of constant density.

Traffic at a Stoplight

Now to solve an actual traffic problem. The simplest problem we can solve is the initial distribution

$$\rho(x, t = 0) = \rho_0(x) = \begin{cases} \rho_m & x < 0 \\ 0 & x > 0 \end{cases} \qquad (7.44)$$

that is, a step function (Figure 7.11). As a traffic problem, this could represent cars at a stoplight. Behind the light (which is at $x = 0$), the traffic is at its maximum density (bumper-to-bumper); there is no traffic on the other side of the light. At time $t = 0$ the light turns green and the cars are free to move. Intuitively, we know that not all cars start moving when the light turns green. The density decreases as the cars separate, but this effect propagates back into the stream of traffic with a finite wave speed (Figure 7.12). In fluid dynamics this is known as a rarefaction wave problem.

Let's start by drawing the characteristic lines on the positive x-axis. These lines will have slope $1/c(0) = 1/v_m$. If we shade the region of constant density, we have the sketch shown in Figure 7.13. The first car through the light will move at the maximum velocity since there are no cars in front of it. The left border of the $\rho(x, t) = 0$ region is the location of the lead car.

Next, we add the characteristic lines for the points on the negative x-axis, as shown in Figure 7.14. Notice that most cars do not begin to move until long after the light has turned green. This is because the disturbance (or wave) can

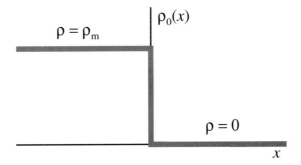

Figure 7.11: Initial density profile for traffic at a stoplight.

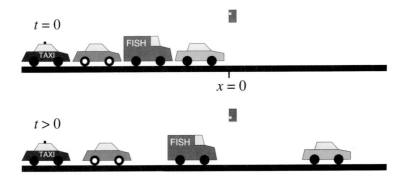

Figure 7.12: Traffic moving after a stoplight turns green. Notice that in the second frame the last car toward the rear has not moved.

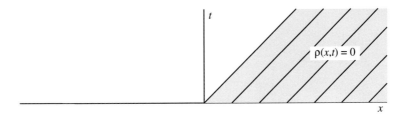

Figure 7.13: Partial construction of $\rho(x,t)$ in the xt plane using characteristic lines. In the shaded region the density $\rho(x,t)$ is zero. The left boundary of this region is given by the position of the lead car.

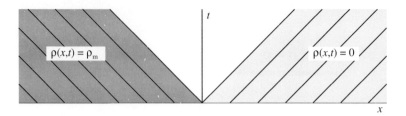

Figure 7.14: Partial construction of $\rho(x,t)$ in the xt plane using characteristic lines. In the shaded region on the left the density $\rho(x,t)$ is maximum (bumper-to-bumper).

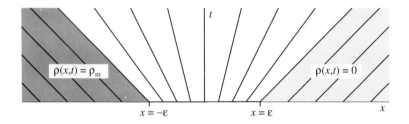

Figure 7.15: Characteristic lines for a continuous initial density profile. This density profile goes to a step function as $\epsilon \to 0$.

only move with velocity $c(\rho_m)$. For our linear relation between v and ρ, we have $c(\rho_m) = -v_m$.

To obtain all the characteristic lines we must remember that our initial condition is discontinuous. Suppose that we modified $\rho_0(x)$ so that it varied continuously from ρ_m to zero in a neighborhood of radius ϵ about $x = 0$. The slopes of the characteristic lines in this neighborhood would vary continuously from $1/v_m$ to $-1/v_m$ (Figure 7.15).

Taking the limit $\epsilon \to 0$, we have our final picture of the characteristic lines

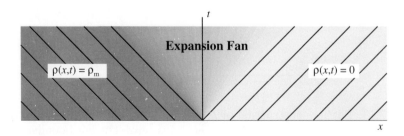

Figure 7.16: Construction of $\rho(x,t)$ in the xt plane using characteristic lines.

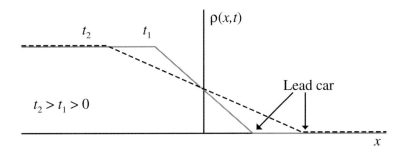

Figure 7.17: Traffic density, $\rho(x, t)$, as a function of position for various times.

as shown in Figure 7.16. The solution may be written as

$$\rho(x,t) = \begin{cases} \rho_{\mathrm{m}} & \text{for} & x \leq -v_{\mathrm{m}}t \\ c^{-1}(x/t) & \text{for} & -v_{\mathrm{m}}t < x < v_{\mathrm{m}}t \\ 0 & \text{for} & x \geq v_{\mathrm{m}}t \end{cases} \qquad (7.45)$$

where $c^{-1}(c(\rho)) = \rho$; that is, c^{-1} is the inverse function of $c(\rho)$. Using Equation (7.40) for $c(\rho)$ we have

$$\rho(x,t) = \begin{cases} \rho_{\mathrm{m}} & \text{for} & x \leq -v_{\mathrm{m}}t \\ \frac{1}{2}\left(1 - \frac{x}{v_{\mathrm{m}}t}\right)\rho_{\mathrm{m}} & \text{for} & -v_{\mathrm{m}}t < x < v_{\mathrm{m}}t \\ 0 & \text{for} & x \geq v_{\mathrm{m}}t \end{cases} \qquad (7.46)$$

Notice that in the region $-v_{\mathrm{m}}t < x < v_{\mathrm{m}}t$, the density varies linearly with position (Figure 7.17).

Traffic Program

Now that we have an analytical solution for a simple traffic problem, let's see how well our numerical methods can do. The equation of continuity is

$$\frac{\partial}{\partial t}\rho(x,t) = -\frac{\partial}{\partial x}F(\rho) \qquad (7.47)$$

where the flow is $F(\rho) = \rho(x,t)v(\rho(x,t))$ and the velocity, $v(\rho)$, is given by Equation (7.35). The FTCS scheme for solving this equation is

$$\rho_i^{n+1} = \rho_i^n - \frac{\tau}{2h}(F_{i+1}^n - F_{i-1}^n) \qquad (7.48)$$

where $F_i^n \equiv F(\rho_i^n)$. The Lax scheme uses the equation

$$\rho_i^{n+1} = \frac{1}{2}(\rho_{i+1}^n + \rho_{i-1}^n) - \frac{\tau}{2h}(F_{i+1}^n - F_{i-1}^n) \qquad (7.49)$$

Table 7.2: Outline of program `traffic`, which computes the equation of continuity for traffic flow.

- Select numerical parameters (τ, h, etc.).

- Set initial condition (7.52) and periodic boundary conditions.

- Initialize plotting variables.

- Loop over desired number of steps.

   - Compute the flow, $F(\rho) = \rho(x,t)v(\rho(x,t))$.

   - Compute new values of density using:
      * FTCS scheme (7.48) **or**;
      * Lax scheme (7.49) **or**;
      * Lax-Wendroff scheme (7.50).

   - Record density for plotting.

   - Display snap-shot of density versus position. [MATLAB only]

- Graph density versus position and time as mesh plot.

- Graph contours of density versus position and time.

See pages 240 and 244 for program listings.

Finally, the Lax-Wendroff scheme uses

$$\rho_i^{n+1} = \rho_i^n - \frac{\tau}{2h}(F_{i+1}^n - F_{i-1}^n) + \frac{\tau^2}{2}\frac{1}{h}\left(c_{i+\frac{1}{2}}\frac{F_{i+1}^n - F_i^n}{h} - c_{i-\frac{1}{2}}\frac{F_i^n - F_{i-1}^n}{h}\right) \tag{7.50}$$

where

$$c_{i\pm\frac{1}{2}} \equiv c(\rho_{i\pm\frac{1}{2}}^n); \qquad \rho_{i\pm\frac{1}{2}}^n \equiv \frac{\rho_{i\pm1}^n + \rho_i^n}{2} \tag{7.51}$$

Notice how the last term of (7.50) is built: We would like to be able to evaluate the function $c(\rho)$ at values between grid points, that is, at $i + \frac{1}{2}$ and $i - \frac{1}{2}$. Since we know the value of ρ only at grid points, we estimate its value between grid points by using a simple average. We use this estimated value for $\rho_{i\pm\frac{1}{2}}$ to evaluate $c_{i\pm\frac{1}{2}}$.

The program called `traffic`, which implements these numerical schemes, is outlined in Table 7.2. As an initial condition we take a square pulse of the form

$$\rho(x, t = 0) = \rho_0(x) = \begin{cases} \rho_{\mathrm{m}} & -L/4 < x < 0 \\ 0 & \text{otherwise} \end{cases} \tag{7.52}$$

This initial value problem is similar to the stoplight problem considered above

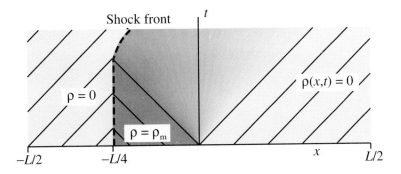

Figure 7.18: Characteristic lines for the finite pulse [see Equation (7.52)].

[see Equation (7.11)], except that the line of cars is of finite length. We take periodic boundary conditions so the problem resembles the start of a race on a circular track. From the solution to the stoplight problem, Equation (7.46), we expect the right side of the pulse to expand with the density varying linearly from ρ_m to zero.

The left edge of the pulse should not move until the density there drops below ρ_{max}. The last car only begins moving when the traffic is no longer bumper-to-bumper. Figure 7.18 shows the characteristic lines for this problem; the discontinuity at $-L/4$ is a shock front. At the shock front, characteristic lines of high density and low density intersect, and the $\rho(x, t)$ is multivalued at the shock. The characteristic line solution is valid as long as we terminate the characteristic lines at the shock. Even if the initial condition is smoothed, this shock will develop since the slopes of low density and high density characteristics lines have opposite sign.

When the last car begins to move, the shock front also moves. Using the condition that the flux, $F(\rho)$, is a continuous function, we may compute the motion of the shock. Our formulation using characteristic lines may then be extended to complete the solution (see Exercise 7.13).

Running the `traffic` program using the FTCS method we obtain the results shown in Figure 7.19. Notice that while the FTCS method appears stable in this case, the solution is not at all satisfactory. The right edge of the pulse is curved, yet it should expand as a straight line (see Figure 7.17). Using the `traffic` program with the Lax method, we get the results shown in Figures 7.20 and 7.21. While the right edge is straighter, its slope is too large. Also the left edge is not maintained constant.

The Lax-Wendroff scheme does an excellent job, as shown in Figures 7.22 and 7.23. The latter is a contour plot of the density in the xt plane; compare this result with the characteristic lines shown in Figure 7.18. By running the program for more time steps, we can observe the evolution of the pulse after the last car starts to move (Figures 7.24 and 7.25). The shock at the left edge of the pulse moves, and its strength begins to decrease. Eventually the density

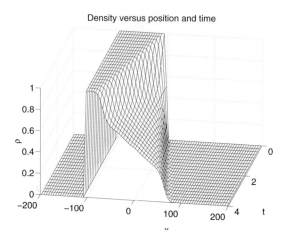

Figure 7.19: Mesh plot of density versus position and time from the `traffic` program using the FTCS method with 80 grid points and a time step of 0.2.

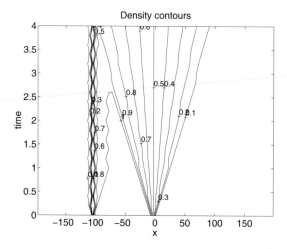

Figure 7.20: Contour plot of density versus position and time from the `traffic` program using the Lax method with 80 grid points and a time step of 0.2.

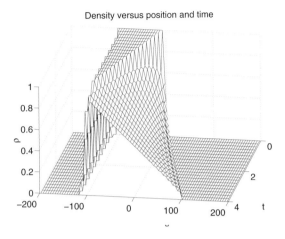

Figure 7.21: Mesh plot of density versus position and time from the `traffic` program using the Lax method with 80 grid points and a time step of 0.2.

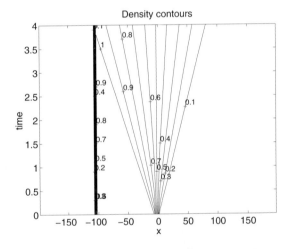

Figure 7.22: Contour plot of density versus position and time from the `traffic` program using the Lax-Wendroff method with 80 grid points and a time step of 0.2.

becomes uniform everywhere.

Shock waves in real traffic are very dangerous. Drivers have finite reaction times, so sudden changes in traffic density can cause accidents. In our traffic model, the local density determines the traffic velocity. Fortunately, under normal visibility conditions, drivers adjust their speed by judging the global traffic conditions (i.e., they look at more than just the car in front of them). This fact introduces a diffusion term into the model that smooths the discontinuous shock fronts.

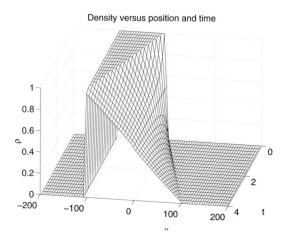

Figure 7.23: Mesh plot of density versus position and time from the `traffic` program using the Lax-Wendroff method with 80 grid points and a time step of 0.2.

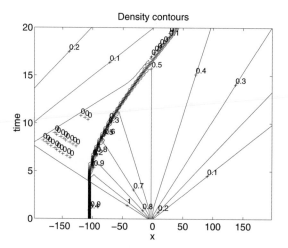

Figure 7.24: Contour plot of density versus position and time from the `traffic` program using the Lax-Wendroff method. Parameters are the same as in Figure 7.22 except the simulation is run five times longer (i.e., the number of time steps is five times larger).

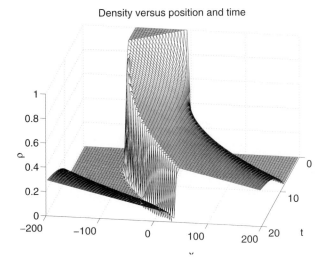

Figure 7.25: Mesh plot of density versus position and time from the `traffic` program using the Lax-Wendroff method. The contour plot for this run is shown in Figure 7.24.

EXERCISES

7.   The flow of traffic is $F(x,t) = \rho(x,t)v(\rho)$. For the stoplight problem, obtain an expression for $F(x,t)$ using the solution (7.46) and $v(\rho) = v_\mathrm{m}(1-\rho/\rho_\mathrm{m})$. Sketch $F(x,t)$ versus x for $t > 0$, and show that it is maximum at $x = 0$ (i.e., at the light). [Pencil]

8.   Call $x_\mathrm{c}(t)$ the position of a given car; then

$$\frac{dx_\mathrm{c}}{dt} = v(\rho(x_\mathrm{c}(t), t)) \tag{7.53}$$

(a) Show that

$$x_\mathrm{c}(t) = \begin{cases} x_\mathrm{c}(0) & t < -x_\mathrm{c}(0)/v_\mathrm{m} \\ v_\mathrm{m}t - 2\sqrt{-x_\mathrm{c}(0)v_\mathrm{m}t} & t > -x_\mathrm{c}(0)/v_\mathrm{m} \end{cases} \tag{7.54}$$

by using the solution to the stoplight problem, Equation (7.46). [Pencil] (b) Plot the trajectories x_c in the xt plane for various $x_\mathrm{c}(0)$. [Computer] (c) Plot the time it takes for a car to reach the intersection as a function of $|x_\mathrm{c}(0)|$. [Computer]

9.   After a time t, the total amount of traffic that has passed through the light is $N(t) = \int_0^\infty \rho(x,t)\,dx$. Show that $N(t) = \int_0^t F(x = 0, t)\,dt$, where $F(x,t) = \rho(x,t)v(x,t)$ is the flow. [Pencil]

10.   Modify the `traffic` program so that it uses a Gaussian pulse of width $L/4$ as an initial distribution for the density. Center the pulse at $x = 0$ with $\rho(0,0) = \rho_\mathrm{m}$. Show how the density evolves with time. Explain why one side of the pulse expands while the other contracts [remember that the wave speed, $c(\rho)$, is not a constant]. Describe what a driver on this racetrack will experience. [Computer]

11. Modify the `traffic` program so that it uses the initial condition

$$\rho(x, t = 0) = \frac{\rho_m}{2}[1 + \cos(4\pi x/L)]$$

(a) Plot the density versus position for a variety of times and show that the cosine wave turns into a sawtooth wave. In nonlinear acoustics this is referred to as an N-wave. If you have ever been to a very loud rock concert, you may have heard one of these. (b) Modify your program to compute the spatial power spectrum of the density (see Section 5.2). Remove the zero wave number component. Initially, the spectrum will contain a single peak, but in time other peaks appear. Use a mesh plot to graph the spectrum versus wave number and time. [Computer]

12.   Suppose that we have a uniform density of traffic with a small congested area. Modify the `traffic` program so that it uses the initial condition

$$\rho(x, t = 0) = \rho_0[1 + \alpha \exp(-x^2/2\sigma^2)]$$

where $\alpha = 1/5$, $\sigma = L/8$, and ρ_0 are a constants. (a) Show that for light traffic (e.g., $\rho_0 = \rho_m/4$) the perturbation moves forward. What is its speed? (b) Show that for heavy traffic (e.g., $\rho_0 = 3\rho_m/4$) the perturbation moves backward. Interpret this result physically. (c) Show that for $\rho_0 = \rho_m/2$ the perturbation is almost stationary; it drifts and distorts slightly. [Computer]

13.   Call $x_s(t)$ the position of the shock wave (see Figures 7.18 and 7.24). The velocity of the shock is given by

$$\frac{dx_s}{dt} = \frac{F(\rho_+) - F(\rho_-)}{\rho_+ - \rho_-} \tag{7.55}$$

where $F(x, t) = \rho(x, t)v(x, t)$ is the flow and $\rho_\pm = \lim_{\epsilon \to 0} \rho(x_s \pm \epsilon)$, that is, the density on each side of the shock front. (a) Show that

$$\frac{dx_s}{dt} = \frac{1}{2}(c(\rho_+) + c(\rho_-)) \tag{7.56}$$

when v is linear in the density. [Pencil] (b) Use the density profile computed by the `traffic` program to compute $x_s(t)$ given that $x_s(0) = -L/4$. Compare your results with the locations of steep gradients in the contour plot produced by `traffic`. [Computer]

BEYOND THIS CHAPTER

In Section 7.2 the method of characteristics is used to obtain an analytical solution to the generalized Burger's equation. The method of characteristics may also be implemented as a numerical scheme for solving hyperbolic equations. For the wave equation we have two sets of characteristic lines (left- and right-moving waves). For more complicated problems (e.g., Euler equations in fluid mechanics) these characteristic lines are computed numerically as trajectories of a nonlinear ODE.[73]

   One of the principal difficulties with numerically solving hyperbolic equations is the formation of shocks. At a shock the solution is discontinuous and our PDE description breaks down. One way to treat the problem is to use an uneven grid and concentrate grid points at the location of the shock. Shock-capturing methods automatically adjust the grid spacing to accomplish this. See Anderson et al. [10] and Fletcher [47] for an extensive discussion of finite difference methods for solving hyperbolic equations. For a presentation of the hydrodynamic equations suitable for a physicist, see Tritton [128].

APPENDIX A: MATLAB LISTINGS

Listing 7A.1 Program `advect`. Solves the advection equation using various numerical schemes.

```
% advect - Program to solve the advection equation
% using the various hyperbolic PDE schemes
clear all;  help advect;  % Clear memory and print header

%* Select numerical parameters (time step, grid spacing, etc.).
method = menu('Choose a numerical method:', ...
         'FTCS','Lax','Lax-Wendroff');
N = input('Enter number of grid points: ');
L = 1.;      % System size
h = L/N;     % Grid spacing
c = 1;       % Wave speed
fprintf('Time for wave to move one grid spacing is %g\n',h/c);
tau = input('Enter time step: ');
coeff = -c*tau/(2.*h);   % Coefficient used by all schemes
coefflw = 2*coeff^2;     % Coefficient used by L-W scheme
fprintf('Wave circles system in %g steps\n',L/(c*tau));
nStep = input('Enter number of steps: ');

%* Set initial and boundary conditions.
sigma = 0.1;              % Width of the Gaussian pulse
k_wave = pi/sigma;        % Wave number of the cosine
x = ((1:N)-1/2)*h - L/2;  % Coordinates of grid points
% Initial condition is a Gaussian-cosine pulse
a = cos(k_wave*x) .* exp(-x.^2/(2*sigma^2));
% Use periodic boundary conditions
ip(1:(N-1)) = 2:N;  ip(N) = 1;      % ip = i+1 with periodic b.c.
im(2:N) = 1:(N-1);  im(1) = N;      % im = i-1 with periodic b.c.

%* Initialize plotting variables.
iplot = 1;             % Plot counter
aplot(:,1) = a(:);     % Record the initial state
tplot(1) = 0;          % Record the initial time (t=0)
nplots = 50;           % Desired number of plots
plotStep = nStep/nplots; % Number of steps between plots

%* Loop over desired number of steps.
for iStep=1:nStep  %% MAIN LOOP %%
```

```
%* Compute new values of wave amplitude using FTCS,
%  Lax or Lax-Wendroff method.
if( method == 1 )        %%% FTCS method %%%
   a(1:N) = a(1:N) + coeff*(a(ip)-a(im));
elseif( method == 2 )  %%% Lax method %%%
   a(1:N) = .5*(a(ip)+a(im)) + coeff*(a(ip)-a(im));
else                     %%% Lax-Wendroff method %%%
   a(1:N) = a(1:N) + coeff*(a(ip)-a(im)) + ...
       coefflw*(a(ip)+a(im)-2*a(1:N));
end

%* Periodically record a(t) for plotting.
if( rem(iStep,plotStep) < 1 )  % Every plot_iter steps record
   iplot = iplot+1;
   aplot(:,iplot) = a(:);        % Record a(i) for ploting
   tplot(iplot) = tau*iStep;
   fprintf('%g out of %g steps completed\n',iStep,nStep);
end
end

%* Plot the initial and final states.
figure(1); clf;  % Clear figure 1 window and bring forward
plot(x,aplot(:,1),'-',x,a,'--'); legend('Initial','Final');
xlabel('x');  ylabel('a(x,t)');
pause(1);     % Pause 1 second between plots

%* Plot the wave amplitude versus position and time
figure(2); clf;  % Clear figure 2 window and bring forward
mesh(tplot,x,aplot); ylabel('Position');  xlabel('Time');
zlabel('Amplitude');
view([-70 50]);  % Better view from this angle
```

Listing 7A.2 Program `traffic`. Solves the equation of continuity for traffic flow.

```
% traffic - Program to solve the generalized Burger
% equation for the traffic at a stop light problem
clear all;  help traffic; % Clear memory and print header

%* Select numerical parameters (time step, grid spacing, etc.).
method = menu('Choose a numerical method:', ...
       'FTCS','Lax','Lax-Wendroff');
N = input('Enter the number of grid points: ');
L = 400;       % System size (meters)
h = L/N;        % Grid spacing for periodic boundary conditions
v_max = 25;    % Maximum car speed (m/s)
fprintf('Suggested timestep is %g\n',h/v_max);
tau = input('Enter time step (tau): ');
```

```
fprintf('Last car starts moving after %g steps\n', ...
                            (L/4)/(v_max*tau));
nstep = input('Enter number of steps: ');
coeff = tau/(2*h);          % Coefficient used by all schemes
coefflw = tau^2/(2*h^2);    % Coefficient used by Lax-Wendroff

%* Set initial and boundary conditions
rho_max = 1.0;                     % Maximum density
Flow_max = 0.25*rho_max*v_max;  % Maximum Flow
% Initial condition is a square pulse from x = -L/4 to x = 0
rho = zeros(1,N); for i=round(N/4):round(N/2-1)
  rho(i) = rho_max;       % Max density in the square pulse
end
rho(round(N/2)) = rho_max/2;   % Try running without this line
% Use periodic boundary conditions
ip(1:N) = (1:N)+1;  ip(N) = 1;   % ip = i+1 with periodic b.c.
im(1:N) = (1:N)-1;  im(1) = N;   % im = i-1 with periodic b.c.

%* Initialize plotting variables.
iplot = 1;
xplot = ((1:N)-1/2)*h - L/2;  % Record x scale for plot
rplot(:,1) = rho(:);          % Record the initial state
tplot(1) = 0;
figure(1); clf;  % Clear figure 1 window and bring forward

%* Loop over desired number of steps.
for istep=1:nstep

  %* Compute the flow = (Density)*(Velocity)
  Flow = rho .* (v_max*(1 - rho/rho_max));

  %* Compute new values of density using FTCS,
  %  Lax or Lax-Wendroff method.
  if( method == 1 )       %%% FTCS method %%%
    rho(1:N) = rho(1:N) - coeff*(Flow(ip)-Flow(im));
  elseif( method == 2 )  %%% Lax method %%%
    rho(1:N) = .5*(rho(ip)+rho(im)) ...
                  - coeff*(Flow(ip)-Flow(im));
  else                    %%% Lax-Wendroff method %%%
    cp = v_max*(1 - (rho(ip)+rho(1:N))/rho_max);
    cm = v_max*(1 - (rho(1:N)+rho(im))/rho_max);
    rho(1:N) = rho(1:N) - coeff*(Flow(ip)-Flow(im)) ...
            + coefflw*(cp.*(Flow(ip)-Flow(1:N)) ...
                  - cm.*(Flow(1:N)-Flow(im)));
  end

  %* Record density for plotting.
  iplot = iplot+1;
  rplot(:,iplot) = rho(:);
  tplot(iplot) = tau*istep;
```

```
  %* Display snap-shot of density versus position
  plot(xplot,rho,'-',xplot,Flow/Flow_max,'--');
  xlabel('x'); ylabel('Density and Flow');
  legend('\rho(x,t)','F(x,t)');
  axis([-L/2, L/2, -0.1, 1.1]);
  drawnow;
end

%* Graph density versus position and time as wire-mesh plot
figure(1); clf;  % Clear figure 1 window and bring forward
mesh(tplot,xplot,rplot) xlabel('t'); ylabel('x'); zlabel('\rho');
title('Density versus position and time');
view([100 30]);  % Rotate the plot for better view point
pause(1);     % Pause 1 second between plots

%* Graph contours of density versus position and time.
figure(2); clf;   % Clear figure 2 window and bring forward
% Use rot90 function to graph t vs x since
% contour(rplot) graphs x vs t.
clevels = 0:(0.1):1;   % Contour levels
cs = contour(xplot,tplot,flipud(rot90(rplot)),clevels);
clabel(cs);              % Put labels on contour levels
xlabel('x');  ylabel('time');  title('Density contours');
```

APPENDIX B: C++ LISTINGS

Listing 7B.1 Program advect. Solves the advection equation using various numerical schemes.

```cpp
// advect - Program to solve the advection equation
// using the various hyperbolic PDE schemes
#include "NumMeth.h"

void main() {

  //* Select numerical parameters (time step, grid spacing, etc.).
  cout << "Choose a numerical method: 1) FTCS, 2) Lax, 3) Lax-Wendroff : ";
  int method; cin >> method;
  cout << "Enter number of grid points: "; int N; cin >> N;
  double L = 1.;     // System size
  double h = L/N;    // Grid spacing
  double c = 1;      // Wave speed
  cout << "Time for wave to move one grid spacing is " << h/c << endl;
  cout << "Enter time step: "; double tau; cin >> tau;
  double coeff = -c*tau/(2.*h);    // Coefficient used by all schemes
```

```
double coefflw = 2*coeff*coeff;  // Coefficient used by L-W scheme
cout << "Wave circles system in " << L/(c*tau) << " steps" << endl;
cout << "Enter number of steps: "; int nStep; cin >> nStep;

//* Set initial and boundary conditions.
const double pi = 3.141592654;
double sigma = 0.1;              // Width of the Gaussian pulse
double k_wave = pi/sigma;        // Wave number of the cosine
Matrix x(N), a(N), a_new(N);
int i,j;
for( i=1; i<=N; i++ ) {
  x(i) = (i-0.5)*h - L/2;  // Coordinates of grid points
  // Initial condition is a Gaussian-cosine pulse
  a(i) = cos(k_wave*x(i)) * exp(-x(i)*x(i)/(2*sigma*sigma));
}
// Use periodic boundary conditions
int *ip, *im;  ip = new int [N+1];  im = new int [N+1];
for( i=2; i<N; i++ ) {
  ip[i] = i+1;    // ip[i] = i+1 with periodic b.c.
  im[i] = i-1;    // im[i] = i-1 with periodic b.c.
}
ip[1] = 2;  ip[N] = 1;
im[1] = N;  im[N] = N-1;

//* Initialize plotting variables.
int iplot = 1;           // Plot counter
int nplots = 50;         // Desired number of plots
double plotStep = ((double)nStep)/nplots;
Matrix aplot(N,nplots+1), tplot(nplots+1);
tplot(1) = 0;        // Record the initial time (t=0)
for( i=1; i<=N; i++ )
  aplot(i,1) = a(i);  // Record the initial state

//* Loop over desired number of steps.
int iStep;
for( iStep=1; iStep<=nStep; iStep++ ) {

  //* Compute new values of wave amplitude using FTCS,
  //  Lax or Lax-Wendroff method.
  if( method == 1 )       ////// FTCS method //////
    for( i=1; i<=N; i++ )
      a_new(i) = a(i) + coeff*( a(ip[i])-a(im[i]) );
  else if( method == 2 )  ////// Lax method //////
    for( i=1; i<=N; i++ )
      a_new(i) = 0.5*( a(ip[i])+a(im[i]) ) +
                coeff*( a(ip[i])-a(im[i]) );
  else                    ////// Lax-Wendroff method //////
    for( i=1; i<=N; i++ )
      a_new(i) = a(i) + coeff*( a(ip[i])-a(im[i]) ) +
                coefflw*( a(ip[i])+a(im[i])-2*a(i) );
```

```
    a = a_new;    // Reset with new amplitude values

    //* Periodically record a(t) for plotting.
    if( fmod((double)iStep,plotStep) < 1 ) {
      iplot++;
      tplot(iplot) = tau*iStep;
      for( i=1; i<=N; i++ )
        aplot(i,iplot) = a(i);        // Record a(i) for ploting
      cout << iStep << " out of " << nStep << " steps completed" << endl;
    }
  }
  nplots = iplot;    // Actual number of plots recorded

  //* Print out the plotting variables: x, a, tplot, aplot
  ofstream xOut("x.txt"), aOut("a.txt"),
         tplotOut("tplot.txt"), aplotOut("aplot.txt");
  for( i=1; i<=N; i++ ) {
    xOut << x(i) << endl;
    aOut << a(i) << endl;
    for( j=1; j<nplots; j++ )
      aplotOut << aplot(i,j) << ", ";
    aplotOut << aplot(i,nplots) << endl;
  }
  for( i=1; i<=nplots; i++ )
    tplotOut << tplot(i) << endl;

  delete [] ip, im;  // Release allocated memory
}
/***** To plot in MATLAB; use the script below *******************
%* Plot the initial and final states.
load x.txt; load a.txt; load tplot.txt; load aplot.txt;
figure(1); clf;  % Clear figure 1 window and bring forward
plot(x,aplot(:,1),'-',x,a,'--'); legend('Initial','Final');
xlabel('x');   ylabel('a(x,t)');
pause(1);     % Pause 1 second between plots
%* Plot the wave amplitude versus position and time
figure(2); clf;  % Clear figure 2 window and bring forward
mesh(tplot,x,aplot); ylabel('Position');   xlabel('Time');
zlabel('Amplitude');
view([-70 50]); % Better view from this angle
********************************************************************/
```

Listing 7B.2 Program traffic. Solves the equation of continuity for traffic flow.

```
// traffic - Program to solve the generalized Burger
// equation for the traffic at a stop light problem
#include "NumMeth.h"
```

```cpp
void main() {

  //* Select numerical parameters (time step, grid spacing, etc.).
  cout << "Choose a numerical method: 1) FTCS, 2) Lax, 3) Lax-Wendroff : ";
  int method; cin >> method;
  cout << "Enter the number of grid points: "; int N; cin >> N;
  double L = 400;        // System size (meters)
  double h = L/N;        // Grid spacing for periodic boundary conditions
  double v_max = 25;     // Maximum car speed (m/s)
  cout << "Suggested timestep is " << h/v_max << endl;
  cout << "Enter time step (tau): "; double tau; cin >> tau;
  cout << "Last car starts moving after "
       << (L/4)/(v_max*tau) << " steps" << endl;
  cout << "Enter number of steps: "; int nStep; cin >> nStep;
  double coeff = tau/(2*h);          // Coefficient used by all schemes
  double coefflw = tau*tau/(2*h*h);  // Coefficient used by Lax-Wendroff
  double cp, cm;         // Variables used by Lax-Wendroff

  //* Set initial and boundary conditions
  double rho_max = 1.0;                     // Maximum density
  double Flow_max = 0.25*rho_max*v_max;  // Maximum Flow
  // Initial condition is a square pulse from x = -L/4 to x = 0
  Matrix rho(N), rho_new(N);
  int i,j, iBack = N/4, iFront = N/2 - 1;
  for( i=1; i<=N; i++ )
    if( iBack <= i && i <= iFront ) rho(i) = rho_max;
    else rho(i) = 0.0;
  rho(iFront+1) = rho_max/2;  // Try running without this line
  // Use periodic boundary conditions
  int *ip, *im;  ip = new int [N+1];  im = new int [N+1];
  for( i=2; i<N; i++ ) {
    ip[i] = i+1;    // ip[i] = i+1 with periodic b.c.
    im[i] = i-1;    // im[i] = i-1 with periodic b.c.
  }
  ip[1] = 2;  ip[N] = 1;
  im[1] = N;  im[N] = N-1;

  //* Initialize plotting variables.
  int iplot = 1;
  Matrix tplot(nStep+1), xplot(N), rplot(N,nStep+1);
  tplot(1) = 0.0;               // Record initial time
  for( i=1; i<=N; i++ ) {
    xplot(i) = (i - 0.5)*h - L/2;  // Record x scale for plot
    rplot(i,1) = rho(i);           // Record the initial state
  }

  //* Loop over desired number of steps.
  Matrix Flow(N);
  int iStep;
```

```
for( iStep=1; iStep<=nStep; iStep++ ) {

  //* Compute the flow = (Density)*(Velocity)
  for( i=1; i<=N; i++ )
    Flow(i) = rho(i) * (v_max*(1.0 - rho(i)/rho_max));

  //* Compute new values of density using FTCS,
  //  Lax or Lax-Wendroff method.
  if( method == 1 )        ////// FTCS method //////
    for( i=1; i<=N; i++ )
      rho_new(i) = rho(i) - coeff*(Flow(ip[i])-Flow(im[i]));
  else if( method == 2 )  ////// Lax method //////
    for( i=1; i<=N; i++ )
      rho_new(i) = 0.5*(rho(ip[i])+rho(im[i]))
                 - coeff*(Flow(ip[i])-Flow(im[i]));
  else                      ////// Lax-Wendroff method //////
    for( i=1; i<=N; i++ ) {
      cp = v_max*(1 - (rho(ip[i])+rho(i))/rho_max);
      cm = v_max*(1 - (rho(i)+rho(im[i]))/rho_max);
      rho_new(i) = rho(i) - coeff*(Flow(ip[i])-Flow(im[i]))
            + coefflw*(cp*(Flow(ip[i])-Flow(i))
                   - cm*(Flow(i)-Flow(im[i])));
    }
  // Reset with new density values
  rho = rho_new;

  //* Record density for plotting.
  cout << "Finished " << iStep << " of " << nStep << " steps" << endl;
  iplot++;
  tplot(iplot) = tau*iStep;
  for( i=1; i<=N; i++ )
    rplot(i,iplot) = rho(i);

}
int nplots = iplot;      // Number of plots recorded

//* Print out the plotting variables: tplot, xplot, rplot
ofstream tplotOut("tplot.txt"), xplotOut("xplot.txt"),
       rplotOut("rplot.txt");
for( i=1; i<=nplots; i++ )
  tplotOut << tplot(i) << endl;
for( i=1; i<=N; i++ ) {
  xplotOut << xplot(i) << endl;
  for( j=1; j<nplots; j++ )
    rplotOut << rplot(i,j) << ", ";
  rplotOut << rplot(i,nplots) << endl;
}

delete [] ip, im;
}
```

```
/***** To plot in MATLAB; use the script below ********************
load tplot.txt; load xplot.txt; load rplot.txt;
%* Graph density versus position and time as wire-mesh plot
figure(1); clf;  % Clear figure 1 window and bring forward
mesh(tplot,xplot,rplot) xlabel('t'); ylabel('x'); zlabel('\rho');
title('Density versus position and time');
view([100 30]);  % Rotate the plot for better view point
pause(1);     % Pause 1 second between plots
%* Graph contours of density versus position and time.
figure(2); clf;   % Clear figure 2 window and bring forward
% Use rot90 function to graph t vs x since
% contour(rplot) graphs x vs t.
clevels = 0:(0.1):1;   % Contour levels
cs = contour(xplot,tplot,flipud(rot90(rplot)),clevels);
clabel(cs);            % Put labels on contour levels
xlabel('x'); ylabel('time'); title('Density contours');
*****************************************************************/
```

Chapter 8

Partial Differential Equations III: Relaxation and Spectral Methods

The two previous chapters covered methods for solving parabolic and hyperbolic equations. Now we consider the third type of partial differential equation, elliptic equations. For this kind of PDE we have to solve a boundary value problem, and the solution is a static field, such as the electric field described by Laplace's equation. Despite the dissimilarities, we find that numerical relaxation algorithms link these problems. With spectral methods, we explore a completely different way of formulating the numerical solution, using a set of basis functions instead of a spatial grid.

8.1   RELAXATION METHODS

Separation of Variables

Our paradigm for an elliptic PDE is Laplace's equation. In two dimensions it may be written as

$$\frac{\partial^2 \Phi(x,y)}{\partial x^2} + \frac{\partial^2 \Phi(x,y)}{\partial y^2} = 0 \tag{8.1}$$

where Φ is the electrostatic potential. Before going into the numerical methods, let's solve this equation analytically for a simple problem. Take a rectangular geometry with boundaries at $x = 0$, $x = L_x$, $y = 0$, and $y = L_y$. In this case, we can solve Laplace's equation by *separation of variables*.[75]

Our first step is to write $\Phi(x,y)$ as the product

$$\Phi(x,y) = X(x)Y(y) \tag{8.2}$$

Inserting this substitution into Laplace's equation and dividing by Φ, we have

$$\frac{1}{X(x)}\frac{d^2X}{dx^2} + \frac{1}{Y(y)}\frac{d^2Y}{dy^2} = 0 \tag{8.3}$$

Since this equation must hold for all x and y, each term must equal a constant; we write separate equations for X and Y,

$$\frac{1}{X(x)}\frac{d^2X}{dx^2} = -k^2; \qquad \frac{1}{Y(y)}\frac{d^2Y}{dy^2} = k^2 \tag{8.4}$$

where k is a complex constant. These equations are ordinary differential equations since X (or Y) only depends on x (or y).

Two notes are needed for those of you who are less familiar with separation of variables. First, we write the constant as k^2 because it simplifies the notation. Second, one equation has k^2 and the other $-k^2$ does not matter, since k is complex. There is no violation of the original symmetry in Laplace's equation.

The solutions of these ODEs for X and Y are well known:

$$\begin{aligned}
X(x) &= C_s \sin(kx) + C_c \cos(kx) \tag{8.5}\\
Y(y) &= C'_s \sinh(ky) + C'_c \cosh(ky) \tag{8.6}
\end{aligned}$$

where C_s, C_c, C'_s, and C'_c are constants. Again, these solutions are the same since k may be complex. In a few lines you will see why I chose to write the solution in this form.

To proceed further, we need to specify boundary conditions. We'll use

$$\begin{aligned}
\Phi(x=0,y) = \Phi(x=L_x,y) &= \Phi(x,y=0) = 0\\
\Phi(x,y=L_y) &= \Phi_0
\end{aligned} \tag{8.7}$$

where Φ_0 is a constant. The potential is zero on three of the sides of the rectangle and Φ_0 on the fourth. The boundary condition at $x = 0$ is satisfied if $C_c = 0$; the $y = 0$ boundary condition is satisfied if $C'_c = 0$. The boundary condition at $x = L_x$ is satisfied if $k = n\pi/L_x$, where n is an integer.

Using the superposition principle, our general solution takes the form

$$\Phi(x,y) = \sum_{n=1}^{\infty} c_n \sin\left(\frac{n\pi x}{L_x}\right) \sinh\left(\frac{n\pi y}{L_x}\right) \tag{8.8}$$

To find the values of the c_n coefficients, we impose the fourth boundary condition, $\Phi(x,y=L_y) = \Phi_0$; hence

$$\Phi_0 = \sum_{n=1}^{\infty} c_n \sin\left(\frac{n\pi x}{L_x}\right) \sinh\left(\frac{n\pi L_y}{L_x}\right) \tag{8.9}$$

Multiply both sides by $\sin(m\pi x/L_x)$ and integrate from $x = 0$ to $x = L_x$,

$$\int_0^{L_x} dx\, \Phi_0 \sin\left(\frac{m\pi x}{L_x}\right) =$$

$$\sum_{n=1}^{\infty} c_n \sinh\left(\frac{n\pi L_y}{L_x}\right) \int_0^{L_x} dx\, \sin\left(\frac{m\pi x}{L_x}\right) \sin\left(\frac{n\pi x}{L_x}\right) \tag{8.10}$$

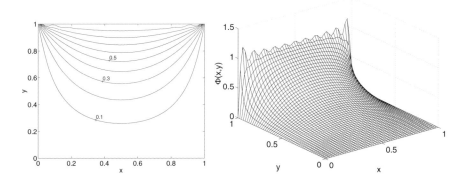

Figure 8.1: Contour and mesh plots of the potential versus x and y as given by the separation of variables solution, Equation (8.15), using terms up through $n = 21$.

The integral on the left-hand side is easily solved,

$$\int_0^{L_x} \sin\left(\frac{m\pi x}{L_x}\right) dx = \begin{cases} 2L_x/\pi m & m \text{ odd} \\ 0 & m \text{ even} \end{cases} \tag{8.11}$$

The sum on the right-hand side may be simplified, since that integral is

$$\int_0^{L_x} \sin\left(\frac{m\pi x}{L_x}\right) \sin\left(\frac{n\pi x}{L_x}\right) dx = \frac{L_x}{2}\delta_{n,m} \tag{8.12}$$

which collapses the sum to a single term.

Equation (8.10) reduces to

$$\Phi_0 \frac{2L_x}{\pi m} = c_m \sinh\left(\frac{m\pi L_y}{L_x}\right)\frac{L_x}{2} \qquad (m \text{ odd}) \tag{8.13}$$

or

$$c_m = \frac{4\Phi_0}{\pi m \sinh(m\pi L_y/L_x)} \qquad (m \text{ odd}) \tag{8.14}$$

Our final expression for the solution is the infinite sum

$$\Phi(x,y) = \Phi_0 \sum_{n=1,3,5,\ldots}^{\infty} \frac{4}{\pi n} \sin\left(\frac{n\pi x}{L_x}\right)\frac{\sinh(n\pi y/L_x)}{\sinh(n\pi L_y/L_x)} \tag{8.15}$$

When we graph this solution we discover that a large number of terms is needed to represent the solution near the $y = L_y$ boundary accurately (Figure 8.1). Near the corners of this boundary we observe *Gibbs' phenomenon*, an oscillation that commonly occurs when a Fourier series is used to represent a discontinuous function.[86]

Jacobi Method

We now develop a numerical method for solving Laplace's equation. To begin, let's go back for a moment to the diffusion equation (Section 6.2). Consider the Fourier equation for the two-dimensional diffusion of temperature,

$$\frac{\partial T(x,y,t)}{\partial t} = \kappa \left(\frac{\partial^2 T}{\partial x^2} + \frac{\partial^2 T}{\partial y^2} \right) \tag{8.16}$$

where κ is the thermal diffusion coefficient. We know from physical intuition that given any initial temperature profile plus stationary boundary conditions, the solution will relax to some steady state, call it $T_s(x, y)$. In other words,

$$\lim_{t \to \infty} T(x, y, t) = T_s(x, y) \tag{8.17}$$

When the temperature profile is at the steady state, then it does not change in time, that is, $\partial T_s / \partial t = 0$. This means that the steady state obeys the equation

$$\frac{\partial^2 T_s}{\partial x^2} + \frac{\partial^2 T_s}{\partial y^2} = 0 \tag{8.18}$$

Does this look familiar? Of course, this is just Laplace's equation.

The idea is that the solution of Laplace's equation is just the solution of the diffusion equation in the limit $t \to \infty$. Algorithms based on this physical principal are called *relaxation methods*. We already know how to solve the diffusion equation using the FTCS scheme. We start from the two-dimensional diffusion equation

$$\frac{\partial \Phi(x,y,t)}{\partial t} = \mu \left(\frac{\partial^2 \Phi}{\partial x^2} + \frac{\partial^2 \Phi}{\partial y^2} \right) \tag{8.19}$$

The value of the constant μ is unimportant because it drops out later. Using the FTCS scheme in two dimensions,

$$\begin{aligned}
\Phi_{i,j}^{n+1} = \Phi_{i,j}^n \ &+ \ \frac{\mu \tau}{h_x^2} \{ \Phi_{i+1,j}^n + \Phi_{i-1,j}^n - 2\Phi_{i,j}^n \} \\
&+ \ \frac{\mu \tau}{h_y^2} \{ \Phi_{i,j+1}^n + \Phi_{i,j-1}^n - 2\Phi_{i,j}^n \}
\end{aligned} \tag{8.20}$$

where $\Phi_{i,j}^n \equiv \Phi(x_i, y_j, t_n)$, $x_i \equiv (i-1)h_x$, $y_j \equiv (j-1)h_y$, and $t_n \equiv (n-1)\tau$. Remember that we are solving an electrostatics problem, so the potential doesn't actually depend on time. We introduce an artificial time dependence only to assist in the construction of the algorithm. A better way to interpret $\Phi_{i,j}^n$ is to call it the nth guess for the potential with (8.20) serving as a formula for improving this guess.

In Section 6.2 we saw that the FTCS scheme can be numerically unstable. In one-dimensional systems the scheme is stable if $\mu\tau/h^2 \leq \frac{1}{2}$; for two-dimensional systems the scheme is stable if

$$\frac{\mu \tau}{h_x^2} + \frac{\mu \tau}{h_y^2} \leq \frac{1}{2} \tag{8.21}$$

(see Exercise 9.5). To simplify the analysis, we take $h_x = h_y = h$ so the condition for stability is $\mu\tau/h^2 \leq \frac{1}{4}$.

Since we are only interested in the steady state solution ($n \to \infty$), we want to use the largest possible time step. Setting $\mu\tau/h^2 = 1/4$, Equation (8.20) becomes

$$\Phi_{i,j}^{n+1} = \frac{1}{4}\{\Phi_{i+1,j}^n + \Phi_{i-1,j}^n + \Phi_{i,j+1}^n + \Phi_{i,j-1}^n\} \tag{8.22}$$

Notice that the diffusion constant, μ, has dropped out and that the $\Phi_{i,j}^n$ terms cancel out on the right-hand side. This equation has a good parentage; our first example of a relaxation scheme is called the *Jacobi method*. It is easy to see that the method involves replacing the value of the potential at a point with the average value of the four nearest neighbors. This result may be thought of as a discrete version of the mean-value theorem for electrostatic potential. Of course, Equation (8.22) is used only for interior points and not when (i, j) is a boundary point.

Gauss-Seidel and Simultaneous Overrelaxation

A simple modification of the Jacobi method improves its rate of convergence. Suppose that we use the updated values of $\Phi_{i,j}$ as they become available. The iteration equation is then

$$\Phi_{i,j}^{n+1} = \frac{1}{4}\{\Phi_{i+1,j}^n + \Phi_{i-1,j}^{n+1} + \Phi_{i,j+1}^n + \Phi_{i,j-1}^{n+1}\} \tag{8.23}$$

The idea is that the updated values of Φ at two of the nearest neighbors have already been computed, so why not use them. With this modification the method is called the *Gauss-Seidel* method. Besides accelerating the convergence, with Gauss-Seidel we do not need to simultaneously store both the Φ^n and Φ^{n+1} matrices, a significant savings in memory.

We can significantly improve our algorithm by overcorrecting the value of Φ at each iteration of the Gauss-Seidel method. This is achieved by using the iteration equation

$$\Phi_{i,j}^{n+1} = (1-\omega)\Phi_{i,j}^n + \frac{\omega}{4}\{\Phi_{i+1,j}^n + \Phi_{i-1,j}^{n+1} + \Phi_{i,j+1}^n + \Phi_{i,j-1}^{n+1}\} \tag{8.24}$$

where the constant ω is called the overrelaxation parameter. This method is called *simultaneous overrelaxation* (SOR).

The trick to using SOR effectively is to select a good value for ω. Notice that using $\omega = 1$ is equivalent to Gauss-Seidel. For $\omega < 1$ we have underrelaxation, and the convergence is slowed. For $\omega > 2$ the SOR method is unstable. There is an ideal value for ω between 1 and 2 that gives the best acceleration. In some geometries this optimal value is known. For example, in an $N_x \times N_y$ rectangular grid,

$$\omega_{\text{opt}} = \frac{2}{1 + \sqrt{1 - r^2}} \tag{8.25}$$

Table 8.1: Outline of program `relax`, which solves Laplace's equation using the Jacobi, Gauss-Seidel, or SOR method.

- Initialize parameters (L, h, etc.).

- Select ω, the over-relaxation factor (SOR only).

- Set initial guess as first term in separation of variables solution, (8.15).

- Loop until desired fractional change per iteration is obtained.

  - Compute new estimate for Φ using:
    * Jacobi method (8.22) **or**;
    * Gauss-Seidel method (8.23) **or**;
    * Simultaneous over-relaxation (SOR) method (8.24).
  - Check if fractional change is small enough to halt the iteration.

- Plot final estimate of $\Phi(x, y)$ as contour and surface plots.

- Plot the fractional change versus iteration.

See pages 268 and 271 for program listings.

where

$$r = \frac{1}{2}\left(\cos\frac{\pi}{N_x} + \cos\frac{\pi}{N_y}\right) \tag{8.26}$$

If $N_x = N_y = N$ (square geometry), this simplifies to

$$\omega_{\text{opt}} = \frac{2}{1 + \sin(\pi/N)} \tag{8.27}$$

with $\omega_{\text{opt}} \approx 1.939$ for $N = 100$. In real-life problems the optimal value for ω is obtained by empirical trial and error. Sophisticated programs will automatically adjust ω according to how well the solution is converging.

A program, called `relax`, that solves Laplace's equation using the Jacobi, Gauss-Seidel, or SOR method, is outlined in Table 8.1. Relaxation algorithms require an initial guess to start the iteration process and the `relax` program uses the first term in the separation of variables solution (8.15). Sometimes the efficiency of the algorithm is greatly influenced by the accuracy of this initial guess. The best way to appreciate this point is to run the program using a poor initial guess (e.g., $\Phi = 0$ in the interior).

The potential, as computed by the `relax` program, is illustrated in Figure 8.2 by a contour map and a mesh figure. Notice that we have no Gibbs' phenomenon (compare with the separation of variables solution, Figure 8.1).

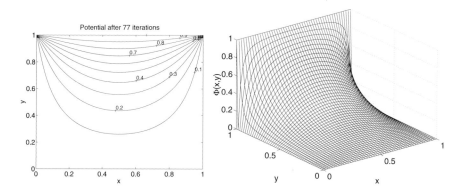

Figure 8.2: Contour and mesh plots of the potential from `relax` using the SOR method. Grid size is $N = 50$ and $\omega = 1.8$ ($\omega_{\text{opt}} \approx 1.88$). Compare with the separation of variables solution, Figure 8.1.

Poisson Equation

The methods developed so far are easy to generalize to solve the Poisson equation. In MKS units,

$$\frac{\partial^2 \Phi(x,y)}{\partial x^2} + \frac{\partial^2 \Phi(x,y)}{\partial y^2} = -\frac{1}{\epsilon_0}\rho(x,y) \tag{8.28}$$

where $\rho(x,y)$ is the charge density and ϵ_0 is the permittivity of free space. In discretized form, we have

$$\frac{1}{h_x^2}\{\Phi_{i+1,j} + \Phi_{i-1,j} - 2\Phi_{i,j}\} + \frac{1}{h_y^2}\{\Phi_{i,j+1} + \Phi_{i,j-1} - 2\Phi_{i,j}\} = -\frac{1}{\epsilon_0}\rho_{i,j} \tag{8.29}$$

Using the analysis presented earlier, we construct the Jacobi relaxation scheme for the Poisson equation as

$$\Phi_{i,j}^{n+1} = \frac{1}{4}\left\{\Phi_{i+1,j}^n + \Phi_{i-1,j}^n + \Phi_{i,j+1}^n + \Phi_{i,j-1}^n + \frac{1}{\epsilon_0}h^2\rho_{i,j}\right\} \tag{8.30}$$

where to simplify the formulation we take $h_x = h_y = h$. The other two schemes considered in this section may also be generalized by the simple addition of the charge density term.

EXERCISES

1. Write a program to evaluate the potential $\Phi(x,y)$ numerically, as given by Equation (8.15), on a 50×50 grid. Take $\Phi_0 = 1$ and graph your solution by mesh and contour plots (see Figure 8.1). Plot your results using terms through $n = 11$, 21, and 51. Estimate how many terms in the infinite sum are needed to obtain about 1% accuracy in the solution. [Computer]

2. (a) Find the solution to the more general boundary value problem,

$$
\begin{aligned}
\Phi(x=0,y) &= \Phi_1 & \Phi(x=L_x,y) &= \Phi_2 \\
\Phi(x,y=0) &= \Phi_3 & \Phi(x,y=L_y) &= \Phi_4
\end{aligned}
$$

where $\Phi_1, \ldots, \Phi_4$ are constants. [Pencil] (b) Write a program to graph your solution by mesh and contour plots. Graph the potential for $\Phi_1 = \Phi_3 = 1$, $\Phi_2 = \Phi_4 = 0$, and for $\Phi_1 = \Phi_2 = 1$, $\Phi_3 = \Phi_4 = 0$. [Computer]

3. (a) Find the solution to the three-dimensional cubic boundary value problem, [75, Problem 2.13]

$$
\begin{aligned}
\Phi(x=0,y,z) &= \Phi(x=L,y,z) &= 0 \\
\Phi(x,y=0,z) &= \Phi(x,y=L,z) &= 0 \\
\Phi(x,y,z=0) &= \Phi(x,y,z=L) &= \Phi_0
\end{aligned}
$$

using separation of variables. [Pencil] (b) Write a program to graph your solution for a given height z. Produce mesh and contour plots of $\Phi(x,y,z)$ for $z = L/4$ and $L/2$. [Computer] (c) Write a three-dimensional version of the `relax` program to solve this problem by relaxation. Produce mesh and contour plots of $\Phi(x,y,z)$ for $z = L/4$ and $L/2$; compare with your results from part (b).

4. A major issue with relaxation methods is their computational speed. (a) Run the `relax` program using the Jacobi method for different-sized systems ($N_x = N_y = 10$ to 50). Graph the number of iterations performed versus system size. Fit the data to a power law and approximate the exponent. (b) Repeat part (a) using a bad initial guess. Set the potential initially to zero everywhere in the interior. (c) Using SOR, repeat parts (a) and (b). Compare the Jacobi and SOR methods (use the optimum value for ω). [Computer]

5. Formulate the Jacobi method without assuming that $h_x = h_y$. Modify the `relax` program to implement this modification. Keep $L_x = L_y$ and the boundary conditions, Equation (8.7), and try grids of 32×32, 64×16, and 16×64. Do you find any significant differences? [Computer]

6. The `relax` program uses a good initial guess for the potential $\Phi(x,y)$. To illustrate its importance, run the program with a variety of initial guesses, including some poor ones (e.g., $\Phi = 0$ in the interior). Also try an initial guess that uses the first few terms of the separation of variables solution (8.15). Compare and comment on your results. [Computer]

7. Modify the `relax` program to plot the electric field, $\mathbf{E} = -\nabla\Phi$. In MATLAB, the functions `gradient` (which computes the gradient) and `quiver` (which produces a field plot; see Figure 8.8) are available. Plot the electric field for the potential shown in Figure 8.2. Try both proportional and equal-length field arrows. [MATLAB]

8. Write a program that uses the SOR method to simulate a Faraday cage (Figure 8.3). Use a square geometry with $N_x = N_y = 60$. Set the left and right walls to $\Phi = 0$ and $\Phi = 100$, respectively. Fix the potential at the top and bottom walls but have it vary linearly across the system. (a) The Faraday cage is represented by the following eight points: $(i,j) = (20,20), (30,20), (40,20), (20,30), (20,40), (30,40), (40,30)$, and $(40,40)$. The potential at these points is fixed at zero. Plot the potential $\Phi_{i,30}$ versus i (i.e., a horizontal cross section through the center), both with and without the cage. (b) Try a cage that has only the four corner points $(20,20), (20,40), (40,20), (40,40)$, and compare with the results from part (a). (c) Try a cage that has only the four

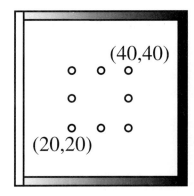

Figure 8.3: Faraday cage.

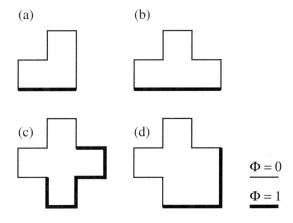

Figure 8.4: Geometries and boundary conditions for Laplace equation.

side points $(20, 30)$, $(30, 20)$, $(40, 30)$, $(30, 40)$, and compare with the results from part (a). [Computer]

9. Write a program that uses the SOR method to solve the electrostatics problems shown in Figure 8.4. For each box, the thin lines indicate a boundary where the potential is fixed at zero; a thick line indicates the potential is fixed at one. [Computer]

10. (a) Write a program that solves the two-dimensional Poisson equation in a square geometry with the Dirichlet boundary conditions $\Phi = 0$ at the boundary. Map the potential for a single charge at the center of the system. Compare with the potential for a charge in free space. Remember that in two dimensions this charge is a line charge and not a point charge (see Figure 8.5). (b) Modify your program to use periodic boundary conditions. Compare with the results from part (a). (Hint: Think.) [Computer]

11. In two dimensions, the Laplace equation may be discretized as

$$\frac{1}{h_x^2}\{\Phi_{i+1,j} + \Phi_{i-1,j} - 2\Phi_{i,j}\} + \frac{1}{h_y^2}\{\Phi_{i,j+1} + \Phi_{i,j-1} - 2\Phi_{i,j}\} = 0$$

(a) Take a very small system that contains only nine interior points (3×3 interior grid). Show that the discretized Laplace equation can be reduced to a system of nine simultaneous equations. [Pencil] (b) Write a program that solves these simultaneous equations using Gaussian elimination. This solution is important because it can be used as an initial guess in multigrid programs. [Computer]

8.2   *SPECTRAL METHODS

Fourier Galerkin Method

At the end of Section 8.1, we saw that the relaxation methods could be used to solve the Poisson equation

$$\nabla^2 \Phi(\mathbf{r}) = -\frac{1}{\epsilon_0}\rho(\mathbf{r}) \tag{8.31}$$

where $\Phi(\mathbf{r})$ is the electrostatic potential at position $\mathbf{r}$, ρ is the charge density, and ϵ_0 is the permittivity of free space. We now develop a very different approach for solving Equation (8.31); for simplicity we'll work in a two-dimensional, square geometry with $0 \leq x \leq L$ and $0 \leq y \leq L$. The algorithms in this section are easily extended to rectangular geometries; in Chapter 10 we consider spherical and cylindrical geometries.

Relaxation methods discretize space and assemble a set of equations for $\Phi_{i,j}$. Let's construct a numerical scheme that represents the potential in a different way. In Section 8.1, using separation of variables, we constructed our analytical solution as an infinite sum of trigonometric functions [see Equation (8.15)]. Suppose that we build our approximate numerical solution using a finite sum of functions,

$$
\begin{aligned}
\Phi(x,y) &= a_1 f_1(x,y) + a_2 f_2(x,y) + \ldots + a_K f_K(x,y) + T(x,y) \\
&= \sum_{k=1}^{K} a_k f_k(x,y) + T(x,y) \\
&= \Phi_{\mathrm{a}}(x,y) + T(x,y)
\end{aligned}
\tag{8.32}
$$

where $\Phi_{\mathrm{a}}(x,y)$ is our approximate solution and $T(x,y)$ is the error term. We'll demand that the trial functions be orthogonal,

$$\int_0^L dx \int_0^L dy\, f_k(x,y) f_{k'}(x,y) = A_k \delta_{k,k'} \tag{8.33}$$

This orthogonality condition is not absolutely necessary, but imposing it simplifies the formulation of the algorithm.

Inserting (8.32) into the Poisson equation gives

$$\nabla^2 \left(\sum_k a_k f_k(x,y) \right) + \frac{1}{\epsilon_0} \rho(x,y) = R(x,y) \tag{8.34}$$

where $R(x,y) = -\nabla^2 T(x,y)$ is the residual. In general, for a partial differential equation of the form $\mathcal{D}\Phi = 0$, where $\mathcal{D}$ is a linear differential operator, the residual is $R = -\mathcal{D}(\Phi - \Phi_a) = \mathcal{D}\Phi_a$. Separation of variables follows a similar procedure, except that we have an infinite sum with no error term and thus zero residual.

Our next step is to obtain an expression for the coefficients, a_k. There are a variety of approaches depending on how we choose to minimize the error. For example, the collocation method sets $R(x_k, y_k) = 0$ at selected locations (x_k, y_k). We'll use the Galerkin method, which imposes the condition

$$\int_0^L dx \int_0^L dy\, f_k(x,y) R(x,y) = 0 \tag{8.35}$$

for all k. In other words, we select the coefficients such that the residual is orthogonal to all the trial functions.

Our choice of trial functions is usually motivated by the geometry and the boundary conditions. For a change of pace, let's solve the Poisson equation with the Neumann boundary conditions, $\nabla\Phi \cdot \hat{\mathbf{n}}$, where $\hat{\mathbf{n}}$ is the unit normal at the boundary. In our square geometry, this condition may be written as

$$\left.\frac{\partial\Phi}{\partial x}\right|_{x=0} = \left.\frac{\partial\Phi}{\partial x}\right|_{x=L} = \left.\frac{\partial\Phi}{\partial y}\right|_{y=0} = \left.\frac{\partial\Phi}{\partial y}\right|_{y=L} = 0 \tag{8.36}$$

With these boundary conditions, the normal component of the electric field is zero at the boundary.

Given these boundary conditions, a natural set of trial functions is

$$f_{m,n}(x,y) = \cos\left[\frac{(m-1)\pi x}{L}\right] \cos\left[\frac{(n-1)\pi y}{L}\right] \tag{8.37}$$

with $m, n = 1, \ldots, M$. It is easy to check that

$$\int_0^L dx \int_0^L dy\, f_{m,n}(x,y) f_{m',n'}(x,y) = \frac{L^2}{4}(1 + \delta_{m,1})(1 + \delta_{n,1})\delta_{m,m'}\delta_{n,n'} \tag{8.38}$$

so these trial functions are orthogonal.

Inserting (8.37) into (8.34) gives

$$-\sum_{m=1}^M \sum_{n=1}^M a_{m,n}[(m-1)^2 + (n-1)^2]\frac{\pi^2}{L^2} f_{m,n}(x,y) + \frac{1}{\epsilon_0}\rho(x,y) = R(x,y) \tag{8.39}$$

To solve for the coefficients, apply

$$\int_0^L dx \int_0^L dy\, f_{m',n'}(x,y) \tag{8.40}$$

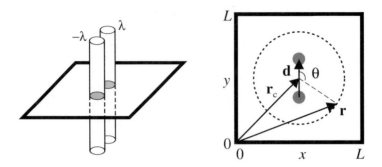

Figure 8.5: Schematic illustration of a two-dimensional dipole. The two line charges, centered at $\mathbf{r}_c$, are separated by a distance d. Their charge densities are $\pm\lambda$ coulombs per unit length.

to both sides of this equation. Using the Galerkin condition (8.35) and orthogonality (8.33), we obtain,

$$
\begin{aligned}
a_{m,n} =\ & \frac{4}{\pi^2\epsilon_0}\frac{1}{(m-1)^2+(n-1)^2}\frac{1}{(1+\delta_{m,1})(1+\delta_{n,1})} \\
& \times \int_0^L dx \int_0^L dy\, \rho(x,y)\cos\left[\frac{(m-1)\pi x}{L}\right]\cos\left[\frac{(n-1)\pi y}{L}\right]
\end{aligned} \quad (8.41)
$$

Finally, having computed the coefficients, our approximate solution is

$$
\Phi_a(x,y) = \sum_{m=1}^{M}\sum_{n=1}^{M} a_{m,n}\cos\left[\frac{(m-1)\pi x}{L}\right]\cos\left[\frac{(n-1)\pi y}{L}\right] \quad (8.42)
$$

Because our trial functions form a complete basis, the solution would be exact if we used an infinite number of terms.

To obtain the coefficients we need to be able to evaluate the integrals in (8.41). If the charge distribution consists of a finite number of line charges, then the integrals are trivial to evaluate because $\rho(\mathbf{r})$ is a sum of Dirac delta functions. Generally, the charge density is not such a simple function, and the integrals in (8.41) have to be evaluated numerically (see Section 10.2).

Dipole Example

As a specific example, consider the charge distribution for a two-dimensional dipole

$$
\rho(\mathbf{r}) = \lambda\left\{\delta(\mathbf{r}-\mathbf{r}_+) - \delta(\mathbf{r}-\mathbf{r}_-)\right\} \quad (8.43)
$$

where λ is the charge per unit length, $\mathbf{r}_\pm = \mathbf{r}_c \pm \frac{1}{2}\mathbf{d}$, $\mathbf{r}_c$ is the location of the dipole, and $\mathbf{d}$ is the separation vector (Figure 8.5). For the purpose of comparison, consider the case where the size of the square box is infinite, that

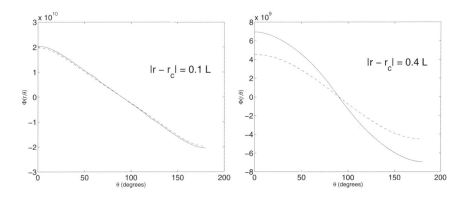

Figure 8.6: Potential as a function of angle for the dipole-in-a-box computed from (8.42), using $M = 100$ terms. For comparison, the potential for the free dipole is plotted with a dashed line. The radial distance is $|\mathbf{r} - \mathbf{r}_c| = 0.1\ L$ (left) and $0.4\ L$ (right) with $L = 1$. The dipole is in the center of the box with charge density $\lambda = 1$.

is, a dipole in free space. The potential for the free dipole is

$$\Phi(\mathbf{r}) = \frac{-\lambda}{2\pi\epsilon_0}\left\{\ln|\mathbf{r} - \mathbf{r}_+| - \ln|\mathbf{r} - \mathbf{r}_-|\right\} \tag{8.44}$$

If the observation point, $\mathbf{r}$, is far from the dipole, that is, if $|\mathbf{r} - \mathbf{r}_c| \gg |\mathbf{d}|$, then

$$\Phi(\mathbf{r}) \approx \frac{\lambda}{2\pi\epsilon_0}\frac{|\mathbf{d}|}{|\mathbf{r} - \mathbf{r}_c|}\cos\theta \tag{8.45}$$

where θ is the angle between $\mathbf{d}$ and $\mathbf{r} - \mathbf{r}_c$.

The potential for the dipole-in-a-box computed by the Galerkin method is shown in Figure 8.6. The potential is evaluated [using Equation (8.42)] on a ring of points equidistant from the center of the dipole. The potential at this radius is plotted along with the potential of the free dipole, (8.44). The width of the box is $L = 1.0$; the dipole parameters are $\lambda = 1$, $\mathbf{r}_c = (L/2)\hat{\mathbf{x}} + (L/2)\hat{\mathbf{y}}$, and $\mathbf{d} = (L/10)\hat{\mathbf{y}}$. Notice in Figure 8.6 the strong influence of the boundary when $|\mathbf{r} - \mathbf{r}_c| = 0.4L$.

Galerkin Method and Separation of Variables

At this point the reader may (incorrectly) have the impression that the Galerkin method is nothing more than using the separation of variables solution retaining only a finite number of terms. For our simple example with the Poisson equation, it turns out that way. However, looking ahead to more complicated partial differential equations, we see that the Galerkin method is more versatile. It gives us great latitude as to our choice of trial functions. With separation of variables, we must first find the general solution of a PDE and then build our particular solution by imposing boundary conditions on these functions. With Galerkin, the trial functions do not have to be the eigenfunctions of the PDE we are solving. Rather, any convenient set of functions that is orthogonal and that matches the boundary conditions may be used.

A more appropriate way of viewing the Galerkin method is as being a spectral transform approach. In our example we represent our solution by its Fourier series, which, due to the boundary conditions, is a cosine series. The coefficients of this series are obtained after we compute the Fourier coefficients of the charge density. This line of thought leads us naturally to our next numerical scheme.

Multiple Fourier Transform (MFT) Method

One advantage of the Galerkin method is that does not use a spatial grid, allowing us to evaluate the potential at only selected points. Contrast this with relaxation methods that require us to compute the potential everywhere inside the system. On the other hand, if we do need to map the potential over the entire system, the Galerkin method, as constructed above, is relatively inefficient.

To understand why the Galerkin method is slow, consider the following problem. Suppose that we partition the space with an $N \times N$ grid with grid points at locations (x_i, y_j). Define the discretized potential, $\Phi_{i,j} = \Phi(x_i, y_j)$, and charge density, $\rho_{i,j} = \rho(x_i, y_j)$. A simple way of computing the integrals in Equation (8.41) is to estimate them as sums,

$$
\begin{aligned}
a_{m,n} &= \frac{4}{\pi^2 \epsilon_0} \frac{1}{(m-1)^2 + (n-1)^2} \frac{1}{(1 + \delta_{m,1})(1 + \delta_{n,1})} \\
&\times \sum_{i=1}^{N} \sum_{j=1}^{N} \rho_{ij} \cos\left[\frac{(m-1)\pi x_i}{L}\right] \cos\left[\frac{(n-1)\pi y_j}{L}\right] h^2 \quad (8.46)
\end{aligned}
$$

for $m, n = 1, \ldots, M$, the grid spacing between points is $h = L/N$. Typically, $M \approx N$, so computing all the coefficients, using (8.46), requires a calculation effort of $O(N^2 M^2) = O(N^4)$. The computation of the potential at all N^2 grid points using (8.42) also requires an effort of $O(N^4)$. In comparison, for simultaneous overrelaxation (SOR) the computation time is $O(N^3)$.

If you think about it, in (8.46) we are taking the two-dimensional (cosine) Fourier transform of the density. After getting the coefficients, $a_{i,j}$, we take the inverse transform to obtain the potential. Yet we know that the fast Fourier transform (FFT) algorithm can do this type of operation very efficiently (see Section 5.2). Although the transform is now two-dimensional, it does not significantly complicate the problem. The discrete Fourier transform is a linear operation, so we may apply it separately in each direction (i.e., it doesn't matter which sum we do first). The FFT algorithm may be adapted to perform sine or cosine transforms. As we have seen, the cosine transform is useful for Neumann boundary conditions. The sine transform is used with the Dirichlet boundary condition $\Phi = 0$. For simplicity, we'll change the problem and use periodic boundary conditions allowing us to use the standard FFT routines.

Discretized on an $N \times N$ square grid, the Poisson equation, (8.28), may be written as

$$\frac{1}{h^2}\left\{\Phi_{i+1,j} + \Phi_{i-1,j} - 2\Phi_{i,j}\right\} + \frac{1}{h^2}\left\{\Phi_{i,j+1} + \Phi_{i,j-1} - 2\Phi_{i,j}\right\} = -\frac{1}{\epsilon_0}\rho_{i,j} \quad (8.47)$$

We define the two-dimensional Fourier transforms of the potential and the charge density as

$$F_{m+1,n+1} = \sum_{i=0}^{N-1}\sum_{j=0}^{N-1}\Phi_{i+1,j+1}e^{-\alpha im}e^{-\alpha jn} \quad (8.48)$$

$$R_{m+1,n+1} = \sum_{i=0}^{N-1}\sum_{j=0}^{N-1}\rho_{i+1,j+1}e^{-\alpha im}e^{-\alpha jn} \quad (8.49)$$

where $\alpha \equiv 2\pi\sqrt{-1}/N$. The inverse transforms are

$$\Phi_{i+1,j+1} = \frac{1}{N^2}\sum_{m=0}^{N-1}\sum_{n=0}^{N-1}F_{m+1,n+1}e^{\alpha im}e^{\alpha jn} \quad (8.50)$$

$$\rho_{i+1,j+1} = \frac{1}{N^2}\sum_{m=0}^{N-1}\sum_{n=0}^{N-1}R_{m+1,n+1}e^{\alpha im}e^{\alpha jn} \quad (8.51)$$

Notice that we have as many Fourier coefficients as grid points, that is, $M = N$. Transforming (8.47),

$$\left\{e^{-\alpha(m-1)} + e^{\alpha(m-1)} + e^{-\alpha(n-1)} + e^{\alpha(n-1)} - 4\right\}F_{m,n} = -\frac{1}{\epsilon_0}h^2 R_{m,n} \quad (8.52)$$

Solving for the matrix **F**, we have

$$F_{m,n} = P_{m,n}R_{m,n} \quad (8.53)$$

where

$$P_{m,n} = \frac{-h^2/2\epsilon_0}{\cos[2\pi(m-1)/N] + \cos[2\pi(n-1)/N] - 2} \quad (8.54)$$

Taking the inverse transform of **F** gives us the potential. This algorithm is called the *multiple Fourier transform* (MFT) method.

The program `fftpoi`, which uses the MFT method to solve the dipole-in-a-box problem with periodic boundary conditions, is outlined in Table 8.2. The functions `fft2` and `ifft2` are used to compute the two-dimensional transforms. In MATLAB, these are built-in functions; the C++ versions are outlined in Table 8.3.

The potential for a dipole, as computed by `fftpoi`, is shown in Figure 8.7. Given the potential, the electric field is $\mathbf{E} = -\nabla\Phi$. In MATLAB, the `gradient` function is used to take the gradient of the potential and the `quiver` function produces a vector arrow plot given E_x and E_y, the x- and y-components of the electric field. For better visualization, we normalize **E** so that its magnitude is unity; the quiver plot shows the direction of the field (Figure 8.8). Try plotting the field without normalizing to see why this is useful.

Table 8.2: Outline of program `fftpoi`, which solves the Poisson equation using the multiple Fourier transform method.

- Initialize parameters (L, h, etc.).

- Set up charge density $\rho_{i,j}$.

- Compute matrix $\mathbf{P}$ using (8.54).

- Compute potential using (8.50) and (8.53).

- Compute electric field as $\mathbf{E} = -\nabla\Phi$.

- Plot potential and electric field.

See pages 270 and 274 for program listings.

Table 8.3: Outline of function `fft2` and `ifft2`, which takes the matrix $\mathbf{A}$ and computes its two-dimensional Fourier transform, $\mathbf{Z}$, using the FFT algorithm. The `ifft2` function is similar but applies the inverse transform.

- *Inputs*: Real($\mathbf{A}$), Imag($\mathbf{A}$).

- *Output*: Real($\mathbf{Z}$), Imag($\mathbf{Z}$).

- Loop over the columns of the matrix.

  − Copy out a column into a vector.
  − Take FFT of the vector.
  − Copy the transformed vector back into the column.

- Loop over the rows of the matrix.

  − Copy out a row into a vector.
  − Take FFT of the vector.
  − Copy the transformed vector back into the row.

See pages 276 and 277 for program listings.

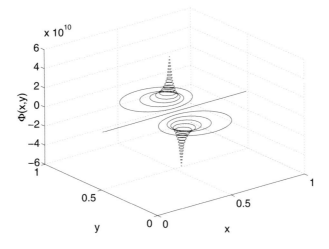

Figure 8.7: Three-dimensional contour plot of the potential from `fftpoi`. Charges of the dipole are located at $[x \ y] = [0.5L \ 0.55L]$ and $[0.5L \ 0.45L]$; $\lambda = 1$ C/m, $L = 1$ m.

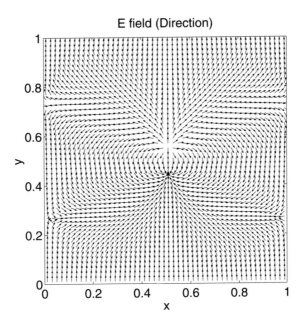

Figure 8.8: Electric field lines plot from `fftpoi`. Parameters as in Figure 8.7.

EXERCISES

12. Derive Equation (8.45) given (8.44). [Pencil]

13. (a) Using the method of images, find an expression for the potential for the dipole-in-a-box problem. [Pencil] (b) Write a program to evaluate this solution at a ring of points centered on the dipole. Compare your results with Figure 8.6. [Computer]

14. Write a program to compute the potential of the dipole-in-a-box by the Galerkin method using Equations (8.41) and (8.42). Reproduce the results shown in Figure 8.6. [Computer]

15. (a) Write a program to compute the potential of the dipole-in-a-box by the Galerkin method using the Dirichlet boundary conditions

$$\Phi(x = 0, y) = \Phi(x = L, y) = \Phi(x, y = 0) = \Phi(x, y = L) = 0$$

Compare the results with those shown in Figure 8.6. [Computer] (b) Using the method of images, find an expression for the potential of a dipole-in-a-box with Dirichlet boundary conditions. [Pencil] (c) Write a program to evaluate the expression obtained in (b) at a ring of points centered on the dipole. Check your answers with those obtained in part (a). [Computer]

16. Consider the trivial ODE $df/dt = f$ with $f(0) = 1$. Suppose we construct an approximate solution as

$$f_a(t) = 1 + \sum_{k=1}^{K} a_k t^k$$

in the interval $0 \le t \le 1$. Using the Galerkin method, find the coefficients, a_k, for $K = 3$. Notice that our basis functions are not orthogonal but the integrals are easy to evaluate. Compare with the Taylor expansion of the true solution. [Pencil]

17. The `fftpoi` program uses a rather coarse method for placing the charges on the grid: It assigns a charge to the nearest grid point. Modify the program so that it proportionally assigns a fraction of the charge to each of the nearest four grid points as $\rho_{ij} = \lambda \delta_x \delta_y / h_x h_y$ (see Figure 8.9). Compare with the unmodified version by plotting $\Phi(x = L/2, y)$ for a dipole with charges at $(x, y) = (L/2, (L + d)/2)$ and $(L/2, (L - d)/2)$. Take $L = 1$ and $d = 1/100$. [Computer]

18. In optical diffraction, the Fraunhofer irradiance is the two-dimensional Fourier transform of the aperture function.[96] Write a program, using `fft2`, that computes the irradiance for a square aperture, as shown in Figure 8.10.[134] In MATLAB you will probably want to use the `fftshift(X)` function that swaps quadrants one and three and quadrants two and four of matrix `X` (i.e., the four corners are mapped to the center). If you are not using MATLAB, consider writing your own version of `fftshift` to shift the origin from the corner to the center. [Computer]

BEYOND THIS CHAPTER

The relaxation methods can be accelerated by using multiple grids.[66, 132] Recall the physical analogy between relaxation and the diffusion equation. The long wavelength modes decay the slowest; this is why it is useful to use the first term of the separation of variables solution as an initial guess. In a multigrid

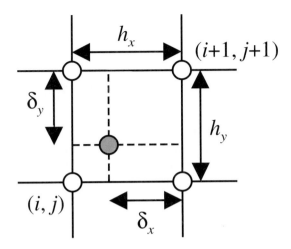

Figure 8.9: Proportional partitioning of charge density on the mesh.

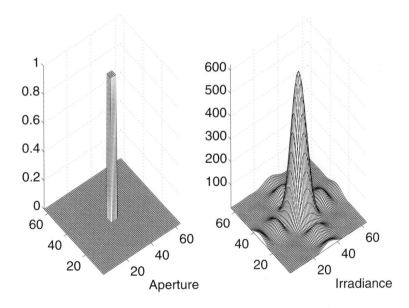

Figure 8.10: Aperture function for a square aperture and its corresponding Fraunhofer irradiance pattern.

algorithm, we start the relaxation process on the finest grid. When the convergence begins to slow, we transfer (by averaging) to a coarser grid. When we have converged on the coarse grid, we transfer back down (by interpolation) to the finer grid. Multigrid schemes can solve the Laplace equation on an $N \times N$ grid in a time $O(N^2)$, as compared with $O(N^4)$ for Jacobi and $O(N^3)$ for SOR.

The Laplace (or Poisson) equation in one dimension is an ordinary differential equation. It should be clear that the methods described in this section may be applied to this type of boundary-value ODE problems. For a detailed discussion, see Ascher et al. [12].

Exercise 8.11 illustrates that the discretized Laplace equation may be written as a large system of linear equations. I say large because the number of unknowns (and equations) equals the number of interior grid points. This approach for solving elliptic PDEs is most useful when the grid size is small (e.g., coarsest grid in a multigrid scheme). However, you can get a lot of extra mileage by making use of the sparseness of the matrix (see Section 9.3). A rapid, iterative algorithm for solving such sparse matrices is the conjugate-gradient method.[59]

Spectral methods have been used extensively to compute the fields in plasma simulations.[22, 72, 124] They are also used in computational fluid dynamics [48], especially in turbulence studies [30]. Haltiner and Williams [68] discuss spectral methods in the context of geophysical problems. Sadiku [110] and Booton [25] review a wide variety of numerical techniques as applied to electromagnetic problems.

APPENDIX A: MATLAB LISTINGS

Listing 8A.1 Program `relax`. Solves the Laplace equation using the Jacobi, Gauss-Seidel, or SOR method.

```
% relax - Program to solve the Laplace equation using
% Jacobi, Gauss-Seidel and SOR methods on a square grid
clear all; help relax;  % Clear memory and print header

%* Initialize parameters (system size, grid spacing, etc.)
method = menu('Numerical Method','Jacobi','Gauss-Seidel','SOR');
N = input('Enter number of grid points on a side: ');
L = 1;          % System size (length)
h = L/(N-1);    % Grid spacing
x = (0:N-1)*h;  % x coordinate
y = (0:N-1)*h;  % y coordinate

%* Select over-relaxation factor (SOR only)
if( method == 3 )
  omegaOpt = 2/(1+sin(pi/N));  % Theoretical optimum
  fprintf('Theoretical optimum omega = %g \n',omegaOpt);
  omega = input('Enter desired omega: ');
end
```

```
%* Set initial guess as first term in separation of variables soln.
phi0 = 1;      % Potential at y=L
phi = phi0 * 4/(pi*sinh(pi)) * sin(pi*x'/L)*sinh(pi*y/L);

%* Set boundary conditions
phi(1,:) = 0;  phi(N,:) = 0;  phi(:,1) = 0;
phi(:,N) = phi0*ones(N,1);
fprintf('Potential at y=L equals %g \n',phi0);
fprintf('Potential is zero on all other boundaries\n');

%* Loop until desired fractional change per iteration is obtained
flops(0);                % Reset the flops counter to zero;
newphi = phi;            % Copy of the solution (used only by Jacobi)
iterMax = N^2;           % Set max to avoid excessively long runs
changeDesired = 1e-4;    % Stop when the change is given fraction
fprintf('Desired fractional change = %g\n',changeDesired);
for iter=1:iterMax
  changeSum = 0;

  if( method == 1 )      %% Jacobi method %%
    for i=2:(N-1)            % Loop over interior points only
      for j=2:(N-1)
        newphi(i,j) = .25*(phi(i+1,j)+phi(i-1,j)+ ...
                           phi(i,j-1)+phi(i,j+1));
        changeSum = changeSum + abs(1-phi(i,j)/newphi(i,j));
      end
    end
    phi = newphi;

  elseif( method == 2 )  %% G-S method %%
    for i=2:(N-1)            % Loop over interior points only
      for j=2:(N-1)
        newphi = .25*(phi(i+1,j)+phi(i-1,j)+ ...
                      phi(i,j-1)+phi(i,j+1));
        changeSum = changeSum + abs(1-phi(i,j)/newphi);
        phi(i,j) = newphi;
      end
    end

  else                   %% SOR method %%
    for i=2:(N-1)            % Loop over interior points only
      for j=2:(N-1)
        newphi = 0.25*omega*(phi(i+1,j)+phi(i-1,j)+ ...
                phi(i,j-1)+phi(i,j+1))   + (1-omega)*phi(i,j);
        changeSum = changeSum + abs(1-phi(i,j)/newphi);
        phi(i,j) = newphi;
      end
    end
  end
```

```
%* Check if fractional change is small enough to halt the iteration
change(iter) = changeSum/(N-2)^2;
if( rem(iter,10) < 1 )
  fprintf('After %g iterations, fractional change = %g\n',...
                       iter,change(iter));
end
if( change(iter) < changeDesired )
  fprintf('Desired accuracy achieved after %g iterations\n',iter);
  fprintf('Breaking out of main loop\n');
  break;
end
end

%* Plot final estimate of potential as contour and surface plots
figure(1); clf;
cLevels = 0:(0.1):1;     % Contour levels
cs = contour(x,y,flipud(rot90(phi)),cLevels);
xlabel('x'); ylabel('y'); clabel(cs);
title(sprintf('Potential after %g iterations',iter));
figure(2); clf;
mesh(x,y,flipud(rot90(phi)));
xlabel('x'); ylabel('y'); zlabel('\Phi(x,y)');

%* Plot the fractional change versus iteration
figure(3); clf;
semilogy(change);
xlabel('Iteration');   ylabel('Fractional change');
title(sprintf('Number of flops = %g\n',flops));
```

Listing 8A.2 Program `fftpoi`. Solves the Poisson equation using the multiple Fourier transform method.

```
% fftpoi - Program to solve the Poisson equation using
% MFT method (periodic boundary conditions)
clear all; help fftpoi;  % Clear memory and print header

%* Initialize parameters (system size, grid spacing, etc.)
eps0 = 8.8542e-12;   % Permittivity (C^2/(N m^2))
N = 50;   % Number of grid points on a side (square grid)
L = 1;   % System size
h = L/N;   % Grid spacing for periodic boundary conditions
x = ((1:N)-1/2)*h;  % Coordinates of grid points
y = x;               % Square grid
fprintf('System is a square of length %g \n',L);

%* Set up charge density rho(i,j)
rho = zeros(N,N);  % Initialize charge density to zero
M = input('Enter number of line charges: ');
```

```
for i=1:M
  fprintf('\n For charge #%g \n',i);
  r = input('Enter position [x y]: ');
  ii=round(r(1)/h + 1/2);    % Place charge at nearest
  jj=round(r(2)/h + 1/2);    % grid point
  q = input('Enter charge density: ');
  rho(ii,jj) = rho(ii,jj) + q/h^2;
end

%* Compute matrix P
cx = cos((2*pi/N)*(0:N-1));
cy = cx;
numerator = -h^2/(2*eps0);
tinyNumber = 1e-20;  % Avoids division by zero
for i=1:N
 for j=1:N
   P(i,j) = numerator/(cx(i)+cy(j)-2+tinyNumber);
 end
end

%* Compute potential using MFT method
rhoT = fft2(rho);    % Transform rho into wavenumber domain
phiT = rhoT .* P;    % Computing phi in the wavenumber domain
phi = ifft2(phiT);   % Inv. transf. phi into the coord. domain
phi = real(phi);     % Clean up imaginary part due to round-off

%* Compute electric field as E = - grad phi
[Ex Ey] = gradient(flipud(rot90(phi)));
magnitude = sqrt(Ex.^2 + Ey.^2);
Ex = -Ex ./ magnitude;     % Normalize components so
Ey = -Ey ./ magnitude;     % vectors have equal length

%* Plot potential and electric field
figure(1); clf;
contour3(x,y,flipud(rot90(phi,1)),35);
xlabel('x'); ylabel('y'); zlabel('\Phi(x,y)');
figure(2); clf;
quiver(x,y,Ex,Ey)          % Plot E field with vectors
title('E field (Direction)'); xlabel('x'); ylabel('y');
axis('square');  axis([0 L 0 L]);
```

APPENDIX B: C++ LISTINGS

Listing 8B.1 Program `relax`. Solves Laplace's equation using the Jacobi, Gauss-Seidel, or SOR method.

```
// relax - Program to solve the Laplace equation using
```

```
// Jacobi, Gauss-Seidel and SOR methods on a square grid
#include "NumMeth.h"

void main() {

  //* Initialize parameters (system size, grid spacing, etc.)
  cout << "Select a numerical method: 1) Jacobi, 2) Gauss-Seidel, 3) SOR : ";
  int method; cin >> method;
  cout << "Enter number of grid points on a side: "; int N; cin >> N;
  double L = 1;           // System size (length)
  double h = L/(N-1);     // Grid spacing
  Matrix x(N), y(N);
  int i,j;
  for( i=1; i<=N; i++ )
    x(i) = (i-1)*h;   // x coordinate
  y = x;                  // y coordinate

  //* Select over-relaxation factor (SOR only)
  double omega, omegaOpt, pi = 3.141592654;
  if( method == 3 ) {
    omegaOpt = 2.0/(1.0+sin(pi/N));   // Theoretical optimum
    cout << "Theoretical optimum omega = " << omegaOpt << endl;
    cout << "Enter desired omega: "; cin >> omega;
  }

  //* Set initial guess as first term in separation of variables soln.
  double phi0 = 1;      // Potential at y=L
  double coeff = phi0 * 4/(pi*sinh(pi));
  Matrix phi(N,N);
  for( i=1; i<=N; i++ )
    for( j=1; j<=N; j++ )
      phi(i,j) = coeff * sin(pi*x(i)/L) * sinh(pi*y(j)/L);

  //* Set boundary conditions
  for( i=1; i<=N; i++ ) {
    phi(i,1) = 0.0;
    phi(i,N) = phi0;
  }
  for( j=1; j<=N; j++ ) {
    phi(1,j) = 0.0;
    phi(N,j) = 0.0;
  }
  cout << "Potential at y=L equals " << phi0 << endl;
  cout << "Potential is zero on all other boundaries" << endl;

  //* Loop until desired fractional change per iteration is obtained
  Matrix newphi(N,N);     // Copy of the solution (used only by Jacobi)
  newphi = phi;
  double phiTemp;         // Temporary value used by GS and SOR
  int iterMax = N*N;              // Set max to avoid excessively long runs
```

```
double changeDesired = 1e-4;  // Stop when the change is given fraction
cout << "Desired fractional change = " << changeDesired << endl;
Matrix change(iterMax); // Record fractional change at each iteration
int iter, nIter;          // Iterations counters
for( iter=1; iter<=iterMax; iter++ ) {

  double changeSum = 0;
  if( method == 1 )  {    //// Jacobi method ////
    for( i=2; i<=(N-1); i++ )  // Loop over interior points only
     for( j=2; j<=(N-1); j++ ) {
       newphi(i,j) = 0.25*(phi(i+1,j)+phi(i-1,j)+
                             phi(i,j-1)+phi(i,j+1));
       changeSum += fabs(1-phi(i,j)/newphi(i,j));
      }
    phi = newphi;    // Copy new values into phi
  }
  else if( method == 2 )  //// G-S method ////
    for( i=2; i<=(N-1); i++ )  // Loop over interior points only
     for( j=2; j<=(N-1); j++ ) {
       phiTemp = 0.25*(phi(i+1,j)+phi(i-1,j)+
                             phi(i,j-1)+phi(i,j+1));
       changeSum += fabs(1-phi(i,j)/phiTemp);
       phi(i,j) = phiTemp;
      }
  else                      //// SOR method ////
    for( i=2; i<=(N-1); i++ )  // Loop over interior points only
     for( j=2; j<=(N-1); j++ ) {
       phiTemp = 0.25*omega*(phi(i+1,j)+phi(i-1,j)+
              phi(i,j-1)+phi(i,j+1))  +  (1-omega)*phi(i,j);
       changeSum += fabs(1-phi(i,j)/phiTemp);
       phi(i,j) = phiTemp;
      }

  //* Check if fractional change is small enough to halt the iteration
  change(iter) = changeSum/((N-2)*(N-2));
  if( (iter%10) < 1 )
    cout << "After " << iter << " iterations, fractional change = "
                << change(iter) << endl;
  if( change(iter) < changeDesired ) {
    cout << "Desired accuracy achieved after " << iter
        << " iterations" << endl;
    cout << "Breaking out of main loop" << endl;
    nIter = iter;
    break;        // Break out of the main loop
  }
}

//* Print out the plotting variables: x, y, phi, change
ofstream xOut("x.txt"), yOut("y.txt"),
        phiOut("phi.txt"), changeOut("change.txt");
```

```
  for( i=1; i<=N; i++ ) {
    xOut << x(i) << endl;
    yOut << y(i) << endl;
    for( j=1; j<N; j++ )
      phiOut << phi(i,j) << ", ";
    phiOut << phi(i,N) << endl;
  }
  for( i=1; i<=nIter; i++ )
    changeOut << change(i) << endl;
}
/***** To plot in MATLAB; use the script below ********************
load x.txt; load y.txt; load phi.txt; load change.txt;
%* Plot final estimate of potential as contour and surface plots
figure(1); clf;
cLevels = 0:(0.1):1;    % Contour levels
cs = contour(x,y,flipud(rot90(phi)),cLevels);
xlabel('x'); ylabel('y'); clabel(cs);
figure(2); clf;
mesh(x,y,flipud(rot90(phi)));
xlabel('x'); ylabel('y'); zlabel('\Phi(x,y)');
%* Plot the fractional change versus iteration
figure(3); clf;
semilogy(change);
xlabel('Iteration');  ylabel('Fractional change');
******************************************************************/
```

Listing 8B.2 Program `fftpoi`. Solves the Poisson equation using the multiple Fourier transform method. Uses `fft2` (Listing 8B.4) and `ifft2` (Listing 8B.5).

```
// fftpoi - Program to solve the Poisson equation using
// MFT method (periodic boundary conditions)
#include "NumMeth.h"

void fft2( Matrix& RealA, Matrix& ImagA);
void ifft2( Matrix& RealA, Matrix& ImagA);

void main() {

  //* Initialize parameters (system size, grid spacing, etc.)
  double eps0 = 8.8542e-12;   // Permittivity (C^2/(N m^2))
  int N = 64;    // Number of grid points on a side (square grid)
  double L = 1;    // System size
  double h = L/N;   // Grid spacing for periodic boundary conditions
  Matrix x(N), y(N);
  int i,j;
  for( i=1; i<=N; i++ )
    x(i) = (i-0.5)*h;  // Coordinates of grid points
    y = x;                // Square grid
    cout << "System is a square of length " << L << endl;
```

```
//* Set up charge density rho(i,j)
Matrix rho(N,N);
rho.set(0.0);      // Initialize charge density to zero
cout << "Enter number of line charges: "; int M; cin >> M;
for( i=1; i<=M; i++ ) {
  cout << "For charge #" << i << endl;
  cout << "Enter x coordinate: "; double xc; cin >> xc;
  cout << "Enter y coordinate: "; double yc; cin >> yc;
  int ii = (int)(xc/h) + 1;    // Place charge at nearest
  int jj = (int)(yc/h) + 1;    // grid point
  cout << "Enter charge density: "; double q; cin >> q;
  rho(ii,jj) += q/(h*h);
}

//* Compute matrix P
const double pi = 3.141592654;
Matrix cx(N), cy(N);
for( i=1; i<=N; i++ )
  cx(i) = cos((2*pi/N)*(i-1));
cy = cx;
Matrix RealP(N,N), ImagP(N,N);
double numerator = -h*h/(2*eps0);
double tinyNumber = 1e-20;  // Avoids division by zero
for( i=1; i<=N; i++ )
 for( j=1; j<=N; j++ )
   RealP(i,j) = numerator/(cx(i)+cy(j)-2+tinyNumber);
ImagP.set(0.0);

//* Compute potential using MFT method
Matrix RealR(N,N), ImagR(N,N), RealF(N,N), ImagF(N,N);
for( i=1; i<=N; i++ )
 for( j=1; j<=N; j++ ) {
   RealR(i,j) = rho(i,j);
   ImagR(i,j) = 0.0;        // Copy rho into R for input to fft2
 }
fft2(RealR,ImagR);   // Transform rho into wavenumber domain
// Compute phi in the wavenumber domain
for( i=1; i<=N; i++ )
 for( j=1; j<=N; j++ ) {
  RealF(i,j) = RealR(i,j)*RealP(i,j) - ImagR(i,j)*ImagP(i,j);
  ImagF(i,j) = RealR(i,j)*ImagP(i,j) + ImagR(i,j)*RealP(i,j);
 }
Matrix phi(N,N);
ifft2(RealF,ImagF);    // Inv. transf. phi into the coord. domain
for( i=1; i<=N; i++ )
 for( j=1; j<=N; j++ )
   phi(i,j) = RealF(i,j);

//* Print out the plotting variables: x, y, phi
```

```
  ofstream xOut("x.txt"), yOut("y.txt"), phiOut("phi.txt");
  for( i=1; i<=N; i++ ) {
    xOut << x(i) << endl;
    yOut << y(i) << endl;
    for( j=1; j<N; j++ )
      phiOut << phi(i,j) << ", ";
    phiOut << phi(i,N) << endl;
  }
}
/***** To plot in MATLAB; use the script below ********************
load x.txt; load y.txt; load phi.txt;
%* Compute electric field as E = - grad phi
[Ex Ey] = gradient(flipud(rot90(phi)));
magnitude = sqrt(Ex.^2 + Ey.^2);
Ex = -Ex ./ magnitude;      % Normalize components so
Ey = -Ey ./ magnitude;      % vectors have equal length
%* Plot potential and electric field
figure(1); clf;
contour3(x,y,flipud(rot90(phi,1)),35);
xlabel('x'); ylabel('y'); zlabel('\Phi(x,y)');
figure(2); clf;
quiver(x,y,Ex,Ey)           % Plot E field with vectors
title('E field (Direction)'); xlabel('x'); ylabel('y');
axis('square');   axis([0 1 0 1]);
*****************************************************************/
```

Listing 8B.3 Function `fft2`. Computes two-dimensional discrete Fourier transform. Uses `fft` (Listing 5B.7).

```
#include "NumMeth.h"

void fft( Matrix& RealA, Matrix& ImagA);

void fft2( Matrix& RealA, Matrix& ImagA) {
// Routine to compute two dimensional Fourier transform
// using FFT algorithm
// Inputs
//    RealA, ImagA        Real and imaginary parts of data array
// Outputs
//    RealA, ImagA        Real and imaginary parts of transform

  int i, j, N = RealA.nRow();
  Matrix RealT(N), ImagT(N);   // Temporary work vector

  //* Loop over the columns of the matrix
  for( j=1; j<=N; j++ ) {
    //* Copy out a column into a vector
    for( i=1; i<=N; i++ ) {
      RealT(i) = RealA(i,j);
```

```
      ImagT(i) = ImagA(i,j);
    }
    //* Take FFT of the vector
    fft(RealT,ImagT);
    //* Copy the transformed vector back into the column
    for( i=1; i<=N; i++ ) {
      RealA(i,j) = RealT(i);
      ImagA(i,j) = ImagT(i);
    }
  }

  //* Loop over the rows of the matrix
  for( i=1; i<=N; i++ ) {
    //* Copy out a row into a vector
    for( j=1; j<=N; j++ ) {
      RealT(j) = RealA(i,j);
      ImagT(j) = ImagA(i,j);
    }
    //* Take FFT of the vector
    fft(RealT,ImagT);
    //* Copy the transformed vector back into the row
    for( j=1; j<=N; j++ ) {
      RealA(i,j) = RealT(j);
      ImagA(i,j) = ImagT(j);
    }
  }
}
```

Listing 8B.4 Function `ifft2`. Computes two-dimensional inverse discrete Fourier transform. Uses `fft` (Listing 5B.7).

```
#include "NumMeth.h"

void fft( Matrix& RealA, Matrix& ImagA);

void ifft2( Matrix& RealA, Matrix& ImagA) {
// Routine to compute inverse two dimensional Fourier transform
// using FFT algorithm
// Inputs
//    RealA, ImagA        Real and imaginary parts of transform array
// Outputs
//    RealA, ImagA        Real and imaginary parts of data array

  int i, j, N = RealA.nRow();
  Matrix RealT(N), ImagT(N);   // Temporary work vector

  //* Loop over the columns of the matrix
  for( j=1; j<=N; j++ ) {
    //* Copy out a column into a vector and take its complex conjugate
```

```
    for( i=1; i<=N; i++ ) {
      RealT(i) = RealA(i,j);
      ImagT(i) = -1.0*ImagA(i,j);
    }
    //* Take FFT of the vector
    fft(RealT,ImagT);
    //* Copy the transformed vector back into the column
    for( i=1; i<=N; i++ ) {
      RealA(i,j) = RealT(i);
      ImagA(i,j) = ImagT(i);
    }
  }

  //* Loop over the rows of the matrix
  double invN2 = 1.0/(N*N);
  for( i=1; i<=N; i++ ) {
    //* Copy out a row into a vector and take its complex conjugate
    for( j=1; j<=N; j++ ) {
      RealT(j) = RealA(i,j);
      ImagT(j) = ImagA(i,j);
    }
    //* Take FFT of the vector
    fft(RealT,ImagT);
    //* Copy the transformed vector back, taking its complex conjugate
    //  and applying the 1/N normalization
    for( j=1; j<=N; j++ ) {
      RealA(i,j) = RealT(j)*invN2;
      ImagA(i,j) = -1.0*ImagT(j)*invN2;
    }
  }
}
```

Chapter 9

Partial Differential Equations IV: Stability and Implicit Methods

Chapters 6 and 7 covered various marching methods for solving partial differential equations. Empirically, we discovered that some methods were numerically unstable when the time step was too large. Section 9.1 presents two techniques for testing numerical stability. Section 9.2 discusses some algorithms that are unconditionally stable but that require inverting large matrices. Section 9.3 covers some specialized routines to handle these matrices.

9.1   STABILITY ANALYSIS

Von Neumann Stability

Consider the `advect` program we used in Section 7.1 to solve the advection equation. Using the FTCS scheme, the method is numerically unstable, as shown in Figure 9.1. The solution looks like a standing wave that rapidly grows in amplitude. In fact, the amplitude of the solution at the last time step is many orders of magnitude larger than the initial condition; this is why the mesh plot looks flat for the earlier times. We get a very similar picture if we employ a large time step $(\tau > h/|c|)$ when solving the advection equation using any of the other methods in Chapter 7.

From the above observations, it is reasonable to use a trial solution that has the form

$$a(x,t) = A(t)e^{ikx} \tag{9.1}$$

where $i = \sqrt{-1}$. This solution is a wave with wave number k and (complex) amplitude $A(t)$. In discretized form, we have

$$a(x_j, t_n) = a_j^n = A^n e^{ikjh} \tag{9.2}$$

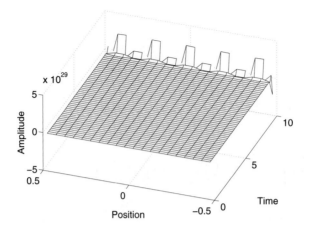

Figure 9.1: Amplitude versus x and t. Mesh plot of the solution of the advection equation obtained by the `advect` program using the FTCS method with $N = 20$ mesh points and time step $\tau = 0.05$. The number of iteration steps was set to `nstep`$= 10L/(c\tau)$, so that the wave circles the system 10 times.

where $x_j = jh$ and $t_n = (n-1)\tau$. Advancing the solution by one step gives

$$a_j^{n+1} = A^{n+1}e^{ikjh} = \xi A^n e^{ikjh} \tag{9.3}$$

The coefficient $\xi = A^{n+1}/A^n$ is called the *amplification factor*. The strategy of the analysis is to insert the trial solution, (9.2), into the numerical scheme and solve for the amplification factor in terms of the grid spacing, h, and the time step, τ. A scheme is unstable if the magnitude of the amplification factor exceeds unity; that is, if $|\xi| > 1$. This approach is called *von Neumann stability analysis*.

Stability of FTCS for the Advection Equation

To illustrate von Neumann analysis, we'll work through some examples. Recall from Section 7.1 that for the advection equation, the FTCS scheme may be written as

$$a_j^{n+1} = a_j^n - \frac{c\tau}{2h}(a_{j+1}^n - a_{j-1}^n) \tag{9.4}$$

where a is the wave amplitude and c is the wave speed. Inserting our trial solution, (9.2) and (9.3), we get

$$\begin{aligned}
\xi A^n e^{ikjh} &= A^n e^{ikjh} - \frac{c\tau}{2h}(A^n e^{ik(j+1)h} - A^n e^{ik(j-1)h}) \\
&= A^n e^{ikjh}\left(1 - \frac{c\tau}{2h}(e^{ikh} - e^{-ikh})\right)
\end{aligned} \tag{9.5}$$

Dividing both sides by $A^n e^{ikjh}$, we find that the amplification factor is

$$\xi = 1 - \frac{c\tau}{2h}(e^{ikh} - e^{-ikh})$$

$$= 1 - i\frac{c\tau}{h}\sin(kh) \tag{9.6}$$

The magnitude of the amplification factor is

$$|\xi| = \sqrt{1 + \left(\frac{c\tau}{h}\right)^2 \sin^2(kh)} \tag{9.7}$$

In general, the magnitude of ξ is greater than one. The solution is unstable since its amplitude grows with each time step.

Most of the modes are numerically unstable, but some grow faster than others. We find the fastest-growing mode, k_{max}, by solving $\sin^2(k_{max}h) = 1$. Since $k = 2\pi/\lambda$, where λ is the wavelength, then $\lambda_{max} = 4h$. Compare this result with the mesh plot in Figure 9.1.

Stability of the Lax Scheme

As a second example, let's apply the von Neumann analysis to the Lax method for solving the advection equation. Recall that the Lax scheme may be written as

$$a_j^{n+1} = \frac{1}{2}(a_{j+1}^n + a_{j-1}^n) - \frac{c\tau}{2h}(a_{j+1}^n - a_{j-1}^n) \tag{9.8}$$

As before, we insert the trial solution, $a_j^n = A^n e^{ikhj}$, and, $a_j^{n+1} = \xi a_j^n$, to get

$$\begin{aligned}
\xi A^n e^{ikjh} &= \frac{1}{2}(A^n e^{ik(j+1)h} + A^n e^{ik(j-1)h}) - \frac{c\tau}{2h}(A^n e^{ik(j+1)h} - A^n e^{ik(j-1)h}) \\
&= A^n e^{ikjh}\left[\frac{1}{2}(e^{ikh} + e^{-ikh}) - \frac{c\tau}{2h}(e^{ikh} - e^{-ikh})\right]
\end{aligned} \tag{9.9}$$

The amplification factor is thus

$$\xi = \cos(kh) - i\frac{c\tau}{h}\sin(kh) \tag{9.10}$$

and its magnitude is

$$|\xi| = \sqrt{\cos^2(kh) + \left(\frac{c\tau}{h}\right)^2 \sin^2(kh)} \tag{9.11}$$

Thus, $|\xi| \leq 1$ if and only if $|c\tau/h| \leq 1$, which is the Courant-Friedrichs-Lewy (CFL) stability criterion discussed in Chapter 7.

Matrix Stability

The von Neumann approach is not the only way to investigate the stability of a scheme but, being the easiest to do, it is the most popular. One of its shortcomings is that it neglects the possible influence of the boundary conditions. To include their effect, we introduce *matrix stability analysis*.[116]

For linear problems, most schemes may be written in the form, $\mathbf{x}^{n+1} = \mathbf{A}\mathbf{x}^n$, where $\mathbf{x}^n$ is the solution at time $t = (n-1)\tau$. Recall from Section 6.2 the FTCS scheme for solving the thermal diffusion equation,

$$T_j^{n+1} = T_j^n + \frac{\tau}{2t_\sigma}(T_{j+1}^n + T_{j-1}^n - 2T_j^n) \tag{9.12}$$

where T is the temperature, $t_\sigma = h^2/2\kappa$, and κ is the diffusion coefficient. For Dirichlet boundary conditions (i.e., values of T_1^n and T_N^n fixed), we may write the FTCS scheme as

$$\begin{aligned}
\mathbf{T}^{n+1} &= \mathbf{T}^n + \frac{\tau}{2t_\sigma}\mathbf{D}\mathbf{T}^n \\
&= \left(\mathbf{I} + \frac{\tau}{2t_\sigma}\mathbf{D}\right)\mathbf{T}^n = \mathbf{A}\mathbf{T}^n
\end{aligned} \tag{9.13}$$

where

$$\mathbf{T}^n = \begin{bmatrix} T_1^n \\ T_2^n \\ T_3^n \\ T_4^n \\ \vdots \\ T_N^n \end{bmatrix} ; \quad \mathbf{D} = \begin{bmatrix} 0 & 0 & 0 & 0 & \cdots & 0 \\ 1 & -2 & 1 & 0 & \cdots & 0 \\ 0 & 1 & -2 & 1 & \cdots & 0 \\ 0 & 0 & 1 & -2 & \cdots & 0 \\ \vdots & \vdots & \vdots & \vdots & \ddots & \vdots \\ 0 & 0 & 0 & 0 & \cdots & 0 \end{bmatrix} \tag{9.14}$$

and $\mathbf{I}$ is the identity matrix ($I_{ij} = \delta_{ij}$). Notice that the matrix $\mathbf{D}$ has the following structure: Because of the Dirichlet boundary conditions the elements of the first and last rows are all zero, guaranteeing that the values of the endpoints (T_1 and T_N) remain unchanged. All the other rows have a -2 on the main diagonal and a 1 at the first off-diagonal elements.

To determine the stability of $\mathbf{T}^{n+1} = \mathbf{A}\mathbf{T}^n$, we consider the eigenvalue problem for the matrix $\mathbf{A}$,

$$\mathbf{A}\mathbf{v}_k = \lambda_k\mathbf{v}_k \tag{9.15}$$

where $\mathbf{v}_k$ is the eigenvector corresponding to the eigenvalue λ_k. We label the eigenvalues in decreasing order, so $|\lambda_1| > |\lambda_2| > \ldots > |\lambda_N|$. Assuming that the eigenvectors form a complete basis, we may write our initial condition as

$$\mathbf{T}^1 = \sum_{k=1}^{N} c_k\mathbf{v}_k \tag{9.16}$$

From Equation (9.13),

$$\mathbf{T}^{n+1} = \mathbf{A}\mathbf{T}^n = \mathbf{A}(\mathbf{A}\mathbf{T}^{n-1}) = \mathbf{A}^n\mathbf{T}^1 \tag{9.17}$$

In other words, the solution at time step $n+1$ may be obtained by repeatedly multiplying the initial condition n times by the matrix $\mathbf{A}$. Using our decomposition, (9.16),

$$\mathbf{T}^{n+1} = \sum_{k=1}^{N} c_k\mathbf{A}^n\mathbf{v}_k = \sum_{k=1}^{N} c_k(\lambda_k)^n\mathbf{v}_k \tag{9.18}$$

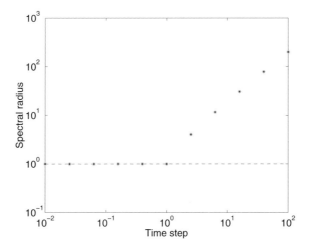

Figure 9.2: Spectral radius $\rho(\mathbf{A})$ as a function of τ for $N = 61$ grid points [see equation (9.13)]. Notice that $\rho(\mathbf{A}) = 1$ for $\tau \leq t_\sigma = 1$.

Clearly, if $|\lambda_k| > 1$ for any eigenvalue, then $|\mathbf{T}^n| \to \infty$ as $n \to \infty$.

The *spectral radius* of the matrix $\mathbf{A}$ is defined as $\rho(\mathbf{A}) = |\lambda_1|$, that is, as the magnitude of the largest eigenvalue. A scheme is matrix stable if the spectral radius is less than or equal to unity. There are many powerful theorems that allow us to set bounds on the spectral radius (e.g., the Gerschgorin circle theorem [93]).

Alternatively, we may obtain the spectral radius by numerically computing the eigenvalues. In MATLAB the eigenvalues of a matrix may be obtained using the built-in `eig` function. With this function, the spectral radius is $\rho(\texttt{A}) = $ `max(abs(eig(A)))`. Figure 9.2 shows the spectral radius of the matrix $\mathbf{A}$ used by the FTCS scheme in solving the diffusion equation with Dirichlet boundary conditions [Equation (9.13)]. Notice that the spectral radius is less than one only if the time step is less than t_σ. This agrees with our empirical findings from Section 7.1.

Power Method

The ideas developed above for matrix stability may be turned around to construct an algorithm for computing eigenvalues and eigenvectors. Consider the general eigenvalue problem

$$\mathbf{M}\mathbf{v}_k = \lambda_k \mathbf{v}_k \qquad (9.19)$$

where $\mathbf{v}_k$ is the (normalized) eigenvector corresponding to the (nondegenerate) eigenvalue λ_k. Take any vector $\mathbf{x}$; write it as*

$$\mathbf{x} = \sum_{k=1}^{N} c_k \mathbf{v}_k \tag{9.20}$$

We assume that $\mathbf{x}$ is not orthogonal to any of the eigenvectors, so $c_k \neq 0$.

The *power method* [3] is a simple technique for computing λ_1, the largest eigenvalue, and $\mathbf{v}_1$, its corresponding eigenvector. First, we repeatedly multiply the vector $\mathbf{x}$ by the matrix $\mathbf{M}$. Doing so n times, we have

$$\mathbf{M}^n \mathbf{x} = \mathbf{M}^n \left(\sum_k c_k \mathbf{v}_k \right) = \sum_k c_k \lambda_k^n \mathbf{v}_k \tag{9.21}$$

Since the λ's are ordered by decreasing magnitude,

$$\mathbf{M}^n \mathbf{x} \approx c_1 \lambda_1^n \mathbf{v}_1 \tag{9.22}$$

as $n \to \infty$. The eigenvectors are normalized, that is, $|\mathbf{v}_k| = 1$, so we obtain the first eigenvector

$$\mathbf{v}_1 = \frac{\mathbf{M}^n \mathbf{x}}{|\mathbf{M}^n \mathbf{x}|} \tag{9.23}$$

as $n \to \infty$. To use the power method we iteratively compute $\mathbf{M}^n \mathbf{x}$ until the value of $\mathbf{v}_1$ has converged to the desired accuracy. Given $\mathbf{v}_1$, use (9.19) to get λ_1.

Using MATLAB interactively, here's a simple example of the power method with $n = 10$:

```
>>M=[2 -1 0;-1 2 -1;0 -1 2];
>>x=[1; 1; 1];
>>v=M^10*x;
>>v=v/norm(v)


v =
    0.5000
   -0.7071
    0.5000


>>mv = M*v;
>>lambda = mv(1)/v(1)


lambda =

    3.4142
```

---

*Here we assume that the eigenvectors form a complete basis. There are exceptional matrices (e.g., Jordan matrices) for which this assumption is not valid. The power method still works, but the derivation is longer.

This eigenvalue problem was considered in Section 5.3; the eigenvalues and eigenvectors are given by (5.61) and (5.63). The power method correctly gives the eigenvector $\mathbf{a}_+$ corresponding to the largest eigenvalue $\omega_+ = 2 + \sqrt{2}$.

There are several ways to modify the power method to accelerate its convergence to the largest eigenvalue. The method may also be extended to obtain the next largest eigenvalue by forming the new matrix

$$\tilde{\mathbf{M}} = \mathbf{M} - \frac{\lambda_1}{\mathbf{v}_1^{\mathrm{T}} \mathbf{v}_1} (\mathbf{v}_1 \mathbf{v}_1^{\mathrm{T}}) \tag{9.24}$$

where $\mathbf{v}_1^{\mathrm{T}}$ is the transpose of $\mathbf{v}_1$. This matrix has the same eigenvalues and eigenvectors as $\mathbf{M}$, except that λ_1 is replaced by zero. This method is called *deflation.*

The power method is useful if we require only the first few largest eigenvalues. If we need to compute all the eigenvalues, then there are more efficient methods. Finally, you could use the power method to compute the spectral radius and determine the matrix stability of a PDE scheme. However, you would essentially be running the scheme and seeing if the solution diverged as $t \to \infty$.

EXERCISES

1. Apply the von Neumann stability analysis to the FTCS scheme for the diffusion equation. Confirm that the method is stable only if $\tau \leq h^2/2\kappa$. [Pencil]

2. Another method for solving the advection equation is the Lax-Wendroff scheme,

$$a_j^{n+1} = a_j^n - \frac{c\tau}{h} \left\{ \frac{1}{2}(a_{j+1}^n - a_{j-1}^n) - \frac{c\tau}{2h}(a_{j+1}^n + a_{j-1}^n - 2a_j^n) \right\}$$

Apply the von Neumann stability analysis to this scheme. Confirm that the method is stable only if $\tau \leq h/|c|$ (i.e., the CFL criterion). [Pencil]

3. Another method for solving the advection equation is the leap-frog scheme

$$a_j^{n+1} = a_j^{n-1} - \frac{c\tau}{h}(a_{j+1}^n - a_{j-1}^n)$$

Apply the von Neumann stability analysis to this scheme; notice that you will have a quadratic equation for ξ. Confirm that the method is stable only if $\tau \leq h/|c|$ (i.e., the CFL criterion). [Pencil]

4. The *Richardson method* for solving the diffusion equation uses centered derivatives in both space and time:

$$\frac{T_i^{n+1} - T_i^{n-1}}{2\tau} = \kappa \frac{T_{i+1}^n + T_{i-1}^n - 2T_i^n}{h^2}$$

Apply the von Neumann stability analysis to this scheme; notice that you will have a quadratic equation for ξ. Show that this scheme is unconditionally unstable. [Pencil]

5. The two-dimensional diffusion equation for temperature (Fourier equation) may be solved using the FTCS scheme as,

$$T_{i,j}^{n+1} = T_{i,j}^n + \frac{\kappa\tau}{h_x^2}(T_{i+1,j}^n + T_{i-1,j}^n - 2T_{i,j}^n) + \frac{\kappa\tau}{h_y^2}(T_{i,j+1}^n + T_{i,j-1}^n - 2T_{i,j}^n)$$

where h_x, h_y are the x and y grid spacings, respectively. Apply the von Neumann stability analysis to this scheme and show that it is stable if $\tau \leq \frac{1}{2\kappa} \left(h_x^{-2} + h_y^{-2} \right)^{-1}$. [Pencil]

6. Write a function that computes the largest eigenvalue of a matrix using the power method. Establish a suitable criterion for when to stop the iteration process. Use this function to evaluate the spectral radius of the matrix $\mathbf{A}$ defined in Equation (9.13) and reproduce Figure 9.2.

7. A stricter condition for matrix stability is that the norm of $\mathbf{A}$, $||\mathbf{A}||$, is less than or equal to unity. This condition is stronger since $\rho(\mathbf{A}) \leq ||\mathbf{A}||$. There are a variety of ways of defining the norm; two of the easiest to compute are the 1-norm,

$$||\mathbf{A}||_1 = \max_{j=1,\ldots,N} \left\{ \sum_{i=1}^{N} |A_{ij}| \right\}$$

and the ∞-norm,

$$||\mathbf{A}||_\infty = \max_{i=1,\ldots,N} \left\{ \sum_{j=1}^{N} |A_{ij}| \right\}$$

Evaluate $||\mathbf{A}||_1$ and $||\mathbf{A}||_\infty$ where $\mathbf{A}$ is given by Equation (9.13). Compare your results with Figure 9.2. [Pencil]

8. The FTCS scheme for the advection equation with periodic boundary conditions may be written as

$$\mathbf{a}^{n+1} = \left(\mathbf{I} - \frac{c\tau}{2h}\mathbf{B} \right) \mathbf{a}^n = \mathbf{A}\mathbf{a}^n$$

where

$$\mathbf{a}^n = \begin{bmatrix} a_1^n \\ a_2^n \\ a_3^n \\ \vdots \\ a_N^n \end{bmatrix} ; \quad \mathbf{B} = \begin{bmatrix} 0 & 1 & 0 & \cdots & 0 & -1 \\ -1 & 0 & 1 & \cdots & 0 & 0 \\ 0 & -1 & 0 & \cdots & 0 & 0 \\ \vdots & \vdots & \vdots & \ddots & \vdots & \vdots \\ 1 & 0 & 0 & \cdots & -1 & 0 \end{bmatrix}$$

Demonstrate that this scheme is unconditionally unstable by finding the spectral radius of $\mathbf{A}$ using: (a) the power method [Computer]; (b) MATLAB's $\texttt{eig}$ eigenvalue function [MATLAB]; (c) $||A||_1$ and $||A||_\infty$ as estimates for the spectral radius (see Exercise 9.7) [Pencil].

9. The Lax scheme for the advection equation with periodic boundary conditions may be written as

$$\mathbf{a}^{n+1} = \left(\frac{1}{2}\mathbf{C} - \frac{c\tau}{2h}\mathbf{B} \right) \mathbf{a}^n = \mathbf{A}\mathbf{a}^n$$

where $\mathbf{a}$ and $\mathbf{B}$ are defined in the previous exercise and

$$\mathbf{C} = \begin{bmatrix} 0 & 1 & 0 & \cdots & 0 & 1 \\ 1 & 0 & 1 & \cdots & 0 & 0 \\ 0 & 1 & 0 & \cdots & 0 & 0 \\ \vdots & \vdots & \vdots & \ddots & \vdots & \vdots \\ 1 & 0 & 0 & \cdots & 1 & 0 \end{bmatrix}$$

Demonstrate that the matrix stability for the Lax scheme is given by the CFL condition. Specifically, find the spectral radius of $\mathbf{A}$ using: (a) the power method [Computer]; (b) MATLAB's $\texttt{eig}$ eigenvalue function [MATLAB]; (c) $||A||_1$ and $||A||_\infty$ as estimates for the spectral radius (see Exercise 9.7) [Pencil].

9.2 IMPLICIT SCHEMES

Schrödinger Equation

As a physicist you need no introduction to the Schrödinger equation. For a particle of mass m in one dimension, it may be written as

$$i\hbar\frac{\partial}{\partial t}\psi(x,t) = -\frac{\hbar^2}{2m}\frac{\partial^2}{\partial x^2}\psi + V(x)\psi \tag{9.25}$$

where $\psi(x,t)$ is the wave function and $V(x)$ is the potential. In operator notation, we may write the Schrödinger equation as

$$i\hbar\frac{\partial\psi}{\partial t} = \mathcal{H}\psi \tag{9.26}$$

where $\mathcal{H}$ is the Hamiltonian operator,

$$\mathcal{H} = -\frac{\hbar^2}{2m}\frac{\partial^2}{\partial x^2} + V(x) \tag{9.27}$$

The formal solution of (9.25) is

$$\psi(x,t) = \exp\left\{-\frac{i}{\hbar}\mathcal{H}t\right\}\psi(x,0) \tag{9.28}$$

As before, we discretize space and time in increments of h and τ, respectively; Planck's constant always appears as $\hbar$, so there should be no confusion with the grid spacing h. In our notation, the discretized wave function is $\psi_j^n = \psi(x_j, t_n)$. The FTCS scheme discretizes the Schrödinger equation as

$$i\hbar\frac{\psi_j^{n+1} - \psi_j^n}{\tau} = -\frac{\hbar^2}{2m}\frac{\psi_{j+1}^n + \psi_{j-1}^n - 2\psi_j^n}{h^2} + V_j\psi_j^n \tag{9.29}$$

where $V_j \equiv V(x_j)$.

Since the Hamiltonian is a linear operator, we may write the previous equation as

$$i\hbar\frac{\psi_j^{n+1} - \psi_j^n}{\tau} = \sum_{k=1}^{N} H_{jk}\psi_k^n \tag{9.30}$$

where the matrix $\mathbf{H}$ is the discretized form of the Hamiltonian operator

$$H_{jk} = -\frac{\hbar^2}{2m}\frac{\delta_{j+1,k} + \delta_{j-1,k} - 2\delta_{jk}}{h^2} + V_j\delta_{jk} \tag{9.31}$$

Solving (9.30) for ψ_j^{n+1} gives us our numerical scheme; in matrix notation it may be written as

$$\Psi^{n+1} = \left(\mathbf{I} - \frac{i\tau}{\hbar}\mathbf{H}\right)\Psi^n \tag{9.32}$$

where Ψ^n is a column vector and $\mathbf{I}$ is the identity matrix. Equation (9.32) is the explicit FTCS scheme for solving the Schrödinger equation. Since $e^{-z} \approx 1 - z$, we can interpret (9.32) as using first term in the Taylor expansion of (9.28) to advance the solution by one time step.

Implicit Schemes

The disadvantage of the FTCS scheme is that it is numerically unstable if the time step is too large. This stability problem motivates us to consider alternative approaches. For example, suppose that we apply the Hamiltonian to the *future value* of ψ,

$$i\hbar \frac{\psi_j^{n+1} - \psi_j^n}{\tau} = \sum_{k=1}^N H_{jk}\psi_k^{n+1} \tag{9.33}$$

or

$$\Psi^{n+1} = \Psi^n - \frac{i\tau}{\hbar}\mathbf{H}\Psi^{n+1} \tag{9.34}$$

Collecting Ψ^{n+1} we have

$$\left(\mathbf{I} + \frac{i\tau}{\hbar}\mathbf{H}\right)\Psi^{n+1} = \Psi^n \tag{9.35}$$

Solving for Ψ^{n+1} we have

$$\Psi^{n+1} = \left(\mathbf{I} + \frac{i\tau}{\hbar}\mathbf{H}\right)^{-1}\Psi^n \tag{9.36}$$

This scheme is called the *implicit FTCS method*; compare it with the explicit FTCS scheme, Equation (9.32). Note that since $(1 + \epsilon)^{-1} \to (1 - \epsilon)$ as $\epsilon \to 0$, our implicit and explicit schemes are equivalent in the limit $\tau \to 0$. Since $e^{-z} = 1/e^z \approx (1 + z)^{-1}$, we can interpret (9.36) as an alternative way of using the first term in the Taylor expansion of (9.28) to advance the solution by one time step.

Our new method requires the evaluation of a matrix inverse; this is a common feature of implicit schemes. Of course we wouldn't even consider doing this extra work without some benefit. The advantage of the implicit FTCS scheme is that it is *unconditionally stable*, as may be shown using von Neumann stability analysis. Unconditional stability is a general feature of implicit schemes.

While the fully implicit scheme is very appealing because of its stability, we also want a method to be accurate. Just because the solution doesn't blow up doesn't mean that it is correct. A more accurate scheme is the *Crank-Nicolson method*. Basically it takes the average between the implicit and explicit FTCS schemes

$$i\hbar \frac{\psi_j^{n+1} - \psi_j^n}{\tau} = \frac{1}{2}\sum_{k=1}^N H_{jk}(\psi_k^n + \psi_k^{n+1}) \tag{9.37}$$

In matrix form it may be written as

$$\Psi^{n+1} = \Psi^n - \frac{i\tau}{2\hbar}\mathbf{H}(\Psi^n + \Psi^{n+1}) \tag{9.38}$$

or

$$\left(\mathbf{I} + \frac{i\tau}{2\hbar}\mathbf{H}\right)\Psi^{n+1} = \left(\mathbf{I} - \frac{i\tau}{2\hbar}\mathbf{H}\right)\Psi^n \tag{9.39}$$

Finally, isolating the Ψ^{n+1} term on the left-hand side we have

$$\Psi^{n+1} = \left(\mathbf{I} + \frac{i\tau}{2\hbar}\mathbf{H}\right)^{-1}\left(\mathbf{I} - \frac{i\tau}{2\hbar}\mathbf{H}\right)\Psi^n \tag{9.40}$$

As nasty as this looks, the Crank-Nicolson scheme is the best of the three schemes since it is unconditionally stable and centered in both space and time.

A Páde approximation for the exponential is

$$e^{-z} \approx \frac{1-z}{1+z} \tag{9.41}$$

so we can interpret (9.40) as an alternative way of using this Páde approximation of the formal solution (9.28). Note that if z is imaginary, then $(e^{-z})^*$ (asterisk denotes the complex conjugate) is the inverse of e^{-z}, which means that e^{-z} is unitary. The operator $\exp\left\{-\frac{i}{\hbar}\mathcal{H}t\right\}$ in (9.28) is unitary. Of the three approximations we have considered for the exponential, $1-z$, $1/(1+z)$, and $(1-z)/(1+z)$, only the Páde approximation retains this unitary property.[57]

Wave Packet for a Free Particle

Before putting together a program to solve the Schrödinger equation, we need to think about what initial conditions we want to use. A reasonable initial condition would be the wave packet for a particle localized about x_0 with a packet width of σ_0 and an average momentum $p_0 = \hbar k_0$ (k_0 is the average wave number).

We will use a Gaussian wave packet; the initial wave function is

$$\psi(x, t = 0) = \frac{1}{\sqrt{\sigma_0\sqrt{\pi}}}e^{ik_0 x}e^{-(x-x_0)^2/2\sigma_0^2} \tag{9.42}$$

Notice that this wave function is normalized so that $\int_{-\infty}^{\infty}|\psi|^2 dx = 1$. The Gaussian wave packet has the special property that the uncertainty product $\Delta x \Delta p$ has its minimum theoretical value of $\hbar/2$.

In free space (i.e., $V(x) = 0$), the wave function evolves as

$$\psi(x, t) = \frac{1}{\sqrt{\sigma_0\sqrt{\pi}}}\frac{\sigma_0}{\alpha}e^{ik_0(x-p_0 t/2m)}e^{-(x-x_0-p_0 t/m)^2/2\alpha^2} \tag{9.43}$$

where $\alpha^2 = \sigma_0^2 + i\hbar t/m$. The probability density $P(x, t) = |\psi(x, t)|^2$ is

$$P(x, t) = \frac{\sigma_0}{|\alpha|^2\sqrt{\pi}}\exp\left[-\left(\frac{\sigma_0}{|\alpha|}\right)^4\frac{(x-x_0-p_0 t/m)^2}{\sigma_0^2}\right] \tag{9.44}$$

thus, $P(x, t)$ remains a Gaussian in time.

By symmetry, the maximum of the Gaussian equals the expectation value $\langle x \rangle = \int_{-\infty}^{\infty} xP(x, t)\, dx$. In time, it moves as $\langle x \rangle = x_0 + p_0 t/m$; that is, the

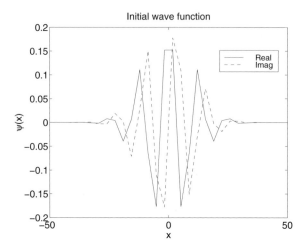

Figure 9.3: Real and imaginary parts of $\psi(x, t = 0)$, as computed by schro for $N = 30$.

packet moves with a velocity p_0/m. The Gaussian spreads in time; its standard deviation is

$$\sigma(t) = \sigma_0 \sqrt{\left(\frac{|\alpha|}{\sigma_0}\right)^4} = \sigma_0 \sqrt{1 + \frac{\hbar^2 t^2}{m^2 \sigma_0^4}} \tag{9.45}$$

The details of this calculation are in any undergraduate quantum mechanics text.[111, 112]

Crank-Nicolson Program for a Free Particle

The program schro solves the Schrödinger equation using the Crank-Nicolson scheme (see Table 9.1). The initial condition is a Gaussian packet (9.42). The boundary conditions are periodic, so when the particle moves out the right side, it reappears on the left. The interior rows of the Hamiltonian matrix are defined according to Equation (9.31); in this version the potential, $V(x)$, is zero. The first and last rows of the Hamiltonian matrix are

$$H_{1,k} = -\frac{\hbar^2}{2m} \frac{\delta_{2,k} + \delta_{N,k} - 2\delta_{1,k}}{h^2} \tag{9.46}$$

$$H_{N,k} = -\frac{\hbar^2}{2m} \frac{\delta_{1,k} + \delta_{N-1,k} - 2\delta_{N,k}}{h^2} \tag{9.47}$$

so as to give periodic boundary conditions.

The wavefunction is complex and we plot the real and imaginary parts separately. For $N = 30$ grid points, the coarsening of the initial condition due to the discretization, as shown in Figure 9.3, is rather noticeable. The program computes $\psi(x, t)$ up to a time such that the pulse should circle the system once and return to the center. As discussed above, the width of the pulse increases

Table 9.1: Outline of program `schro`, which computes the evolution of a Gaussian wave packet by solving the Schrödinger equation using the Crank-Nicolson scheme.

- Initialize parameters (h, τ, etc.).

- Set up the Hamiltonian operator matrix (9.31).

- Compute the Crank-Nicolson matrix $\left(\mathbf{I} + \frac{i\tau}{2\hbar}\mathbf{H}\right)^{-1}\left(\mathbf{I} - \frac{i\tau}{2\hbar}\mathbf{H}\right)$.

- Initialize the wave function (9.42).

- Plot the initial wave function (real and imaginary parts).

- Initialize loop and plot variables.

- Loop over desired number of steps (wave packet circles system once).

  - Compute new wave function using the Crank-Nicolson scheme (9.40).
  - Periodically record values for plotting.

- Plot probability $P(x,t)$ versus position at various times.

See pages 300 and 302 for program listings.

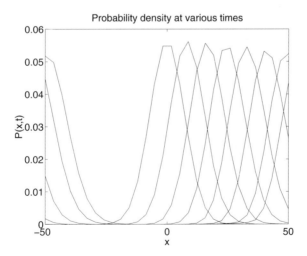

Figure 9.4: Probability density for the particle as a function of position for various times for $N = 30$. Notice that the packet moves to the right and, due to the periodic boundary conditions, reappears from the left. The time step is $\tau = 1.0$.

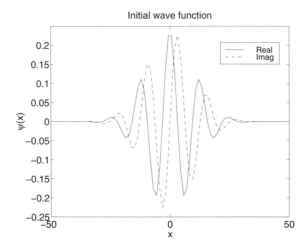

Figure 9.5: Real and imaginary parts of $\psi(x, t = 0)$ as computed by `schro` for $N = 80$.

with time as given by Equation (9.45). The plot of $|\psi(x,t)|^2$ versus x for various values of t is shown in Figure 9.4. Notice that the evolution appears normal, except that the pulse travels only about half the expected distance. If we lower the time step, the result is not significantly affected.

However, if we increase the number of grid points to $N = 80$, the spatial discretization is less prominent; the plot of the wave function is smoother (Figure 9.5). The probability density, $|\psi(x,t)|^2$, versus x for various values of t, is shown in Figure 9.6. This result looks much better because the pulse almost returns to the origin. If we further increase N, we get even better results.

Our error, when $N = 30$, arises from how well we are representing the initial condition. The spatial discretization suppresses the shorter wavelengths. Because of this suppression of the higher wave number modes, the discretized Gaussian pulse ψ_i^n has a lower momentum than $\psi(x,t)$. This error arises from the same aliasing problem we encountered in Section 5.2. Our highest wave number is limited by the grid spacing, so to obtain an accurate solution requires using a finer grid. Unfortunately, we run into memory problems storing our large matrices and the computation time for inverting an $N \times N$ matrix rapidly increases as N^3. In the next section we reformulate the Crank-Nicolson scheme to avoid these difficulties.

EXERCISES

10.   Show that the Schrödinger equation, (9.25), is a parabolic partial differential equation. [Pencil]

11.   Write a program that uses Equation (9.44) to compute and plot $P(x,t) = |\psi(x,t)|^2$ versus x for various values of t. Compare with the results from `schro`. [Computer]

12.   (a) Write a program that solves the diffusion equation using the implicit FTCS

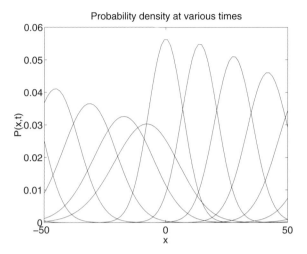

Figure 9.6: Probability density for the particle as a function of position for various times for $N = 80$. Notice that the packet moves to the right and, due to the periodic boundary conditions, reappears from the left. The time step is $\tau = 1.0$.

scheme. Run your program for the parameters given in Figures 6.7 and 6.8 and comment on the results. (b) Repeat part (a) using the Crank-Nicolson scheme. [Computer]

13. (a) Using von Neumann stability analysis, show that the Crank-Nicolson scheme for solving the diffusion equation is unconditionally stable. [Pencil] (b) Show that the Crank-Nicolson scheme for solving the diffusion equation with periodic boundary conditions is matrix stable by plotting the spectral radius versus time step (see Figure 9.2). [Computer]

14. (a) Modify the schro program to compute the energy of the particle as

$$\langle E \rangle = \frac{\int dx\, \psi^*(x,t)\mathcal{H}\psi(x,t)}{\int dx\, \psi^*(x,t)\psi(x,t)} \quad \Rightarrow \quad \frac{\sum_{j,k}(\psi_j^n)^* H_{jk}\psi_k^n}{\sum_{jk}(\psi_j^n)^*\psi_k^n}$$

Plot $\langle E \rangle$ versus time for various values of N. Is energy conserved? (b) Obtain an expression for the total momentum of the particle. Modify schro to compute and graph the total momentum as a function of time; is it conserved? (c) Repeat parts (a) and (b) using the Dirichlet boundary conditions, $\psi(x = \pm L/2) = 0$. [Computer]

15. Modify the schro program to include the delta function potential $V(x) = U\delta(x - L/2)$. Vary the amplitude U and do runs where it is less than, equal to, and more than $E = \hbar^2 k_0^2/2m$, the energy of the particle. Show that some of the wave function penetrates the potential even when $E < U$. If memory allows, increase L, the system size, to distinctly separate the reflected and transmitted waves. [Computer]

16. An important PDE from nonlinear acoustics is Burger's equation,

$$\frac{\partial a}{\partial t} = -a\frac{\partial a}{\partial x} + \kappa\frac{\partial^2 a}{\partial x^2}$$

Write a program that solves it by the explicit/implicit scheme

$$\frac{a_j^{n+1} - a_j^n}{\tau} = -D_j a_j^n$$
$$+ \frac{1}{2}\kappa \left(\frac{a_{j+1}^n + a_{j-1}^n - 2a_j^n}{h^2} + \frac{a_{j+1}^{n+1} + a_{j-1}^{n+1} - 2a_j^{n+1}}{h^2} \right)$$

where

$$D_j = \frac{a_{j+1}^n - a_{j-1}^n}{2h}$$

Take the initial condition: $a(x,0) = 1$ if $x < 0$ and $a(x,0) = -1$ if $x > 0$. Use the Dirichlet boundary conditions: $a(\pm L/2, t) = \mp 1$; try $L = 10$, $\kappa = 1$. Compare your results with the exact (for $L \to \infty$) solution,

$$a(x,t) = \kappa \frac{F(x,t) - F(-x,t)}{F(x,t) + F(-x,t)}$$

where

$$F(x,t) \equiv \frac{1}{2} e^{t-x} \left\{ 1 - \text{erf}\left(\frac{x - 2t}{2\sqrt{t}} \right) \right\}$$

and $\text{erf}(x)$ is the error function. [Computer]

17.   An important equation from the theory of solitons is the *Korteweg-de Vries* (KdV) equation [42],

$$\frac{\partial \rho}{\partial t} = -6\rho \frac{\partial \rho}{\partial x} - \frac{\partial^3 \rho}{\partial x^3}$$

Write a program that solves it using the explicit/implicit scheme

$$\frac{\rho_j^{n+1} - \rho_j^n}{\tau} = -6 D_j \rho_j^n - \frac{1}{2} \left(\frac{\rho_{j+2}^n - 2\rho_{j+1}^n + 2\rho_{j-1}^n - \rho_{j-2}^n}{2h^3} \right.$$
$$+ \left. \frac{\rho_{j+2}^{n+1} - 2\rho_{j+1}^{n+1} + 2\rho_{j-1}^{n+1} - \rho_{j-2}^{n+1}}{2h^3} \right)$$

where

$$D_j = \frac{\rho_{j+1}^n - \rho_{j-1}^n}{2h}$$

Use Dirichlet boundary conditions, $\rho(x = \pm L/2) = 0$. Test your program for the solitary wave solution of the KdV equations: $\rho(x,t) = 2 \text{ sech}^2(x - 4t)$. [Computer]

9.3   *SPARSE MATRICES

General Properties

As the complexity of our problems increases we find ourselves working with larger and larger matrices. Not only do these large matrices occupy a large amount of memory, they are computationally expensive to manipulate (multiply, invert, etc.). However, you probably noticed that the Hamiltonian matrix used in the previous section is very sparse (i.e., almost all the elements of the matrix are zero). In this section we examine how to exploit this feature to allow us to work with larger systems.

Sparse matrices fall into two categories, depending on their structure. The more general case is when the nonzero elements are arbitrarily distributed, such as in the matrix sketched below:

$$
\begin{bmatrix}
0 & * & 0 & 0 & * & 0 & 0 & 0 \\
* & 0 & 0 & * & * & 0 & 0 & 0 \\
0 & * & 0 & 0 & 0 & 0 & 0 & 0 \\
* & * & * & 0 & 0 & 0 & 0 & * \\
0 & 0 & * & 0 & 0 & * & * & 0 \\
0 & 0 & 0 & 0 & * & 0 & 0 & 0 \\
* & * & 0 & 0 & 0 & 0 & * & * \\
0 & 0 & 0 & * & 0 & 0 & 0 & 0
\end{bmatrix}
$$

where the nonzero elements are indicated by asterisks. Such matrices may be stored in a compressed format by recording the values of the nonzero elements and their locations. Typically this is done using a linked list.[43]

The simpler and, fortunately, more common case is when the matrix has a definite, known structure. Some examples of such matrices are sketched below:

$$
\begin{bmatrix}
* & * & 0 & 0 & 0 & 0 & 0 & 0 \\
0 & * & * & 0 & 0 & 0 & 0 & 0 \\
0 & 0 & * & * & 0 & 0 & 0 & 0 \\
0 & 0 & 0 & * & * & 0 & 0 & 0 \\
0 & 0 & 0 & 0 & * & * & 0 & 0 \\
0 & 0 & 0 & 0 & 0 & * & * & 0 \\
* & * & * & * & * & * & * & * \\
0 & 0 & 0 & 0 & 0 & 0 & 0 & *
\end{bmatrix}
\qquad
\begin{bmatrix}
* & * & 0 & 0 & 0 & 0 & 0 & 0 \\
* & * & 0 & 0 & 0 & 0 & 0 & 0 \\
0 & 0 & 0 & 0 & 0 & 0 & 0 & 0 \\
0 & 0 & 0 & * & * & * & 0 & 0 \\
0 & 0 & 0 & * & * & * & 0 & 0 \\
0 & 0 & 0 & * & * & * & 0 & 0 \\
0 & 0 & 0 & 0 & 0 & 0 & * & * \\
0 & 0 & 0 & 0 & 0 & 0 & * & *
\end{bmatrix}
$$

The first matrix is an example of a banded matrix and the second is a block diagonal matrix.

The solution of sparse matrix problems is so important that a significant industry has arisen in the numerical analysis community.[100] It would be far beyond the scope of this book to go into these specialized methods, but there is one special case that is so simple and so common that I believe it is valuable for you to learn it. It also gives you a bit of a flavor of what is involved when working with sparse matrices.

Tridiagonal Matrices

The special case we consider is the tridiagonal matrix; it has the following structure:

$$
\mathbf{A} =
\begin{bmatrix}
\beta_1 & \gamma_1 & 0 & \cdots & 0 \\
\alpha_1 & \beta_2 & \gamma_2 & \cdots & 0 \\
0 & \alpha_2 & \beta_3 & \cdots & 0 \\
\vdots & \vdots & \vdots & \ddots & \vdots \\
0 & 0 & 0 & \cdots & \beta_N
\end{bmatrix}
\tag{9.48}
$$

Since only the elements on the main diagonal (the β's) and on the first sub and superdiagonals (the α's and γ's) are nonzero, we may store the matrix in a compressed (or packed) form using the matrix

$$
\mathbf{A}_c =
\begin{bmatrix}
? & \beta_1 & \gamma_1 \\
\alpha_1 & \beta_2 & \gamma_2 \\
\alpha_2 & \beta_3 & \gamma_3 \\
\vdots & \vdots & \vdots \\
\alpha_{N-1} & \beta_N & ?
\end{bmatrix}
\tag{9.49}
$$

The two corner elements marked with question marks are unused.

We now reformulate the Gaussian elimination algorithm, but specialized for the case of tridiagonal matrices. The basic method requires no major modification; many operations may be skipped, since most elements of the matrix are zero. To solve the linear system $\mathbf{Ax} = \mathbf{b}$, the forward elimination stage requires only that we modify the values on the main diagonal. Thus $\alpha_i' = \alpha_i$, $\gamma_i' = \gamma_i$, where the prime indicates the value after forward elimination, and

$$
\beta_i' = \beta_i - \frac{\alpha_{i-1}}{\beta_{i-1}'}\gamma_{i-1} \qquad i = 2, \ldots, N
\tag{9.50}
$$

with $\beta_1' = \beta_1$. The elements of $\mathbf{b}$ are

$$
b_i' = b_i - \frac{\alpha_{i-1}}{\beta_{i-1}'}b_{i-1}' \qquad i = 2, \ldots, N
\tag{9.51}
$$

with $b_1' = b_1$. For the backsubstitution stage we may easily obtain $\mathbf{x}$ using $x_N = b_N'/\beta_N'$ and the downward recursion relation

$$
x_i = \frac{b_i' - \gamma_i x_{i+1}}{\beta_i'} \qquad i = N - 1, \ldots, 1
\tag{9.52}
$$

This formulation of Gaussian elimination for a tridiagonal matrix is sometimes called the *Thomas algorithm*. The function tri_ge (Table 9.2) performs Gaussian elimination on a packed tridiagonal matrix.

You might expect that we would next assemble a program to compute the inverse of a tridiagonal matrix. There is only one problem: The inverse of a tridiagonal matrix is not necessarily sparse. Try using the routines from Chapter 4.2 to invert some sparse matrices constructed at random. You'll find that the inverse is almost always a full matrix.

Crank-Nicolson for Tridiagonal Matrices

Returning to the Schrödinger equation, we want to take the Crank-Nicolson scheme

$$
\Psi^{n+1} = \left(\mathbf{I} + \frac{i\tau}{2\hbar}\mathbf{H}\right)^{-1}\left(\mathbf{I} - \frac{i\tau}{2\hbar}\mathbf{H}\right)\Psi^n
\tag{9.53}
$$

Table 9.2: Outline of function `tri_ge`, which performs Gaussian elimination for tridiagonal matrices.

- *Inputs*: $\mathbf{A}_c$, $\mathbf{b}$.

- *Output*: $\mathbf{x}$.

- Check that dimensions of $\mathbf{A}_c$ and $\mathbf{b}$ are compatible.

- Unpack diagonals of triangular matrix into the vectors α, β, and γ.

- Perform forward elimination using (9.50) and (9.51).

- Perform back substitution using (9.52).

See pages 301 and 305 for program listings.

and rewrite it in such a way that we do not have to compute a matrix inverse. Rearranging terms gives

$$
\begin{aligned}
\Psi^{n+1} &= \left(\mathbf{I} + \frac{i\tau}{2\hbar}\mathbf{H}\right)^{-1}\left[2\mathbf{I} - \left(\mathbf{I} + \frac{i\tau}{2\hbar}\mathbf{H}\right)\right]\Psi^n \\
&= \left[2\left(\mathbf{I} + \frac{i\tau}{2\hbar}\mathbf{H}\right)^{-1} - \mathbf{I}\right]\Psi^n \qquad (9.54)
\end{aligned}
$$

or

$$
\begin{aligned}
\Psi^{n+1} &= (\mathbf{Q}^{-1} - \mathbf{I})\Psi^n \\
&= \mathbf{Q}^{-1}\Psi^n - \Psi^n \qquad (9.55)
\end{aligned}
$$

where $\mathbf{Q} = \frac{1}{2}[\mathbf{I} + (i\tau/2\hbar)\mathbf{H}]$.

The computation of a matrix inverse is avoided by splitting the problem into two stages. First we solve the following linear system for the vector χ,

$$
\mathbf{Q}\chi = \Psi^n \qquad (9.56)
$$

and then update our solution as

$$
\Psi^{n+1} = \chi - \Psi^n \qquad (9.57)
$$

Notice that while we do not have to take the inverse of a matrix, we do have to solve a linear system, Equation (9.56), at each time step.

Figure 9.7 shows a Gaussian wave packet computed by the sparse matrix Crank-Nicolson algorithm described above. In this case we have Dirichlet boundary conditions, $\psi_1^n = \psi_N^n = 0$. Setting the wave function to zero at $\pm L/2$ is equivalent to having an infinite potential at the boundaries (particle in a box).

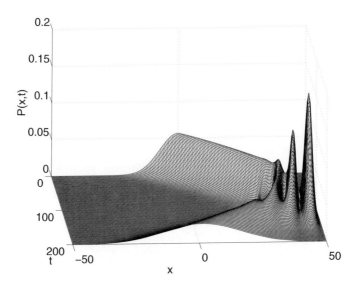

Figure 9.7: Square amplitude of the wave function $\psi(x,t)$ as a function of position and time. Boundary conditions are $\psi_1^n = \psi_N^n = 0$. The number of grid points is $N = 200$, and the time step is $\tau = 1$.

Notice the interesting structure in the wave function as it rebounds off the reflecting wall. After it moves away from the wall, the wave packet regains its original Gaussian shape (with the appropriate spreading). For a collection of pictures showing wave packets interacting with potentials, see Saxon [111].

EXERCISES

18. Solve the following problem by hand using the Thomas algorithm,

$$\begin{bmatrix} 1 & 1 & 0 & 0 & 0 \\ 1 & 2 & 0 & 0 & 0 \\ 0 & -1 & 3 & 2 & 0 \\ 0 & 0 & 0 & 4 & 1 \\ 0 & 0 & 0 & -1 & 2 \end{bmatrix} \begin{bmatrix} x_1 \\ x_2 \\ x_3 \\ x_4 \\ x_5 \end{bmatrix} = \begin{bmatrix} 3 \\ 5 \\ 15 \\ 21 \\ 6 \end{bmatrix}$$

What do the matrix and the right-hand side look like at the end of forward elimination? [Pencil]

19. Modify the schro program to use the sparse matrix Crank-Nicolson scheme and reproduce Figure 9.7.

20. Using the tri_ge function for the Crank-Nicolson scheme is inefficient for two reasons. The first part of forward elimination (9.50) is repeated at every time step even though the matrix **Q** is fixed. Second, several terms are recomputed at every time step even though they remain constant. Improve the efficiency by breaking up the tri_ge function into two separate functions. The first function will be invoked once outside the main loop and the second function will be invoked at each iteration. You will essentially be implementing LU decomposition. [Computer]

21. Modify the `schro` program to use the sparse matrix Crank-Nicolson scheme using the potential,

$$V(x) = U_0[\delta(x + L/4) + \delta(x - L/4)] \quad \Rightarrow \quad V_i = \begin{cases} U_0/h & i = N/4, i = 3N/4 \\ 0 & \text{otherwise} \end{cases}$$

which makes the center of the system a "box." Due to tunneling, the particle is not contained by the box even when its energy is less than U_0. Compute the probability that the particle is inside the box,

$$P(t_n) = \sum_{i=N/4}^{3N/4} (\psi_i^n)^* \psi_i^n$$

where $t_n \equiv (n-1)\tau$. Plot $P(t)$ versus t for various values of U_0. [Computer]

22. For periodic boundary conditions the Hamiltonian matrix is not tridiagonal. The elements at the opposite corners, `ham(1, N)` and `ham(N, 1)`, are nonzero. Derive a modified version of the Thomas algorithm that can perform Gaussian elimination on matrices of this type. Write a function that implements this algorithm and demonstrate its use in a modified version of `schro`. [Computer]

23. (a) Derive a modified version of the Thomas algorithm that applies to pentadiagonal matrices, that is, matrices for which only elements on the five central diagonals are nonzero. [Pencil] (b) Write a computer routine that implements your algorithm from part (a). [Computer]

BEYOND THIS CHAPTER

Our two stability analyses are suitable only for linear partial differential equations. On the other hand, most interesting research problems involve nonlinear equations. We may still use von Neumann or matrix analysis by linearizing our PDE about a reference state. Also, the stability criteria we've seen have a physical basis (e.g., the CFL condition is given by the time it takes a wave to move one grid spacing). Going back to the original physical problem, you can usually find some characteristic time scale to guide your selection of a time step. Finally, there are some specialized techniques (e.g., energy stability analysis) that can sometimes be used with nonlinear PDEs. See Richtmyer and Morton [107] for a more complete discussion.

This chapter covers two techniques for studying stability. A related problem is determining the dissipation and dispersion of a numerical scheme. We saw in Section 7.1 that the Lax scheme had an undesirably large numerical dissipation when the time step was too small. Furthermore, we want our numerical scheme to preserve the same dispersion relation as the original PDE. Both dissipation and dispersion may be studied by a simple extension of von Neumann stability analysis; see Anderson, et al. [10] for details.

Implicit techniques are more difficult to use in higher-dimensional problems. This is because the conventional extension would require us to manipulate huge matrices. A more efficient approach is to use operator splitting to separately perform the implicit step in each direction. This is known as alternating direction implicit (ADI).[98]

APPENDIX A: MATLAB LISTINGS

Listing 9A.1 Program schro. Computes the motion of a Gaussian wave packet by solving the Schrödinger equation using the Crank-Nicolson scheme.

```
%  schro - Program to solve the Schrodinger equation
%  for a free particle using the Crank-Nicolson scheme
clear all;  help schro;   % Clear memory and print header

%* Initialize parameters (grid spacing, time step, etc.)
i_imag = sqrt(-1);   % Imaginary i
N = input('Enter number of grid points: ');
L = 100;             % System extends from -L/2 to L/2
h = L/(N-1);         % Grid size
x = h*(0:N-1) - L/2;  % Coordinates  of grid points
h_bar = 1;   mass = 1; % Natural units
tau = input('Enter time step: ');

%* Set up the Hamiltonian operator matrix
ham = zeros(N);  % Set all elements to zero
coeff = -h_bar^2/(2*mass*h^2);
for i=2:(N-1)
  ham(i,i-1) = coeff;
  ham(i,i) = -2*coeff;  % Set interior rows
  ham(i,i+1) = coeff;
end
% First and last rows for periodic boundary conditions
ham(1,N) = coeff;    ham(1,1) = -2*coeff; ham(1,2) = coeff;
ham(N,N-1) = coeff; ham(N,N) = -2*coeff; ham(N,1) = coeff;

%* Compute the Crank-Nicolson matrix
dCN = ( inv(eye(N) + .5*i_imag*tau/h_bar*ham) * ...
             (eye(N) - .5*i_imag*tau/h_bar*ham) );

%* Initialize the wavefunction
x0 = 0;              % Location of the center of the wavepacket
velocity = 0.5;  % Average velocity of the packet
k0 = mass*velocity/h_bar;       % Average wavenumber
sigma0 = L/10;   % Standard deviation of the wavefunction
Norm_psi = 1/(sqrt(sigma0*sqrt(pi)));  % Normalization
psi = Norm_psi * exp(i_imag*k0*x') .* ...
                    exp(-(x'-x0).^2/(2*sigma0^2));

%* Plot the initial wavefunction
figure(1); clf;
```

```
plot(x,real(psi),'-',x,imag(psi),'--');
title('Initial wave function');
xlabel('x');  ylabel('\psi(x)'); legend('Real','Imag');
drawnow;  pause(1);

%* Initialize loop and plot variables
max_iter = L/(velocity*tau);      % Particle should circle system
plot_iter = max_iter/20;          % Produce 20 curves
p_plot(:,1) = psi.*conj(psi);     % Record initial condition
iplot = 1;
figure(2); clf;
axisV = [-L/2 L/2 0 max(p_plot)]; % Fix axis min and max

%* Loop over desired number of steps (wave circles system once)
for iter=1:max_iter

  %* Compute new wave function using the Crank-Nicolson scheme
  psi = dCN*psi;

  %* Periodically record values for plotting
  if( rem(iter,plot_iter) < 1 )
    iplot = iplot+1;
    p_plot(:,iplot) = psi.*conj(psi);
    plot(x,p_plot(:,iplot));       % Display snap-shot of P(x)
    xlabel('x'); ylabel('P(x,t)');
    title(sprintf('Finished %g of %g iterations',iter,max_iter));
    axis(axisV); drawnow;
  end

end

%* Plot probability versus position at various times
pFinal = psi.*conj(psi);
plot(x,p_plot(:,1:3:iplot),x,pFinal);
xlabel('x'); ylabel('P(x,t)');
title('Probability density at various times');
```

Listing 9A.2 Function tri_ge. Gaussian elimination routine for tridiagonal matrices.

```
function x = tri_ge(a,b)
% Function to solve b = a*x by Gaussian elimination where
% the matrix a is a packed tridiagonal matrix
% Inputs
%   a    Packed tridiagonal matrix, N by N unpacked
%   b    Column vector of length N
% Output
%   x    Solution of b = a*x; Column vector of length N
```

```
%* Check that dimensions of a and b are compatible
[N,M] = size(a);
[NN,MM] = size(b);
if( N ~= NN | MM ~= 1)
  error('Problem in tri_GE, inputs are incompatible');
end


%* Unpack diagonals of triangular matrix into vectors
alpha(1:N-1) = a(2:N,1);
beta(1:N) = a(1:N,2);
gamma(1:N-1) = a(1:N-1,3);


%* Perform forward elimination
for i=2:N
  coeff = alpha(i-1)/beta(i-1);
  beta(i) = beta(i) - coeff*gamma(i-1);
  b(i) = b(i) - coeff*b(i-1);
end


%* Perform back substitution
x(N) = b(N)/beta(N);
for i=N-1:-1:1
  x(i) = (b(i) - gamma(i)*x(i+1))/beta(i);
end
x = x.';    % Transpose x to a column vector
return;
```

APPENDIX B: C++ LISTINGS

Listing 9B.1 Program schro. Computes the motion of a Gaussian wave packet by solving the Schrödinger equation using the Crank-Nicolson scheme. Uses cinv (Listing 9B.3).

```
//  schro - Program to solve the Schrodinger equation
//  for a free particle using the Crank-Nicolson scheme
#include "NumMeth.h"

void cinv( Matrix RealA, Matrix ImagA,
           Matrix& RealAinv, Matrix& ImagAinv );

void main() {

  //* Initialize parameters (grid spacing, time step, etc.)
  cout << "Enter number of grid points: "; int N; cin >> N;
  double L = 100;        // System extends from -L/2 to L/2
  double h = L/(N-1);    // Grid size
```

```
double h_bar = 1;   double mass = 1; // Natural units
cout << "Enter time step: "; double tau; cin >> tau;
Matrix x(N);
int i, j, k;
for( i=1; i<=N; i++ )
  x(i) = h*(i-1) - L/2;  // Coordinates  of grid points

//* Set up the Hamiltonian operator matrix
Matrix eye(N,N), ham(N,N);
eye.set(0.0);  // Set all elements to zero
for( i=1; i<=N; i++ ) // Identity matrix
  eye(i,i) = 1.0;
ham.set(0.0);  // Set all elements to zero
double coeff = -h_bar*h_bar/(2*mass*h*h);
for( i=2; i<=(N-1); i++ ) {
  ham(i,i-1) = coeff;
  ham(i,i) = -2*coeff;  // Set interior rows
  ham(i,i+1) = coeff;
}
// First and last rows for periodic boundary conditions
ham(1,N) = coeff;   ham(1,1) = -2*coeff; ham(1,2) = coeff;
ham(N,N-1) = coeff; ham(N,N) = -2*coeff; ham(N,1) = coeff;

//* Compute the Crank-Nicolson matrix
Matrix RealA(N,N), ImagA(N,N), RealB(N,N), ImagB(N,N);
for( i=1; i<=N; i++ )
 for( j=1; j<=N; j++ ) {
   RealA(i,j) = eye(i,j);
   ImagA(i,j) = 0.5*tau/h_bar*ham(i,j);
   RealB(i,j) = eye(i,j);
   ImagB(i,j) = -0.5*tau/h_bar*ham(i,j);
 }
Matrix RealAi(N,N), ImagAi(N,N);
cout << "Computing matrix inverse ... " << flush;
cinv( RealA, ImagA, RealAi, ImagAi );  // Complex matrix inverse
cout << "done" << endl;
Matrix RealD(N,N), ImagD(N,N); // Crank-Nicolson matrix
for( i=1; i<=N; i++ )
 for( j=1; j<=N; j++ ) {
  RealD(i,j) = 0.0;              // Matrix (complex) multiplication
  ImagD(i,j) = 0.0;
  for( k=1; k<=N; k++ ) {
    RealD(i,j) += RealAi(i,k)*RealB(k,j) - ImagAi(i,k)*ImagB(k,j);
    ImagD(i,j) += RealAi(i,k)*ImagB(k,j) + ImagAi(i,k)*RealB(k,j);
  }
 }

//* Initialize the wavefunction
const double pi = 3.141592654;
double x0 = 0;             // Location of the center of the wavepacket
```

```
double velocity = 0.5;   // Average velocity of the packet
double k0 = mass*velocity/h_bar;        // Average wavenumber
double sigma0 = L/10;   // Standard deviation of the wavefunction
double Norm_psi = 1/(sqrt(sigma0*sqrt(pi)));  // Normalization
Matrix RealPsi(N), ImagPsi(N), rpi(N), ipi(N);
for( i=1; i<=N; i++ ) {
  double expFactor = exp(-(x(i)-x0)*(x(i)-x0)/(2*sigma0*sigma0));
  RealPsi(i) = Norm_psi * cos(k0*x(i)) * expFactor;
  ImagPsi(i) = Norm_psi * sin(k0*x(i)) * expFactor;
  rpi(i) = RealPsi(i);    // Record initial wavefunction
  ipi(i) = ImagPsi(i);    // for plotting
}

//* Initialize loop and plot variables
int nStep = (int)(L/(velocity*tau));  // Particle should circle system
int nplots = 20;                      // Number of plots to record
double plotStep = nStep/nplots;       // Iterations between plots
Matrix p_plot(N,nplots+2);
for( i=1; i<=N; i++ )       // Record initial condition
  p_plot(i,1) = RealPsi(i)*RealPsi(i) + ImagPsi(i)*ImagPsi(i);
int iplot = 1;

//* Loop over desired number of steps (wave circles system once)
int iStep;
Matrix RealNewPsi(N), ImagNewPsi(N);
for( iStep=1; iStep<=nStep; iStep++ ) {

  //* Compute new wave function using the Crank-Nicolson scheme
  RealNewPsi.set(0.0);  ImagNewPsi.set(0.0);
  for( i=1; i<=N; i++ )          // Matrix multiply D*psi
    for( j=1; j<=N; j++ ) {
      RealNewPsi(i) += RealD(i,j)*RealPsi(j) - ImagD(i,j)*ImagPsi(j);
      ImagNewPsi(i) += RealD(i,j)*ImagPsi(j) + ImagD(i,j)*RealPsi(j);
    }
  RealPsi = RealNewPsi;  // Copy new values into Psi
  ImagPsi = ImagNewPsi;

  //* Periodically record values for plotting
  if( fmod(iStep,plotStep) < 1 ) {
    iplot++;
    for( i=1; i<=N; i++ )
      p_plot(i,iplot) = RealPsi(i)*RealPsi(i) + ImagPsi(i)*ImagPsi(i);
    cout << "Finished " << iStep << " of " << nStep << " steps" << endl;
  }
}
// Record final probability density
iplot++;
for( i=1; i<=N; i++ )
  p_plot(i,iplot) = RealPsi(i)*RealPsi(i) + ImagPsi(i)*ImagPsi(i);
nplots = iplot;   // Actual number of plots recorded
```

```
  //* Print out the plotting variables:  x, rpi, ipi, p_plot
  ofstream xOut("x.txt"), rpiOut("rpi.txt"), ipiOut("ipi.txt"),
           p_plotOut("p_plot.txt");
  for( i=1; i<=N; i++ ) {
    xOut << x(i) << endl;
    rpiOut << rpi(i) << endl;
    ipiOut << ipi(i) << endl;
    for( j=1; j<nplots; j++ )
      p_plotOut << p_plot(i,j) << ", ";
    p_plotOut << p_plot(i,nplots) << endl;
  }
}
/***** To plot in MATLAB; use the script below ********************
load x.txt; load rpi.txt; load ipi.txt; load p_plot.txt;
%* Plot the initial wavefunction
figure(1); clf;
plot(x,rpi,x,ipi);
title('Initial wave function');
xlabel('x');  ylabel('\psi(x)'); legend('Real','Imag');
%* Plot probability versus position at various times
figure(2); clf;
[mp np] = size(p_plot);
plot(x,p_plot(:,1:3:np),x,p_plot(:,np));
xlabel('x'); ylabel('P(x,t)');
title('Probability density at various times');
axisV = [-1/2 1/2 0 max(p_plot)]; % Fix axis min and max
****************************************************************/
```

Listing 9B.2 Function `tri_ge`. Gaussian elimination routine for tridiagonal matrices.

```
#include "NumMeth.h"

double trige( Matrix A, Matrix b, Matrix& x) {
// Function to solve b = A*x by Gaussian elimination where
// the matrix A is a packed tridiagonal matrix
// Inputs
//   A       Packed tridiagonal matrix, N by N unpacked
//   b       Column vector of length N
// Output
//   x       Solution of b = A*x; Column vector of length N
//   determ  Determinant of A

  //* Check that dimensions of a and b are compatible
  int N = A.nRow();
  assert( N == b.nRow() && A.nCol() == 3 );

  //* Unpack diagonals of triangular matrix into vectors
```

```
Matrix alpha(N), beta(N), gamma(N);
int i;
for( i=1; i<=(N-1); i++ ) {
  alpha(i) = A(i+1,1);
  beta(i) = A(i,2);
  gamma(i) = A(i,3);
}
beta(N) = A(N,2);

//* Perform forward elimination
for( i=2; i<=N; i++ ) {
  double coeff = alpha(i-1)/beta(i-1);
  beta(i) -= coeff*gamma(i-1);
  b(i) -= coeff*b(i-1);
}

//* Compute determinant as product of diagonal elements
double determ = 1.0;
for( i=1; i<=N; i++ )
  determ *= beta(i);

//* Perform back substitution
x(N) = b(N)/beta(N);
for( i=N-1; i>=1; i-- )
  x(i) = (b(i) - gamma(i)*x(i+1))/beta(i);

return( determ );
}
```

Listing 9B.3 Subroutine cinv. Computes the inverse of a complex matrix using Gaussian elimination with pivoting.

```
#include "NumMeth.h"

// Compute inverse of complex matrix
void cinv( Matrix RealA, Matrix ImagA,
           Matrix& RealAinv, Matrix& ImagAinv )
// Inputs
//   RealA  -   Real part of matrix A (N by N)
//   ImagA  -   Imaginary part of matrix A (N by N)
// Outputs
//   RealAinv -   Real part of inverse of matrix A (N by N)
//   ImagAinv -   Imaginary part of A inverse (N by N)
{

  int N = RealA.nRow();
  assert( N == RealA.nCol() && N == ImagA.nRow()
                   && N == ImagA.nCol());
  RealAinv = RealA; // Copy matrices to ensure they are same size
```

```
    ImagAinv = ImagA;

    int i, j, k;
    Matrix scale(N);    // Scale factor
    int *index;  index = new int [N+1];

    //* Matrix B is initialized to the identity matrix
    Matrix RealB(N,N), ImagB(N,N);
    RealB.set(0.0);  ImagB.set(0.0);
    for( i=1; i<=N; i++ )
      RealB(i,i) = 1.0;

    //* Set scale factor, scale(i) = max( |a(i,j)| ), for each row
    for( i=1; i<=N; i++ ) {
      index[i] = i;                // Initialize row index list
      double scaleMax = 0.;
      for( j=1; j<=N; j++ ) {
        double MagA = RealA(i,j)*RealA(i,j) + ImagA(i,j)*ImagA(i,j);
        scaleMax = (scaleMax > MagA) ? scaleMax : MagA;
      }
      scale(i) = scaleMax;
    }

    //* Loop over rows k = 1, ..., (N-1)
    for( k=1; k<=N-1; k++ ) {
      //* Select pivot row from max( |a(j,k)/s(j)| )
      double ratiomax = 0.0;
      int jPivot = k;
      for( i=k; i<=N; i++ ) {
        double MagA = RealA(index[i],k)*RealA(index[i],k) +
                      ImagA(index[i],k)*ImagA(index[i],k);
        double ratio = MagA/scale(index[i]);
        if( ratio > ratiomax ) {
          jPivot=i;
          ratiomax = ratio;
        }
      }
      //* Perform pivoting using row index list
      int indexJ = index[k];
      if( jPivot != k ) {          // Pivot
        indexJ = index[jPivot];
        index[jPivot] = index[k];  // Swap index jPivot and k
        index[k] = indexJ;
      }
      //* Perform forward elimination
      for( i=k+1; i<=N; i++ ) {
        double denom = RealA(indexJ,k)*RealA(indexJ,k)
                    + ImagA(indexJ,k)*ImagA(indexJ,k);
        double RealCoeff = (RealA(index[i],k)*RealA(indexJ,k)
                       + ImagA(index[i],k)*ImagA(indexJ,k))/denom;
```

```
      double ImagCoeff = (ImagA(index[i],k)*RealA(indexJ,k)
                      - RealA(index[i],k)*ImagA(indexJ,k))/denom;
      for( j=k+1; j<=N; j++ ) {
        RealA(index[i],j) -= RealCoeff*RealA(indexJ,j)
                        - ImagCoeff*ImagA(indexJ,j);
        ImagA(index[i],j) -= RealCoeff*ImagA(indexJ,j)
                        + ImagCoeff*RealA(indexJ,j);
      }
      RealA(index[i],k) = RealCoeff;
      ImagA(index[i],k) = ImagCoeff;
      for( j=1; j<=N; j++ ) {
        RealB(index[i],j) -= RealA(index[i],k)*RealB(indexJ,j)
                        - ImagA(index[i],k)*ImagB(indexJ,j);
        ImagB(index[i],j) -= RealA(index[i],k)*ImagB(indexJ,j)
                        + ImagA(index[i],k)*RealB(indexJ,j);
      }
    }
  }
}

//* Perform backsubstitution
for( k=1; k<=N; k++ ) {
  double denom = RealA(index[N],N)*RealA(index[N],N)
              + ImagA(index[N],N)*ImagA(index[N],N);
  RealAinv(N,k) = (RealB(index[N],k)*RealA(index[N],N)
              + ImagB(index[N],k)*ImagA(index[N],N))/denom;
  ImagAinv(N,k) = (ImagB(index[N],k)*RealA(index[N],N)
              - RealB(index[N],k)*ImagA(index[N],N))/denom;
  for( i=N-1; i>=1; i-- ) {
    double RealSum = RealB(index[i],k);
    double ImagSum = ImagB(index[i],k);
    for( j=i+1; j<=N; j++ ) {
      RealSum -= RealA(index[i],j)*RealAinv(j,k)
              - ImagA(index[i],j)*ImagAinv(j,k);
      ImagSum -= RealA(index[i],j)*ImagAinv(j,k)
              + ImagA(index[i],j)*RealAinv(j,k);
    }
    double denom = RealA(index[i],i)*RealA(index[i],i)
                + ImagA(index[i],i)*ImagA(index[i],i);
    RealAinv(i,k) = (RealSum*RealA(index[i],i)
                + ImagSum*ImagA(index[i],i))/denom;
    ImagAinv(i,k) = (ImagSum*RealA(index[i],i)
                - RealSum*ImagA(index[i],i))/denom;
  }
}

delete [] index;  // Release allocated memory
}
```

Chapter 10

Special Functions and Quadrature

You can go quite far with the elementary transcendental functions (exponential, sine, etc.). However, eventually you will find it useful to add more functions to your toolbox. This chapter discusses two important special functions: Legendre polynomials and Bessel functions. The second topic of this chapter is quadrature, a fancy term for evaluating integrals numerically. Two general-purpose methods are covered: Romberg and Gaussian integration.

10.1 SPECIAL FUNCTIONS

Eigenfunctions

In Section 8.1 we solved the Laplace equation in rectangular coordinates using separation of variables. Our PDE was separated into ODEs, all of which were of the form

$$\frac{d^2}{dx^2}f(x) + k^2 f(x) = 0 \tag{10.1}$$

The general solution of this simple equation is a linear combination of trigonometric functions,

$$f(x) = A\cos(kx) + B\sin(kx) \tag{10.2}$$

where the coefficients A and B are determined by the boundary conditions.

This ODE is a special case of the *Sturm-Liouville equation*,

$$\mathcal{L}f_i(x) - \lambda_i \rho(x) f_i(x) = 0 \tag{10.3}$$

where λ_i is the eigenvalue and f_i is its corresponding eigenfunction. The linear differential operator $\mathcal{L}$ is

$$\mathcal{L} = \frac{d}{dx}p(x)\frac{d}{dx} + q(x) \tag{10.4}$$

and $\rho(x)$ is a weight function.

It is not difficult to show that this operator, with homogeneous boundary conditions* in the interval $[a, b]$, is Hermitian,

$$\int_a^b f_i^*(x) \mathcal{L} f_j(x) \, dx = \int_a^b f_j^*(x) \mathcal{L} f_i(x) \, dx \qquad (10.5)$$

where the asterisk denotes complex conjugate. This Hermitian property leads to the two important results: (1) the eigenvalues λ_i are real (i.e., $\lambda_i = \lambda_i^*$), and (2) the eigenfunctions are orthogonal,

$$\int_a^b \rho(x) f_i^*(x) f_j(x) \, dx = \mathcal{N}_i \delta_{i,j} \qquad (10.6)$$

where $\mathcal{N}_i$ is the normalization. If this sounds vaguely familiar, you probably recall that in quantum mechanics the Hamiltonian operator (which is Hermitian) has real eigenvalues. These eigenvalues are the energy levels, and the eigenfunctions are the wave functions of those states.

When separation of variables is performed in a nonrectangular coordinate system (e.g., spherical, cylindrical), we commonly obtain ODEs of the form given by (10.3). The solutions of these more complicated problems are important enough to be studied as named functions. In this section we cover two of these special functions: Legendre polynomials and Bessel functions. Special functions are also discussed in the standard mathematical physics texts, such as Boas [24] and Arfken [11]; many useful identities may be found in Abramowitz and Stegun [2].

Legendre Polynomials

Laplace's equation is $\nabla^2 \Phi(\mathbf{r}) = 0$; in spherical coordinates it may be written as

$$\left(\frac{1}{r} \frac{\partial^2}{\partial r^2} r + \frac{1}{r^2 \sin\theta} \frac{\partial}{\partial \theta} \sin\theta \frac{\partial}{\partial \theta} + \frac{1}{r^2 \sin^2\theta} \frac{\partial^2}{\partial \phi^2} \right) \Phi(r, \theta, \phi) = 0 \qquad (10.7)$$

We'll assume that our problem is azimuthally symmetric, so Φ is independent of the angle ϕ. To use separation of variables, we insert

$$\Phi(r, \theta) = U(r) P(\theta) \qquad (10.8)$$

into (10.7) and obtain the pair of equations

$$\frac{1}{\sin\theta} \frac{d}{d\theta} \left(\sin\theta \frac{dP}{d\theta} \right) + \lambda P = 0 \qquad (10.9)$$

$$r^2 \frac{d^2}{dr^2} U + 2r \frac{dU}{dr} - \lambda U = 0 \qquad (10.10)$$

---

*The boundary condition is homogeneous if $f = 0$ (Dirichlet) or $df/dx = 0$ (Neumann) or a linear combination of f and df/dx is zero (mixed) at the boundary.

Table 10.1: Legendre polynomials P_0 through P_5.

$P_0(x) = 1$	$P_3(x) = \frac{1}{2}(5x^3 - 3x)$
$P_1(x) = x$	$P_4(x) = \frac{1}{8}(35x^4 - 30x^2 + 3)$
$P_2(x) = \frac{1}{2}(3x^2 - 1)$	$P_5(x) = \frac{1}{8}(63x^5 - 70x^3 + 15x)$

The former equation may be solved by power series expansion in $\cos\theta$. We find that the solution is finite at $\theta = 0$ and $\theta = \pi$ only if $\lambda = n(n+1)$, where n is an integer.

The solution of the radial equation, (10.10), is

$$U(r) = c_1 r^n + c_2 r^{-(n+1)} \tag{10.11}$$

where the constants c_1 and c_2 are determined by the boundary conditions.

It is convenient to rewrite (10.9) as

$$\frac{d}{dx}(1 - x^2)\frac{d}{dx}P_n(x) + n(n+1)P_n(x) = 0 \tag{10.12}$$

by using the change of variable $x = \cos\theta$. Note that this is the Sturm-Liouville equation (10.3) with $p(x) = 1 - x^2$, $q(x) = 0$, $\lambda_n = n(n+1)$, and $\rho(x) = 1$. The power series solution of (10.12) terminates after a finite number of terms, so $P_n(x)$ is a polynomial of degree n.

The most compact way to write the *Legendre polynomial* $P_n(x)$ is by the Rodrigues formula

$$P_n(x) = \frac{1}{2^n n!}\left(\frac{d}{dx}\right)^n (x^2 - 1)^n \tag{10.13}$$

The first few polynomials are listed in Table 10.1 and plotted in Figure 10.1. The Legendre polynomials are orthogonal in the interval $[-1, 1]$ with the normalization

$$\int_{-1}^{1} P_m(x)P_n(x)\,dx = \frac{2}{2n+1}\delta_{m,n} \tag{10.14}$$

Many other Legendre polynomial identities are compiled in Abramowitz and Stegun.

For the purpose of numerical computation, the most useful identity is the recursion relation (see Exercise 10.3),

$$(n+1)P_{n+1}(x) = (2n+1)xP_n(x) - nP_{n-1}(x) \tag{10.15}$$

Since the first two polynomials are trivial to compute $[P_0(x) = 1; P_1(x) = x]$, we may use this recursion relation to bootstrap up to the desired P_n. The

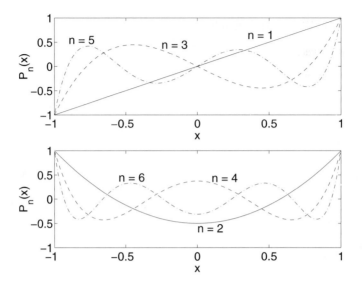

Figure 10.1: Graph of the first few Legendre polynomials, $P_n(x)$. Solid line indicates $n = 1$ and $n = 2$; dashed line is $n = 3$ and $n = 4$; dash-dot line is $n = 5$ and $n = 6$.

function `legndr` returns a vector containing the values $[P_0(x)\ P_1(x)\ \ldots\ P_n(x)]$ (see Table 10.2). To compute P_n using (10.15), we need to compute all the lower index values, so we might as well return them since often they are also needed (e.g., in evaluating the series solution (10.31)). Note that MATLAB has a built-in function, `legendre`, which computes the associated Legendre functions.

Bessel Functions

A ubiquitous PDE in mathematical physics is the Helmholtz equation,

$$\nabla^2 \psi(\mathbf{r}) + k^2 \psi = 0 \qquad (10.16)$$

In cylindrical coordinates it is

$$\left(\frac{1}{\rho} \frac{\partial}{\partial \rho} \rho \frac{\partial}{\partial \rho} + \frac{1}{\rho^2} \frac{\partial^2}{\partial \phi^2} + \frac{\partial^2}{\partial z^2} \right) \psi(\rho, \phi, z) + k^2 \psi = 0 \qquad (10.17)$$

Using the separation of variables substitution, $\psi(\rho, \phi, z) = R(r)Q(\phi)Z(z)$, we find that the equations for Q and Z have solutions

$$
\begin{aligned}
Q(\phi) &= c_1 \cos(m\phi) + c_2 \sin(m\phi) & (10.18) \\
Z(z) &= c_3 \cos(\alpha z) + c_4 \sin(\alpha z) & (10.19)
\end{aligned}
$$

where $c_1, \ldots, c_4$, m, and α are constants fixed by the boundary conditions.

Table 10.2: Outline of function `legndr`, which computes the values of Legendre polynomials $[P_0(x), \ldots, P_n(x)]$ using upward recursion.

- *Inputs*: n, x.

- *Output*: $[P_0(x), \ldots, P_n(x)]$.

- Perform upward recursion using (10.15), starting from $P_0(x) = 1$ and $P_1(x) = x$.

See pages **334** and **336** for program listings.

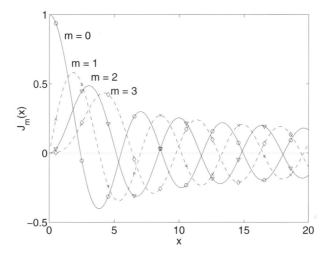

Figure 10.2: Bessel function $J_m(x)$ for $m = 0$ to 3.

The radial component is given by Bessel's equation

$$\rho^2 \frac{d^2 R}{d\rho^2} + \rho \frac{dR}{d\rho} + [(k^2 - \alpha^2)\rho^2 - m^2]R = 0 \qquad (10.20)$$

If we require that R be regular on the z-axis (i.e., finite for $\rho = 0$), the solution is the *Bessel function* of the first kind

$$R(\rho) = J_m(\sqrt{k^2 - \alpha^2}\,\rho) \qquad (10.21)$$

See Figure 10.2 for a plot of $J_m(x)$ for the first few values of m.

To evaluate $J_m(x)$ numerically we make use of the recursion relation (see Exercise 10.7)

$$J_{m-1}(x) = (2m/x)J_m(x) - J_{m+1}(x) \qquad (10.22)$$

Table 10.3: Outline of function `bess`, which returns values of Bessel functions $[J_0(x) \ldots J_m(x)]$.

- *Inputs*: m, x.

- *Output*: $[J_0(x), \ldots, J_m(x)]$.

- Perform downward recursion (10.22) from initial guess.

- Normalize using (10.24) and return requested values.

See pages 334 and 337 for program listings.

There are two reasons why this equation is not as easy to use as the recursion relation for Legendre polynomials. First, the functions $J_0(x)$ and $J_1(x)$ are not as simple to evaluate as the first two Legendre polynomials. There are, however, tabulated polynomial approximations for the low-order Bessel functions.

The more serious difficulty is that when $m > x$ upward recursion is numerically unstable. However, the recursion relation is stable if we iterate downward. To illustrate how this works, let's evaluate $J_0(0.5)$. The idea is to take advantage of the fact that

$$ J_m(x) \approx \frac{1}{\sqrt{2\pi m}} \left(\frac{ex}{2m} \right)^m \qquad \text{as } m \to \infty \qquad (10.23) $$

thus, $J_m(x) \ll 1$ if $m \gg x$. We start the recursion using the (incorrect) values

$$ J_5(0.5) = 0; \qquad J_4(0.5) = 1 $$

The values at this stage are arbitrary since we are going to renormalize the result in a moment. Using (10.22) we obtain

$$ J_3(0.5) = 16; \quad J_2(0.5) = 191; \quad J_1(0.5) = 1512; \quad J_0(0.5) = 5857 $$

Finally, we normalize the values by using the identity (see Exercise 10.8),

$$ J_0(x) + 2J_2(x) + 2J_4(x) + \ldots = 1 \qquad (10.24) $$

Our final result is $J_0(0.5) \approx 5857/6241 = 0.938471$; tables give 0.938470. Of course, our estimate for $J_4(0.5) \approx 1/6241 = 1.6023 \times 10^{-4}$ is not as accurate (tables give 1.6074×10^{-4}). The function `bess`, which computes $[J_0(x), J_1(x),$ $\ldots, J_m(x)]$ using downward recursion, is outlined in Table 10.3. Note that MATLAB has several built-in functions (`besselj`, `bessely`, `besselh`, etc.) that compute the various flavors of the Bessel function.

Zeros of the Bessel Function

The Bessel function $J_m(x)$ is oscillatory in a fashion similar to the trigonometric functions. This fact is evident from the graph of the function (Figure 10.2) and from the asymptotic formula

$$J_m(x) \approx \sqrt{\frac{2}{\pi x}} \cos(x - \frac{\pi}{2}m - \frac{\pi}{4}) \tag{10.25}$$

as $x \to \infty$. Like the trigonometric functions, the Bessel function has an infinite number of zeros, but the zeros of J_m are not evenly spaced.

The sine function satisfies the well-known orthogonality relation

$$\int_0^L \sin(\alpha_i x/L) \sin(\alpha_j x/L)\, dx = \frac{L}{2}\delta_{i,j} \tag{10.26}$$

where $\alpha_i = \pi i$ is the ith zero of $\sin(x)$. The Bessel function, $J_m(x)$, satisfies a similar orthogonality relation

$$\int_0^R J_m(\zeta_{m,s}\rho/R)J_m(\zeta_{m,t}\rho/R)\rho\, d\rho = \frac{R^2}{2}J_{m+1}^2(\zeta_{m,s})\delta_{s,t} \tag{10.27}$$

where $\zeta_{m,s}$ is the sth zero of $J_m(x)$.

Roots of the Bessel function may be computed using Newton's method (Section 4.3). Specifically, the iteration

$$z_{n+1} = z_n - \frac{J_m(z_n)}{J_m'(z_n)}; \qquad J_m'(z) \equiv \frac{d}{dz}J_m(z) \tag{10.28}$$

converges to $z_n = \zeta_{m,s}$ as $n \to \infty$, so long as $z_1 \approx \zeta_{m,s}$ (i.e., initial guess is close to the desired root). For the initial guess, we use the asymptotic formula

$$\zeta_{m,s} \approx \beta - \frac{\mu - 1}{8\beta} - \frac{4(\mu - 1)(7\mu - 31)}{3(8\beta)^3} \tag{10.29}$$

where $\beta = (s + \frac{1}{2}m - \frac{1}{4})\pi$ and $\mu = 4m^2$. This formula is valid for $s \gg m$. If $m \ll s$, then (10.29) is not an accurate estimate for $\zeta_{m,s}$. However, it lands us close enough to the root that we converge after only a few iterations.

Newton's method needs the derivative of $J_m(x)$; this is easy to obtain from the recurrence relation (see Exercise 10.9)

$$J_m'(x) = -J_{m+1}(x) + \frac{m}{x}J_m(x) \tag{10.30}$$

The function `zeroj`, which computes $\zeta_{m,s}$ using Newton's method, is outlined in Table 10.4. For a more advanced algorithm, see Temme [125].

In the next two sections we use special functions to solve some physics problems. You'll discover that we need to solve integrals of special functions, motivating us to find a way of computing them numerically.

Table 10.4: Outline of function `zeroj`, which returns the sth zero of $J_m(x)$.

- *Inputs*: m, s.

- *Output*: $\zeta_{m,s}$.

- Use asymtotic formula (10.29) for initial guess.

- Use Newton's method to locate the root.

See pages 335 and 338 for program listings.

EXERCISES

1. (a) Show that the diffusion equation, $\partial T/\partial t = \kappa \nabla^2 T$, gives the Helmoltz equation after the separation of variables substitution $T(\mathbf{r}, t) = \Theta(t)\psi(\mathbf{r})$. (b) Show that the wave equation, $\partial^2 a/\partial t^2 = c^2 \nabla^2 a$ gives the Helmoltz equation after the separation of variables substitution $a(\mathbf{r}, t) = \Theta(t)\psi(\mathbf{r})$. [Pencil]

2. One of the most useful identities for Legendre polynomials is

$$\frac{1}{\sqrt{1 - 2hx + h^2}} = \sum_{n=0}^{\infty} h^n P_n(x)$$

where the left-hand side is called the *generating function* for $P_n(x)$. Using this identity, show that

$$\frac{1}{|\mathbf{r} - \mathbf{r}'|} = \sum_{n=0}^{\infty} \frac{r_<^n}{r_>^{n+1}} P_n(\cos\theta)$$

where $\mathbf{r}$ and $\mathbf{r}'$ are three-dimensional vectors, $\cos\theta = \mathbf{r} \cdot \mathbf{r}'/|\mathbf{r}||\mathbf{r}'|$, $r_< = \min(|\mathbf{r}|, |\mathbf{r}'|)$, and $r_> = \max(|\mathbf{r}|, |\mathbf{r}'|)$. [Pencil]

3. Using the generating function (see Exercise 10.2), derive the recursion relation (10.15). (Hint: Differentiate with respect to h.) [Pencil]

4. Using the generating function (see Exercise 10.2), show that if n is even, then

$$P_n(0) = \frac{(-1)^{n/2}(n-1)!!}{2^{n/2}(n/2)!}$$

where $n!! = n \times (n-2) \times \ldots \times 5 \times 3 \times 1$ and $P_n(0) = 0$ if n is odd. [Pencil]

5. Using the Rodrigues formula, show that if n is odd, then

$$\int_0^1 P_n(x)\, dx = \frac{(-1)^{(n-1)/2}(n-2)!!}{2^{(n+1)/2}((n+1)/2)!}$$

where $n!! = n \times (n-2) \times \ldots \times 5 \times 3 \times 1$ and $\int_0^1 P_n(x)\, dx = 0$ if n is even. [Pencil]

6. Write a function that finds $\zeta_{n,i}$, the ith root of $P_n(x)$, using Newton's method. The derivative of the Legendre polynomials may be found using,

$$(x^2 - 1)P_n'(x) = nxP_n(x) - nP_{n-1}(x)$$

Since a good initial guess is crucial for locating the right root, you may want to use the following facts: (1) $\zeta_{1,1} = 0$; (2) all the roots are real; and (3) the roots are intertwined, so $\zeta_{n+1,i} < \zeta_{n,i} < \zeta_{n+1,i+1}$. Compare your results with the Gauss-Legendre quadrature nodes (see Table 10.7). [Computer]

7. A useful Bessel function identity is

$$\exp\left[\frac{1}{2}x\left(h - \frac{1}{h}\right)\right] = \sum_{m=-\infty}^{\infty} J_m(x)h^m$$

where the left-hand side is called the generating function of $J_m(x)$. Using this identity derive the recursion relation, Equation (10.22). (Hint: Differentiate with respect to h.) [Pencil]

8. Using the generating function (see Exercise 10.7), derive the normalization identity, Equation (10.24). [Hint: $J_{-m}(x) = (-1)^m J_m(x)$.] [Pencil]

9. Using the generating function (see Exercise 10.7), derive the recursion relation, Equation (10.30). [Pencil]

10. Modify the function bess to use polynomial approximation (see [2]) with upward recursion when $m < x$. Compute $J_2(x)$ using the old and new routines and plot the absolute difference for $0 \le x \le 10$. [Computer]

11. The spherical Bessel function of the first kind is defined as

$$j_m(x) = \sqrt{\frac{\pi}{2x}} J_{m+\frac{1}{2}}(x)$$

Write a function that computes $j_m(x)$ using the recursion relation

$$j_{m-1}(x) + j_{m+1}(x) = \frac{2m+1}{x} j_m(x)$$

Use upward recursion with the starting values $j_0(x) = \sin x/x$ and $j_1(x) = \sin x/x^2 - \cos x/x$. Show that this scheme works well except when $x \ll m$. [Computer]

12. The second solution to Bessel's equation is $Y_m(x)$, the Bessel function of the second kind. Write a function to compute $Y_m(x)$ using upward recursion

$$Y_{m+1} = \frac{2m}{x} Y_m(x) - Y_{m-1}(x)$$

To obtain the starting values for recursion, use the identities

$$Y_0(x) = \frac{2}{\pi}\{\ln(x/2) + \gamma\}J_0(x) - \frac{4}{\pi}\sum_{k=1}^{\infty}(-1)^k \frac{J_{2k}(x)}{k}$$

and

$$J_1(x)Y_0(x) - J_0(x)Y_1(x) = \frac{2}{\pi x}$$

where $\gamma \approx 0.577215664$. Demonstrate your routine by producing plots of $Y_m(x)$ for $0 < x < 50$ and various m. [Computer]

10.2   BASIC NUMERICAL INTEGRATION

Laplace Equation in Spherical Coordinates

As an application of our special functions, we consider the following electrostatics problem. Take a sphere of radius R; the outer surface of the sphere is held at the fixed potential $V(\theta)$. Using (10.8), the solution of Laplace's equation in spherical coordinates for azimuthally symmetric problems is [75]

$$\Phi(r,\theta) = \sum_{n=0}^{\infty}[A_n r^n + B_n r^{-(n+1)}]P_n(\cos\theta) \qquad (10.31)$$

To find the potential everywhere outside the sphere, we need to obtain the coefficients A_n and B_n that match the boundary conditions.

The implicit boundary condition at infinity requires that the potential goes to zero as $r \to \infty$. To meet this requirement, the A_n's must all be zero. Matching the potential at the surface of the sphere

$$V(\theta) = \sum_{n=0}^{\infty} B_n R^{-(n+1)} P_n(\cos\theta) \qquad (10.32)$$

To solve for B_n, we multiply both sides by $P_m(\cos\theta)$ and integrate,

$$
\begin{aligned}
\int_0^\pi & d\theta\,\sin\theta P_m(\cos\theta)V(\theta) \\
&= \int_0^\pi d\theta\,\sin\theta P_m(\cos\theta)\sum_{n=0}^{\infty} B_n R^{-(n+1)}P_n(\cos\theta) \qquad (10.33) \\
&= \sum_{n=0}^{\infty} B_n R^{-(n+1)}\int_0^\pi d\theta\,\sin\theta P_m(\cos\theta)P_n(\cos\theta)
\end{aligned}
$$

Using the orthogonality relation, equation (10.14), we may solve for B_n as

$$
\begin{aligned}
B_n &= \frac{2n+1}{2}R^{n+1}\int_\pi^0 V(\theta)P_n(\cos\theta)\,d(\cos\theta) \\
&= \frac{2n+1}{2}R^{n+1}\int_{-1}^1 V(x)P_n(x)\,dx \qquad (10.34)
\end{aligned}
$$

The problem is now reduced to solving this integral to obtain the B's.

Unfortunately, (10.34) is not always simple to evaluate for an arbitrary potential $V(\theta)$. One example that is not so difficult is the split hemisphere potential

$$V(\theta) = \begin{cases} +V_0 & 0 \le \theta \le \pi/2 \\ -V_0 & \pi/2 < \theta \le \pi \end{cases} \qquad (10.35)$$

where V_0 is a constant. In this case, (see Exercise 10.5) we obtain

$$B_n = V_0 R^{n+1}\left(-\frac{1}{2}\right)^{(n-1)/2}\frac{(2n+1)(n-2)!!}{2[\frac{1}{2}(n+1)]!} \qquad (n \text{ odd}) \qquad (10.36)$$

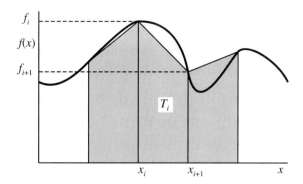

Figure 10.3: General trapezoidal rule for estimating integrals.

and $B_n = 0$ for n even.

Ideally, we would like to compute the coefficients for an arbitrary potential $V(\theta)$. In fact, we may not even know this potential as a function; we may just have a table of values for selected angles. This motivates our study of numerical integration.

Trapezoidal Rule

Consider the integral

$$I = \int_a^b f(x)dx \tag{10.37}$$

Our strategy for estimating I is to evaluate $f(x)$ at a few points and fit a simple curve (e.g., piecewise linear) through these points. First, subdivide the interval $[a, b]$ into $N - 1$ subintervals. Define the points x_i as

$$x_1 = a, \quad x_N = b, \quad x_1 < x_2 < \ldots < x_{N-1} < x_N \tag{10.38}$$

The function is only evaluated at these points, so we use the short-hand notation $f_i \equiv f(x_i)$.

The simplest, most practical quadrature scheme is the *trapezoidal rule*. As illustrated in Figure 10.3, straight lines connect the points, and this piecewise linear function serves as our fitting curve. The integral of this fitting function is easy to compute since it is the sum of the areas of trapezoids. The area of a single trapezoid is

$$T_i = \frac{1}{2}(x_{i+1} - x_i)(f_{i+1} + f_i) \tag{10.39}$$

The true integral is estimated as the sum of the areas of the trapezoids, so

$$I \approx I_T = T_1 + T_2 + \ldots + T_{N-1} \tag{10.40}$$

Notice that the last term in the sum is $N - 1$ since there is one fewer panel than grid point.

The general formula simplifies if we take equally spaced grid points. The spacing is $h = \frac{b-a}{N-1}$, so $x_i = a + (i-1)h$. Our formula for the area of a trapezoid reduces to

$$T_i = \frac{1}{2}h(f_{i+1} + f_i) \tag{10.41}$$

The trapezoidal rule for equally spaced points is

$$
\begin{aligned}
I_T(h) &= \frac{1}{2}hf_1 + hf_2 + hf_3 + \ldots + hf_{N-1} + \frac{1}{2}hf_N \\
&= \frac{1}{2}h(f_1 + f_N) + h\sum_{i=2}^{N-1} f_i \tag{10.42}
\end{aligned}
$$

Notice that for all the interior points the coefficient is h, while on the two exterior points ($i = 1$ and $i = N$) it is $h/2$. This is because each interior point appears in two trapezoids; it is on the right of one trapezoid and on the left of the neighboring trapezoid.

A quick example shows you that something as simple as trapezoidal rule does quite well. Consider the error function

$$\mathrm{erf}(x) = \frac{2}{\sqrt{\pi}} \int_0^x e^{-y^2} dy \tag{10.43}$$

For $x = 1$, $\mathrm{erf}(1) \approx 0.842701$. The trapezoidal rule with $N = 5$ gives a value of 0.83837, which is good to about two decimal places. Of course, the integrand in this example is very smooth and well behaved.

Most numerical analysis texts give the truncation error for trapezoidal rule as

$$I - I_T(h) = -\frac{1}{12}(b-a)h^2 f''(\zeta) \tag{10.44}$$

for some ζ in $[a, b]$. An alternative way of writing the truncation error makes use of the Euler-Maclaurin formula

$$I - I_T(h) = -\frac{1}{12}h^2[f'(b) - f'(a)] + O(h^4) \tag{10.45}$$

Notice that the error is proportional to h^2, and the latter expression warns you that the trapezoidal rule will have difficulties if the derivative diverges at the end points. For example, the integral $\int_0^b \sqrt{x}\,dx$ is problematic (see Exercise 10.13).

Romberg Integration

A common question is, "How many panels should I use?" One way to decide on the number of panels is to repeat the calculation with a smaller interval. If the answer doesn't change significantly, then we accept it as correct. We might get tricked by pathological functions or in unusual scenarios, but don't be paranoid about this. With trapezoidal rule, if the number of panels is a power of two, we can halve the interval size without having to recompute all the points.

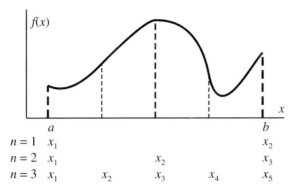

Figure 10.4: Intervals used by recursive trapezoidal rule.

Define the sequence of interval sizes,

$$h_1 = (b - a), \quad h_2 = \frac{1}{2}(b - a), \quad \ldots \quad h_n = \frac{1}{2^{n-1}}(b - a) \tag{10.46}$$

For $n = 1$ we have only one panel, so

$$I_T(h_1) = \frac{1}{2}(b - a)[f(a) + f(b)] = \frac{1}{2}h_1[f(a) + f(b)] \tag{10.47}$$

For $n = 2$, an interior point is added (Figure 10.4) so

$$
\begin{aligned}
I_T(h_2) &= \frac{1}{2}h_2[f(a) + f(b)] + h_2 f(a + h_2) \\
&= \frac{1}{2}I_T(h_1) + h_2 f(a + h_2) \tag{10.48}
\end{aligned}
$$

There is a simple recursive formula for calculating $I_T(h_n)$ using $I_T(h_{n-1})$:

$$I_T(h_n) = \frac{1}{2}I_T(h_{n-1}) + h_n \sum_{i=1}^{2^{n-2}} f[a + (2i - 1)h_n] \tag{10.49}$$

The second term of the right-hand side gives the contribution from the interior points that are added when the interval size is halved (Figure 10.4).

By using the recursive method described above, we can keep adding panels until the answer appears to converge. However, we can greatly improve this process by using a method called *Romberg integration*. I'll first describe the mechanics of Romberg integration and then show you why it works. The method computes a lower-triangular table of the form:

$$
\mathbf{R} = \begin{matrix}
R_{1,1} & - & - & - \\
R_{2,1} & R_{2,2} & - & - \\
R_{3,1} & R_{3,2} & R_{3,3} & - \\
\vdots & \vdots & \vdots & \ddots
\end{matrix} \tag{10.50}
$$

Table 10.5: Outline of function `rombf`, which computes integrals using the Romberg algorithm.

- *Inputs*: a, b, N, $f(x; \lambda)$, λ.

- *Output*: **R**.

- Compute the first term $R_{1,1}$.

- Loop over the desired number of rows, $i = 2, \ldots, N$.

    - Compute the summation in the recursive trapezoidal rule (10.49).
    - Compute Romberg table entries $R_{i,1}, \ldots, R_{i,i}$ using (10.52).

See pages 335 and 338 for program listings.

Table 10.6: Outline of function `errintg`, which returns the integrand of the error function integral.

- *Inputs*: x, λ (not used).

- *Output*: $f = \exp(-x^2)$

See pages 336 and 339 for program listings.

The formula for the first column is just the recursive trapezoidal rule

$$R_{i,1} = I_T(h_i) \tag{10.51}$$

The successive columns to the right are computed using the Richardson extrapolation formula

$$R_{i+1,j+1} = R_{i+1,j} + \frac{1}{4^j - 1}[R_{i+1,j} - R_{i,j}] \tag{10.52}$$

The most accurate estimate for the integral is $R_{N,N}$, the value at the bottom-right corner of the table.

Romberg Integration Routine

The function `rombf` performs Romberg integration for a given integrand and interval (Table 10.5). The integrand, $f(x; \lambda)$, is defined as a separate function with an optional parameter λ. For example, the simple routine `errintg`, outlined in Table 10.6, returns the integrand of the error function (10.43). Working interactively from the command line in MATLAB, we obtain the small Romberg table shown below:

```
>>format long  % Print answer to full precision
>>2/sqrt(pi)*rombf(0,1,3,'errintg',0)

ans =

   0.77174333225805             0                   0
   0.82526295559675    0.84310283004298             0
   0.83836777744121    0.84273605138936    0.84271159947912
```

Our best estimate of the integral is given by the bottom right entry in the table, $R_{3,3}$. Comparing it with the exact result (0.842701), we find that we have almost five digits of accuracy using only four panels! Again, this is a very smooth integrand; life is not always so kind.

It is useful that the function returns the entire table and not just the last entry, since this gives us an estimate on the error. One should not be too eager to use an excessive amount of computer time to make the table as large as possible. Eventually, round-off error begins to degrade the answer (see Exercise 10.13), so it is better to quit while you're ahead.

Why Romberg Works

To understand why the Romberg scheme works, consider the truncation error for trapezoidal rule, $E_T(h_n) = I - I_T(h_n)$. Using (10.45),

$$E_T(h_n) = -\frac{1}{12}h_n^2[f'(b) - f'(a)] + O(h_n^4) \tag{10.53}$$

Since $h_{n+1} = h_n/2$,

$$E_T(h_{n+1}) = -\frac{1}{48}h_n^2[f'(b) - f'(a)] + O(h_n^4) \tag{10.54}$$

Consider the second column of the Romberg table. The truncation error for $R(n + 1, 2)$ is

$$
\begin{aligned}
I - R(n+1,2) &= I - \left\{ I_T(h_{n+1}) + \frac{1}{3}[I_T(h_{n+1}) - I_T(h_n)] \right\} \\
&= E_T(h_{n+1}) + \frac{1}{3}[E_T(h_{n+1}) - E_T(h_n)] \tag{10.55} \\
&= -\left[\frac{1}{48} + \frac{1}{3}\left(\frac{1}{48} - \frac{1}{12} \right) \right] h_n^2[f'(b) - f'(a)] + O(h_n^4) \\
&= O(h_n^4)
\end{aligned}
$$

Notice how the h_n^2 term serendipitously cancels out, leaving us with a truncation error that is of order h_n^4. The next (third) column of the Romberg table removes this term, and so forth.

Returning to the electrostatics problem from the beginning of this section, we wanted to evaluate (10.34) numerically. We could quickly write a program to compute the coefficients B_n using our existing Romberg function. However, remember how the Legendre polynomials are computed using the recursion relation. To get $P_n(x)$ we also compute $P_{n-1}(x)$, ..., $P_0(x)$. It would be wasteful not to make use of these values. In fact, it's not difficult to construct a program that computes all the coefficients, B_n, simultaneously. I'll leave that as an exercise.

EXERCISES

13. Use Romberg integration to numerically evaluate the integrals below:

(a) $\int_0^1 e^x \, dx$ (b) $\int_0^{2\pi} \sin^4(8x)\, dx$ (c) $\int_0^1 \sqrt{x}\, dx$

(d) $\int_0^1 \sqrt{1-x^2}\, dx$ (e) $\int_{-1}^1 P_{10}(x)\, dx$ (f) $\int_{-1}^1 P_{10}^2(x)\, dx$

In each case, evaluate the integral analytically and graph the absolute error for the main diagonal of the Romberg table, $R_{i,i}$, versus i. Show that the error normally decreases with increasing i, but can increase due to round-off. [Computer]

14. A popular integration scheme is Simpson's rule,

$$\int_a^b f(x)\, dx \approx \frac{h}{3}[f(a) + 4f(a+h) + 2f(a+2h) + \ldots$$
$$+ 2f(b-2h) + 4f(b-h) + f(b)]$$

Show that this rule is equivalent to the second column of Romberg integration, that is, $R_{i,2}$. [Pencil]

15. Richardson extrapolation can be used to improve our formulas for estimating derivatives. Take the centered first derivative approximation,

$$D_{i,1} = \frac{f(x+h_i) - f(x-h_i)}{2h_i} = f'(x) + O(h_i^2)$$

with $h_{i+1} = \frac{1}{2}h_i$ and define the Richardson extrapolation

$$D_{i+1,j+1} = D_{i+1,j} + \frac{1}{4^j - 1}[D_{i+1,j} - D_{i,j}]$$

(a) Using Taylor expansion show that $|f'(x) - D_{i,2}| = O(h_i^4)$. [Pencil] (b) Write a function, similar to rombf, that computes the Richardson extrapolation table for derivatives. Test the function by graphing $|f'(x) - D_{i,1}|$ and $|f'(x) - D_{i,i}|$ versus i for $f(x) = \exp(x)$ at $x = 10$ taking $h_1 = 1$. [Computer]

16. Debye theory tells us that the heat capacity of a solid is

$$C_V(T) = 9kN\frac{T^3}{\theta_D^3} \int_0^{\theta_D/T} \frac{x^4 e^x}{(e^x - 1)^2}\, dx$$

where θ_D is the Debye temperature, N is the number of atoms, and k is Boltzmann's constant. Produce a graph of the molar specific heat of copper ($\theta_D = 309$ K) from $T = 0$ K to 1083 K (melting point). [Computer]

17. Write a program to compute and graph $K(x)$, the complete elliptic integral of the first kind (see Section 2.2). [Computer]

18. In Fresnel diffraction you meet the Fresnel integrals,

$$C(w) = \int_0^w \cos(\frac{1}{2}\pi x^2)\, dx \qquad S(w) = \int_0^w \sin(\frac{1}{2}\pi x^2)\, dx$$

Write functions that compute $C(w)$ and $S(w)$, and produce a graph of $S(w)$ versus $C(w)$ for $w = 0$ to 5. Your plot will be a Cornu spiral. [Computer]

19. Write a program to compute the coefficients, B_n, for Equation (10.34). Don't do it by brute force using `rombf`. Instead, write a new Romberg routine designed to use `legndr`. Your program should compute all the coefficients simultaneously. Test your program with the split-sphere potential. [Computer]

20. An azimuthally symmetric potential has a dipole moment of B_1, [see Equation (10.34)]. Modify your program from the previous exercise to evaluate the potentials:

$$\text{(a) } V(\theta) = \cos\theta \qquad \text{(b) } V(\theta) = \cos^3\theta$$

$$\text{(c) } V(\theta) = \begin{cases} 1 & \text{if} \quad \theta < \pi/4 \\ -1 & \text{if} \quad \theta > 3\pi/4 \\ 0 & \text{otherwise} \end{cases}$$

Using the coefficients, produce a contour plot of $\Phi(r, \theta)$. Compare it with the potential for a point dipole with the same dipole moment. [Computer]

21. Consider the following electrostatics problem: A hollow cylinder has radius R and height L. The potential on the top disk is an arbitrary function $V(\rho)$. All other sides are held at zero potential. Show that the separation of variables solution is

$$\Phi(\rho, z) = \sum_{s=1}^{\infty} A_s J_0\left(\zeta_{0,s}\frac{\rho}{R}\right) \sinh\left(\zeta_{0,s}\frac{z}{R}\right)$$

where $\zeta_{0,s}$ is the sth zero of $J_0(x)$. Obtain an explicit expression for the coefficients A_s in terms of $V(\rho)$. [Pencil]

22. Write a program that numerically evaluates the electrostatic potential in the previous exercise by numerically evaluating the integrals and summing the series. Produce a contour plot of $\Phi(\rho, z)$ for the potential (a) $V(\rho) = 1$; (b) $V(\rho) = 1 - \rho/R$; (c) $V(\rho) = e^{-\rho/R}$. [Computer]

10.3 *GAUSSIAN QUADRATURE

Basic Idea

Our original formulation of the trapezoidal rule allows arbitrary values for the grid points x_i. For simplicity, we used evenly spaced points, but can anything be gained if we use uneven intervals? Is there some optimal choice for the location of these grid points? If so, should some panels carry more weight than others? In other words, for an integration formula of the form

$$\int_a^b f(x)\, dx \approx w_1 f(x_1) + \ldots + w_N f(x_N) \tag{10.56}$$

is there an optimal choice for the grid points (or nodes) x_i and the weights w_i?

The questions above lead us to formulate a new class of integration formulas, known collectively as *Gaussian quadrature*. We will use only the most common formula, namely Gauss-Legendre quadrature. There are many other kinds of Gaussian quadrature that treat specific types of integrands. For example, Gauss-Laguerre is optimal for integrals of the form $\int_0^\infty e^{-x} f(x)\, dx$. The derivation of the other Gaussian formulas is similar to our analysis of Gauss-Legendre quadrature.

The theory of Gaussian integration is based on the following theorem. Let $q(x)$ be a polynomial of degree N, such that

$$\int_a^b q(x)\rho(x)x^k\, dx = 0 \tag{10.57}$$

where $k = 0, 1, \ldots, N - 1$ and $\rho(x)$ is a specified weight function. Call x_1, x_2, $\ldots$, x_N the roots of the polynomial $q(x)$. Using these roots as grid points, plus a set of weights w_1, w_2, $\ldots$, w_N, we construct an integration formula of the form

$$\int_a^b f(x)\rho(x)\, dx \approx w_1 f(x_1) + w_2 f(x_2) + \ldots + w_N f(x_N) \tag{10.58}$$

There exists a set of w's for which the integral formula will be *exact* if $f(x)$ is a polynomial of degree $< 2N$.

Think about this for a moment. In general, if we have N data values, we can fit an $N - 1$ degree polynomial to the points. This gives us an integration formula that is exact for polynomials of degree $< N$. However, using Gaussian grid points (along with their weights), we have a formula that is exact for polynomials of degree $< 2N$. If our integrand is well approximated by a high-degree polynomial, then our integral approximation should be very accurate.

Three-Point Gauss-Legendre Rule

To demonstrate the construction of a Gaussian quadrature rule we'll work out the formula for three grid points in the interval $[-1, 1]$ with $\rho(x) = 1$. This gives us a Gaussian-Legendre formula. For integrals in the interval $[a, b]$, it is easy to transform them as

$$\int_a^b f(x)\, dx = \frac{b - a}{2} \int_{-1}^1 f(z)\, dz \tag{10.59}$$

using the change of variable $x = \frac{1}{2}(b + a) + \frac{1}{2}(b - a)z$.

The first step is to find the polynomial $q(x)$. We want a three-point rule, so $q(x)$ is a cubic

$$q(x) = c_0 + c_1 x + c_2 x^2 + c_3 x^3 \tag{10.60}$$

From the theorem, Equation (10.57), we know that

$$\int_{-1}^1 q(x)\, dx = \int_{-1}^1 x q(x)\, dx = \int_{-1}^1 x^2 q(x)\, dx = 0 \tag{10.61}$$

Plugging in and doing each integral, we get the equations

$$2c_0 + \frac{2}{3}c_2 = \frac{2}{3}c_1 + \frac{2}{5}c_3 = \frac{2}{3}c_0 + \frac{2}{5}c_2 = 0 \tag{10.62}$$

A solution of the above equations gives us the polynomial[†]

$$q(x) = \frac{5}{2}x^3 - \frac{3}{2}x \tag{10.63}$$

Notice that this is just the Legendre polynomial $P_3(x)$, a result we might have anticipated given the orthogonality property of these polynomials.

Next we need to find the roots of $q(x) = P_3(x)$. This cubic is easy to factor and its roots are $x_1 = -\sqrt{3/5}$, $x_2 = 0$, $x_3 = \sqrt{3/5}$. Using these grid points in Equation (10.58) gives us

$$\int_{-1}^{1} f(x)dx \approx w_1 f\left(-\sqrt{\frac{3}{5}}\right) + w_2 f(0) + w_3 f\left(\sqrt{\frac{3}{5}}\right) \tag{10.64}$$

Finally, to find the weights, we know that the above formula must be exact for $f(x) = 1, x, \ldots, x^5$. We can use this to work out the values of w_1, w_2, and w_3. It turns out to be sufficient to consider just $f(x) = 1$, x, and x^2. For these three cases, after some computation, we arrive at the three equations

$$\begin{aligned}
2 &= w_1 + w_2 + w_3 \\
0 &= -\sqrt{\frac{3}{5}}w_1 + \sqrt{\frac{3}{5}}w_3 \\
\frac{2}{3} &= \frac{3}{5}w_1 + \frac{3}{5}w_3
\end{aligned} \tag{10.65}$$

This linear system of equations is easy to solve; the solution is $w_1 = \frac{5}{9}$, $w_2 = \frac{8}{9}$, $w_3 = \frac{5}{9}$. An alternative way of finding the weights is to use the identity

$$w_i = \frac{2}{(1 - x_i^2)\{(d/dx)P_N(x_i)\}^2} \qquad i = 1, \ldots, N \tag{10.66}$$

This formula may be derived from the recurrence relation for Legendre polynomials. For our error function example, Equation (10.43), the three-point formula (10.64) gives 0.842690, almost five digits of accuracy!

After working out the grid points and weights in the above example, I must confess that I usually look these values up in tables. Grid points and weights for various values of N are given in Table 10.7; for more extensive tables see Abramowitz and Stegun [2] or Stroud and Secrest [121]. If for some reason you need to compute these, your principal challenge will be to locate all the roots of the polynomial $q(x)$.

There are various advantages and disadvantages in using Gaussian integration: The main benefit is that a very high-order accuracy is obtained for just a

---

[†]The general solution is $c_0 = 0$, $c_1 = -a$, $c_2 = 0$, $c_3 = 5a/3$, where a is some constant. This arbitrary constant cancels out in the second step.

Table 10.7: Grid points and weights for Gauss-Legendre integration.

$\pm x_i$	w_i	$\pm x_i$	w_i
$N = 2$		$N = 8$	
0.5773502692	1.0000000000	0.1834346425	0.3626837834
$N = 3$		0.5255324099	0.3137066459
0.0000000000	0.8888888889	0.7966664774	0.2223810345
0.7745966692	0.5555555556	0.9602898565	0.1012285363
$N = 4$		$N = 12$	
0.3399810436	0.6521451549	0.1252334085	0.2491470458
0.8611363116	0.3478548451	0.3678314990	0.2334925365
$N = 5$		0.5873179543	0.2031674267
0.0000000000	0.5688888889	0.7699026742	0.1600783285
0.5384693101	0.4786286705	0.9041172564	0.1069393260
0.9061798459	0.2369268850	0.9815606342	0.0471753364

few points; often the method yields excellent results, using fewer than 10 points. This is especially useful if $f(x)$ is expensive to compute. There are two main disadvantages: (1) The node points and weights must be computed or obtained from tables. This step is nontrivial if you want to use many node points. Using more than $N = 20$ points is rarely worth it, since badly behaved functions will spoil the results in any case. (2) Unlike Romberg integration, the method does not lend itself to iteration, nor is it easy to estimate the error.

Quantum Perturbation Theory

As a final example of the use of quadrature we consider quantum perturbation theory. The basic idea of perturbation theory is to start with a problem that is easy to solve, for example, the hydrogen atom. Next we change (perturb) the problem slightly; for example, we apply a weak external field. The new problem is often significantly more difficult to solve, even though the solution changes only slightly. Perturbation theory approximates the correction to the solution by making use of the fact that the change is small. The short discussion in this section is only an introduction to the theory; for more details, see any of the standard quantum mechanics texts, such as Saxon [111] or Schiff [112].

We start with the time-independent Schrödinger equation for a particle of mass m_a in a potential $V(\mathbf{r})$

$$\mathcal{H}\psi_n = E_n\psi_n(\mathbf{r}) \tag{10.67}$$

where $\mathcal{H}$ is the Hamiltonian

$$\mathcal{H} = -\frac{\hbar^2}{2m_a}\nabla^2 + V(\mathbf{r}) \tag{10.68}$$

The energy levels and their corresponding wave functions are E_n and ψ_n, respectively. For simplicity, we assume these states are nondegenerate.

Suppose that we know the solution to (10.67) for a given Hamiltonian, $\mathcal{H}^0$, and want to compute an approximate solution for a slightly different Hamiltonian. We'll write our Hamiltonian as

$$\mathcal{H} = \mathcal{H}^0 + \mathcal{H}' \tag{10.69}$$

where $\mathcal{H}'$ is the perturbation. For $\mathcal{H}^0$, the energies and wave functions are

$$\mathcal{H}^0 \psi_n^0 = E_n^0 \psi_n^0 \tag{10.70}$$

The wave functions are assumed to be orthogonal, so

$$\int \psi_n^{0*}(\mathbf{r}) \psi_m^0(\mathbf{r}) \, d\mathbf{r} = \langle \psi_n^0 | \psi_m^0 \rangle = 0 \tag{10.71}$$

if $n \neq m$.

First-order perturbation theory approximates E_n and ψ_n as

$$E_n \approx E_n^0 + E_n' \tag{10.72}$$

$$\psi_n \approx \psi_n^0 + \sum_m a_{mn}' \psi_m^0 \tag{10.73}$$

Using (10.72) and (10.73) in (10.67) we get

$$(\mathcal{H}^0 + \mathcal{H}') \left(\psi_n^0 + \sum_m a_{mn}' \psi_m^0 \right) = (E_n^0 + E_n') \left(\psi_n^0 + \sum_m a_{mn}' \psi_m^0 \right) \tag{10.74}$$

or

$$\mathcal{H}^0 \psi_n^0 + \underline{\mathcal{H}' \psi_n^0} + \underline{\mathcal{H}^0 \sum a_{mn}' \psi_m^0} + \underline{\underline{\mathcal{H}' \sum a_{mn}' \psi_m^0}} =$$
$$E_n^0 \psi_n^0 + \underline{E_n' \psi_n^0} + \underline{E_n^0 \sum a_{mn}' \psi_m^0} + \underline{\underline{E_n' \sum a_{mn}' \psi_m^0}} \tag{10.75}$$

where the first-order terms are underlined and the second-order terms are double underlined. Using (10.70), the zeroth-order terms drop out. Retaining only first-order terms

$$\mathcal{H}' \psi_n^0 + \sum a_{mn}' E_m^0 \psi_m^0 = E_n' \psi_n^0 + E_n^0 \sum a_{mn}' \psi_m^0 \tag{10.76}$$

Applying $\int d\mathbf{r} \, \psi_n^{0*}$ to both sides and knowing that the wave functions are orthogonal

$$E_n' = \frac{\int \psi_n^{0*} \mathcal{H}' \psi_n^0 \, d\mathbf{r}}{\int \psi_n^{0*} \psi_n^0 \, d\mathbf{r}} = \frac{\langle \psi_n^0 | \mathcal{H}' | \psi_n^0 \rangle}{\langle \psi_n^0 | \psi_n^0 \rangle} \tag{10.77}$$

The first-order energy shift due to the perturbation is thus equal to the expectation value of $\mathcal{H}'$.

Particle in a Can

Let's work through an example using perturbation theory. Consider the "particle in a box problem" using cylindrical geometry (i.e., the particle in a can). The container has radius R and height L. Because the particle is confined inside the can, the boundary conditions are

$$\psi(\rho = R, \phi, z) = \psi(\rho, \phi, z = 0) = \psi(\rho, \phi, z = L) = 0 \qquad (10.78)$$

that is, the wave function goes to zero at the interior surface of the can. This boundary condition is equivalent to having a potential that is zero inside the can and infinite at the boundary.

Since the potential inside the can is zero, the Schrödinger equation, (10.67), is the Helmholtz equation, (10.16), with $k^2 = 2m_{\mathrm{a}}E/\hbar^2$. Separation of variables tells us the solution must be of the form [see Equations (10.18), (10.19), and (10.21)]

$$\psi^0(\rho, \phi, z) = J_m(\sqrt{k^2 - \alpha^2}\rho) \quad \times \quad [c_1 \cos(m\phi) + c_2 \sin(m\phi)]$$
$$\times \quad [c_3 \cos(\alpha z) + c_4 \sin(\alpha z)] \qquad (10.79)$$

The boundary condition at $z = 0$ requires that $c_3 = 0$; the condition at $z = L$ tells us that $\alpha = l\pi/L$ where $l = 1, 2, \ldots$. Finally, the boundary condition at $\rho = R$ requires that

$$\sqrt{k^2 - \alpha^2}R = \zeta_{m,n} \qquad (10.80)$$

where $\zeta_{m,n}$ is the nth zero of $J_m(x)$ (see Section 10.1). Thus

$$E_{lmn}^0 = \frac{\hbar^2}{2m_{\mathrm{a}}} \left[\left(\frac{\zeta_{m,n}}{R}\right)^2 + \left(\frac{l\pi}{L}\right)^2 \right] \qquad (10.81)$$

are the unperturbed energy levels for the particle in a can. You can easily check that the lowest energy level occurs when $l = 1$, $m = 0$, $n = 1$. The (unnormalized) ground state wave function is

$$\psi_{101}^0 = J_0\left(\zeta_{0,1}\frac{\rho}{R}\right) \sin\left(\pi\frac{z}{L}\right) \qquad (10.82)$$

If we take the radius and height of the can to be one Bohr radii, the ground state energy for an electron is $E_{101}^0 = 214$ eV.

Now let's apply the perturbation

$$V'(\mathbf{r}) = V_{\mathrm{c}}'\left(\frac{\rho}{R}\right)^\gamma \qquad (10.83)$$

where V_{c}' is a constant. Using (10.77) and (10.82), we find the perturbation of the ground state to be

$$E_{101}' = \frac{\int_0^R d\rho\rho \int_0^{2\pi} d\phi \int_0^L dz (V_{\mathrm{c}}'\rho^\gamma/R^\gamma) J_0^2(\zeta_{0,1}\rho/R) \sin^2(\pi z/L)}{\int_0^R d\rho\rho \int_0^{2\pi} d\phi \int_0^L dz J_0^2(\zeta_{0,1}\rho/R) \sin^2(\pi z/L)} \qquad (10.84)$$

or

$$E'_{101} = \frac{2V'_c}{R^{\gamma+2}} \frac{1}{J_1^2(\zeta_{0,1})} \int_0^R \rho^{1+\gamma} J_0^2(\zeta_{0,1}\rho/R)\, d\rho \qquad (10.85)$$

The problem is now reduced to quadrature, that is, to evaluating the integral in (10.85). I'll leave it for you to finish up (see Exercise 10.28).

EXERCISES

23. Estimate the integrals below using Gaussian quadrature:

(a) $\int_0^5 e^{-x}\, dx$ (b) $\int_0^1 \sqrt{1-x^2}\, dx$ (c) $\int_0^1 \frac{dx}{x}$

(d) $\int_0^1 \frac{\ln x}{x+1}\, dx$ (e) $\int_{-1}^1 P_{10}(x)\, dx$ (f) $\int_{-1}^1 P_{10}^2(x)\, dx$

using the Gauss-Legendre quadrature formula with $N = 4$, 8, and 12 nodes. Compare the error in each case with the exact value of the integral. Note that some of the integrals have singularities. [Computer]

24. Compute the weights and grid points for the two-point Gauss-Laguerre formula,

$$\int_0^\infty e^{-x} f(x)\, dx \approx w_1 f(x_1) + w_2 f(x_2)$$

Test your formula by estimating the integral $\int_0^\infty e^{-x} \cos x\, dx = \frac{1}{2}$. [Pencil]

25. Any polynomials $f(x)$ (degree $< n$) and $g(x)$ (degree $< 2n$) may be written as

$$f(x) = \sum_{i=1}^n \prod_{\substack{j=1 \\ j\neq i}}^n \frac{x - x_j}{x_i - x_j} f(x_i)$$

and $g(x) = Q(x)P_n(x) + f(x)$, where $Q(x)$ is a polynomial of degree $< n$ and $P_n(x)$ is a Legendre polynomial. From this, prove the Gauss-Legendre quadrature theorem: The integral

$$\int_{-1}^1 g(x)\, dx = \sum_{i=1}^n w_i g(x_i)$$

where

$$w_i = \int_{-1}^1 \prod_{\substack{j=1 \\ j\neq i}}^n \frac{x - x_j}{x_i - x_j}\, dx$$

and $x_1, \ldots, x_n$ are the zeros of $P_n(x)$. [Pencil]

26. (a) Show that the period of oscillation for a particle of mass m moving in a potential $V(x)$, which is symmetric about the origin, may be found by solving the integral (see Section 2.2)

$$T = \sqrt{8m} \int_0^{x_m} \frac{dx}{\sqrt{V(x_m) - V(x)}}$$

where $x_m = \max(x)$. (b) Write a program to evaluate this integral using Gaussian quadrature for the potential $V(x) = |x|^\beta$. Produce a contour plot of the integral for $0 < x_m < 4$ and $0 < \beta < 4$. [Computer]

27. Find the 10 lowest energy states of the particle in a can (take $R = L$) by writing a program to compute and sort through all the possibilities. [Computer]

28. (a) Write a program to find the shift in the ground state energy for the perturbed particle in a can [see Equation (10.85)]. Use Gaussian quadrature to evaluate the integral for $\gamma = \frac{1}{2}$, 1, 2, 3, and 4. (b) Repeat part (a) using the perturbation $V'(\mathbf{r}) = V'_c |x/R|^\gamma$ for $\gamma = 1, 2, 3$, and 4. [Computer]

29. (a) Consider a particle in a rectangular box of dimensions $L_x \times L_y \times L_z$. Use separation of variables to solve the Schrödinger equation for the free particle ($V(\mathbf{r}) = 0$ inside the box). Find the eigenfunctions and energy levels. Set up your coordinate system so the origin is in a corner of the box. [Pencil] (b) Using your results from part (a), find the first order energy shift for the ground state due to the perturbation potential $V(x, y, z) = V'_c x / L_x$, where V'_c is a constant. [Pencil] (c) Using your results from part (a), write a program that computes the energy shift, E', for an arbitrary separable potential, i.e., for potentials of the form $V(x, y, z) = V_x(x) V_y(y) V_z(z)$. Set up your program to find the energy shift for any state, not just the ground state. Use your program to find the energy shift in the first excited state for the potential $V(\mathbf{r}) = V'_c \exp(-r^2)$ with $L_x = 1$, $L_y = 2$, and $L_z = 3$. [Computer]

30. Consider the two-dimensional integral

$$I = \int_a^b dx \int_c^d dy \, f(x, y)$$

Write a program that numerically estimates this integral by dividing it into a pair of integrals,

$$I = \int_a^b F(x) \, dx \qquad \text{where} \qquad F(x) = \int_c^d f(x, y) \, dy$$

Test your program by evaluating $\int_0^\pi dx \int_0^\pi dy \, \cos(x + y)$ and $\int_0^1 dx \int_0^1 dy \, (x + y + 1)^{-1}$ using Gaussian quadrature.

31. Using your program from the previous exercise, evaluate the rotational inertia of a thin wedge (Figure 10.5) with $H \ll L$, $H \ll W$. Take $L = 10$, $W = 3$, and the mass $M = 1$. The axis of rotation is perpendicular to the plane of the wedge and through: (a) the center of mass of the wedge; (b) the geometric center of the wedge; (c) one of the corners on the thick edge. Check your answers with the parallel axis theorem. [Computer]

BEYOND THIS CHAPTER

There are many more special functions besides the two discussed in this chapter; there is even a rich family of Bessel functions of which $J_m(x)$ is just one member. Baker presents algorithms for evaluating many special functions and their auxiliaries (e.g., zeros of functions).[13] Recently, special functions have been used increasingly for solving PDEs in nonrectangular coordinate systems by spectral methods.[30]

Recall that our original formulation of the trapezoidal rule, (10.39), allowed us to place grid points at arbitrary locations. Consider the function in Figure 10.6. To evaluate $\int_a^b f(x) \, dx$ accurately, we should use a fine grid spacing

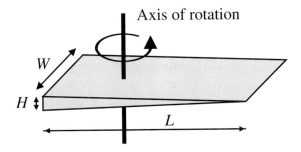

Figure 10.5: Rotating wedge.

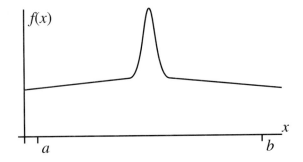

Figure 10.6: Function suitable for adaptive quadrature.

near the center of the interval. On the sides, the function is almost constant; even using a handful of grid points would give us an accurate answer. Integrals like this are suitable for adaptive integration schemes.[39] The idea is to start at one end and lay down grid points as we move across the interval. As we go, we test if the grid size is adequate, increasing or decreasing it as needed. The most commonly used scheme is adaptive Simpson's rule.

The standard quadrature methods may be extended to multidimensional integrals (sometimes called cubature).[120] As long as the number of dimensions is small (six or fewer), their efficiency is competitive. Multidimensional integration can be computation intensive, so high-accuracy techniques, such as Gaussian quadrature, are especially useful. For even higher-dimensional problems it turns out to be more efficient to essentially use the general trapezoidal rule and select the location of the grid points at random. This technique is known as Monte Carlo integration.[61, 79]

The truncation error for Monte Carlo integration is $O(N^{-1/2})$, where N is the number of grid points. For one-dimensional integrals this is very poor, as compared with trapezoidal rule with evenly spaced grid points. The good news is that Monte Carlo integration's truncation error is always $O(N^{-1/2})$, while the truncation error for deterministic rules deteriorates with dimension. For example, the truncation error for trapezoidal rule with evenly spaced grid points is $O(N^{-2/d})$ for a d-dimensional integral.[76]

APPENDIX A: MATLAB LISTINGS

Listing 10A.1 Function `legndr`. Computes Legendre polynomials $[P_n(x) \ldots P_0(x)]$.

```
function p = legndr(n,x)
% Legendre polynomials function
% Inputs
%    n = Highest order polynomial returned
%    x = Value at which polynomial is evaluated
% Output
%    p = Vector containing P(x) for order 0,1,...,n

%* Perform upward recursion
p(1)=1;      % P(x) for n=0
if(n == 0) return; end
p(2)=x;      % P(x) for n=1
for i=3:n+1  % Use upward recursion to obtain other n's
  p(i) = ((2*i-3)*x*p(i-1) - (i-2)*p(i-2))/(i-1);
end
return;
```

Listing 10A.2 Function `bess`. Computes values of Bessel functions $[J_m(x) \ldots J_0(x)]$.

```
function jj = bess(m_max,x)
% Bessel function
% Inputs
%    m_max = Largest desired order
%    x = Value at which Bessel function J(x) is evaluated
% Output
%    jj = Vector of J(x) for all orders <= m_max

%* Perform downward recursion from initial guess
m_top = max(m_max,x)+15;    % Top value of m for recursion
m_top = 2*ceil( m_top/2 );  % Round up to an even number
j(m_top+1) = 0;
j(m_top) = 1;
for m=m_top-2:-1:0          % Downward recursion
  j(m+1) = 2*(m+1)/(x+eps)*j(m+2) - j(m+3);
end

%* Normalize using identity and return requested values
norm = j(1);                % NOTE: Be careful, m=0,1,... but
for m=2:2:m_top             % vector goes j(1),j(2),...
```

```
   norm = norm + 2*j(m+1);
end
for m=0:m_max              % Send back only the values for
   jj(m+1) = j(m+1)/norm;  % m=0,...,m_max and discard values
end                        % for m=m_max+1,...,m_top
```

Listing 10A.3 Function zeroj. Computes the sth zero of $J_m(x)$.

```
function z = zeroj(m_order,n_zero)
% Zeros of the Bessel function J(x)
% Inputs
%   m_order = Order of the Bessel function
%   n_zero  = Index of the zero (first, second, etc.)
% Output
%   z = The "n_zero th" zero of the Bessel function

%* Use asymtotic formula for initial guess
beta = (n_zero + 0.5*m_order - 0.25)*pi;
mu = 4*m_order^2;
z = beta - (mu-1)/(8*beta) - 4*(mu-1)*(7*mu-31)/(3*(8*beta)^3);

%* Use Newton's method to locate the root
for i=1:5
   jj = bess(m_order+1,z);
   % Use the recursion relation to evaluate derivative
   deriv = -jj(m_order+2) + m_order/z * jj(m_order+1);
   z = z - jj(m_order+1)/deriv;   % Newton's root finding
end
return;
```

Listing 10A.4 Function rombf. Computes integrals using the Romberg algorithm.

```
function R = rombf(a,b,N,func,param)
%  Function to compute integrals by Romberg algorithm
%  R = rombf(a,b,N,func,param)
%  Inputs
%    a,b     Lower and upper bound of the integral
%    N       Romberg table is N by N
%    func    Name of integrand function in a string such as
%            func='errintg'.  The calling sequence is func(x,param)
%    param   Set of parameters to be passed to function
%  Output
%    R       Romberg table; Entry R(N,N) is best estimate of
%            the value of the integral

%* Compute the first term R(1,1)
h = b - a;         % This is the coarsest panel size
```

```
np = 1;              % Current number of panels
R(1,1) = h/2 * (feval(func,a,param) + feval(func,b,param));

%* Loop over the desired number of rows, i = 2,...,N
for i=2:N

  %* Compute the summation in the recursive trapezoidal rule
  h = h/2;              % Use panels half the previous size
  np = 2*np;            % Use twice as many panels
  sumT = 0;
  for k=1:2:np-1     % This for loop goes k=1,3,5,...,np-1
    sumT = sumT + feval(func, a + k*h, param);
  end

  %* Compute Romberg table entries R(i,1), R(i,2), ..., R(i,i)
  R(i,1) = 1/2 * R(i-1,1) + h * sumT;
  m = 1;
  for j=2:i
    m = 4*m;
    R(i,j) = R(i,j-1) + (R(i,j-1) - R(i-1,j-1))/(m-1);
  end
end
return;
```

Listing 10A.5 Function errintg. Defines the error function integrand for rombf.

```
function f = errintg(x,param)
% Error function integrand
% Inputs
%    x         Value where integrand is evaluated
%    param     Parameter list (not used)
% Output
%    f         Integrand of the error function
f = exp(-x^2);
return;
```

APPENDIX B: C++ LISTINGS

Listing 10B.1 Function legndr. Computes Legendre polynomials $[P_n(x) \dots P_0(x)]$.

```
#include "NumMeth.h"

void legndr( int n, double x, Matrix& p) {
```

```
// Legendre polynomials function
// Inputs
//    n      Highest order polynomial returned
//    x      Value at which polynomial is evaluated
// Output
//    p      Vector containing P(x) for order 0,1,...,n

  //* Perform upward recursion
  p(1) = 1;        // P(x) for n=0
  if(n == 0) return;
  p(2) = x;        // P(x) for n=1
  // Use upward recursion to obtain other n's
  int i;
  for( i=3; i<=(n+1); i++ )
    p(i) = ((2*i-3)*x*p(i-1) - (i-2)*p(i-2))/(i-1);
}
```

Listing 10B.2 Function bess. Computes values of Bessel functions $[J_m(x) \dots J_0(x)]$.

```
#include "NumMeth.h"

void bess( int m_max, double x, Matrix& jj ) {
// Bessel function
// Inputs
//    m_max  Largest desired order
//    x = Value at which Bessel function J(x) is evaluated
// Output
//    jj = Vector of J(x) for order m = 0, 1, ..., m_max

  //* Perform downward recursion from initial guess
  int maxmx = (m_max > x) ? m_max : ((int)x);  // Max(m,x)
  // Recursion is downward from m_top (which is even)
  int m_top = 2*((int)( (maxmx+15)/2 + 1 ));
  Matrix j(m_top+1);
  j(m_top+1) = 0.0;
  j(m_top) = 1.0;
  double tinyNumber = 1e-16;
  int m;
  for( m=m_top-2; m>=0; m--)          // Downward recursion
    j(m+1) = 2*(m+1)/(x+tinyNumber)*j(m+2) - j(m+3);

  //* Normalize using identity and return requested values
  double norm = j(1);          // NOTE: Be careful, m=0,1,... but
  for( m=2; m<=m_top; m+=2 ) // vector goes j(1),j(2),...
    norm += 2*j(m+1);
  for( m=0; m<=m_max; m++ )   // Send back only the values for
    jj(m+1) = j(m+1)/norm;    // m=0,...,m_max and discard values
}
```

Listing 10B.3 Function zeroj. Computes the sth zero of $J_m(x)$.

```
#include "NumMeth.h"

void bess( int m_max, double x, Matrix& jj ) ;

double zeroj( int m_order, int n_zero) {
// Zeros of the Bessel function J(x)
// Inputs
//   m_order    Order of the Bessel function
//   n_zero     Index of the zero (first, second, etc.)
// Output
//   z          The "n_zero"th zero of the Bessel function

  //* Use asymtotic formula for initial guess
  double beta = (n_zero + 0.5*m_order - 0.25)*(3.141592654);
  double mu = 4*m_order*m_order;
  double beta8 = 8*beta;
  double z = beta - (mu-1)/beta8
            - 4*(mu-1)*(7*mu-31)/(3*beta8*beta8*beta8);

  //* Use Newton's method to locate the root
  Matrix jj(m_order+2);
  int i;  double deriv;
  for( i=1; i<=5; i++ ) {
    bess( m_order+1, z, jj );  // Remember j(1) is J_0(z)
    // Use the recursion relation to evaluate derivative
    deriv = -jj(m_order+2) + m_order/z * jj(m_order+1);
    z -= jj(m_order+1)/deriv;  // Newton's root finding
  }
  return(z);
}
```

Listing 10B.4 Function rombf. Computes integrals using the Romberg algorithm.

```
#include "NumMeth.h"

void rombf( double a, double b, int N,
           double (*func)( double x, Matrix param ),
           Matrix param, Matrix& R) {
//  Function to compute integrals by Romberg algorithm
//  R = rombf(a,b,N,func,param)
//  Inputs
//     a,b    Lower and upper bound of the integral
//     N      Romberg table is N by N
//     func   Integrand function; the calling sequence
//            is: double (*func)( double x, Matrix param )
```

```
//    param  Set of parameters to be passed to function
//  Output
//    R      Romberg table; Entry R(N,N) is best estimate of
//           the value of the integral

  //* Compute the first term R(1,1)
  double h = b - a;      // This is the coarsest panel size
  int np = 1;            // Current number of panels
  R(1,1) = h/2 * ((*func)(a,param) + (*func)(b,param));

  //* Loop over the desired number of rows, i = 2,...,N
  int i,j,k;
  for( i=2; i<=N; i++ ) {

    //* Compute the summation in the recursive trapezoidal rule
    h /= 2.0;            // Use panels half the previous size
    np *= 2;             // Use twice as many panels
    double sumT = 0.0;
    for( k=1; k<=(np-1); k+=2 )
      sumT += (*func)( a + k*h, param);

    //* Compute Romberg table entries R(i,1), R(i,2), ..., R(i,i)
    R(i,1) = 0.5 * R(i-1,1) + h * sumT;
    int m = 1;
    for( j=2; j<=i; j++ ) {
      m *= 4;
      R(i,j) = R(i,j-1) + (R(i,j-1) - R(i-1,j-1))/(m-1);
    }
  }
}
```

Listing 10B.5 Function errintg. Defines the error function integrand for rombf.

```
#include "NumMeth.h"

double errintg( double x, Matrix param) {
// Error function integrand
// Inputs
//    x      Value where integrand is evaluated
//    param  Parameter list (not used)
// Output
//    f      Integrand of the error function
  double f = exp(-x*x);
  return( f );
}
```

Chapter 11

Stochastic Methods

Many methods in computational physics involve a stochastic or random element. Not surprisingly, most applications of stochastic methods are in statistical mechanics. These algorithms are sometimes called Monte Carlo methods in honor of the famous casino in that European city-state. Central to any stochastic method is the generation of random numbers. In this chapter we discuss some basic stochastic techniques and apply them to problems in the kinetic theory of gases.

11.1   KINETIC THEORY

Molecular Dynamics

One of the first applications of probability theory in physics was in the kinetic theory of dilute gases.[*] Consider the following model for a monatomic gas: a system of volume V contains N particles. These particles interact, but since the gas is dilute, the interactions are always two-body collisions. The criterion for a gas to be dilute is that the distance between the particles[†] is large compared to d, the effective diameter of the particles. This effective diameter may be measured, for example, by scattering experiments. Our criterion for a gas to be considered dilute may be written as

$$d \ll \sqrt[3]{V/N} \tag{11.1}$$

An alternative view of this criterion is to say that a gas is dilute if the volume occupied by the particles is a small fraction of the total volume.

The interactions between particles in a dilute gas may be accurately modeled using classical mechanics. Assume the particles interact by a pairwise force that

---

[*]If you're a little rusty on probability theory, you may want to review one of the standard texts, for example Feller [45].

[†]Actually we should say the average distance between the particles, since the particles are not uniformly spaced. We already see the probabilistic formulation creeping in.

depends only on the relative separation

$$\mathbf{F}_{ij} = \mathbf{F}(\mathbf{r}_i - \mathbf{r}_j) = -\mathbf{F}_{ji} \tag{11.2}$$

where $\mathbf{F}_{ij}$ is the force on particle i due to particle j; the positions of the particles are $\mathbf{r}_i$ and $\mathbf{r}_j$, respectively. The explicit form for $\mathbf{F}$ may either be approximated from experimental data or computed theoretically using quantum mechanics.

Once we fix the interparticle force, the dynamics is given by the equation of motion

$$\frac{d^2}{dt^2}\mathbf{r}_i = \frac{1}{m}\sum_{\substack{j=1 \\ j \neq i}}^{N} \mathbf{F}_{ij} \tag{11.3}$$

where m is the mass of a particle. From the initial conditions, in principle, the future state can be computed by evaluating this system of ODEs. This numerical approach is called *molecular dynamics*, and it has been very successful in computing microscopic properties of fluids.[6, 9, 67]

In Boltzmann's time there was no hope of evaluating (11.3) numerically, and even today molecular dynamics is limited to very small systems. To understand the scale of the problem, consider that in a dilute gas at standard temperature and pressure, the number of particles in a cubic centimeter, Loschmidt's number, is 2.687×10^{19}. A molecular dynamics simulation of a dilute gas containing a million particles represents a volume of 0.037 cubic microns. Even on a supercomputer, an hour of computer time will evolve the system for only a few nanoseconds of physical time.

Maxwell-Boltzmann Distribution

Instead of being overwhelmed by the huge numbers, we can use them to our advantage. The basic idea of statistical mechanics is to abandon any attempt to predict the instantaneous state of a single particle. Instead, we obtain probabilities and compute average quantities, for example, the average speed of a particle. The large numbers of particles now work in our favor because even in a very small volume we are averaging over a very large sample.

For a dilute gas we usually take the gas to be ideal; that is, we assume that a particle's energy is all kinetic energy,

$$E(\mathbf{r}, \mathbf{v}) = \frac{1}{2}m|\mathbf{v}|^2 \tag{11.4}$$

In a dilute gas this is a good approximation, since the interparticle forces are short-ranged.

Our starting point is the fundamental axiom of the canonical ensemble [105]: Consider a system at thermodynamic equilibrium with temperature T. The probability that a particle in this system is at a position between $\mathbf{r}$ and $\mathbf{r} + d\mathbf{r}$ with a velocity between $\mathbf{v}$ and $\mathbf{v} + d\mathbf{v}$ is

$$P(\mathbf{r}, \mathbf{v})\, d\mathbf{r} d\mathbf{v} = A \exp(-E(\mathbf{r}, \mathbf{v})/kT)\, d\mathbf{r} d\mathbf{v} \tag{11.5}$$

where $k = 1.38 \times 10^{-23}$ J/K is Boltzmann's constant. The constant A is a normalization that is fixed by the condition that the integral of the probability over all possible states must equal unity. The differential elements, $d\mathbf{r}d\mathbf{v}$, on each side of the equation serve to remind us that $P(\mathbf{r}, \mathbf{v})$ is a *probability density*.

Since a particle's energy is independent of $\mathbf{r}$, the probability density may be written as

$$
\begin{aligned}
P(\mathbf{r}, \mathbf{v}) \, d\mathbf{r}d\mathbf{v} &= [P_{\mathbf{r}}(\mathbf{r})d\mathbf{r}][P_{\mathbf{v}}(\mathbf{v})d\mathbf{v}] \\
&= \left[\frac{1}{V}d\mathbf{r}\right][P_{\mathbf{v}}(\mathbf{v})d\mathbf{v}]
\end{aligned}
\tag{11.6}
$$

The particle is equally likely to be anywhere inside the volume V. For example, suppose that we demark a subregion α inside our system. The probability that the particle is inside α is

$$
\int\int\int_\alpha P_{\mathbf{r}}(\mathbf{r}) \, d\mathbf{r} = \frac{1}{V} \int\int\int_\alpha d\mathbf{r} = \frac{V_\alpha}{V}
\tag{11.7}
$$

where V_α is the volume of subregion α.

We may further simplify our expression for the probability by making use of the isotropy of the distribution. In spherical coordinates, the probability that a particle has a velocity between $\mathbf{v}$ and $\mathbf{v} + d\mathbf{v}$ is

$$
\begin{aligned}
P_{\mathbf{v}}(\mathbf{v}) \, d\mathbf{v} &= P_{\mathbf{v}}(v, \theta, \phi)v^2 \sin\theta \, dv \, d\theta \, d\phi \\
&= A(e^{-\frac{1}{2}mv^2/kT}v^2 \, dv)(\sin\theta \, d\theta)(d\phi)
\end{aligned}
\tag{11.8}
$$

Since the distribution of velocities is isotropic, the angular parts can be integrated to give

$$
P_v(v) \, dv = 4\pi \left(\frac{m}{2\pi kT}\right)^{3/2} v^2 e^{-\frac{1}{2}mv^2/kT} dv
\tag{11.9}
$$

where $P_v(v)dv$ is the probability that a particle's speed is between v and $v + dv$. Notice that we finally fixed the normalization constant A by imposing the condition that $\int_0^\infty P_v(v)dv = 1$. This velocity distribution is known as the *Maxwell-Boltzmann distribution* (see Figure 11.1).

Using (11.9), it is not difficult to compute various average quantities. For example, the average particle speed

$$
\langle v \rangle = \int_0^\infty v P_v(v) \, dv = \frac{2\sqrt{2}}{\sqrt{\pi}} \sqrt{\frac{kT}{m}}
\tag{11.10}
$$

and the root mean square (r.m.s.) particle speed

$$
\sqrt{\langle v^2 \rangle} = \sqrt{\int_0^\infty v^2 P_v(v) \, dv} = \sqrt{3}\sqrt{\frac{kT}{m}}
\tag{11.11}
$$

From this, the average kinetic energy of a particle is,

$$
\langle K \rangle = \langle \frac{1}{2}mv^2 \rangle = \frac{3}{2}kT
\tag{11.12}
$$

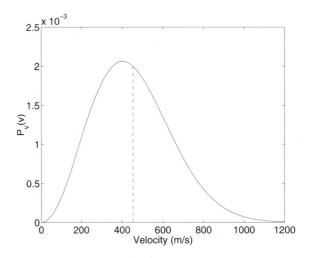

Figure 11.1: Maxwell-Boltzmann distribution of particle speed for nitrogen at $T = 273$ K. The dashed line marks the average speed, $\langle v \rangle$.

in agreement with the equipartition theorem.

Finally, the most probable speed, v_{mp}, is not an average, but rather is the speed at which $P_v(v)$ has a maximum. Solving

$$\left. \frac{d}{dv} P_v(v) \right|_{v=v_{\mathrm{mp}}} = 0 \tag{11.13}$$

gives

$$v_{\mathrm{mp}} = \sqrt{2} \sqrt{\frac{kT}{m}} \tag{11.14}$$

Notice that $v_{\mathrm{mp}} < \langle v \rangle < \sqrt{\langle v^2 \rangle}$, but they are all of comparable magnitude and approximately equal to the speed of sound

$$v_{\mathrm{s}} = \sqrt{\gamma} \sqrt{\frac{kT}{m}} \tag{11.15}$$

where $\gamma = c_{\mathrm{p}}/c_{\mathrm{v}}$ is the ratio of specific heats. In a monatomic gas, $\gamma = 5/3$.

Collision Frequency and Mean Free Path

In general, the particles in a dilute gas interact when their separation is of the order of their effective diameter. While the interaction between particles is continuous, it is also short-ranged, so it is useful to think of the particles as colliding. In the *hard-sphere model* we picture the dilute gas as a cloud of tiny billiard balls of diameter d. Particles collide elastically when their separation equals this diameter. We use this model throughout this chapter because it does a surprisingly good job of representing a real gas.

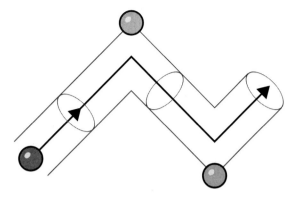

Figure 11.2: Test particle moving amid a field of stationary particles.

The average number of collisions per particle per unit time is called the *collision frequency*, f. A related quantity is the *mean free path*, λ, which is the average distance traveled by a particle between collisions. To compute these two quantities for a hard-sphere gas, consider the following picture. A test particle moves with speed v_r amid a sea of stationary particles (Figure 11.2). The particle travels a zigzag path much like the ball in a pinball machine.[‡] In a time increment t_0, the test particle travels a distance $l = v_r t_0$.

Imagine a cylindrical tube of radius d centered on the path of the test particle. This tube has "elbows" at the locations of collisions, but we approximate its volume as $\pi d^2 l$. The number of stationary particles contained within this cylinder equals the number of collisions experienced by the test particle. On the other hand, since the gas is homogeneous, the number of particles in the tube is

$$
\begin{aligned}
M_{\text{tube}} &= \text{(number of particles per unit volume)} \times \text{(volume of tube)} \\
&= (N/V)(\pi d^2 v_r t_0)
\end{aligned}
\tag{11.16}
$$

which is also the number of collisions in a time t_0.

The collision frequency is

$$
f = \frac{\langle M_{\text{tube}} \rangle}{t_0} = \frac{N}{V} \pi d^2 \langle v_r \rangle
\tag{11.17}
$$

There remains one problem: We don't really have just one moving particle; all particles move. This issue is resolved by identifying $\langle v_r \rangle$ as the average relative speed between particles

$$
\langle v_r \rangle = \langle |\mathbf{v}_1 - \mathbf{v}_2| \rangle = \int \int |\mathbf{v}_1 - \mathbf{v}_2| P_{\mathbf{v}}(\mathbf{v}_1) P_{\mathbf{v}}(\mathbf{v}_2) \, d\mathbf{v}_1 \, d\mathbf{v}_2
$$

[‡]A primitive mechanical entertainment device in common use before the advent of video games.

$$= \frac{4}{\sqrt{\pi}} \sqrt{\frac{kT}{m}} \qquad (11.18)$$

where $P_{\mathbf{v}}(\mathbf{v})$ is given by (11.8). From the collision frequency, the mean free path is obtained as

$$\lambda = \text{(average particle speed)} \times \text{(average time between collisions)}$$

$$= \langle v \rangle \frac{1}{f} = \frac{V}{N\pi d^2} \frac{\langle v \rangle}{\langle v_r \rangle} \qquad (11.19)$$

Using (11.10) and (11.19),

$$\lambda = \frac{V}{\sqrt{2}N\pi d^2} \qquad (11.20)$$

Notice that the mean free path depends only on density and particle diameter; it is independent of temperature.

Using kinetic theory, we can design a numerical simulation of a dilute gas. Instead of solving the deterministic equations of motion, we will build a stochastic model. The probability arguments discussed in this section give us the framework for the numerical scheme. Section 11.2 discusses how to generate random numbers, the foundation of any stochastic method. In Section 11.3, we bring it all together to formulate the Monte Carlo simulation of a dilute gas.

EXERCISES

1.   Plot $\sqrt[3]{V/N}$ as a function of temperature for a dilute gas at one atmosphere of pressure (use ideal gas law). Use a temperature range of 0 K to 500 K; mark the liquification temperatures of nitrogen and oxygen. The effective diameters of N_2 and O_2 are $d = 3.78$ Å and 3.64 Å, respectively. Show that inequality (11.1) is satisfied by air, but not by a wide margin. [Computer]

2.   Using the identities

$$\int_0^\infty e^{-x^2/a^2} dx = \frac{\sqrt{\pi}a}{2}; \qquad \int_0^\infty xe^{-x^2/a^2} dx = \frac{a^2}{2}$$

(a) Confirm that the Maxwell-Boltzmann distribution is correctly normalized. (b) Derive the average speed, (11.10). (c) Derive the r.m.s. speed, (11.11). [Pencil]

3.   Derive the expression for the average relative speed, (11.18), by explicitly solving the integrals. You will probably want to make the change of variable to center-of-mass coordinates. [Pencil]

4.   Define v_a by $\int_0^{v_a} P_v(v)\, dv = a$. In words, the probability that a particle has a speed less than v_a is a; the median velocity is $v_{1/2}$. Write a program that uses quadrature to compute v_a. For nitrogen, plot v_a as a function of temperature for $a = 0.01, 0.5$, and 0.99; also plot $\langle v \rangle$ on the same graph. [Computer]

5.   (a) Plot the mean free path in nitrogen as a function of pressure from 10^{-6} atmospheres to 100 atmospheres. The effective diameter of N_2 is $d = 3.78$ Å; assume $T = 300$ K. (b) Plot the number of particles in a cubic mean free path as a function of pressure. Explain why the number of particles decreases with increasing pressure.

(c) Plot the mean free path in nitrogen as a function of temperature for a pressure of one atmosphere. Find the temperature at which $\lambda = d$ and compare it with the boiling point temperature, 77 K. [Computer]

6. An important model in kinetic theory, and one that is often used in molecular dynamics simulations, is the *hard disk gas*. This is the two-dimensional analog of the hard-sphere gas; the particles are elastic disks moving in a plane. For a dilute hard disk gas, find (a) the most probable speed; (b) the r.m.s. speed; (c) the average relative speed; and (d) the mean free path. [Pencil]

11.2 RANDOM NUMBER GENERATORS

Uniform Deviates

To write a computer program that implements a stochastic algorithm, we first need to know how to generate random numbers. Most languages include a random number generator as one of the functions in their math library.[§] In MAT-LAB, `rand(n)` returns an n×n matrix with each element set to an independent random value. C++ has a random number generator in the `<stdlib.h>` but it is not intended for scientific programming. We'll use our own simple generator, `double rand( long& seed )`, which returns a random value given an integer "seed."

Both the MATLAB and C++ versions of `rand` generate uniform deviates, which means they return random numbers in the interval $[0, 1)$. The distribution is uniform so all values in the interval are equally probable. Using the variable $\Re$ to refer to a uniform deviate

$$P_{\Re}(\Re) = \left\{ \begin{array}{ll} 1 & 0 \leq \Re < 1 \\ 0 & \text{otherwise} \end{array} \right. \tag{11.21}$$

is probability density of $\Re$.

A simple way to generate uniform deviates is by the *linear congruential method*.[81] Given an initial (seed) integer value, I_1, a sequence of integers, I, is generated using the mapping

$$I_{\text{new}} = (aI_{\text{old}} + c) \bmod M \tag{11.22}$$

where a, c, and M are integer constants. As a simple example, if $a = 7$, $c = 0$, and $M = 10$, then one possible sequence is $I = \{3, 1, 7, 9, 3, 1, \ldots\}$. The uniform deviate is computed as $\Re = I_n/M$.

In MATLAB, (11.22) could be computed as

```
I_new  =  floor( rem( a*I_old + c, M ) );
I_old  =  I_new;
R      =  I_new/M;
```

[§]Because these generators use a deterministic algorithm, they are sometimes referred to as pseudorandom number generators. Since the definition of random is problematic, I prefer to avoid these randomer-than-thou arguments.

Since MATLAB has no integer arithmetic, the `rem` (remainder) function is used in place of modulo. See the listing of `rand` (page 395) to see how this is implemented in C++. A possible numerical pitfall is that the integer arithmetic might overflow, that is, exceed the range of allowed integers.

The quality of this generator is highly dependent on the choice of a, c, and M. There is no single, ideal choice because there are many tests for validating generators. A good choice, justified at length by Park and Miller [94], is $a = 7^5$, $c = 0$, and $M = 2^{31} - 1$. If you write your own implementation of this generator, be sure to check that for an initial seed of one the generator returns a seed of 1043618065 after 10000 calls. Notice that if $I_{\text{old}} \neq 0$, then $I_{\text{new}} \neq 0$, since M is a Mersenne prime (do *not* set the seed to zero).

There is considerable superstition regarding how one should set the initial seed. There three schools of thought. (1) Use a simple initial seed such as $I_1 = 1$. (2) Use a large integer. I sometimes use my social security number (which happens to be prime!). (3) Select the seed in a "blind" fashion, for example, by reading the computer's internal clock. I don't feel you can make a convincing argument why any of these is superior. However, no matter how you select the initial seed, you should record its value. For debugging purposes, we often want to run a program using identical conditions, that is, with the same set of random numbers.

Beware of generators whose seed is shorter than 4 bytes. They are unsuitable for scientific work because they have a short period. For example, most implementations of the uniform deviate generator in `<stdlib.h>` repeat the same sequence of numbers after about 33,000 calls.[101] Using $a = 7^5$, $c = 0$, and $M = 2^{31} - 1$, the linear congruential generator has a full period; that is, it repeats after M calls. MATLAB's built-in generator uses a 35 element seed and has a period of $2^{1492} \approx 10^{450}$.

Finally, resist the temptation to "improve" a generator by building a Rube Goldberg machine; for a cautionary tale see Knuth [81]. One allowed exception is to generate a set of numbers and then shuffle them.[104]

Invertible Distributions

The uniform deviate is the basic building block in the construction of most random number generators. Let's start with some simple examples of how it can be transformed to deliver a variety of distributions.

As a simple example, a single random number, x, which is uniformly distributed in the interval $[a, b)$, may be obtained as

$$x = a + (b - a)\Re \tag{11.23}$$

Given two independent uniform deviates, $\Re_1$ and $\Re_2$, their sum, $y = \Re_1 + \Re_2$, is triangle distributed in $[0, 2)$ as

$$P_y(y) = \begin{cases} y & 0 \le y \le 1 \\ 2 - y & 1 \le y \le 2 \end{cases} \tag{11.24}$$

This result may be extended to construct a Gaussian distributed random variable (see Exercise 11.15).

Uniform deviates may be easily transformed to generate random numbers from invertible distributions. A simple example is the exponential distribution

$$P_u(u) = \frac{1}{\lambda} e^{-u/\lambda} \tag{11.25}$$

where $0 \leq u < \infty$. This distribution has mean value $\langle u \rangle = \lambda$ and variance $\langle (u - \langle u \rangle)^2 \rangle = \lambda^2$. Consider a new random variable, R, defined as

$$u = -\lambda \ln(1 - R) \tag{11.26}$$

so

$$R = 1 - e^{-u/\lambda}; \qquad dR = \frac{1}{\lambda} e^{-u/\lambda} du \tag{11.27}$$

Performing this change of variable just as we normally do in integral calculus

$$P_u(u)\, du = 1 \cdot dR = P_R(R)\, dR \tag{11.28}$$

Thus the variable R is uniformly distributed in $[0, 1)$, that is, it is a uniform deviate and $R = \Re$. Using (11.26), an exponentially distributed random value u may be computed as

```
u  =  - lambda * log( 1 - rand(1) );
```

in MATLAB.

A more common distribution is the Gaussian (or normal) distribution

$$P_x(x)\, dx = \frac{1}{\sqrt{2\pi}\sigma} e^{-(x-\mu)^2/2\sigma^2}\, dx \tag{11.29}$$

which has mean value, $\langle x \rangle = \mu$, and a variance, $\langle (x - \langle x \rangle)^2 \rangle = \sigma^2$. You are probably familiar with the polar transformation trick [105] used for integrating a Gaussian; to make the Gaussian an invertible distribution, we play the same game. Consider the product of two similar Gaussian distributions,

$$
\begin{aligned}
P_x(x) P_y(y)\, dx\, dy &= \frac{1}{2\pi\sigma^2} e^{-(x-\mu)^2/2\sigma^2} e^{-(y-\mu)^2/2\sigma^2}\, dx\, dy \\
&= \frac{1}{2\pi\sigma^2} e^{-[(x-\mu)^2+(y-\mu)^2]/2\sigma^2}\, dx\, dy
\end{aligned}
\tag{11.30}
$$

Introducing the polar coordinates, $x = \rho\cos\theta + \mu$ and $y = \rho\sin\theta + \mu$, we have

$$P_\rho(\rho) P_\theta(\theta) \rho\, d\rho\, d\theta = \frac{1}{2\pi\sigma^2} e^{-\rho^2/2\sigma^2} \rho\, d\rho\, d\theta \tag{11.31}$$

If we define a supplementary change of variable,

$$u = \rho^2/2\sigma^2; \qquad R = \frac{1}{2\pi}\theta \tag{11.32}$$

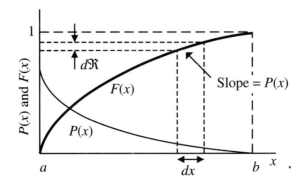

Figure 11.3: Probability distribution $P(x)$ (light line) and its cumulative distribution function $F(x)$ (heavy line). The interval dR is mapped into the interval dx.

then

$$P_u(u)P_R(R)\,du\,dR = (e^{-u}\,du)(1\,dR) \tag{11.33}$$

The variable u is exponentially distributed, while the variable R is uniformly distributed in $[0, 1)$.

This procedure for obtaining Gaussian distributed random numbers is known as the *Box-Muller transformation*. This transformation is used by the C++ function **randn** to generate Gaussian distributed random numbers (see the listing on page 395). MATLAB has a built-in Gaussian generator, **randn**, with a syntax similar to **rand**. Both the C++ and MATLAB generators return Gaussian distributed random values with $\mu = 0$ and $\sigma = 1$. For the general case, transform these values using **sigma*randn(1) + mu** in MATLAB and **sigma*randn(seed) + mu** in C++.

To understand why these transformations work, consider a probability distribution, $P_x(x)$, where x is in the range $[a, b]$. We introduce the cumulative distribution function,

$$F_x(x) = \int_a^x P_x(x')\,dx' \tag{11.34}$$

Note that $F_x(a) = 0$ and $F_x(b) = 1$. Figure 11.3 illustrates a typical distribution $P_x(x)$ and its corresponding $F_x(x)$. Using the cumulative distribution function, we map the interval $[0, 1)$ into the interval $[a, b]$. Where the slope of F is small, the interval $d\Re$ gets mapped into a large interval dx. In this way the transformation correctly maps the uniform deviate $\Re$ into the random variable x.

Once again, consider the exponential distribution (11.25), whose cumulative distribution function is

$$F_u(u) \quad = \quad \int_0^u \frac{1}{\lambda} e^{-u'/\lambda}\,du'$$

$$= \left[-e^{-u'/\lambda}\right]_0^u = 1 - e^{-u/\lambda} \tag{11.35}$$

Setting $F_u(u) = \Re$ and solving for u gives (11.26), our previous transformation for the generation of the exponential distribution. Although the method works in general, if the function $F_x(x)$ is difficult to evaluate or to invert, that is, if either $F_x(x)$ or $F_x^{-1}(\Re)$ does not have a simple form, other techniques may be more efficient.

Discrete Distributions

So far we have considered continuous probability distributions where the random variable is a real number. However, some random processes have only a discrete set of outcomes. Say that the random variable i takes on integer values in the interval $[a, b]$ and is distributed with probability $P_i[i]$. For example, with a die roll, $P_i[1] = P_i[2] = \ldots P_i[6] = \frac{1}{6}$. As a more complicated example, the probability of getting k "heads" when flipping N coins (or one coin N times) is given by the binomial distribution,

$$P_k[k] = \frac{N!}{k!(N-k)!}\left(\frac{1}{2}\right)^N \tag{11.36}$$

where $k = 0, \ldots, N$.

For the die roll example, the random variable i may be generated as $i = \lceil 6\Re \rceil$, where $\Re$ is a uniform deviate in $[0, 1)$. The ceiling of x, $\lceil x \rceil$, is the smallest integer greater than x (i.e., round-up x to an integer). In C++, the random variable i may be generated as

```
int i  =  ceil(6*rand(seed));
```

For the coin toss example, call j the outcome of a single toss. We may select it as $j = \lfloor 2\Re \rfloor$; the floor of x, $\lfloor x \rfloor$, is the largest integer less than x. In MATLAB, we may generate j using

```
j   =  floor(2*rand(1));
```

If k is the number of "heads" out of N tosses, it may be selected as

```
k=0;
for i=1:N
   k = k + floor(2*rand(1));
end
```

or more compactly, k = sum(floor(2*rand(N,1))), in MATLAB.

Another algorithm for evaluating a single coin toss is

```
int j;
if( rand(seed) < 0.5 )
   j = 0;  // Tails
else
   j = 1;  // Heads
```

in C++. This second approach may seem cumbersome, but it has the advantage that it may be easily generalized to handle any discrete probability distribution. A simple algorithm for selecting a random variable i with distribution $P_i[i]$ is to find the value of i that satisfies the condition

$$\sum_{j=a}^{i-1} P_i[j] \leq \Re < \sum_{j=a}^{i} P_i[j] \tag{11.37}$$

with $P_i[a-1] \equiv 0$. In MATLAB, this could be implemented as

```
R = rand(1);   % Uniform deviate in [0,1)
sum = 0;
for j=a:b
  sum = sum + P(j);  % Cumulative sum of P(i)
  if( R < sum )
    i = j;  % Pick this value
    break;  % Jump out of the "for" loop
  end
end
```

We usually need many random values drawn from a distribution. In that case, this algorithm is more efficient if we use the discrete cumulative distribution

$$F_i[i] = \sum_{j=a}^{i} P_i[j] \tag{11.38}$$

We compute F_i once and use it as follows:

```
// Define a, b, and F[j]
...
double R = rand(seed);   // Uniform deviate in [0,1)
int i,j;
for( j=a; j<=b; j++ )
  if( R < F[j] ) {
    i = j;     // Pick this value
    break;     // Jump out of the "for" loop
  }
}
```

The random variable i is selected by the condition

$$F_i[i-1] \leq \Re < F_i[i] \tag{11.39}$$

(Figure 11.4). The simple search scheme above requires, on average, $O(N)$ operations, where N is the number of possible values for i (i.e., $N = b - a + 1$). Typically, a more efficient search algorithm can reduce this to $O(\ln N)$ operations.

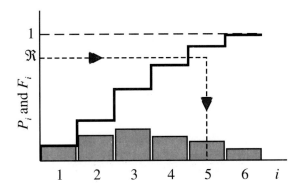

Figure 11.4: Selection of a discrete random number using the generating function. Shaded histogram is $P_i[i]$ and dark staircase is $F_i[i]$.

Acceptance-Rejection

Acceptance-rejection is a useful technique for building generators of arbitrary distributions. It works equally well for both continuous and discrete random variables. The general idea is analogous to throwing darts at a dartboard. There is a low probability of hitting the bull's-eye because its area is a small fraction of the area of the board.

Consider a continuous random variable x distributed in $[a, b)$ with a probability distribution $P_x(x)$. We select a value P_x^{max} with the condition

$$P_x^{max} \geq P_x(x) \tag{11.40}$$

for all x. The scheme for selecting a random value for x is: (1) pick a trial value $x_{try} = a + (b - a)\Re_1$; (2) compute $P(x_{try})$; (3) accept x_{try} as the generated random number if

$$\frac{P_x(x_{try})}{P_x^{max}} \geq \Re_2 \tag{11.41}$$

where $\Re_1$ and $\Re_2$ are independent uniform deviates; and (4) if this condition is not satisfied, x_{try} is rejected, and we return to step (1) and try again.

Figure 11.5 shows a geometric interpretation of this scheme. Picture a rectangle bounded by $x = [a, b)$ and $y = [0, P_x^{max})$. We select a random point (x_{try}, y_{try}) inside this rectangle, where $y_{try} = P_x^{max}\Re_2$. If this point lands in the shaded region [i.e., below the curve $P_x(x)$], then it is accepted. The larger the value of $P_x(x_{try})$, the more likely it is that we'll accept x_{try}. The acceptance-rejection scheme is exact if P_x^{max} satisfies (11.40). However, it is most efficient when $P_x^{max} = \max(P_x(x))$, since this minimizes the number of rejections. Finally, the scheme is easy to adapt to discrete random variables; replace the curve in Figure 11.5 with the histogram of the distribution.

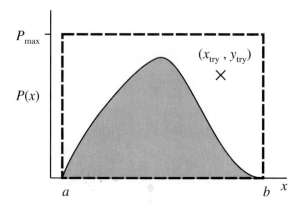

Figure 11.5: Schematic illustrating acceptance-rejection method.

EXERCISES

7. A common way of displaying the distribution of a random variable is by a histogram. Consider the interval $[a,b)$ divided into M sub-intervals (bins) of length $\Delta x = (b-a)/M$. Given a set of N random values of x, call N_j the number of values that fall within the jth interval. The expected value of N_j is

$$\langle N_j \rangle = N \int_{a+(j-1)\Delta x}^{a+j\Delta x} P_x(x)\,dx \approx \frac{N\Delta x}{2}[P_x(a+(j-1)\Delta x) + P_x(a+j\Delta x)]$$

where $P_x(x)$ is the distribution for x. (a) Show that the values returned by the `rand` function are uniformly distributed by counting the number in each bin and plotting the histogram of N_j versus j. Generate $N = 10^3$, 10^4, and 10^6 random numbers, and use $M = 20$ bins. Also plot the expected value $\langle N_j \rangle$ for each bin. (b) Repeat part (a) for exponentially distributed random values generated using (11.26). Take $\lambda = 1$ and $[a,b) = [0,5\lambda)$. (c) Repeat part (a) for Gaussian distributed random values generated using the `randn` function. Take $\mu = 0$, $\sigma = 1$, and $[a,b) = [-4\sigma, 4\sigma)$. [Computer]

8. The moments of a distribution are defined as

$$\langle x^i \rangle = \int_a^b x^i P_x(x)\,dx$$

where the random variable, x, takes values in the interval $[a,b]$. Obtain the moments for the following distributions: (a) uniform deviate; (b) exponential distribution, (11.25); (c) Gaussian distribution, (11.29) for $\mu = 0$. (d) Show that the variance may be written in terms of the first and second moments, $\langle (x - \langle x \rangle)^2 \rangle = \langle x^2 \rangle - \langle x \rangle^2$. Compute the variance of each of the distributions from parts (a) to (c). [Pencil]

9. The moments of a distribution may be estimated given a sample of random numbers from that distribution. Given the numbers x_j, this estimate may be computed as,

$$\langle x^i \rangle \approx \frac{1}{N} \sum_{j=1}^{N} x_j^i$$

Write a program that computes this sum to estimate $i = 1, \ldots, 6$. Compare your numerical estimates with the analytic results from the previous exercise for $N = 10$, 10^2, and 10^4. [Computer]

10. (a) Write a program that generates a vector of 1024 Gaussian distributed random values, computes the discrete Fourier transform using the FFT, and plots the power spectrum (see Section 5.2). This time series is an example of white noise. Produce at least four plots each using a different initial seed. (b) Assemble a time series consisting of white noise plus a sinusoid of amplitude α and a period of 20 data points. Compute the power spectrum for a variety of values of α. In your judgment, what is the minimum value of α for which the sinusoid is distinctly seen in the spectrum. [Computer]

11. An extension of the exponential distribution is the *gamma distribution*,

$$P_x(x)\, dx = \frac{e^{-x} x^{m-1}}{(m-1)!}\, dx$$

where $0 \le x < \infty$. Show that x may be generated using

$$x = -\sum_{i=1}^{m} \ln(1 - \Re_i)$$

where $\Re_i$ is a uniform deviate. [Pencil]

12. Consider a random variable $0 \le x < b$ that is distributed as

$$P_x(x)\, dx = \frac{(n+1)x^n}{b^{n+1}}\, dx$$

Find the transformation that maps the uniform deviate $\Re$ into x. [Pencil]

13. Consider a random variable $0 \le x < \infty$ that is distributed as

$$P_x(x)\, dx = \frac{2}{a^2} x e^{-x^2/a^2}\, dx$$

Find the transformation that maps the uniform deviate $\Re$ into x. [Pencil]

14. The probability distribution for points $\mathbf{r} = (x, y)$ uniformly distributed within a circle of radius R is

$$P_{\mathbf{r}}(\mathbf{r}) = \begin{cases} \frac{1}{\pi R^2} & r \le R \\ 0 & \text{otherwise} \end{cases}$$

Prove that these points may be generated as $x = \sqrt{\Re_1}\cos(2\pi\Re_2)$ and $y = \sqrt{\Re_1}\sin(2\pi\Re_2)$, where $\Re_1$ and $\Re_2$ are independent uniform deviates. [Pencil]

15. One way to obtain a Gaussian distributed random number, x, is to make use of the central limit theorem and compute

$$x = \frac{12}{M} \sum_{i=1}^{M} \left(\Re_i - \frac{1}{2} \right)$$

where the $\Re_i$ is a uniform deviate. (a) Show that $\langle x \rangle = 0$ and $\langle x^2 \rangle = 1$. [Pencil] (b) Write a program that generates 10^6 values of x for $M = 2, 6, 12$, and 24. Plot a histogram of each sequence and show that x is approximately Gaussian distributed when M is sufficiently large. [Computer]

16. The *Poisson distribution* is a discrete probability distribution common in statistical mechanics. It is defined as

$$P_i[i] = \frac{e^{-\lambda}\lambda^i}{i!}$$

where $0 \leq i < \infty$. (a) Write a function that uses the cumulative distribution to generate Poisson-distributed random integers. Assume that λ is never very large so that a simple search algorithm is adequate. Test your function by showing that the mean value $\langle i \rangle = \lambda$. (b) Modify your function to use a more sophisticated search algorithm for large values of λ. For what values of λ does the advanced method pay off? [Computer]

17. (a) Write a function that uses acceptance-rejection to generate the distribution

$$P_x(x)\, dx = \frac{3}{4}(1 - x^2)\, dx$$

where $-1 \leq x \leq 1$. Test your routine by generating 10^6 values and plotting the histogram (see Exercise 11.7). (b) Repeat part (a) for the binomial distribution [Equation (11.36)]. (c) Repeat part (a) for Poisson-distributed random numbers (see Exercise 11.16). [Computer]

18. Consider the dice game known as craps. On the first throw, if you roll 7 or 11 you win; otherwise the roll establishes your "mark." You continue throwing until either you roll your mark (and win) or roll a 7 or an 11 (and lose). Write a program that simulates the continuous playing of craps. Determine (a) the probability of winning; (b) the average number of dice rolls in a game; (c) the probability of rolling 10 times without hitting your mark; (d) the probability of winning if the dice are "loaded" so that the probability of rolling a 1 or 6 is twice as probable as any other die roll. [Computer]

11.3   DIRECT SIMULATION MONTE CARLO

General Algorithm

We now turn to the problem of constructing a numerical simulation for a dilute gas. Again, we don't want to compute the trajectory of every particle. Instead, we'll use kinetic theory to build a stochastic model. The scheme is loosely based on the Boltzmann equation; it was popularized as a practical numerical algorithm by G. A. Bird. He named it direct simulation Monte Carlo (DSMC) [21], and it has been called "the dominant predictive tool in rarefied gas dynamics for the past decade."[90]

The DSMC algorithm is like molecular dynamics in that the state of the system is given by the positions and velocities of the particles, $\{\mathbf{r}_i, \mathbf{v}_i\}$, for $i = 1, \ldots, N$. A useful concept in these types of simulations is that of representative particles. If each particle were to represent only a single molecule, a simulation of ambient air would need about 27 million particles per cubic micron. Instead, each particle in the simulation is assumed to represent N_{ef} molecules in the physical system that are roughly at the same position with roughly the same velocity. The totally democratic dynamics of the real system is represented in the simulation by a parliamentary subset. Of course, the simulation will not be accurate if the number of particles, N, is too small. Surprisingly, using 20 or more particles per cubic mean free path is usually sufficient. The concept of representative particles allows us to rescale length and time to model larger systems. For example, the system volume is $V = (NN_{ef})/n$, where n is the number density.

The evolution of the system is integrated in time steps, τ, which are typically on the order of the mean collision time for a particle. At each time step, the particles are first moved as if they did not interact with each other. Every particle's position is reset as $\mathbf{r}_i(t + \tau) = \mathbf{r}_i(t) + \mathbf{v}_i(t)\tau$. In this section we study homogeneous problems, but formulate the DSMC algorithm for inhomogeneous systems, in anticipation of the next section. After the particles move, some are selected to collide. The rules for this random selection process are obtained from kinetic theory. After the velocities of all colliding particles have been reset, the process is repeated for the next time step.

Collisions

Intuitively, we would want to select only particles that were near each other as collision partners. In other words, particles on opposite sides of the system should not be allowed to interact. To implement this condition, the particles are sorted into spatial cells and only particles in the same cell are allowed to collide. We could invent more complicated schemes, but this one works well, as long as the dimension of a cell is no larger than a mean free path.

In each cell, a set of representative collisions is processed at each time step. All pairs of particles in a cell are considered to be candidate collision partners, regardless of their positions within the cell. In the hard-sphere model, the collision probability for the pair of particles, i and j, is proportional to their relative speed,

$$P_{\text{coll}}[i, j] = \frac{|\mathbf{v}_i - \mathbf{v}_j|}{\sum_{m=1}^{N_c} \sum_{n=1}^{m-1} |\mathbf{v}_m - \mathbf{v}_n|} \qquad (11.42)$$

where N_c is the number of particles in the cell [see Equation (11.17)]. Notice that the denominator serves to normalize this discrete probability distribution.

It would be computationally expensive to use (11.42) directly, because of the double sum in the denominator. Instead, the following acceptance-rejection scheme is used to select collision pairs:

1. A pair of candidate particles, i and j, is chosen at random.

2. Their relative speed, $v_r = |\mathbf{v}_i - \mathbf{v}_j|$, is computed.

3. The pair is accepted as collision partners if $v_r > v_r^{\text{max}}\Re$, where v_r^{max} is the maximum relative velocity in the cell and $\Re$ is a uniform deviate in $[0, 1)$.

4. If the pair is accepted, the collision is processed and the velocities of the particles are reset.

5. After the collision is processed or if the pair is rejected, return to step 1.

This acceptance-rejection procedure exactly selects collision pairs according to (11.42). The method is also exact if we overestimate the value of v_r^{new}, although it is less efficient in the sense that more candidates are rejected. On the whole, it is computationally cheaper to make an intelligent guess that overestimates v_r^{new} rather than recompute it at each time step.

After the collision pair is chosen, their postcollision velocities, $\mathbf{v}_i^*$ and $\mathbf{v}_j^*$, need to be evaluated. Conservation of linear momentum tells us that the center of mass velocity remains unchanged by the collision,

$$\mathbf{v}_{cm} = \frac{1}{2}(\mathbf{v}_i + \mathbf{v}_j) = \frac{1}{2}(\mathbf{v}_i^* + \mathbf{v}_j^*) = \mathbf{v}_{cm}^* \tag{11.43}$$

From conservation of energy, the magnitude of the relative velocity is also unchanged by the collision,

$$v_r = |\mathbf{v}_i - \mathbf{v}_j| = |\mathbf{v}_i^* - \mathbf{v}_j^*| = v_r^* \tag{11.44}$$

Equations (11.43) and (11.44) give us four constraints for the six unknowns in $\mathbf{v}_i^*$ and $\mathbf{v}_j^*$.

The two remaining unknowns are fixed by the angles, θ and ϕ, for the relative velocity

$$\mathbf{v}_r^* = v_r[(\sin\theta\cos\phi)\hat{\mathbf{x}} + (\sin\theta\sin\phi)\hat{\mathbf{y}} + \cos\theta\hat{\mathbf{z}}] \tag{11.45}$$

For the hard-sphere model, these angles are uniformly distributed over the unit sphere. The azimuthal angle is uniformly distributed between 0 and 2π, so it is selected as $\phi = 2\pi\Re_1$. The θ angle is distributed according to the probability density,

$$P_\theta(\theta)\,d\theta = \tfrac{1}{2}\sin\theta\,d\theta \tag{11.46}$$

Using the change of variable $q = \sin\theta$, we have $P_q(q)\,dq = (\tfrac{1}{2})\,dq$, so q is uniformly distributed in the interval $[-1, 1]$. We don't really need to find θ; instead we compute

$$\begin{aligned}
q &= 2\Re_2 - 1 \\
\cos\theta &= q \\
\sin\theta &= \sqrt{1 - q^2}
\end{aligned} \tag{11.47}$$

to use in (11.45). The post-collision velocities are set as

$$\begin{aligned}
\mathbf{v}_i^* &= \mathbf{v}_{cm}^* + \frac{1}{2}\mathbf{v}_r^* \\
\mathbf{v}_j^* &= \mathbf{v}_{cm}^* - \frac{1}{2}\mathbf{v}_r^*
\end{aligned} \tag{11.48}$$

and we go on to select the next collision pair.

Finally we ask, "How many total collisions should take place in a cell during a time step?" From the collision frequency (11.17), the total number of collisions in a cell during a time τ is

$$M_{\text{coll}} = \frac{1}{2} N_c N_{\text{ef}} f \tau = \frac{N_c^2 N_{\text{ef}} \pi d^2 \langle v_r \rangle \tau}{2 V_c} \tag{11.49}$$

where V_c is the volume of the cell. Each collision between simulation particles represents N_{ef} collisions among molecules in the physical system. However, we don't really want to compute $\langle v_r \rangle$, since that involves doing a sum over all $\frac{1}{2} N_c^2$ pairs of particles in the cell.

Recall that collision candidates go through an acceptance-rejection procedure. The ratio of total accepted to total candidates is

$$\frac{M_{\text{coll}}}{M_{\text{cand}}} = \frac{\langle v_r \rangle}{v_r^{\text{max}}} \tag{11.50}$$

since the probability of accepting a pair is proportional to their relative velocity. Using (11.49) and (11.50),

$$M_{\text{cand}} = \frac{N_c^2 N_{\text{ef}} \pi d^2 v_r^{\text{max}} \tau}{2 V_c} \tag{11.51}$$

which tells us how many candidates we should select over a time step τ. Notice that if we set v_r^{max} too high, we still process the same number of collisions on average, but the program is inefficient because many candidates are rejected.

DSMC Program

The program dsmceq, which uses the DSMC algorithm to compute the relaxation of a monatomic gas to thermodynamic equilibrium, is outlined in Table 11.1. The system is assumed to be homogeneous in the y- and z-directions, so only the x-component of position is recorded. While the problem we study in this section is also homogeneous in the x-direction, it is better to construct the more general algorithm for use in the next section. The boundaries at $x = 0$ and $x = L$ are periodic. If a particle crosses the right boundary, it reappears on the left and vice versa (Figure 11.6).

In the dsmceq program, all the particles (argon atoms) have the same initial speed. The y- and z-components of velocity are initially zero, while the x-component is set to $\pm v_{\text{init}}$, where the sign is selected randomly for each particle. We wouldn't want to set all the particle velocities equal, because then the relative velocities would all be zero and collisions would never take place (remember that the boundaries are periodic).

The system is divided into cells along the x direction. The width of a cell, L_c, should be set to a fraction of a mean free path to ensure that a cell is locally homogeneous. The time step is selected as $\tau = a L_c / \langle v \rangle$, where the value of a is set to a fraction less than one ($a = 0.2$ in dsmceq). Thus a particle, on average, will spend several time steps in a cell.

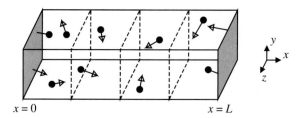

Figure 11.6: Schematic of the dilute gas system simulated by `dsmceq`. Notice that the boundaries at $x = 0, L$ are periodic.

Table 11.1: Outline of program `dsmceq`, which simulates relaxation to equilibrium in a dilute monatomic gas using the DSMC algorithm.

- Initialize constants (m, d, N, etc.).

- Assign random positions and velocities to the particles.

- Plot (MATLAB) or record (C++) the initial speed distribution.

- Initialize the variables used for evaluating collisions (e.g., v_r^{max}).

- Declare structure (MATLAB) or object (C++) for lists used in sorting.

- Loop for the desired number of time steps.

    - Move all the particles ballistically.
    - Sort the particles into cells (see `sorter`, Table 11.2).
    - Evaluate collisions among the particles (see `colider`, Table 11.3).
    - Periodically display the current progress.

- Plot (MATLAB) or record (C++) the final speed distribution.

See pages 375 and 383 for program listings.

Table 11.2: Outline of program `sorter`, which produces sorted lists used to select random particles from a cell.

- *Inputs:* $\{\mathbf{x}_i\}$, L, [sorting Lists].

- *Output:* [sorting Lists].

- Find the cell address for each particle.

- Count the number of particles in each cell.

- Build the index list as cumulative sum of the number of particles in each cell.

- Build cross-reference list.

See pages 376 and 386 for program listings.

Table 11.3: Outline of function `colider`, which is called by `dsmceq` and `dsmcne` to evaluate collisions using the DSMC algorithm.

- *Inputs:* $\{\mathbf{v}_i\}$, $v_r^{\max}$, τ, $M_{\text{cand}}^{\text{extra}}$, $[\frac{1}{2}N_{\text{ef}}\pi d^2 \tau / V_c]$, [sorting lists].

- *Outputs:* $\{\mathbf{v}_i\}$, $v_r^{\max}$, $M_{\text{cand}}^{\text{extra}}$, M_{coll}.

- Loop over cells, processing collisions in each cell.

  − Skip cells with only one particle.

  − Determine number of candidate collision pairs to be selected in this cell.

  − Loop over total number of candidate collision pairs.

    ∗ Pick two particles at random out of this cell.
    ∗ Calculate pair's relative speed.
    ∗ Accept or reject candidate pair according to relative speed.
    ∗ If pair accepted, select post-collision velocities.

See pages 377 and 387 for program listings.

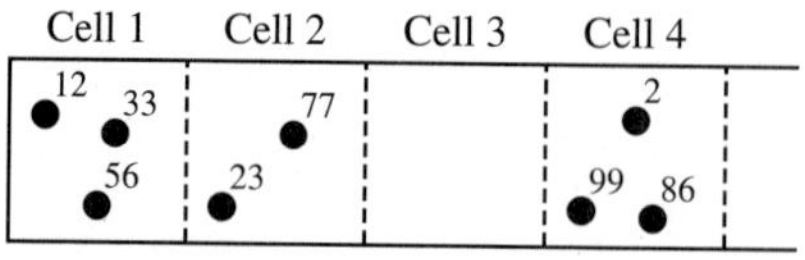

Figure 11.7: Illustration of particle sorting as done by `sorter` function.

The particles are sorted into these cells by the function `sorter` (Table 11.2). This function creates three lists that are used to select particles at random from cells. Figure 11.7 illustrates how the three lists are built. The cross-reference list, `Xref`, is just a list of particle names sorted by their x-coordinate. The number of particles in a cell is given by `cell_n`. Finally, `index` is just the cumulative sum of `cell_n`. When drawing particles at random from a given cell, `index` and `cell_n` tell us where in the cross-reference list `Xref` to look. In the example illustrated in Figure 11.7, suppose that we wanted a random particle from cell 4. We should choose one from `Xref` between 6 (=index(4)) and 8 (=index(4) + cell_n(4) −1). The three candidates are `Xref`(6)=99, `Xref`(7)=2, and `Xref`(8)=86.

The sorting lists are collected into a *structure* in the MATLAB version and into a *class* in the C++ version. This simplifies passing the lists in and out of routines. In MATLAB the structure is declared and initialized as

```
sortData = struct('ncell',ncell,     ...
                  'npart',npart,      ...
                  'cell_n',zeros(ncell,1),  ...
                  'index',zeros(ncell,1),      ...
                  'Xref',zeros(npart,1));
```

The declaration is more complicated in C++ (see the listing on page 396). For both MATLAB and C++, the data elements are accessed as

```
ObjectName.DataElement
```

for example, `sortData.Xref(i)` in MATLAB and `sortData.Xref[i]` in C++. An additional advantage of using a class in C++ is that the memory allocated for these lists is automatically released by the destructor when the class goes out of scope.

The function `colider`, which processes collisions using the DSMC algorithm, is outlined in Table 11.3. For each cell, we first determine the number of collision candidates to be selected. Each candidate pair is drawn at random from the particles in the cell. Given their relative speed, the pair is accepted or rejected; if the pair is accepted, the particles are said to collide. The post-collision velocities of the particles are computed using (11.45) and (11.48).

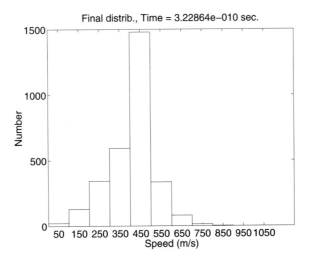

Figure 11.8: Speed distribution as obtained from `dsmceq` for $N = 3000$ particles. After 10 time steps, there have been 2720 collisions.

Initially all particles in the `dsmceq` program have a speed of 413 m/s. Figure 11.8 shows the distribution after 10 steps (and 2720 collisions) for a system of 3000 particles. At this point, the distribution has already significantly relaxed toward equilibrium despite the extremely improbable initial condition and despite the fact that each particle has only been in fewer than two collisions. Figure 11.9 shows the distribution after 50 steps (and 14,555 collisions). This latter histogram shows that the system has almost completely relaxed to equilibrium in about a nanosecond.

EXERCISES

19. Show that in a collision, the magnitude of the relative velocity remains unchanged. Is this result modified if the particles have dissimilar masses? [Pencil]

20. Modify `dsmceq` to compute the expected equilibrium speed distribution histogram using the Maxwell-Boltzmann distribution (see Exercise 11.7). Plot this distribution along with the measured speed distribution histogram and demonstrate that the program correctly approaches equilibrium. [Computer]

21. Modify `dsmceq` to compute

$$H(t) = \sum_{\text{bins}} \Delta v \frac{N_h(v)}{N} \ln \frac{N_h(v)}{N}$$

where $N_h(v)$ is the number of particles in a histogram bin of width Δv (see Exercise 11.7). This H-function is proportional to the entropy in the system.[15] Show that for a system initially out of equilibrium, H decreases with time until the system equilibrates. [Computer]

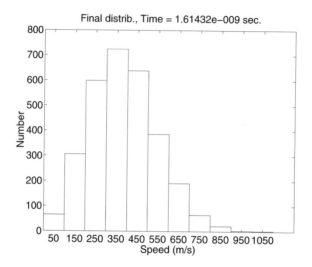

Figure 11.9: Speed distribution as obtained from `dsmceq` for $N = 3000$ particles. After 50 time steps, there have been 14,555 collisions.

22. Modify `dsmceq` to use specular walls instead of periodic boundaries at $x = 0, L$. At a specular wall, a particle is reflected elastically. The pressure at a wall is defined as the time-averaged change in momentum of particles that strike the wall per unit area. Initialize the particles with a Maxwell-Boltzmann distribution and measure the pressure at the walls. Compare with the expected value as given by the ideal gas law. [Computer]

23. Modify your program from the previous exercise to measure the x-velocity distribution of particles that strike a wall. Plot this distribution as a histogram (see Exercise 11.7). Show that particles arriving at a wall are distributed according to the biased Maxwell-Boltzmann distribution,

$$P_{v_x}(v_x) = \pm \frac{m}{kT} v_x e^{-mv_x^2/2kT}$$

with the sign being plus for the right wall and minus for the left wall. [Computer]

24. Modify `dsmceq` to measure the mean free path, λ, of the particles. Note that the program only records the x-component of position while λ is the average three-dimensional distance traveled by a particle between collisions. Confirm that your measurement agrees with (11.20). [Computer]

25. While the total number of particles in the `dsmceq` program remains constant, the number of particles in a given cell fluctuates. Sample and compute the correlation in number density between cells. Compare with the theoretical result,

$$\langle \Delta N_i \Delta N_j \rangle = \langle N_i \rangle \delta_{i,j} - \frac{\langle N_i \rangle \langle N_j \rangle}{\sum_k \langle N_k \rangle}$$

where $\langle N_i \rangle$ is the average number of particles in cell i and ΔN_i is the fluctuation in the number of particles (i.e., $\Delta N_i = N_i - \langle N_i \rangle$). [Computer]

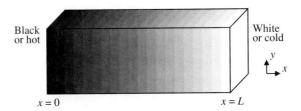

Figure 11.10: Schematic illustrating a nonequilibrium steady state with a constant pigment (or temperature) gradient.

11.4 *NONEQUILIBRIUM STATES

Steady States

The statistical mechanics of equilibrium systems is well developed, resting on the firm foundation of ensemble theory. Unfortunately, we have no similar general theory for nonequilibrium systems. As such, it would be overly ambitious to start off trying to tackle a complex problem such as turbulence. In this section we consider simple systems that are out of equilibrium, but at a steady state. In other words, quantities such as density and temperature may vary in space but are stationary in time.

As a first example of a nonequilibrium steady state, consider a dilute gas in a box of length L and cross section A. Suppose that the particles are tinted either black or white. Particles that reflect off the left wall are turned black, while those contacting the right wall are turned white. A particle's pigmentation is unaffected by reflections off the other walls or by collisions. After a time, we reach a steady state, as illustrated in Figure 11.10.

In this system, black particles diffuse to the right and white particles diffuse to the left. This means there is a net flux of pigment in the system. If we assume that the flux, F_ρ, is proportional to the gradient of pigment, then

$$F_\rho = -D\frac{\partial}{\partial x}\rho(x,t) \tag{11.52}$$

where $\rho(x,t)$ is the density of pigment and the constant of proportionality, D, is the coefficient of diffusion. Notice the negative sign on the right-hand side of this equation; if pigment increases from right to left (negative gradient), then the flux is from left to right (positive flux).

The time evolution is given by the equation of continuity,

$$\frac{\partial}{\partial t}\rho(x,t) \;=\; -\frac{\partial}{\partial x}F_\rho \tag{11.53}$$

$$=\; D\frac{\partial^2}{\partial x^2}\rho \tag{11.54}$$

At the steady state, the flux must be constant across the system. Thus,

$$\rho(x) = 1 - x/L \tag{11.55}$$

given the boundary conditions $\rho(0) = 1$ and $\rho(L) = 0$.

Consider Figure 11.10 again, but instead of having the walls of different pigment, set them at different temperatures. Particles leaving the hot, left wall have, on average, a large kinetic energy as compared with those leaving the cold, right wall. The scenario is slightly more complicated because, unlike pigment, kinetic energy is exchanged in collisions. The general picture, however, remains the same.

We define the number density, $n(x, t)$, as the number of particles per unit volume and the energy density, $e(x, t)$, as the kinetic energy per unit volume. At the particle level, they are defined as

$$n(x, t) = \frac{1}{A dx} \sum_{i=1}^{N} \delta[x \le x_i < x + dx] \tag{11.56}$$

$$e(x, t) = \frac{1}{A dx} \sum_{i=1}^{N} \frac{1}{2} m v_i^2 \delta[x \le x_i < x + dx] \tag{11.57}$$

where

$$\delta[x \le x_i < x + dx] = \begin{cases} 1 & x \le x_i < x + dx \\ 0 & \text{otherwise} \end{cases} \tag{11.58}$$

The sums are over all N particles, but with the Kronecker delta functions only particles located between x and $x + dx$ are counted. These are strictly mechanical variables, so there is no problem with their definition.

Next, we use the equipartition theorem, (11.12), to define a local, instantaneous temperature as

$$T(x, t) \equiv \frac{2}{3k} \frac{e(x, t)}{n(x, t)} \tag{11.59}$$

Aside from a conversion factor involving Boltzmann's constant k, this temperature is the average kinetic energy per particle. If you've had a rigorous training in equilibrium statistical mechanics, you should instinctively cringe at (11.59). The proper thermodynamic definition of temperature is based on entropy and involves an average over an ensemble of states. All the same, it is useful to extend definitions of thermodynamic quantities, such as temperature, to nonequilibrium systems by using equilibrium identities, such as the equipartition theorem.[87]

Returning to the problem at hand, the energy flux through the system is

$$F_e = -\alpha \frac{\partial}{\partial x} T(x, t) \tag{11.60}$$

where α is the thermal conductivity. A related quantity is the thermal diffusion coefficient, κ (for a dilute, monatomic gas, $\kappa = 2\alpha/3kn$). If the thermal conductivity is a constant, there is a linear temperature gradient across the system.

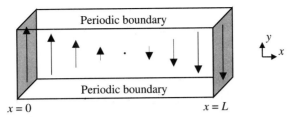

Figure 11.11: Planar Couette flow. Left and right walls move at constant velocities in opposite directions. The steady state velocity profile in the fluid is linear [Equation (11.62)].

Viscosity

Consider a dilute gas contained between two walls moving in opposite directions, with velocities $\pm u_{\mathrm{w}}$ in the y-direction (Figure 11.11). You can picture the walls as infinite planes or take the boundaries perpendicular to the walls to be periodic. This simple flow problem is called planar Couette flow.

The momentum density per unit volume is defined as

$$\mathbf{p}(x,t) = \frac{1}{A\,dx} \sum_{i=1}^{N} m\mathbf{v}_i \delta[x \leq x_i < x + dx] \qquad (11.61)$$

where $\mathbf{v}_i$ is the velocity of particle i. The fluid velocity is defined as $\mathbf{u}(x,t) = \mathbf{p}(x,t)/mn(x,t)$. At the steady state the velocity of the fluid is

$$\mathbf{u}(x) = u_{\mathrm{w}}\left(\frac{2x}{L} - 1\right)\hat{\mathbf{y}} \qquad (11.62)$$

that is, we have a linear velocity profile across the system. Particles leave the left (right) wall with a net downward (upward) momentum, and this y-momentum diffuses across the system. Assuming the net flux of y-momentum varies linearly with the velocity gradient, we may write it as

$$F_{p_y} = -\eta \frac{\partial}{\partial x} u_y(x,t) \qquad (11.63)$$

where u_y is the y-component of the fluid velocity and η is the *viscosity* of the fluid.

Before continuing, let's reconcile this definition with your intuitive notions about viscosity. Picture a highly viscous fluid, say syrup, in a cup. If we quickly stir the syrup then let it relax, the motion quickly comes to a halt. The reason is that the syrup quickly transports its momentum to the sides of the cup. The faster the rate of transport, the more viscous the fluid.

We can obtain an approximate expression for the viscosity of a dilute gas using a heuristic argument first proposed by Maxwell. Consider a vertical plane located at $x = x^*$ (Figure 11.12). From purely dimensional arguments, we

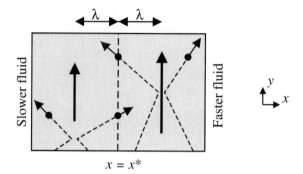

Figure 11.12: Schematic for Maxwell's back-of-the-envelope estimate of viscosity.

know that the total flux of particles crossing this plane from right to left is $a\langle v\rangle n$, where n is the number density and a is a dimensionless constant of order unity.

Particles crossing from right to left had their last contact with other particles at a distance of about one mean free path from the plane (see Figure 11.12). Since the y-velocity of the fluid is $u_y(x)$, these particles, on average, carry a y-momentum of $mu_y(x^* + \lambda)$. Similarly, particles crossing from left to right, on average, carry a y-momentum of $mu_y(x^* - \lambda)$. Assembling our results, the y-momentum flux is approximately

$$F_{p_y}(x^*) \approx [a\langle v\rangle nmu_y(x^* - \lambda)] - [a\langle v\rangle nmu_y(x^* + \lambda)]$$

$$= -2a\langle v\rangle nm\lambda \left(\frac{u_y(x^* + \lambda) - u_y(x^* - \lambda)}{2\lambda} \right) \tag{11.64}$$

$$\approx -2a\langle v\rangle nm\lambda \left. \frac{du_y}{dx}\right|_{x=x^*} \tag{11.65}$$

From (11.63), the viscosity is

$$\eta \approx 2anm\langle v\rangle\lambda \tag{11.66}$$

Using slightly more sophisticated derivations we find that a lies between $\frac{1}{6}$ and $\frac{1}{4}$. Using a significantly more rigorous approach (Chapman-Enskog theory) we find

$$\eta = \frac{5\pi}{32}nm\langle v\rangle\lambda \tag{11.67}$$

for a hard-sphere gas.[87]

DSMC Nonequilibrium Program

The program dsmcne, which simulates planar Couette flow in a dilute gas, is outlined in Table 11.4. The particles (argon atoms) are initialized near the steady

Table 11.4: Outline of program `dsmcne`, which simulates planar Couette flow in a dilute gas using the DSMC algorithm.

- Initialize constants (m, d, N, etc.).

- Assign random positions and velocities to particles.

- Initialize variables used for evaluating collisions (e.g., v_r^{max}).

- Declare structure (MATLAB) or object (C++) for lists used in sorting.

- Initialize structure and variables used in statistical sampling.

- Loop for the desired number of time steps.

  - Move all the particles (see `mover`, Table 11.5).
  - Sort the particles into cells (see `sorter`, Table 11.2).
  - Evaluate collisions among the particles (see `colider`, Table 11.3).
  - After initial transient, accumulate statistical samples (see `sampler`, Table 11.6).
  - Periodically display the current progress.

- Normalize the accumulated statistics.

- Compute viscosity from drag force on the walls.

- Plot average density, velocity and temperature.

See pages 379 and 389 for program listings.

state with temperature T. Their thermal velocities are set as Gaussian distributed random numbers with $\sigma = \sqrt{kT/m}$. Furthermore, a linear y-velocity profile (11.62) is set up across the system. The wall speed is entered in terms of Mach number, $\text{Ma} \equiv u_w/v_s$, where v_s is the sound speed. We want to use a high wall speed (e.g., $\text{Ma} = 0.2$) to make the velocity profile noticeable above the random fluctuations in the system (remember that we use only a few thousand particles).

As in the program from Section 11.3, the routine `sorter` (Table 11.2) is used to sort the particles into cells and the routine `colide` (Table 11.3) evaluates collisions in those cells. The function `mover` (Table 11.5) moves the particles and evaluates reflections off the thermal walls at $x = 0, L$. When a particle reaches a wall, its velocity is reset according to the biased Maxwellian distribution,

$$P_{v_x}(v_x) = \pm \frac{m}{kT_w} v_x e^{-mv_x^2/2kT_w} \tag{11.68}$$

$x = 0$ 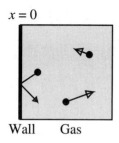 $x = 0$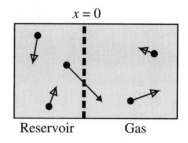

Wall   Gas   Reservoir   Gas

Figure 11.13: Equivalence of a thermal wall and a thermal reservoir.

$$P_{v_y}(v_y) \quad = \quad \sqrt{\frac{m}{2\pi kT_\mathrm{w}}} e^{-m(v_y - u_\mathrm{w})^2 / 2kT_\mathrm{w}} \tag{11.69}$$

$$P_{v_z}(v_z) \quad = \quad \sqrt{\frac{m}{2\pi kT_\mathrm{w}}} e^{-mv_z^2 / 2kT_\mathrm{w}} \tag{11.70}$$

where u_w and T_w are the y-velocity and temperature of the wall, respectively. The sign on the x-velocity is positive for the left wall and negative for the right wall. After a particle's velocity is thermalized, it is allowed to move away from the wall for whatever fraction of the time step remains.

To understand why the v_x distribution is biased, consider Figure 11.13. On the left we have a fluid at equilibrium with a thermal wall. The picture on the right is similar, except the wall has been replaced with a reservoir of fluid held at the same temperature as the wall. Particles reflected off a thermal wall should have the same distribution as particles entering the system from a thermal reservoir at temperature T_w. Clearly, the distribution is biased toward particles with a higher x-component of velocity since those are more likely to cross the boundary. If it is still not clear how this works, do Exercise 11.23.

After an initial relaxation period, the `dsmcne` program calls the routine `sampler` (Table 11.6) to sample the cells. This routine measures the instantaneous number density, fluid velocity, and temperature in each cell and accumulates the results as running sums. As with the sorting lists, a structure (in MATLAB) or class (in C++) is used to collect the sampling data into a single object. At the end of the run, this data is normalized by the number of measured samples and used to plot number density, fluid velocity, and temperature versus x.

Notice that the instantaneous thermal kinetic energy density in cell j is defined as

$$e_j(t) = \frac{1}{V_c} \sum_{i \text{ inside } j} \frac{1}{2} m |\mathbf{v}_i - \mathbf{u}_j|^2 \tag{11.71}$$

where the sum runs over all the particles within cell j and $\mathbf{u}_j$ is the instantaneous fluid velocity in the cell. Since the fluid is moving, we have to remove the center of mass kinetic energy when computing the thermal kinetic energy. This energy density is used to obtain the instantaneous temperature from (11.59).

Table 11.5: Outline of function `mover`, which is called by the `dsmcne` program to update particle positions. It also evaluates particles' impacts with the thermal walls.

- *Inputs:* $\{\mathbf{x}_i\}$, $\{\mathbf{v}_i\}$, N, L, v_{mp}, v_{wall}, τ.

- *Outputs:* $\{\mathbf{x}_i\}$, $\{\mathbf{v}_i\}$, M_{strikes}, Δv_{wall}.

- Move all particles, pretending walls are absent.

- Loop over all particles.

  - Test if particle strikes either wall.

  - If particle strikes a wall,

    * Reset velocity components as biased Maxwellian, (11.68), (11.69), and (11.70).
    * Reset position after leaving wall.
    * Record velocity change for force measurement.

See pages 381 and 392 for program listings.

Table 11.6: Outline of function `sampler`, which is called by the `dsmcne` program to sample the number density, fluid velocity, and temperature in the cells.

- *Inputs:* $\{\mathbf{x}_i\}$, $\{\mathbf{v}_i\}$, N, L, [sampling lists].

- *Outputs:* [sampling lists].

- Compute cell location for each particle.

- Initialize running sums of number, velocity and v^2.

- For each particle, accumulate running sums for its cell.

- Use current sums to update sample number, velocity, and temperature for each cell.

See pages 382 and 394 for program listings.

The total y-momentum flux, F_{p_y}, may be measured from the change in momentum of particles that reflect off the walls. From the momentum-impulse theorem, this flux is related to the time-average drag force on a wall as

$$\langle f_{\text{drag}} \rangle = -\frac{1}{t} \sum m \Delta v_y = -\langle F_{p_y} \rangle \tag{11.72}$$

where Δv_y is the change in y-velocity for a particle striking the wall. The sum is over all particle collisions with the wall over a time t. The change in velocity is measured by the routine mover. The average viscosity is then

$$\eta = \frac{\langle f_{\text{drag}} \rangle}{du_y / dx} \tag{11.73}$$

The dsmcne program computes a viscosity from the measured drag force at each wall.

For the density and temperature used in the simulation, Chapman-Enskog theory predicts a viscosity for argon gas of $\eta = 2.08 \times 10^{-5}$ N $\cdot$ s/m^2. For a short run (1000 steps) using 3000 particles and a wall speed of $u_w = 0.2$ Ma, the dsmcne program obtains the estimate of $\eta = 2.29 \pm 0.55 \times 10^{-5}$ N $\cdot$ s/m^2; the answer is reasonable but the error bar is unacceptably large. Doing a longer run (50,000 steps), we get the more satisfying value of $\eta = 2.12 \pm 0.08 \times 10^{-5}$ N $\cdot$ s/m^2. You should come to the conclusion that Monte Carlo simulations, by their statistical nature, often require long runs to accumulate enough statistical samples.

EXERCISES

26. In a dilute hard-sphere gas, the thermal diffusivity varies with temperature as $\kappa(T) = \kappa_0 \sqrt{T}$, where κ_0 is a constant. (a) Solve the diffusion equation,

$$\frac{\partial T}{\partial t} = \frac{\partial}{\partial x} \kappa \frac{\partial}{\partial x} T(x, t)$$

and find the steady state temperature profile in a one-dimensional system with boundary conditions $T(x = 0) = T_a$ and $T(x = L) = T_b$. [Pencil] (b) Plot your solution for $T_a = 300$K, $T_b = 400$K, and compare with the linear profile obtained when we assume κ is a constant. [Computer]

27. Modify dsmcne so that particles are labeled "black" or "white." Particles that reflect off a wall are turned black with probability q and white with probablity $(1 - q)$. Set the walls at equal temperature and make them stationary; give them different values of q to set up a pigmentation gradient across the system (see Figure 11.10). Measure the average pigment flux, and compute the self-diffusion coefficient using (11.54). Compare your results with

$$D = \frac{6\pi}{32} \langle v \rangle \lambda$$

the value given by Chapman-Enskog theory. [Computer]

28. Modify dsmcne to measure energy flux, F_e, in a system with a temperature gradient. Set up your simulation with stationary walls at different temperatures.

Compute thermal conductivity, α, and compare your results with $\alpha = 15\eta k/4m$, the value given by Chapman-Enskog theory. [Computer]

29. For the small systems simulated by the dsmcne program, our definition of temperature does not exactly reproduce the correct thermodynamic temperature. (a) Do several runs at thermodynamic equilibrium (i.e., zero wall speed) and show that the time average of the instantaneous temperature is

$$\langle T \rangle = \frac{\langle N_c \rangle}{\langle N_c \rangle + 1} T_w$$

where $\langle N_c \rangle$ is the average number of particles in a cell. Set $\langle N_c \rangle = 20$ to produce a more noticeable effect. (b) When $\langle N_c \rangle$ is very small ($\langle N_c \rangle < 10$), another problem arises. Explain what causes it and how to avoid it. [Computer]

30. As mentioned in the previous exercise, the average instantaneous temperature does not equal the thermodynamic temperature. The correct measurement of temperature is

$$T(y) = \frac{2m}{3k} \left(\frac{\langle E(y) \rangle}{m \langle n(y) \rangle} - \tfrac{1}{2}[\langle u_x(y) \rangle^2 + \langle u_y(y) \rangle^2 + \langle u_z(y) \rangle^2)] \right)$$

where

$$E_j(t) = \frac{1}{V_c} \sum_{i \text{ inside } j} \frac{1}{2} m |\mathbf{v}_i|^2$$

is the total energy density in cell j and the angle brackets indicate time-average. Modify dsmcne to measure temperature this way, and show that it produces the correct value at thermodynamic equilibrium, $T(y) = T_w$. [Computer]

31. In Couette flow, the velocity of a fluid near a wall does not exactly equal the velocity of the wall; this phenomenon is known as *slip*. Maxwell predicted this effect and estimated that

$$u_y(x = 0) \approx -u_w + \lambda \frac{du_y}{dx}$$

$$u_y(x = L) \approx u_w - \lambda \frac{du_y}{dx}$$

where u_y is the y-component of the fluid velocity. Do a variety of runs using dsmcne to verify this estimate. Be sure your system is at least 10 mean free paths wide. [Computer]

32. Consider the following simple one-dimensional flow problem: A constant acceleration, g, is applied to the particles in the y-direction. The walls are fixed at constant temperature and are stationary. This is called planar *Poiseuille flow*. (a) Modify dsmcne to simulate planar Poiseuille flow and confirm that the velocity profile is

$$u_y(x) = \frac{mng}{2\eta} \left[\frac{L^2}{4} - (x - L/2)^2 \right] + u_w^{\text{slip}}$$

where u_w^{slip} is the velocity of the fluid at the wall (see Exercise 11.31). Select a value of g that gives a maximum fluid speed of about Ma = 0.5. (b) Estimate the viscosity by fitting the velocity profile to a quadratic. [Computer]

33. In Couette flow, the velocity gradient in the fluid produces viscous heating. The temperature profile is parabolic and given by,

$$T(x) = \frac{\eta \gamma^2}{2\alpha}((L/2)^2 - x^2) + T_0$$

where $\gamma = du_y/dx$ is the velocity gradient and $T_0 = T(0) = T(L)$ is the temperature of the fluid at the walls. Modify `dsmcne` and fit the temperature profile to the above quadratic. From your fit, estimate the ratio of thermal conductivity to viscosity and compare your result with $\alpha/\eta = 15k/4m$, the value given by Chapman-Enskog theory. [Computer]

BEYOND THIS CHAPTER

I picture my readers' eyebrows rising to the tops of their heads as they discover that this chapter does not cover such topics as the Ising model or quantum Monte Carlo. Yet, I believe that the kinetic theory of gases is easier to understand and just as important. Of course a proper coverage of stochastic methods really requires a full-length book. Some of the topics I have omitted are discussed by Gould and Tobochnik [61]. The Metropolis algorithm and its application to the Ising model is covered in depth by Binder [19, 20] and Heermann [71]. Several introductory articles on the various flavors of quantum Monte Carlo have appeared in articles in *Computers in Physics* [84, 106, 126, 127]. In the more general field of stochastic processes, Gardiner [53] presents an excellent introduction.

We've seen two different ways to model a fluid: using partial differential equations and, on a more microscopic level, using particles. In general, the latter is computationally much more expensive. However, particle simulations thrive in certain "ecological niches." For example, the PDE description sometimes breaks down. Define the Knudsen number

$$\text{Kn} \equiv \frac{\lambda}{L} = \frac{(\text{mean free path})}{(\text{characteristic length})} \tag{11.74}$$

The continuum description of a fluid begins to break down when $\text{Kn} > 1/10$. Three important cases where this occurs are: (1) flow in narrow channels, such as the flow under the write head of a disk drive; (2) sharp fronts, such as shock waves; and (3) rarefied gas flows, such as high-altitude flight. The DSMC algorithm is ideally suited for these scenarios.

This chapter presents only very basic DSMC algorithms; there are many possible extensions and improvements.[21] To model true gases more realistically, you can use a more sophisticated potential than hard-spheres. One successful model is the variable hard-sphere potential for which the effective cross section of the particles is a function of their relative speed. The scattering angles, θ and ϕ, are still selected according to the hard-sphere distribution. The DSMC method can also simulate chemistry by including an extra selection process at each collision. Particles react chemically when their relative kinetic energy surpasses the activation energy of the reaction.[64] Finally, the DSMC method can be extended to simulate dense gases [7] and liquids [8].

APPENDIX A: MATLAB LISTINGS

Listing 11A.1 Program `dsmceq`. Simulates relaxation to equilibrium in a dilute gas using the DSMC algorithm. Uses `sorter` (Listing 11A.2) and `colider` (Listing 11A.3).

```matlab
% dsmceq - Dilute gas simulation using DSMC algorithm
% This version illustrates the approach to equilibrium
clear all;  help dsmceq;   % Clear memory and print header

%* Initialize constants  (particle mass, diameter, etc.)
boltz = 1.3806e-23;     % Boltzmann's constant (J/K)
mass = 6.63e-26;        % Mass of argon atom (kg)
diam = 3.66e-10;        % Effective diameter of argon atom (m)
T = 273;                % Temperature (K)
density = 1.78;         % Density of argon at STP (kg/m^3)
L = 1e-6;               % System size is one micron
npart = input('Enter number of simulation particles: ');
eff_num = density/mass*L^3/npart;
fprintf('Each particle represents %g atoms\n',eff_num);

%* Assign random positions and velocities to particles
rand('state',0);          % Initialize random number generator
x = L*rand(npart,1);      % Assign random positions
v_init = sqrt(3*boltz*T/mass);   % Initial speed
v = zeros(npart,3);       % Only x-component is non-zero
v(:,1) = v_init * (1 - 2*floor(2*rand(npart,1)));

%* Plot the initial speed distribution
figure(1);  clf;
vmag = sqrt(v(:,1).^2 + v(:,2).^2 + v(:,3).^2);
vbin = 50:100:1050;    % Bins for histogram
hist(vmag,vbin);  title('Initial speed distribution');
xlabel('Speed (m/s)');  ylabel('Number');

%* Initialize variables used for evaluating collisions
ncell = 15;                    % Number of cells
tau = 0.2*(L/ncell)/v_init;    % Set timestep tau
vrmax = 3*v_init*ones(ncell,1); % Estimated max rel. speed
selxtra = zeros(ncell,1);      % Used by routine "colider"
coeff = 0.5*eff_num*pi*diam^2*tau/(L^3/ncell);
coltot = 0;                    % Count total collisions

%* Declare structure for lists used in sorting
sortData = struct('ncell',ncell,    ...
                  'npart',npart,    ...
                  'cell_n',zeros(ncell,1),  ...
                  'index',zeros(ncell,1),   ...
                  'Xref',zeros(npart,1));
```

```
%* Loop for the desired number of time steps
nstep = input('Enter total number of time steps: ');
for istep = 1:nstep

  %* Move all the particles ballistically
  x(:) = x(:) + v(:,1)*tau; % Update x position of particle
  x = rem(x+L,L);           % Periodic boundary conditions

  %* Sort the particles into cells
  sortData = sorter(x,L,sortData);

  %* Evaluate collisions among the particles
  [v, vrmax, selxtra, col] = ...
                 colider(v,vrmax,tau,selxtra,coeff,sortData);
  coltot = coltot + col;

  %* Periodically display the current progress
  if( rem(istep,10) < 1 )
    figure(2); clf;
    vmag = sqrt(v(:,1).^2 + v(:,2).^2 + v(:,3).^2);
    hist(vmag,vbin);
    title(sprintf('Done %g of %g steps; %g collisions',...
                                    istep,nstep,coltot));
    xlabel('Speed (m/s)');  ylabel('Number');
    drawnow;
  end
end

%* Plot the histogram of the final speed distribution
figure(2); clf;
vmag = sqrt(v(:,1).^2 + v(:,2).^2 + v(:,3).^2);
hist(vmag,vbin);
title(sprintf('Final distrib., Time = %g sec.',nstep*tau));
xlabel('Speed (m/s)');  ylabel('Number');
```

Listing 11A.2 Subroutine sorter. Produces sorted lists used by colider to select random particles from a cell.

```
function sD = sorter(x,L,sD)
% sorter - Function to sort particles into cells
% sD = sorter(x,L,sD)
% Inputs
%    x        Positions of particles
%    L        System size
%    sD       Structure containing sorting lists
% Output
%    sD       Structure containing sorting lists
```

```
%* Find the cell address for each particle
npart = sD.npart;
ncell = sD.ncell;
jx = floor(x*ncell/L) + 1;
jx = min( jx, ncell*ones(npart,1) );

%* Count the number of particles in each cell
sD.cell_n = zeros(ncell,1);
for ipart=1:npart
  sD.cell_n( jx(ipart) ) = sD.cell_n( jx(ipart) ) + 1;
end

%* Build index list as cumulative sum of the
%  number of particles in each cell
m=1;
for jcell=1:ncell
  sD.index(jcell) = m;
  m = m + sD.cell_n(jcell);
end

%* Build cross-reference list
temp = zeros(ncell,1);      % Temporary array
for ipart=1:npart
  jcell = jx(ipart);        % Cell address of ipart
  k = sD.index(jcell) + temp(jcell);
  sD.Xref(k) = ipart;
  temp(jcell) = temp(jcell) + 1;
end

return;
```

Listing 11A.3 Subroutine `colider`. Called by `dsmceq` and `dsmcne` to evaluate collisions using the DSMC algorithm.

```
function [v,crmax,selxtra,col] = ...
                 colider(v,crmax,tau,selxtra,coeff,sD)
% colide - Function to process collisions in cells
% [v,crmax,selxtra,col] = colider(v,crmax,tau,selxtra,coeff,sD)
% Inputs
%    v         Velocities of the particles
%    crmax     Estimated maximum relative speed in a cell
%    tau       Time step
%    selxtra   Extra selections carried over from last timestep
%    coeff     Coefficient in computing number of selected pairs
%    sD        Structure containing sorting lists
% Outputs
%    v         Updated velocities of the particles
%    crmax     Updated maximum relative speed
%    selxtra   Extra selections carried over to next timestep
```

```
%    col        Total number of collisions processed
ncell = sD.ncell;
col = 0;            % Count number of collisions

%* Loop over cells, processing collisions in each cell
for jcell=1:ncell

  %* Skip cells with only one particle
  number = sD.cell_n(jcell);
  if( number > 1 )

    %* Determine number of candidate collision pairs
    %  to be selected in this cell
    select = coeff*number^2*crmax(jcell) + selxtra(jcell);
    nsel = floor(select);          % Number of pairs to be selected
    selxtra(jcell) = select-nsel;  % Carry over any left-over fraction
    crm = crmax(jcell);            % Current maximum relative speed

    %* Loop over total number of candidate collision pairs
    for isel=1:nsel

      %* Pick two particles at random out of this cell
      k = floor(rand(1)*number);
      kk = rem(ceil(k+rand(1)*(number-1)),number);
      ip1 = sD.Xref(k+sD.index(jcell));       % First particle
      ip2 = sD.Xref(kk+sD.index(jcell));      % Second particle

      %* Calculate pair's relative speed
      cr = norm( v(ip1,:)-v(ip2,:) );  % Relative speed
      if( cr > crm )          % If relative speed larger than crm,
        crm = cr;             % then reset crm to larger value
      end

      %* Accept or reject candidate pair according to relative speed
      if( cr/crmax(jcell) > rand(1) )
        %* If pair accepted, select post-collision velocities
        col = col+1;                      % Collision counter
        vcm = 0.5*(v(ip1,:) + v(ip2,:));  % Center of mass velocity
        cos_th = 1 - 2*rand(1);           % Cosine and sine of
        sin_th = sqrt(1 - cos_th^2);      % collision angle theta
        phi = 2*pi*rand(1);               % Collision angle phi
        vrel(1) = cr*cos_th;              % Compute post-collision
        vrel(2) = cr*sin_th*cos(phi);     % relative velocity
        vrel(3) = cr*sin_th*sin(phi);
        v(ip1,:) = vcm + 0.5*vrel;        % Update post-collision
        v(ip2,:) = vcm - 0.5*vrel;        % velocities
      end

    end % Loop over pairs
```

```
  crmax(jcell) = crm;      % Update max relative speed
 end
end   % Loop over cells
return;
```

Listing 11A.4 Program `dsmcne`. Measures viscosity in a dilute gas using the DSMC algorithm. Uses `sorter` (Listing 11A.2), `colider` (Listing 11A.3), `mover` (Listing 11A.5), and `sampler` (Listing 11A.6).

```
% dsmcne - Program to simulate a dilute gas using DSMC algorithm
% This version simulates planar Couette flow
clear all;  help dsmcne;   % Clear memory and print header

%* Initialize constants  (particle mass, diameter, etc.)
boltz = 1.3806e-23;    % Boltzmann's constant (J/K)
mass = 6.63e-26;       % Mass of argon atom (kg)
diam = 3.66e-10;       % Effective diameter of argon atom (m)
T = 273;               % Initial temperature (K)
density = 2.685e25;    % Number density of argon at STP (m^-3)
L = 1e-6;              % System size is one micron
Volume = L^3;          % Volume of the system (m^3)
npart = input('Enter number of simulation particles: ');
eff_num = density*Volume/npart;
fprintf('Each simulation particle represents %g atoms\n',eff_num);
mfp = Volume/(sqrt(2)*pi*diam^2*npart*eff_num);
fprintf('System width is %g mean free paths \n',L/mfp);
mpv = sqrt(2*boltz*T/mass);  % Most probable initial velocity
vwall_m = input('Enter wall velocity as Mach number: ');
vwall = vwall_m * sqrt(5/3 * boltz*T/mass);
fprintf('Wall velocities are %g and %g m/s \n',-vwall,vwall);

%* Assign random positions and velocities to particles
rand('state',1);         % Initialize random number generators
randn('state',1);
x = L*rand(npart,1);     % Assign random positions
% Assign thermal velocities using Gaussian random numbers
v = sqrt(boltz*T/mass) * randn(npart,3);
% Add velocity gradient to the y-component
v(:,2) = v(:,2) + 2*vwall*(x(:)/L) - vwall;

%* Initialize variables used for evaluating collisions
ncell = 20;                     % Number of cells
tau = 0.2*(L/ncell)/mpv;        % Set timestep tau
vrmax = 3*mpv*ones(ncell,1);    % Estimated max rel. speed in a cell
selxtra = zeros(ncell,1);       % Used by collision routine "colider"
coeff = 0.5*eff_num*pi*diam^2*tau/(Volume/ncell);

%* Declare structure for lists used in sorting
sortData = struct('ncell', ncell,    ...
```

```
                          'npart', npart,     ...
                          'cell_n', zeros(ncell,1),  ...
                          'index', zeros(ncell,1),    ...
                          'Xref', zeros(npart,1));

%* Initialize structure and variables used in statistical sampling
sampData = struct('ncell', ncell,     ...
                          'nsamp', 0,     ...
                          'ave_n', zeros(ncell,1), ...
                          'ave_u', zeros(ncell,3), ...
                          'ave_T', zeros(ncell,1));
tsamp = 0;                      % Total sampling time
dvtot = zeros(1,2);             % Total momentum change at a wall
dverr = zeros(1,2);             % Used to find error in dvtot

%* Loop for the desired number of time steps
colSum = 0;   strikeSum = [0 0];
nstep = input('Enter total number of timesteps: ');
for istep = 1:nstep

  %* Move all the particles
  [x, v, strikes, delv] = mover(x,v,npart,L,mpv,vwall,tau);
  strikeSum = strikeSum + strikes;

  %* Sort the particles into cells
  sortData = sorter(x,L,sortData);

  %* Evaluate collisions among the particles
  [v, vrmax, selxtra, col] = ...
        colider(v,vrmax,tau,selxtra,coeff,sortData);
  colSum = colSum + col;

  %* After initial transient, accumulate statistical samples
  if(istep > nstep/10)
    sampData = sampler(x,v,npart,L,sampData);
    dvtot = dvtot + delv;
    dverr = dverr + delv.^2;
    tsamp = tsamp + tau;
  end

  %* Periodically display the current progress
  if( rem(istep,10) < 1 )
    fprintf('Finished %g of %g steps, Collisions = %g\n', ...
                                    istep,nstep,colSum);
    fprintf('Total wall strikes: %g (left)  %g (right)\n', ...
                              strikeSum(1),strikeSum(2));
  end
end

%* Normalize the accumulated statistics
```

```
nsamp = sampData.nsamp;
ave_n = (eff_num/(Volume/ncell))*sampData.ave_n/nsamp;
ave_u = sampData.ave_u/nsamp;
ave_T = mass/(3*boltz) * (sampData.ave_T/nsamp);
dverr = dverr/(nsamp-1) - (dvtot/nsamp).^2;
dverr = sqrt(dverr*nsamp);

%* Compute viscosity from drag force on the walls
force = (eff_num*mass*dvtot)/(tsamp*L^2);
ferr = (eff_num*mass*dverr)/(tsamp *L^2);
fprintf('Force per unit area is \n');
fprintf('Left wall:   %g +/- %g \n',force(1),ferr(1));
fprintf('Right wall:  %g +/- %g \n',force(2),ferr(2));
vgrad = 2*vwall/L;  % Velocity gradient
visc = 1/2*(-force(1)+force(2))/vgrad;  % Average viscosity
viscerr = 1/2*(ferr(1)+ferr(2))/vgrad;  % Error
fprintf('Viscosity = %g +/- %g N s/m^2\n',visc,viscerr);
eta = 5*pi/32*mass*density*(2/sqrt(pi)*mpv)*mfp;
fprintf('Theoretical value of viscoisty is %g N s/m^2\n',eta);

%* Plot average density, velocity and temperature
figure(1); clf;
xcell = ((1:ncell)-0.5)/ncell * L;
plot(xcell,ave_n); xlabel('position');  ylabel('Number density');
figure(2); clf;
plot(xcell,ave_u); xlabel('position');  ylabel('Velocities');
legend('x-component','y-component','z-component');
figure(3); clf;
plot(xcell,ave_T); xlabel('position');  ylabel('Temperature');
```

Listing 11A.5 Function mover. Used by the dsmcne program to update particle positions. It also processes particles striking the thermal walls.

```
function [x,v,strikes,delv] = mover(x,v,npart, ...
                                  L,mpv,vwall,tau)
% mover - Function to move particles by free flight
%         Also handles collisions with walls
% Inputs
%    x        Positions of the particles
%    v        Velocities of the particles
%    npart    Number of particles in the system
%    L        System length
%    mpv      Most probable velocity off the wall
%    vwall    Wall velocities
%    tau      Time step
% Outputs
%    x,v      Updated positions and velocities
%    strikes  Number of particles striking each wall
%    delv     Change of y-velocity at each wall
```

```
%* Move all particles pretending walls are absent
x_old = x;                % Remember original position
x(:) = x_old(:) + v(:,1)*tau;

%* Loop over all particles
strikes = [0 0];  delv = [0 0];
xwall = [0 L];  vw = [-vwall vwall];
direction = [1 -1];   % Direction of particle leaving wall
stdev = mpv/sqrt(2);
for i=1:npart

  %* Test if particle strikes either wall
  if( x(i) <= 0 )
    flag=1; % Particle strikes left wall
  elseif( x(i) >= L )
    flag=2; % Particle strikes right wall
  else
    flag=0;  % Particle strikes neither wall
  end

  %* If particle strikes a wall, reset its position
  %  and velocity. Record velocity change.
  if( flag > 0 )
    strikes(flag) = strikes(flag) + 1;
    vyInitial = v(i,2);
    %* Reset velocity components as biased Maxwellian,
    %  Exponential dist. in x; Gaussian in y and z
    v(i,1) = direction(flag)*sqrt(-log(1-rand(1))) * mpv;
    v(i,2) = stdev*randn(1) + vw(flag); % Add wall velocity
    v(i,3) = stdev*randn(1);
    % Time of flight after leaving wall
    dtr = tau*(x(i)-xwall(flag))/(x(i)-x_old(i));
    %* Reset position after leaving wall
    x(i) = xwall(flag) + v(i,1)*dtr;
    %* Record velocity change for force measurement
    delv(flag) = delv(flag) + (v(i,2) - vyInitial);
  end
end
```

Listing 11A.6 Function sampler. Used by the dsmcne program to sample the number density, fluid velocity, and temperature in the cells.

```
function sampD = sampler(x,v,npart,L,sampD)
% sampler - Function to sample density, velocity and temperature
% Inputs
%    x        Particle positions
%    v        Particle velocities
%    npart    Number of particles
```

```
%    L        System size
%      sampD  Structure with sampling data
% Outputs
%      sampD  Structure with sampling data

%* Compute cell location for each particle
ncell = sampD.ncell;
jx=ceil(ncell*x/L);

%* Initialize running sums of number, velocity and v^2
sum_n = zeros(ncell,1);
sum_v = zeros(ncell,3);
sum_v2 = zeros(ncell,1);

%* For each particle, accumulate running sums for its cell
for ipart=1:npart
  jcell = jx(ipart);  % Particle ipart is in cell jcell
  sum_n(jcell) = sum_n(jcell)+1;
  sum_v(jcell,:) = sum_v(jcell,:) + v(ipart,:);
  sum_v2(jcell) = sum_v2(jcell) + ...
            v(ipart,1)^2 + v(ipart,2)^2 + v(ipart,3)^2;
end

%* Use current sums to update sample number, velocity
%  and temperature
for i=1:3
  sum_v(:,i) = sum_v(:,i)./sum_n(:);
end
sum_v2 = sum_v2./sum_n;
sampD.ave_n = sampD.ave_n + sum_n;
sampD.ave_u = sampD.ave_u + sum_v;
sampD.ave_T = sampD.ave_T + sum_v2 - ...
        (sum_v(:,1).^2 + sum_v(:,2).^2 + sum_v(:,3).^2);
sampD.nsamp = sampD.nsamp + 1;
return;
```

APPENDIX B: C++ LISTINGS

Listing 11B.1 Program dsmceq. Simulates relaxation to equilibrium in a dilute gas using the DSMC algorithm. Uses sorter (Listing 11B.2), colider (Listing 11B.3), and rand (Listing 11B.7).

```
// dsmceq - Dilute gas simulation using DSMC algorithm
// This version illustrates the approach to equilibrium

#include "NumMeth.h"
```

```cpp
#include "SortList.h"

double rand( long& seed );
int colider( Matrix& v, Matrix& crmax, double tau, long& seed,
             Matrix& selxtra, double coeff, SortList& sD );
void sorter( Matrix& x, double L, SortList &sD );

void main() {

  //* Initialize constants  (particle mass, diameter, etc.)
  const double pi = 3.141592654;
  const double boltz = 1.3806e-23;     // Boltzmann's constant (J/K)
  double mass = 6.63e-26;        // Mass of argon atom (kg)
  double diam = 3.66e-10;        // Effective diameter of argon atom (m)
  double T = 273;                // Temperature (K)
  double density = 1.78;         // Density of argon at STP (kg/m^3)
  double L = 1e-6;               // System size is one micron
  cout << "Enter number of simulation particles: ";
  int npart; cin >> npart;
  double eff_num = density/mass*L*L*L/npart;
  cout << "Each particle represents " << eff_num << " atoms" << endl;

  //* Assign random positions and velocities to particles
  long seed = 1;          // Initial seed for rand (DO NOT USE ZERO)
  double v_init = sqrt(3.0*boltz*T/mass);    // Initial speed
  Matrix x(npart), v(npart,3);
  int i;
  for( i=1; i<=npart; i++ ) {
    x(i) = L*rand(seed);   // Assign random positions
    int plusMinus = (1 - 2*((int)(2*rand(seed))));
    v(i,1) = plusMinus * v_init;
    v(i,2) = 0.0;   // Only x-component is non-zero
    v(i,3) = 0.0;
  }

  //* Record inital particle speeds
  Matrix vmagI(npart);
  for( i=1; i<=npart; i++ )
    vmagI(i) = sqrt( v(i,1)*v(i,1) + v(i,2)*v(i,2) + v(i,3)*v(i,3) );

  //* Initialize variables used for evaluating collisions
  int ncell = 15;                        // Number of cells
  double tau = 0.2*(L/ncell)/v_init;     // Set timestep tau
  Matrix vrmax(ncell), selxtra(ncell);
  vrmax.set(3*v_init);      // Estimated max rel. speed
  selxtra.set(0.0);         // Used by routine "colider"
  double coeff = 0.5*eff_num*pi*diam*diam*tau/(L*L*L/ncell);
  int coltot = 0;           // Count total collisions

  //* Declare object for lists used in sorting
```

```cpp
  SortList sortData(ncell,npart);

  //* Loop for the desired number of time steps
  cout << "Enter total number of time steps: ";
  int istep, nstep; cin >> nstep;
  for( istep = 1; istep<=nstep; istep++ ) {

    //* Move all the particles ballistically
    for( i=1; i<=npart; i++ ) {
      x(i) += v(i,1)*tau;           // Update x position of particle
      x(i) = fmod(x(i)+L,L);        // Periodic boundary conditions
    }
    //* Sort the particles into cells
    sorter(x,L,sortData);

    //* Evaluate collisions among the particles
    int col = colider(v,vrmax,tau,seed,selxtra,coeff,sortData);
    coltot += col;  // Increment collision count

    //* Periodically display the current progress
    if( (istep%10) < 1 )
      cout << "Done " << istep << " of " << nstep << " steps; " <<
              coltot << " collisions" << endl;
  }

  // Record final particle speeds
  Matrix vmagF(npart);
  for( i=1; i<=npart; i++ )
    vmagF(i) = sqrt( v(i,1)*v(i,1) + v(i,2)*v(i,2) + v(i,3)*v(i,3) );

  //* Print out the plotting variables: vmagI, vmagF
  ofstream vmagIOut("vmagI.txt"), vmagFOut("vmagF.txt");
  for( i=1; i<=npart; i++ ) {
    vmagIOut << vmagI(i) << endl;
    vmagFOut << vmagF(i) << endl;
  }
}
/***** To plot in MATLAB; use the script below ********************
load vmagI.txt; load vmagF.txt;
%* Plot the histogram of the initial speed distribution
vbin = 50:100:1050;    % Bins for histogram
hist(vmagI,vbin);  title('Initial speed distribution');
xlabel('Speed (m/s)');  ylabel('Number');
%* Plot the histogram of the final speed distribution
figure(2); clf;
hist(vmagF,vbin);
title(sprintf('Final speed distribution'));
xlabel('Speed (m/s)');  ylabel('Number');
*****************************************************************/
```

Listing 11B.2 Subroutine `sorter`. Produces sorted lists used by `colider` to select random particles from a cell.

```
#include "NumMeth.h"
#include "SortList.h"

void sorter( Matrix& x, double L, SortList &sD ) {

// sorter - Function to sort particles into cells
// Inputs
//    x          Positions of particles
//    L          System size
//    sD         Object containing lists used in sorting
// Output
//    sD         Object containing lists used in sorting

  //* Find the cell address for each particle
  int ncell = sD.ncell;
  int npart = sD.npart;
  int ipart, *jx;
  jx = new int [npart+1];
  for( ipart=1; ipart<=npart; ipart++ ) {
    int j = (int)(x(ipart)*ncell/L) + 1;
    jx[ipart] = ( j <= ncell ) ? j : ncell;
  }

  //* Count the number of particles in each cell
  int jcell;
  for( jcell=1; jcell<=ncell; jcell++ )
    sD.cell_n[ jcell ] = 0;
  for( ipart=1; ipart<=npart; ipart++ )
    sD.cell_n[ jx[ipart] ]++;

  //* Build index list as cumulative sum of the
  //  number of particles in each cell
  int m=1;
  for( jcell=1; jcell<=ncell; jcell++ ) {
    sD.index[jcell] = m;
    m += sD.cell_n[jcell];
  }

  //* Build cross-reference list
  int *temp;
  temp = new int [ncell+1];    // Temporary array
  for( jcell=1; jcell<=ncell; jcell++ )
    temp[jcell] = 0;
  for( ipart=1; ipart<=npart; ipart++ ) {
    jcell = jx[ipart];         // Cell address of ipart
    int k = sD.index[jcell] + temp[jcell];
```

```
    sD.Xref[k] = ipart;
    temp[jcell] = temp[jcell] + 1;
  }

  delete [] jx;
  delete [] temp;

}
```

Listing 11B.3 Subroutine `colider`. Called by `dsmceq` and `dsmcne` to evaluate collisions using the DSMC algorithm. Uses `rand` (Listing 11B.7).

```
#include "NumMeth.h"
#include "SortList.h"

double rand( long& seed );

int colider( Matrix& v, Matrix& crmax, double tau, long& seed,
             Matrix& selxtra, double coeff, SortList& sD ) {

// colide - Function to process collisions in cells
// Inputs
//    v          Velocities of the particles
//    crmax      Estimated maximum relative speed in a cell
//    tau        Time step
//    seed       Current random number seed
//    selxtra    Extra selections carried over from last timestep
//    coeff      Coefficient in computing number of selected pairs
//    sD         Object containing sorting lists
// Outputs
//    v          Updated velocities of the particles
//    crmax      Updated maximum relative speed
//    selxtra    Extra selections carried over to next timestep
//    col        Total number of collisions processed   (Return value)

  // General variables
  int ncell = sD.ncell;
  int col = 0;             // Count number of collisions
  const double pi = 3.141592654;

  //* Loop over cells, processing collisions in each cell
  int jcell;
  for( jcell=1; jcell<=ncell; jcell++ ) {

    //* Skip cells with only one particle
    int number = sD.cell_n[jcell];
    if( number < 2 ) continue;  // Skip to the next cell

    //* Determine number of candidate collision pairs
```

```
    //  to be selected in this cell
    double select = coeff*number*number*crmax(jcell) + selxtra(jcell);
    int nsel = (int)(select);        // Number of pairs to be selected
    selxtra(jcell) = select-nsel;    // Carry over any left-over fraction
    double crm = crmax(jcell);       // Current maximum relative speed

    //* Loop over total number of candidate collision pairs
    int isel;
    for( isel=1; isel<=nsel; isel++ ) {

      //* Pick two particles at random out of this cell
      int k = (int)(rand(seed)*number);
      int kk = ((int)(k+rand(seed)*(number-1))+1) % number;
      int ip1 = sD.Xref[ k+sD.index[jcell] ];      // First particle
      int ip2 = sD.Xref[ kk+sD.index[jcell] ];     // Second particle

      //* Calculate pair's relative speed
      double cr = sqrt( pow(v(ip1,1)-v(ip2,1),2) +
                        pow(v(ip1,2)-v(ip2,2),2) +   // Relative speed
                        pow(v(ip1,3)-v(ip2,3),2) );
      if( cr > crm )            // If relative speed larger than crm,
        crm = cr;              // then reset crm to larger value

      //* Accept or reject candidate pair according to relative speed
      if( cr/crmax(jcell) > rand(seed) ) {
        //* If pair accepted, select post-collision velocities
        col++;                        // Collision counter
        Matrix vcm(3), vrel(3);
        int k;
        for( k=1; k<=3; k++ )
          vcm(k) = 0.5*(v(ip1,k) + v(ip2,k));       // Center of mass velocity
        double cos_th = 1.0 - 2.0*rand(seed);       // Cosine and sine of
        double sin_th = sqrt(1.0 - cos_th*cos_th);  // collision angle theta
        double phi = 2.0*pi*rand(seed);             // Collision angle phi
        vrel(1) = cr*cos_th;             // Compute post-collision
        vrel(2) = cr*sin_th*cos(phi);    // relative velocity
        vrel(3) = cr*sin_th*sin(phi);
        for(  k=1; k<=3; k++ ) {
          v(ip1,k) = vcm(k) + 0.5*vrel(k);  // Update post-collision
          v(ip2,k) = vcm(k) - 0.5*vrel(k);  // velocities
        }

    } // Loop over pairs
    crmax(jcell) = crm;        // Update max relative speed
  }
} // Loop over cells
return( col );
}
```

Listing 11B.4 Program dsmcne. Measures viscosity in a dilute gas using the DSMC algorithm. Uses sorter (Listing 11B.2), colider (Listing 11B.3), mover (Listing 11B.5), sampler (Listing 11B.6), and rand (Listing 11B.7).

```cpp
// dsmcne - Program to simulate a dilute gas using DSMC algorithm
// This version simulates planar Couette flow

#include "NumMeth.h"
#include "SortList.h"
#include "SampList.h"

double rand( long& seed );
double randn( long& seed );
int colider( Matrix& v, Matrix& crmax, double tau, long& seed,
             Matrix& selxtra, double coeff, SortList& sD );
void sorter( Matrix& x, double L, SortList &sD );
void mover( Matrix& x, Matrix& v, int npart, double L,
            double mpv, double vwall, double tau,
            Matrix& strikes, Matrix& delv, long& seed );
void sampler( Matrix& x, Matrix& v, int npart, double L,
            SampList& sampD );

void main() {

  //* Initialize constants  (particle mass, diameter, etc.)
  const double pi = 3.141592654;
  const double boltz = 1.3806e-23;    // Boltzmann's constant (J/K)
  double mass = 6.63e-26;       // Mass of argon atom (kg)
  double diam = 3.66e-10;       // Effective diameter of argon atom (m)
  double T = 273;               // Temperature (K)
  double density = 2.685e25;    // Number density of argon at STP (m^-3)
  double L = 1e-6;              // System size is one micron
  double Volume = L*L*L;        // Volume of the system
  cout << "Enter number of simulation particles: ";
  int npart; cin >> npart;
  double eff_num = density*L*L*L/npart;
  cout << "Each particle represents " << eff_num << " atoms" << endl;
  double mfp = Volume/(sqrt(2.0)*pi*diam*diam*npart*eff_num);
  cout << "System width is " << L/mfp << " mean free paths" << endl;
  double mpv = sqrt(2*boltz*T/mass);  // Most probable initial velocity
  cout << "Enter wall velocity as Mach number: ";
  double vwall_m; cin >> vwall_m;
  double vwall = vwall_m * sqrt(5./3. * boltz*T/mass);
  cout << "Wall velocities are " << -vwall << " and "
       << vwall << " m/s" << endl;

  //* Assign random positions and velocities to particles
  long seed = 1;         // Initial seed for rand (DO NOT USE ZERO)
  Matrix x(npart), v(npart,3);
  int i;
```

```
for( i=1; i<=npart; i++ ) {
  x(i) = L*rand(seed);         // Assign random positions
  // Initial velocities are Maxwell-Boltzmann distributed
  v(i,1) = sqrt(boltz*T/mass) * randn(seed);
  v(i,2) = sqrt(boltz*T/mass) * randn(seed);
  v(i,3) = sqrt(boltz*T/mass) * randn(seed);
  // Add velocity gradient to the y-component
  v(i,2) += vwall * (x(i)/L - 0.5);
}

//* Initialize variables used for evaluating collisions
int ncell = 20;                      // Number of cells
double tau = 0.2*(L/ncell)/mpv;      // Set timestep tau
Matrix vrmax(ncell), selxtra(ncell);
vrmax.set(3*mpv);     // Estimated max rel. speed
selxtra.set(0.0);         // Used by routine "colider"
double coeff = 0.5*eff_num*pi*diam*diam*tau/(L*L*L/ncell);

//* Declare object for lists used in sorting
SortList sortData(ncell,npart);

//* Initialize object and variables used in statistical sampling
SampList sampData(ncell);
double tsamp = 0;               // Total sampling time
Matrix dvtot(2), dverr(2);
dvtot.set(0.0);                 // Total momentum change at a wall
dverr.set(0.0);                 // Used to find error in dvtot

//* Loop for the desired number of time steps
int colSum = 0;            // Count total collisions
Matrix strikes(2), strikeSum(2);
strikeSum.set(0.0);       // Count strikes on each wall
cout << "Enter total number of time steps: ";
int istep, nstep; cin >> nstep;
for( istep = 1; istep<=nstep; istep++ ) {

  //* Move all the particles
  Matrix delv(2);  delv.set(0.0);
  mover( x, v, npart, L, mpv, vwall,
         tau, strikes, delv, seed );
  strikeSum(1) += strikes(1);
  strikeSum(2) += strikes(2);

  //* Sort the particles into cells
  sorter(x,L,sortData);

  //* Evaluate collisions among the particles
  int col = colider(v,vrmax,tau,seed,selxtra,coeff,sortData);
  colSum += col;  // Increment collision count
```

```
//* After initial transient, accumulate statistical samples
if(istep > nstep/10) {
  sampler(x,v,npart,L,sampData);
  // Cummulative velocity change for particles striking walls
  dvtot(1) += delv(1);            dvtot(2) += delv(2);
  dverr(1) += delv(1)*delv(1);  dverr(2) += delv(2)*delv(2);
  tsamp += tau;
}

//* Periodically display the current progress
if( (istep%100) < 1 )  {
  cout << "Done " << istep << " of " << nstep << " steps; " <<
        colSum << " collisions" << endl;
  cout << "Total wall strikes: " << strikeSum(1) << " (left) "
      << strikeSum(2) << " (right)" << endl;
}
}

//* Normalize the accumulated statistics
int nsamp = sampData.nsamp;
for( i=1; i<=ncell; i++ ) {
  sampData.ave_n[i]  *= (eff_num/(Volume/ncell))/nsamp;
  sampData.ave_ux[i] /= nsamp;
  sampData.ave_uy[i] /= nsamp;
  sampData.ave_uz[i] /= nsamp;
  sampData.ave_T[i]  *= mass/(3*boltz*nsamp);
}
dverr(1) = dverr(1)/(nsamp-1) - (dvtot(1)/nsamp)*(dvtot(1)/nsamp);
dverr(1) = sqrt(dverr(1)*nsamp);
dverr(2) = dverr(2)/(nsamp-1) - (dvtot(2)/nsamp)*(dvtot(2)/nsamp);
dverr(2) = sqrt(dverr(2)*nsamp);

//* Compute viscosity from drag force on the walls
Matrix force(2), ferr(2);
force(1) = (eff_num*mass*dvtot(1))/(tsamp*L*L);
force(2) = (eff_num*mass*dvtot(2))/(tsamp*L*L);
ferr(1) = (eff_num*mass*dverr(1))/(tsamp*L*L);
ferr(2) = (eff_num*mass*dverr(2))/(tsamp*L*L);
cout << "Force per unit area is" << endl;
cout << "Left wall:  " << force(1) << " +/- " << ferr(1) << endl;
cout << "Right wall: " << force(2) << " +/- " << ferr(2) << endl;
double vgrad = 2*vwall/L;    // Velocity gradient
double visc = 0.5*(-force(1)+force(2))/vgrad;  // Average viscosity
double viscerr = 0.5*(ferr(1)+ferr(2))/vgrad;  // Error
cout << "Viscosity = " << visc << " +/- " << viscerr
    << "N s/m^2" << endl;
double eta = 5.*pi/32.*mass*density*(2./sqrt(pi)*mpv)*mfp;
cout << "Theoretical value of viscoisty is " << eta
    << "N s/m^2" << endl;
```

```
//* Print out the plotting variables:
//     xcell, ave_n, ave_ux, ave_uy, ave_uz, ave_T
  ofstream xcellOut("xcell.txt"), ave_nOut("ave_n.txt"),
            ave_uxOut("ave_ux.txt"), ave_uyOut("ave_uy.txt"),
            ave_uzOut("ave_uz.txt"), ave_TOut("ave_T.txt");
  for( i=1; i<=ncell; i++ ) {
    xcellOut << (i-0.5)*L/ncell << endl;
    ave_nOut << sampData.ave_n[i] << endl;
    ave_uxOut << sampData.ave_ux[i] << endl;
    ave_uyOut << sampData.ave_uy[i] << endl;
    ave_uzOut << sampData.ave_uz[i] << endl;
    ave_TOut << sampData.ave_T[i] << endl;
  }
}
/***** To plot in MATLAB; use the script below ********************
load xcell.txt;  load ave_n.txt;    load ave_ux.txt;
load ave_uy.txt; load ave_uz.txt;   load ave_T.txt;
figure(1); clf;
plot(xcell,ave_n); xlabel('position');  ylabel('Number density');
figure(2); clf;
plot(xcell,ave_ux,xcell,ave_uy,xcell,ave_uz);
xlabel('position');  ylabel('Velocities');
legend('x-component','y-component','z-component');
figure(3); clf;
plot(xcell,ave_T); xlabel('position');  ylabel('Temperature');
****************************************************************/
```

Listing 11B.5 Function mover. Used by the dsmcne program to update particle positions. It also evaluates collisions between the particles and the thermal walls. Uses rand (Listing 11B.7).

```
#include "NumMeth.h"

double rand( long& seed );
double randn( long& seed );

void mover( Matrix& x, Matrix& v, int npart, double L,
            double mpv, double vwall, double tau,
            Matrix& strikes, Matrix& delv, long& seed ) {

// mover - Function to move particles by free flight
//         Also handles collisions with walls
// Inputs
//    x        Positions of the particles
//    v        Velocities of the particles
//    npart    Number of particles in the system
//    L        System length
//    mpv      Most probable velocity off the wall
```

```
//    vwall      Wall velocities
//    tau        Time step
//    seed       Random number seed
// Outputs
//    x,v        Updated positions and velocities
//    strikes    Number of particles striking each wall
//    delv       Change of y-velocity at each wall
//    seed       Random number seed

  //* Move all particles pretending walls are absent
  Matrix x_old(npart);
  x_old = x;                // Remember original position
  int i;
  for( i=1; i<= npart; i++ )
    x(i) = x_old(i) + v(i,1)*tau;

  //* Check each particle to see if it strikes a wall
  strikes.set(0.0);   delv.set(0.0);
  Matrix xwall(2), vw(2), direction(2);
  xwall(1) = 0;     xwall(2) = L;    // Positions of walls
  vw(1) = -vwall;   vw(2) = vwall;   // Velocities of walls
  double stdev = mpv/sqrt(2.);
  // Direction of particle leaving wall
  direction(1) = 1;  direction(2) = -1;
  for( i=1; i<=npart; i++ ) {

    //* Test if particle strikes either wall
    int flag = 0;
    if( x(i) <= 0 )
      flag=1;         // Particle strikes left wall
    else if( x(i) >= L )
      flag=2;         // Particle strikes right wall

    //* If particle strikes a wall, reset its position
    //  and velocity. Record velocity change.
    if( flag > 0 )  {
      strikes(flag)++;
      double vyInitial = v(i,2);
      //* Reset velocity components as biased Maxwellian,
      //  Exponential dist. in x; Gaussian in y and z
      v(i,1) = direction(flag)*sqrt(-log(1.-rand(seed))) * mpv;
      v(i,2) = stdev*randn(seed) + vw(flag); // Add wall velocity
      v(i,3) = stdev*randn(seed);
      // Time of flight after leaving wall
      double dtr = tau*(x(i)-xwall(flag))/(x(i)-x_old(i));
      //* Reset position after leaving wall
      x(i) = xwall(flag) + v(i,1)*dtr;
      //* Record velocity change for force measurement
      delv(flag) += (v(i,2) - vyInitial);
    }
```

```
    }
}
```

Listing 11B.6 Function `sampler`. Used by the `dsmcne` program to sample the
number density, fluid velocity, and temperature in the cells.

```
#include "NumMeth.h"
#include "SampList.h"

void sampler( Matrix& x, Matrix& v, int npart, double L,
            SampList& sampD ) {

// sampler - Function to sample density, velocity and temperature
// Inputs
//    x        Particle positions
//    v        Particle velocities
//    npart    Number of particles
//    L        System size
//    sampD    Object with sampling data
// Outputs
//    sampD    Structure with sampling data

  //* Compute cell location for each particle
  int ncell = sampD.ncell;
  int *jx; jx = new int [npart+1];
  int i;
  for( i=1; i<=npart; i++ )
    jx[i] = (int)ceil(ncell*x(i)/L);

  //* Initialize running sums of number, velocity and v^2
  Matrix sum_n(ncell), sum_vx(ncell), sum_vy(ncell),
         sum_vz(ncell), sum_v2(ncell);
  sum_n.set(0.0);
  sum_vx.set(0.0);
  sum_vy.set(0.0);
  sum_vz.set(0.0);
  sum_v2.set(0.0);

  //* For each particle, accumulate running sums for its cell
  for( i=1; i<=npart; i++ ) {
    int jcell = jx[i];  // Particle i is in cell jcell
    sum_n(jcell)++;
    sum_vx(jcell) += v(i,1);
    sum_vy(jcell) += v(i,2);
    sum_vz(jcell) += v(i,3);
    sum_v2(jcell) += v(i,1)*v(i,1) +
                     v(i,2)*v(i,2) + v(i,3)*v(i,3);
  }
```

```
//* Use current sums to update sample number, velocity
//   and temperature
for( i=1; i<=ncell; i++ ) {
  sum_vx(i) /= sum_n(i);
  sum_vy(i) /= sum_n(i);
  sum_vz(i) /= sum_n(i);
  sum_v2(i) /= sum_n(i);
  sampD.ave_n[i] += sum_n(i);
  sampD.ave_ux[i] += sum_vx(i);
  sampD.ave_uy[i] += sum_vy(i);
  sampD.ave_uz[i] += sum_vz(i);
  sampD.ave_T[i] += sum_v2(i) - (sum_vx(i)*sum_vx(i) +
        sum_vy(i)*sum_vy(i) + sum_vz(i)*sum_vz(i));
}
sampD.nsamp++;

delete [] jx;
}
```

Listing 11B.7 Function **rand**. Returns random numbers uniformly distributed in [0,1) (i.e., uniform deviates).

```
#include "NumMeth.h"

// Random number generator; Uniform dist. in [0,1)
double rand( long& seed ) {
// Input
//    seed     Integer seed (DO NOT USE A SEED OF ZERO)
// Output
//    rand     Random number uniformly distributed in [0,1)

  const double a = 16807.0;
  const double m = 2147483647.0;
  double temp = a * seed;
  seed = (long)(fmod(temp,m));
  double rand = seed/m;
  return( rand );
}
```

Listing 11B.8 Function **randn**. Returns normal (Gaussian) distributed random numbers with zero mean and unit variance. Uses **rand** (Listing 11B.7).

```
#include "NumMeth.h"

double rand( long& seed );

// Random number generator; Normal (Gaussian) dist.
double randn( long& seed ) {
```

```
// Input
//    seed      Integer seed   (DO NOT USE A SEED OF ZERO)
// Output
//    randn     Random number, Gaussian distributed

  double randn = sqrt( -2.0*log(1.0 - rand(seed)) )
           * cos( 6.283185307 * rand(seed) );
  return( randn );
}
```

Listing 11B.9 Class SortList. Used by **dsmceq** and **dsmcne** to manage sorting lists.

```
class SortList {

public:

// Class data (sorting lists)
int ncell, npart, *cell_n, *index, *Xref;

// Default Constructor.
SortList() {
  initLists(1,1);
}

// Regular Constructor.
SortList(int ncell_in, int npart_in) {
  initLists(ncell_in,npart_in);
}


// Destructor. Called when a SortList object goes out of scope.
~SortList() {
  delete [] cell_n;    // Release allocated memory
  delete [] index;
  delete [] Xref;
}

//*********************************************************

private:

// Initialization routine
void initLists(int ncell_in, int npart_in) {
  ncell = ncell_in;
  npart = npart_in;
  cell_n = new int [ncell+1];   // Allocate memory
  index = new int [ncell+1];
  Xref = new int [npart+1];
```

```
  int i;
  for( i=1; i<=ncell; i++ ) {
    cell_n[i] = 0;
    index[i] = 0;
  }
  for( i=1; i<=npart; i++ )
    Xref[i] = 0;
}

}; // Class SortList
```

Listing 11B.10 Class SampList. Used by **dsmcne** to manage sampling data vectors.

```
class SampList {

public:

// Class data (sorting lists)
int ncell, nsamp;
double *ave_n, *ave_ux, *ave_uy, *ave_uz, *ave_T;

// Default Constructor.
SampList() {
  initLists(1);
}

// Regular Constructor.
SampList(int ncell_in) {
  initLists(ncell_in);
}


// Destructor. Called when a SampList object goes out of scope.
~SampList() {
  delete [] ave_n;    // Release allocated memory
  delete [] ave_ux;
  delete [] ave_uy;
  delete [] ave_uz;
  delete [] ave_T;
}

//**********************************************************

private:

// Initialization routine
void initLists(int ncell_in) {
  ncell = ncell_in;
```

```
  nsamp = 0;
  ave_n = new double [ncell+1];   // Allocate memory
  ave_ux = new double [ncell+1];
  ave_uy = new double [ncell+1];
  ave_uz = new double [ncell+1];
  ave_T = new double [ncell+1];
  int i;
  for( i=1; i<=ncell; i++ ) {
    ave_n[i] = 0;
    ave_ux[i] = 0;
    ave_uy[i] = 0;
    ave_uz[i] = 0;
    ave_T[i] = 0;
  }
}

}; // Class SampList
```

Bibliography

[1] M.B. Abbot, *An Introduction to the Method of Characteristics* (New York: American Elsevier, 1966).

[2] M. Abramowitz and I. Stegun, *Handbook of Mathematical Functions* (New York: Dover, 1972).

[3] F.S. Acton, *Numerical Methods that Work* (New York: Harper & Row, 1970).

[4] R.K. Adair, *The Physics of Baseball* (New York: Harper & Row, 1990).

[5] C.G. Alder and B.L. Coulter, "Galileo and the Tower of Pisa experiment," *Am. J. Phys.*, **46**, 199–201 (1978).

[6] B.J. Alder and T.E. Wainwright, "Studies in molecular dynamics. I. General method," *J. Chem. Phys.*, **31**, 459–66 (1959).

[7] F.J. Alexander, A.L. Garcia, and B.J. Alder, "The consistent Boltzmann algorithm," *Phys. Rev. Lett.* **74** 5212–5 (1995).

[8] F.J. Alexander, A.L. Garcia, and B.J. Alder, "The consistent Boltzmann algorithm for the van der Waals equation of state", *Physica A*, **240**, 196–201 (1997).

[9] M. Allen and D. Tildesley, *Computer Simulation of Liquids* (Oxford: Clarendon Press, 1987).

[10] D. Anderson, J. Tannehill, and R. Pletcher, *Computational Fluid Mechanics and Heat Transfer* (New York: Hemisphere, 1984).

[11] G. Arfken, *Mathematical Methods for Physicists* (New York: Academic Press, 1970).

[12] U.M. Ascher, R.M.M. Mattheij, and R.D. Russell, *Numerical Solution of Boundary Value Problems for Ordinary Differential Equations* (Upper Saddle River, N.J.: Prentice Hall, 1988).

[13] L. Baker, *C Mathematical Function Handbook* (New York: McGraw-Hill, 1992).

[14] D.M. Bates and D.G. Watts, *Nonlinear Regression Analysis and Its Applications* (New York: Wiley, 1988).

[15] A. Bellemans and J. Orban, "Velocity-inversion and irreversibility in a dilute gas of hard disks," *Phys. Lett.*, **24A**, 620–1 (1967).

[16] E. Benton and G. Platzman, "A table of solutions of the one-dimensional Burgers equation," *Q. Appl. Math.*, **30**, 195–212 (1972).

[17] R.E. Berg and T.S. Marshall, "Wilberforce pendulum oscillations and normal modes," *Am. J. Phys.*, **59**, 32–8 (1991).

[18] P. Bevington, *Data Reduction and Error Analysis for the Physical Sciences* 2d ed. (New York: McGraw-Hill, 1992).

[19] K. Binder ed., *Monte Carlo Methods in Statistical Physics*, Topics Current Physics, vol. 7 (Berlin: Springer, 1979).

[20] K. Binder ed., *Applications of the Monte Carlo Method in Statistical Physics* (Berlin: Springer, 1984).

[21] G.A. Bird, *Molecular Gas Dynamics and the Direct Simulation of Gas Flows* (Oxford: Clarendon Press, 1994).

[22] C.K. Birdsall and A.B. Langdon, *Plasma Physics via Computer Simulation* (New York: McGraw-Hill, 1985)

[23] J.A. Blackburn, H.J.T. Smith, N. Grønbech-Jensen, "Stability and Hopf bifurcations in an inverted pendulum," *Am. J. Phys.*, **60**, 903–8 (1992).

[24] M.L. Boas, *Mathematical Methods in the Physical Sciences*, 2nd ed. (New York: Wiley & Sons, 1983).

[25] R.C. Booton, *Computational Methods for Electromagnetics and Microwaves* (New York: Wiley, 1992).

[26] S. Brandt, *Statistical and Computational Methods in Data Analysis* (Amsterdam: North-Holland, 1970).

[27] E.O. Brigham, *The Fast Fourier Transform and Its Applications* (Upper Saddle River, N.J.: Prentice Hall, 1988).

[28] C.G. Broyden, in *Numerical Methods for Unconstrained Optimization*, edited by W. Murray, (New York: Academic Press, 1972).

[29] R.L. Burden and J.D. Faires, *Numerical Analysis*, 4th ed., (Boston: PWS-Kent, 1989).

[30] C. Canuto, M.Y. Hussaini, A. Quarteroni, and T.A. Zang, *Spectral Methods in Fluid Dynamics* (Berlin: Springer-Verlag, 1988).

[31] D.G. Childers, ed. *Modern Spectrum Analysis* (New York: IEEE Press, 1978).

[32] B.V. Chirikov and V.V. Vecheslavov, "Chaotic dynamics of comet Halley," *Astron. Astrophys.*, **221**, 146–54 (1989).

[33] S. Conte and C. de Boor, *Elementary Numerical Analysis* (New York: McGraw-Hill, 1980).

[34] J.W. Cooley and J.W. Tukey, "An algorithm for the machine calculation of the complex Fourier series," *Math. Comput.*, **19**, 297–301 (1965).

[35] R. Courant and D. Hilbert, *Methods of Mathematical Physics*, vol. II (New York: Interscience, 1962).

[36] A. Cromer, "Stable solutions using the Euler approximation," *Am. J. Phys.*, **49**, 455–9 (1981).

[37] J.M.A. Danby, *Fundamentals of Celestial Mechanics*, 2nd ed. (Richmond, VA: William-Bell Inc., 1988).

[38] S.R. Davis, *C++ for Dummies* (Foster City, Calf.: IDG Books, 1994).

[39] P.J. Davis and P. Rabinowitz, *Numerical Integration* (Waltham: Blaisdell, 1967).

[40] C. de Boor, *A Practical Guide to Splines* (New York: Springer-Verlag, 1978).

[41] J.J. Dongarra, J.R. Bunch, C.B. Moler, and G.W. Stewart, *LINPACK Users' Guide* (Philadelphia: Society for Industrial and Applied Mathematics [SIAM], 1979).

[42] P.G. Drazin and R.S. Johnson, *Solitons, An Introduction* (Cambridge: Cambridge University Press, 1989).

[43] I.S. Duff, A.M. Erisman, and J.K. Reid, *Direct Methods for Sparse Matrices* (Oxford: Clarendon Press, 1989).

[44] D. Etter, *Introduction to MATLAB 5* (Upper Saddle River, N.J.: Prentice Hall, 1999).

[45] W. Feller, *An Introduction to Probability Theory and Its Applications* (New York: Wiley, 1971).

[46] R.P. Feynman, R.B. Leighton, and M. Sands, *The Feynman Lectures on Physics*, vol. I (Reading, Mass.: Addison-Wesley, 1963).

[47] C.A.J. Fletcher, *Computational Techniques for Fluid Dynamics*, vol. I (Berlin: Springer-Verlag, 1988).

[48] C.A.J. Fletcher, *Computational Galerkin Methods* (New York: Springer-Verlag, 1984).

[49] G.E. Forsythe, M.A. Malcolm, and C.B. Moler, *Computer Methods for Mathematical Computations*, (Upper Saddle River, N.J.: Prentice Hall, 1977).

[50] G.E. Forsythe and C.B. Moler, *Computer Solution of Linear Algebraic Systems* (Upper Saddle River, N.J.: Prentice-Hall, 1967).

[51] C. Frohlich, "Aerodynamic drag crisis and its possible effect on the flight of baseballs," *Am. J. Phys.*, **52**, 325–34 (1984).

[52] G. Galilei, *Two New Sciences*, translated by Stillman Drake (Madison: University of Wisconsin Press, 1974).

[53] C.W. Gardiner, *Handbook of Stochastic Methods for Physics, Chemistry and the Natural Sciences* (Berlin: Springer-Verlag, 1985).

[54] C.W. Gear, *Numerical Initial Value Problems in Ordinary Differential Equations* (Upper Saddle River, N.J.: Prentice-Hall, 1971).

[55] N.J. Giordano, *Computational Physics* (Upper Saddle River, N.J.: Prentice Hall, 1997).

[56] J. Gleick, *Chaos, Making a New Science* (New York: Viking Press, 1987).

[57] A. Goldberg, H. Schey and J. Schwartz, "Computer-generated motion pictures of one-dimensional quantum-mechanical transmission and reflection phenomena," *Am. J. Phys.*, **35**, 177–86 (1967).

[58] H.H. Goldstine, *A History of Numerical Analysis from the 16th through the 19th Century* (New York: Springer-Verlag, 1977).

[59] G.H. Golub and C.F. Van Loan, *Matrix Computations*, 2d ed. (Baltimore: Johns Hopkins University Press, 1989).

[60] A. Gore, *Earth in the Balance, Ecology and the Human Spirit* (New York: Plume, 1992).

[61] H. Gould and J. Tobochnik, *An Introduction to Computer Simulation Methods*, 2nd ed. (Reading, Mass.: Addison-Wesley, 1996).

[62] I.S. Gradshteyn and I.M. Ryzhik, *Table of Integrals, Series and Products* (New York: Academic Press, 1965).

[63] J. Guckenheimer and P. Holmes, *Nonlinear Oscillations, Dynamical Systems and Bifurcations of Vector Fields* (New York: Springer-Verlag, 1983).

[64] B.L. Haas and J.D. McDonald, "Validation of chemistry models employed in a particle simulation method," *J. Therm. and Heat Transfer*, **7**, 42–8 (1993).

[65] R. Haberman, *Mathematical Models* (Upper Saddle River, N.J.: Prentice Hall, 1977).

[66] W. Hackbusch, *Multi-Grid Methods and Applications* (Berlin: Springer-Verlag, 1985).

[67] J.M. Haile, *Molecular Dynamics Simulation* (New York: Wiley, 1992).

[68] G.J. Haltiner and R.T. Williams, *Numerical Prediction and Dynamic Meteorology*, 2nd ed. (New York: Wiley, 1980).

[69] R.W. Hamming, *Digital Filters* (Upper Saddle River, N.J.: Prentice Hall, 1977).

[70] D.C. Hanselman and B.C. Littlefield *Mastering MATLAB 5: A Comprehensive Tutorial and Reference* (Upper Saddle River, N.J.: Prentice Hall, 1997).

[71] D. Heermann, *Computer Simulation Methods in Theoretical Physics* (Berlin: Springer, 1986).

[72] R.W. Hockney and J.W. Eastwood, *Computer Simulation Using Particles* (Bristol: Adam Hilger, 1988).

[73] M. Holt, *Numerical Methods in Fluid Dynamics*, (Berlin: Springer-Verlag, 1977).

[74] P.J. Huber, *Robust Statistics* (New York: Wiley, 1981).

[75] J.D. Jackson, *Classical Electrodynamics*, 2d ed. (New York: Wiley, 1975).

[76] F. James, "Monte Carlo theory and practice," *Rep. Prog. Phys.*, **43**, 1147–89 (1980).

[77] G. Jenkins and D. Watts, *Spectral Analysis and Its Applications* (San Francisco: Holden-Day, 1968).

[78] T.P. Jorgensen, *The Physics of Golf* (New York: AIP Press, 1994).

[79] M.H. Kalos and P.A. Whitlock, *Monte Carlo Methods* (New York: Wiley, 1986).

[80] B.W. Kernighan and D.M. Ritchie, *The C Programming Language* (Upper Saddle River, N.J.: Prentice Hall, 1978).

[81] D. Knuth, *Seminumerical Algorithms*, vol. 2 of *The Art of Computer Programming* (Reading Mass.: Addison-Wesley, 1981).

[82] P. Lancaster and K. Salkavskas, *Curve and Surface Fitting* (London: Academic Press, 1986).

[83] L. Landau and E. Lifshitz, *Mechanics* (Oxford: Pergamon, 1976).

[84] M. Lee and K. Schmidt, "Green's Function Monte Carlo," *Comput. Phys.*, **6** 192–7 (1992).

[85] A. Luehrmann, "Orbits in the Solar Wind–a Mini-Research Problem," *Am. J. Phys.*, **42**, 361–71 (1974).

[86] J. Mathews and R. Walker, *Mathematical Methods of Physics* (Menlo Park, Calif.: W. A. Benjamin, 1970).

[87] J. McLennan, *Introduction to Non-Equilibrium Statistical Mechanics* (Upper Saddle River, N.J.: Prentice Hall, 1989).

[88] W. Mendenhall, R.L. Scheaffer, and D.D. Wackerly, *Mathematical Statistics with Applications* (Boston: Duxbury Press, 1981).

[89] P. Morse and H. Feshbach, *Methods of Theoretical Physics*, vol. 1 (New York: McGraw-Hill, 1953).

[90] E.P. Muntz, "Rarefied gas dynamics," *Ann. Rev. Fluid Mech.*, **21**, 387–417 (1989).

[91] S.G. Nash, ed. *A History of Scientific Computing* (New York: ACM Press, 1990).

[92] G. Nicolis and I. Prigogine, *Self-Organization in Nonequilibrium Systems* (New York: Wiley, 1977).

[93] J. Ortega, *Numerical Analysis–A Second Course* (New York: Academic Press, 1972).

[94] S.K. Park and K.W. Miller, "Random number generators: good ones are hard to find," *Comm. A.C.M.*, **32**, 1192-1201 (1988).

[95] C. Penland, M. Ghil, and K.M. Weickmann, "Adaptive filtering and maximum entropy spectra with application to changes in atmospheric angular momentum," *J. Geo. Res.*, **96**, 659–71 (1991).

[96] F.L. Pedrotti and L.S. Pedrotti, *Introduction to Optics*, 2nd ed. (Upper Saddle River, N.J.: Prentice-Hall, 1993).

[97] T. Y. Petrosky and R. Broucke, "Area-preserving mappings and deterministic chaos for nearly parabolic motions," *Celestial Mech.*, **42**, 53–75 (1988).

[98] R. Peyret and T.D. Taylor, *Computational Methods for Fluid Flow* (New York: Springer-Verlag, 1983).

[99] E.C. Pielou, *An Introduction to Mathematical Ecology* (New York: Wiley, 1969).

[100] S. Pissanetsky, *Sparse Matrix Technology* (London: Academic Press, 1984).

[101] P.J. Plauger, *The Standard C Library* (Upper Saddle River, N.J.: Prentice Hall, 1992).

[102] P.J. Plauger, *The Draft Standard C++ Library* (Upper Saddle River, N.J.: Prentice Hall, 1995).

[103] I. Pohl, *C++ for FORTRAN Programmers* (Reading, Mass.: Addison-Wesley, 1997).

[104] W. Press, B. Flannery, S. Teukolsky and W. Vetterling, *Numerical Recipes in FORTRAN*, 2nd ed. (Cambridge: Cambridge University Press, 1992).

[105] F. Reif, *Fundamentals of Statistical and Thermal Physics* (New York: McGraw-Hill, 1965).

[106] P. Reynolds, J. Tobochnik, and H. Gould, "Diffusion Monte Carlo," *Comput. Phys.*, **4**, 662–8 (1990).

[107] R.D. Richtmyer and K.W. Morton, *Difference Methods for Initial Value Problems*, 2nd ed. (New York: Wiley, 1967).

[108] W. Rosser, *An Introduction to Statistical Physics* (Chichester: Ellis Horwood, 1986).

[109] P.J. Rousseeuw and A.M. Leroy, *Robust Regression and Outlier Detection* (New York: Wiley, 1987).

[110] M.N.O. Sadiku, *Numerical Techniques in Electromagnetics* (Boca Raton, Fla.: CRC Press, 1992).

[111] D. Saxon, *Elementary Quantum Mechanics* (San Francisco: Holden-Day, 1968).

[112] L. Schiff, *Quantum Mechanics* (New York: McGraw-Hill, 1968).

[113] G.A.F. Seber and C.J. Wild, *Nonlinear Regression* (New York: Wiley, 1989).

[114] R. Serber, *The Los Alamos Primer, The First Lectures on How to Build an Atomic Bomb* (Berkeley: University of California Press, 1992).

[115] R. Seydel, *From Equilibrium to Chaos, Practical Bifurcation and Stability Analysis* (New York: Elsevier, 1988).

[116] G.D. Smith, *Numerical Solution of Partial Differential Equations: Finite Difference Methods*, 3d ed. (Oxford: Oxford University Press, 1985).

[117] C. Sparrow, *The Lorenz Equations: Bifurcations, Chaos, and Strange Attractors* (New York: Springer-Verlag, 1982).

[118] J. Stoer and R. Bulirsch, *Introduction to Numerical Analysis* (New York: Springer-Verlag, 1980).

[119] B. Stroustrup, *The C++ Programming Language*, 2nd ed. (Reading, Mass.: Addison-Wesley, 1991).

[120] A.H. Stroud, *Approximate Calculation of Multiple Integrals* (Upper Saddle River, N.J.: Prentice Hall, 1971).

[121] A.H. Stroud and D. Secrest, *Gaussian Quadrature Formulas* (Upper Saddle River, N.J.: PrenticeHall, 1966).

[122] W.C. Swope, H.C. Andersen, P.H. Berens, and K.R. Wilson, "A computer simulation method for the calculation of equilibrium constants for the formation of physical clusters of molecules: application to small water clusters," *J. Chem. Phys.*, **76**, 637–49 (1982).

[123] K. Symon, *Mechanics* (Reading Mass.: Addison-Wesley, 1971).

[124] T. Tajima, *Computational Plasma Physics: With Applications to Fusion and Astrophysics* (Redwood City, Calif.: Addison-Wesley, 1989).

[125] N.M. Temme, "An algorithm with ALGOL 60 program for the computation of the zeros of ordinary Bessel functions and those of their derivatives," *J. Comp. Phys.*, **32**, 270 (1979).

[126] J. Tobochnik, G. Batrouni, and H. Gould, "Quantum Monte Carlo on a lattice," *Comput. Phys.*, **6**, 673–80 (1992).

[127] J. Tobochnik, H. Gould, and K. Mulder, "An introduction to quantum Monte Carlo," *Comput. Phys.*, **4**, 431–5 (1990).

[128] D.J. Tritton, *Physical Fluid Dynamics*, 2d ed. (Oxford: Clarendon Press, 1988).

[129] R.S. Varga, *Matrix Iterative Analysis* (Upper Saddle River, N.J.: Prentice Hall, 1962).

[130] L. Verlet, "Computer experiments on classical fluids. I. Thermodynamical properties of Lennard–Jones molecules," *Phys. Rev.* **159**, 98–103 (1967).

[131] R.G. Watts and A.T. Bahill, *Keep Your Eye on the Ball* (New York: W. H. Freeman and Co., 1990).

[132] P. Wesseling, *An Introduction to Multigrid Methods* (Chichester: Wiley, 1992).

[133] J. Wilkinson, *Rounding Errors in Algebraic Processes* (Upper Saddle River, N.J.: Prentice Hall, 1963).

[134] R.G. Wilson, S.M. McCreary and F.L. Thompson, "Optical transformations in three-space: Simulations with a PC", *Am. J. Phys.*, **60**, 49–56 (1992).

Selected Solutions

Chapter 1

1.4: For the first matrix, inverse is

$$\begin{bmatrix} 1.0000 & -0.5000 & -0.0833 \\ 0 & 0.2500 & -0.2083 \\ 0 & 0 & 0.1667 \end{bmatrix}$$

and eigenvalues are 1, 4, and 6.

1.8: (a) 6.1875; (b) 0.0909091.

1.18:

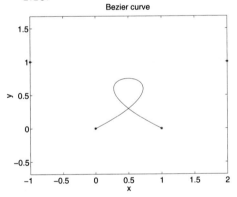

1.26:

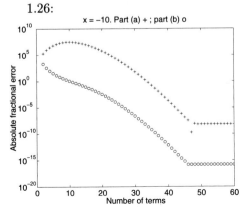

Chapter 2

2.2(e):

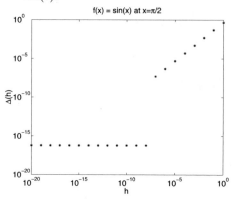

2.5:

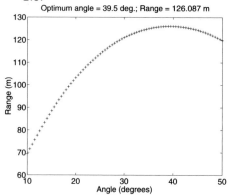

2.17:

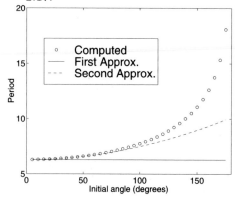

2.21: For $A_0 = 100g$, $T_d = 0.2$, $\tau = 0.004$, and $g/L = 1$,

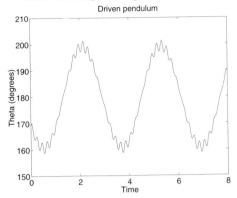

Chapter 3

3.7: For $\mathbf{v}_0 = [0\ 1\ 0]$ m/s, $\mathbf{E} = [0\ 1\ 0]$ V/m, $\mathbf{B} = [0\ 0\ 1]$ Tesla, $\tau = 10^{-14}$ s, the expected drift velocity is $\mathbf{u}_{\text{drift}} = [1\ 0\ 0]$ m/s; the measured value from data below is $[1.09415\ \text{-}0.0164728\ 0]$.

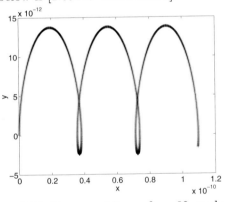

3.13: For $z_0 = 10$ cm, $\theta_0 = 0°$, and $\tau = 0.01$,

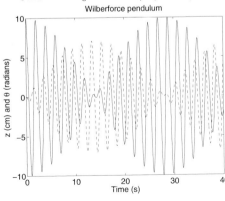

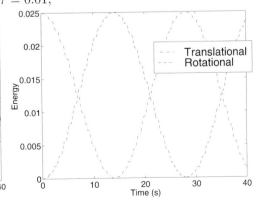

3.14: For $\mathbf{r}_0 = [1 \ 0]$ AU, $\mathbf{v}_0 = [0 \ \pi/2]$ AU/yr, and $\alpha = 0.02$, the expected precession is $-46.7°$ per revolution.

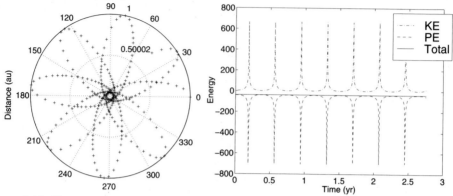

3.25: For $\sigma = 10$, $b = 8/3$, $r = 28$, and $\tau = 5 \times 10^{-3}$,

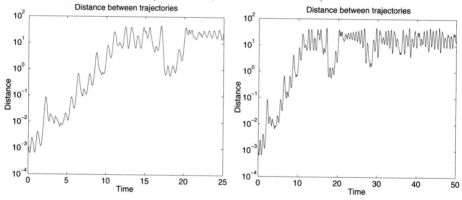

Chapter 4

4.8(a):

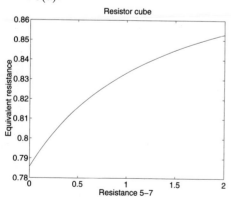

4.13(b):

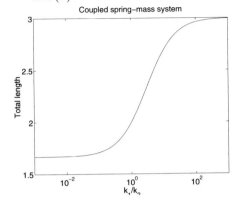

4.18: The first four energy levels are -13.524 eV, -13.300 eV, -12.9154 eV, and -12.384 eV.

4.24: Steady state position is $x = 6.245$ cm and $y = 12.65$ cm.

Chapter 5

5.4: $\alpha = (\Sigma xy)/(\Sigma x^2)$ and $\sigma_\alpha^2 = 1/(\Sigma x^2)$.

5.12(b): The year 2003.

5.19:

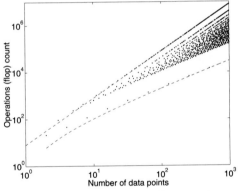

5.23(a): Normal modes frequencies are given by

$$\omega_\pm^2 = \frac{1}{2}(\omega_z^2 + \omega_\theta^2) \pm \frac{1}{2}\sqrt{(\omega_z^2 - \omega_\theta^2)^2 + \epsilon^2/mI}$$

where $\omega_z^2 = k/m$ and $\omega_\theta^2 = \delta/I$.

Chapter 6

6.6(c): For $\tau = 1.0 \times 10^{-4}$ and $N = 61$,

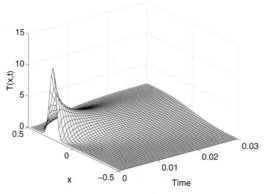 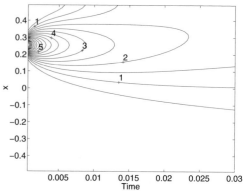

6.9: For $\tau = 1.5 \times 10^{-4}$ and $N = 61$,

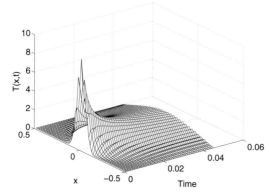 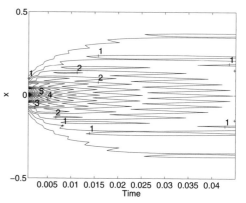

6.14: For $a = 2$, $L_c \approx 1.74$.

Chapter 7

7.2: For $\tau = 0.015$, $N = 50$, $\omega = 10\pi$, using: Lax (left); Lax-Wendroff (right),

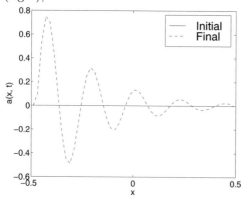 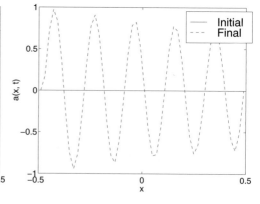

7.11: For $\tau = 0.02$, $N = 80$, using Lax-Wendroff,

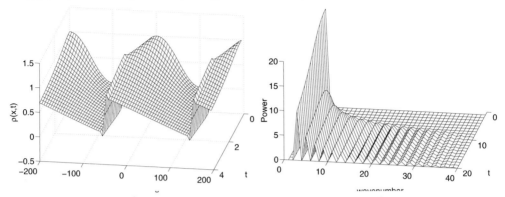

7.12(b): For $\rho_0 = \frac{3}{4}\rho_{\rm m}$, $\tau = 0.02$, $N = 80$, using Lax-Wendroff,

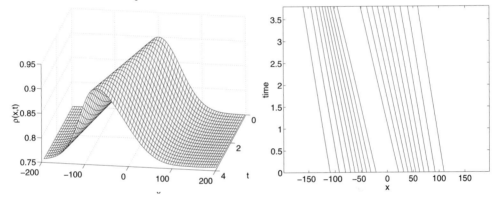

Chapter 8

8.3(a): From separation of variables,

$$\Phi(x, y, z) = \sum_{n=1}^{\infty} \sum_{m=1}^{\infty} c_{n,m} \sin\left(\frac{n\pi x}{L}\right) \sin\left(\frac{m\pi y}{L}\right) \cosh\left[\frac{\sqrt{n^2 + m^2}\pi(z - L/2)}{L}\right]$$

where

$$c_{n,m} = \frac{16\Phi_0}{nm\pi^2}\operatorname{sech}(\sqrt{n^2 + m^2}\pi/2)$$

for m and n odd, $c_{n,m} = 0$ otherwise.

8.8(a): For the 8 point Faraday cage,

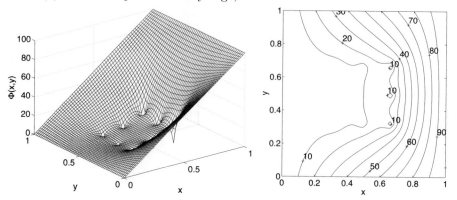

8.15(b): The method of images solution is

$$\Phi(\mathbf{r}) = \sum_{i=-\infty}^{\infty} \sum_{j=-\infty}^{\infty} (-1)^i \Phi_{\mathrm{f}}(\mathbf{r}; \mathbf{r}_+^{i,j}, \mathbf{r}_-^{i,j})$$

where

$$\mathbf{r}_\pm^{i,j} = \left(\frac{L}{2} + iL\right)\hat{\mathbf{x}} + \left(\frac{L \pm d}{2} + jL\right)\hat{\mathbf{y}}$$

and $\Phi_{\mathrm{f}}(\mathbf{r}; \mathbf{r}_+, \mathbf{r}_-)$ is the potential for a free dipole.

Chapter 9

9.2: The amplitude factor is given by,

$$|\xi|^2 = 1 + \left[\left(\frac{c\tau}{h}\right)^4 - \left(\frac{c\tau}{h}\right)^2\right](1 - \cos kh)^2$$

9.7: For $\tau \le t_\sigma$, $\|A\|_1 = 1 + \tau/2t_\sigma$ and for $\tau > t_\sigma$, $\|A\|_1 = \max\{1 + \tau/2t_\sigma, 2\tau/t_\sigma - 1\}$.

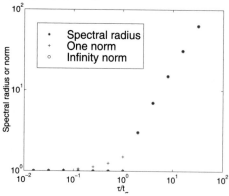

9.17: For $N = 80$, $L = 20$, and $\tau = 5 \times 10^{-3}$,

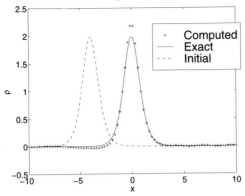

9.21: For $U_0 = 0$ (left) and $U_0 = 2$ (right); $N = 200$, $L = 100$, and $\tau = 1$,

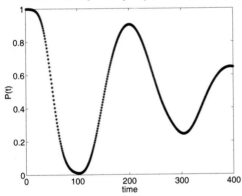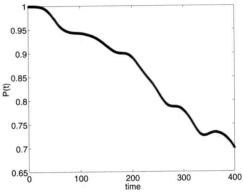

Chapter 10

10.11:

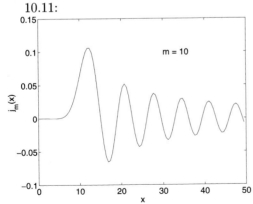

10.16:

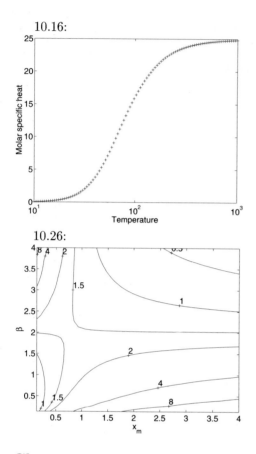

10.26:

Chapter 11

11.4:

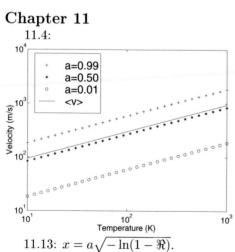

11.13: $x = a\sqrt{-\ln(1 - \Re)}$.

11.15: For $N = 10000$ random values, and $M = 12$,

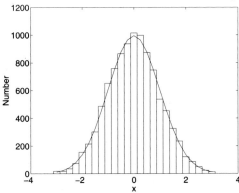

11.21: For $N = 500$ particles, and $\Delta v = 50$ m/s,

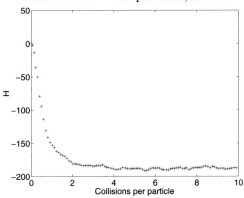

Index